ALSO BY MATTHEW FOX

ONE RIVER, MANY WELLS

Wisdom Springing from Global Faiths

MATTHEW FOX

JEREMY P. TARCHER/PENGUIN
a member of Penguin Group (USA) Inc.
New York

Most Tarcher/Penguin books are available at special quantity
discounts for bulk purchase for sales promotions, premiums,
fund-raising, and educational needs. Special books or book excerpts
also can be created to fit specific needs. For details, write Penguin
Group (USA) Inc. Special Markets, 375 Hudson Street,
New York, NY 10014.

Jeremy P. Tarcher/Penguin
a member of
Penguin Group (USA) Inc.
375 Hudson Street
New York, NY 10014
www.penguin.com

First trade paperback edition 2004

The Library of Congress cataloged the hardcover edition as follows:

Fox, Matthew, date.
One river, many wells : wisdom springing from global faiths/
Matthew Fox.
p.   cm.
ISBN 1-58542-047-6
1. Spirituality.   2. Religions—Quotations, maxims, etc.
I. Title.
BL624.F684   2000   00-030227
291.4—dc21

ISBN 1-58542-326-2 (paperback edition)

Printed in the United States of America

11   13   15   17   19   20   18   16   14   12

Book design by Jennifer Ann Daddio

CONTENTS

*"God is a great underground river that no one
can dam up and no one can stop."*
—MEISTER ECKHART

*This book is gratefully dedicated
to my brothers Thich Nhat Hanh, Howard Thurman,
and Rabbi Zalman Schachter-Shalomi
and to my sisters M. C. Richards and Marija Gimbutas.*

"[What happened in the first century] was an explosion of imagination
that we would call myth-making. . . . But as it turns out, it was hardly
the myth or the message that generated Christianity. It was the attraction
of participating in a group experimenting with a new social vision."
—BURTON L. MACK, THE LOST GOSPEL:
THE BOOK OF Q & CHRISTIAN ORIGINS

ACKNOWLEDGMENTS

I wish to acknowledge the many deep ecumenists of my life and learning, including my brother Meister Eckhart whose spirituality holds such uncanny resemblance to Hinduism, Buddhism, Judaism, and the faith of indigenous peoples and who first led me to the realization of the unity of the mystical dimensions of faith and who was so rudely treated by certain guardians of his own tradition but whose truth outlives them all. Also, to Thomas Aquinas and Nicholas of Cusa, Howard Thurman, and Rabbi Abraham Joshua Heschel. And to living exemplars of deep ecumenism including the Dalai Lama, Thich Nhat Hanh, Bishop William Swing, Buck Ghosthorse, Jose Hobday, Joanna Macy, and others. And to scholars of the most neglected traditions, especially Marija Gimbutas, Dr. Molefi Kete Asante, Joseph Campbell, John O'Donohue, Ana Matt, Danny Matt, Luisah Teish, and Dona Richards, Andrew Harvey, Raimon Panikkar, Russill Paul. And to scientists and activists who are reconnecting to the wisdom of earth and cosmos including Thomas Berry, Brian Swimme, Rupert Sheldrake, Arne Wyler, Wes Jackson, David Brower, Fritjof Capra, Julia Butterfly, and others. I wish also to express my deep gratitude to my agent, Ned Leavitt, and my editors at Jeremy Tarcher, Joel Fotinos and Mitch Horowitz, and copyeditor Timothy Meyer for their support and positive criticism. And my gratitude to the faculty, staff, and students at the University of Creation Spirituality and Naropa-Oakland with special thanks to Mel Bricker, Dorsey Blake, and Russill Paul.

Introduction

"FINALLY,

RELIGION 1999"

It is not easy being a human being. Unlike other species, we are not born with enough programmed DNA to see us through our survival. The best choices we make must come from intuition, cooperation, and learning. We depend on traditions and elders to teach us—and, of course, on experience, trial and error, and creativity as well. We find ourselves up against many obstacles not only to surviving but to living lives of quality and happiness: wars, strife, famine, hurricanes, floods, fires, catastrophes of many kinds, divorce, death, sickness, poverty, abuse, slavery, oppression, betrayals. The human journey is not easy.

Nor is it simple. Our strongest assets—our intelligence and our creative powers—can also get us into our deepest quagmires. Is not much of the ecological peril that we face today due to our inventions that have warmed the climate, put holes in the ozone, and polluted the waters?

One thing that can make human existence meaningful and give us the courage and creativity to navigate our ways is healthy spirituality. When religion is true to itself and is itself healthy, it is about spirituality, for spirituality is meant to be the core of religion. But religion, like everything else that humans touch, can become distorted and misused. It can develop its own institutional ego, even while preaching to individuals about the need to humble their personal egos. This happens. It has often happened. Therefore, it is evident that one can also be spiritual without religion.

In times like ours, when the planet is reeling from abuse and misuse at the hands of humans, when human inventions and discoveries have shrunk time and space so that we can communicate by Internet and satellites instantaneously with others around the globe, when livable space for our own and other species is dwindling and being depleted, it ought to prove especially beneficial to look to spirituality to help us find our way back (and forward!) to what it means to be human.

In this book I try to go to the core of human religious traditions as we know them to find the spirituality that is there. It is clear that once we return to the depth or core of religion we find much more than dogmas, concepts, institutions, commands. We find a striving for experience of the Divine, however, that can be spoken of, we find both form and formlessness, male and female, experience and practice. We also find that in their core and depth we do not encounter many different religions so much as one experience that is expressed variously and with great diversity and color flowing in the name of different traditions and cultures.

This is what the fifteenth-century theologian Nicholas of Cusa recognized. Cusa was a scientist and mystic and even a cardinal in the Roman Catholic Church. Well-steeped in the mystical teachings of Meister Eckhart and a compatriot of Hildegard of Bingen, who lived three centuries previously, he foresaw the times we are living in today and the spiritual demands of our times. He wrote: "Humanity will find that it is not a diversity of creeds, but the very same creed which is everywhere proposed. . . . Even though you are designated in terms of different religions, yet you presuppose in all this diversity one religion which you call wisdom." In our own time, the Dalai Lama expressed similar views when he said in an interview: "I believe deeply that we must find, all of us together, a new spirituality. [Interviewer: Which wouldn't be 'religious'?] Certainly not. This new concept ought to be elaborated alongside the religions, in such a way that all people of good will could adhere to it. [Interviewer: Even if they have no religion, or are against religion?] Absolutely. We need a new concept, a lay spirituality. We ought to promote this concept with the help of scientists."

But the Dalai Lama, true to his own tradition, insists that work is necessary for this new spirituality to emerge. The work he speaks of is an *inner* work, one that develops the seeds of peace within each of us. "Everything starts with us, with each of us. The indispensable qualities are peace of mind and compassion. Without them it's useless even to try. Those qualities are indispensable; they are also inevitable. I've told you: We will surely find them in ourselves, if we take the trouble to search for them. We can reject every form of religion, but we can't reject and cast off compassion and peace of mind." Inner work, that which learns compassion and peace of mind, is key to being human and is the key practice in spiritual traditions.

This book does not intend to offer a course in comparative religions—such studies are readily available. Rather, what I offer here is hopefully an interactive book, a book that itself elicits experience—*an experience in experiential dimensions of faith, namely spirituality.* How do I do this? My method is to choose sayings from the world's spiritual traditions and group them by common themes, themes that I believe are of interest and importance to all peoples in our perilous times. The citations are not complete or exhaustive, nor are they intended to be. They are intended to be *suggestive* and invitational in order to elicit interaction from the reader. I hope this interactive approach stirs the reader's thinking and imagination to think and to act. As the Buddhist monk Thich Nhat Hanh put it, what matters "is not a matter of faith; it is a matter of practice." I trust that this book and the structure of it will contribute to shared practice more than to doctrinal differences. We have had enough of them.

But practice leads to ideas and includes categories, themes, or concepts, and so this book's concepts are carefully chosen and situated. There lies a kind of subtle logic between the connection of the chapters. Each of the themes chosen interacts with other themes (for example, the relation between joy and beauty or between Creation and community).

Father Bede Griffiths, a Benedictine monk who lived for over half a century in India running an ashram for Christians and Hindus, said that the time has come "to share one another's spiritual riches." That is my goal in this book. Isn't it time that instead of trying to convert one another we delved into one another's spiritual riches? We get to the core of religion by going to the heart experience, not by dwelling on doctrines that so easily divide even within religious traditions. As Griffiths put it, "If one starts with doctrines, the arguments are endless. . . . But when one comes to the level of interior experience, that is where the meeting takes place. . . . It is in this cave of the heart that the meeting has to take place. That is the challenge." My hope is that the themes chosen in this book and the sayings in them will take us into the cave of our hearts.

What is Deep Ecumenism? I begin with an observation from Meister Eckhart, who says that "Divinity is an Underground river that no one can stop and no one can dam up." There is one underground river—but there are many wells into that river: an African well, a Taoist well, a Buddhist well, a Jewish well, a Muslim well, a goddess well, a Christian well, and aboriginal wells. Many wells but one river. To go down a well is to practice a tradition, but we would make a grave mistake (an idolatrous one) if we confused the well itself with the flowing waters of the underground river. Many wells, one river. That is Deep Ecumenism. This book is an effort to get us into the wells and hopefully deeper into their source.

Father Bede offered another metaphor for Deep Ecumenism: Look at your fingers. If you look at their top side, you see five distinct entities, each waving in the breeze. But if you follow them down to their origin, they all merge in the palm of the hand. So, too, with our religions. If we just look at their top side, they appear distinct and independent and autonomous. But if you look at their source, they all come from the same center. Each of these images of Deep Ecumenism, the well and the palm of the hand, is telling a common story: It is necessary to *travel deeper*, to let the superficial go, to go to the center, the cave, if we are to connect to the underground river. This is what mystics mean when they instruct us to seek out our *inner* person as opposed to our *outer* selves.

Wherever possible I use primary sources that include various scriptural texts of our religions but also the mystical writings and, in some cases, the pottery, poetry, funeral texts, and other findings that lay bare the efforts of our ancestors to express their wisdom about life, spirit, and the mysteries of being human. In some way this book is a *Source Book*. A return to our sources that name our spiritual experience can lead us to a return to Source itself however we name it.

In this book I deliberately let the spiritual traditions *speak on their own to the hearts and minds of the reader*. I have tried to interfere as little as possible. I quote from the texts of ancient Kemet or Egypt in calling upon African wisdom, from the Bhagavad Gita, from the Hebrew and the Christian Bible, from the Qur'an, from the Tao Te Ching, from Buddhist Scriptures and Celtic authors and indigenous seers and scientists. These quotes will be **in bold.** But I also cite great mystics from these traditions, and their citations will also be **in bold.** I hope the citations alert the imagination of the reader to make her or his connections. I follow no particular order in presenting citations from various traditions—this, too, is deliberate. I want to ensure mixing at many levels of our awareness.

In this book I find myself to be a weaver and a mixer. My job is to weave threads from different spiritual traditions into a common web, a common tapestry, that still values color, diversity, and difference. This task of weaving and mixing does not surprise me, for the post-modern times we live in are a time of *mixing.* The Internet is mixing people of all cultures, ages, and religions. Ecumenism is a recognition of religion's need to mix. We are finding more and more what an amazing *mix* this universe is: our bodies (containing hydrogen atoms from fourteen billion years ago is quite a mix); our DNA, our societies. Consider, for example, what an amazing *mix* is found in African-American culture, where African spirituality, slave history, protest songs, drumming cadences, and creative music all combine with European influences to create a unique expression of spirit and transcendence.

This book is a mixing, a stirring together of the "essence" of religion, namely, spirituality. The third millennium ought to be a time of mixing, not of conquering, mixing, not converting. The mixing includes a mixing with science and with Creation. Perhaps this book represents a start at putting together a Scripture for the twenty-first century. It offers a kind of distillation of the best of our spiritual traditions and a grouping of them according to themes that strike me as pertinent to our soul and social needs. (Carl Jung said that it is to the mystics that we owe what is best in humanity.)

We have to bear in mind, of course, that the most ancient religions on our planet are not of a textual nature but of an *oral* lineage. I try to make up for this lack with story. Dr. Molefi Kete Asante, a scholar of African religions and culture, makes some very important points about the general neglect of indigenous wisdom by Western theologians. "A powerful, expressive modality allows Westerners and, increasingly, Asians to speak of the 'great religions' and mean by such an expression

Buddhism, Christianity, Islam, and Judaism. . . . When the way to transcendence is found in peoples' lives as they deify their own nationalism and history, that becomes sufficiency and greatness for them." Asante points out that human civilization is so ancient in the Nile valley that it antedates the Arab invasions by five thousand years and this resulted in the "dispersal of the secret societies to various other places on the African continent," where an oral tradition survives to this day among the Yoruba Ifa, the Shona Mbira, and the Asante Okyeame systems. "The Arab *jihads* swept out of Arabia and conquered North Africa, stamping out, for the most part, the indigenous Egyptian language and establishing Islam as religion and Arabic as language." Asante's lament could apply to indigenous religions the world over in one form or other. Among the sayings I choose, I also include today's science along with many spiritual traditions, for many scientists in our time are seeing wisdom once again in a recognition of the mystery and wonder of the new cosmology. They are the teachers of nature's wisdom. While not being exhaustive, I also try to avoid exhaustion. By this I mean that not every tradition will be cited for every theme. Ultimately, however, each tradition will be heard for its wisdom.

This is not just a book for Westerners to learn about other traditions, but hopefully to learn more about their own. The Dalai Lama warns that the biggest obstacle to interfaith sharing is people's unhealthy relationships to their own faith. The citations from Western spiritual sources predominate in this book because that is where so much unhealth lies. So many people I encounter have been wounded by their own tradition. So many are ignorant of the deepest spiritual teachings of that same tradition. Many Westerners do not even know their own mystical tradition or spiritual practice.

At times I will mix insights of several traditions in one paragraph, but mostly I let them speak for themselves on separate pages, and I invite the reader to participate by mixing.

If pursued in depth and used to unite instead of to separate our various wisdom traditions, the themes of this book can assist the simplifying of our religions, stripping them down to their essentials, that is, to spirituality. The Dalai Lama has observed that "the reality is that the majority of people today are unpersuaded of the need for religion." He calls, however, for a "spiritual revolution." The task of awakening to our spiritual heritage as a species is an important one as our species weighs into unprecedented challenges and possibilities in the future that calls us on.

Recently, after one of our Techno Cosmic Masses, a twenty-one-year-old came up to me and said: "Finally, Religion 1999. I've been waiting for this all my life." When I asked him what was key to the experience for him he replied: "When I experienced a Jewish rabbi, a Muslim woman prayer leader and preacher, a Christian priest, and an African song leader all at the altar together leading us in prayers of gratitude, I said to myself, 'Finally, religion is catching up. Finally, Religion 1999.'"

This young man is correct. It is time for religions to quit bickering and start contributing. As the Dalai Lama puts it, "Now more than ever we need to show our children that distinctions between 'my country' and 'your country,' 'my religion' and 'your religion' are secondary considerations. . . . In today's increasingly complex and interdependent world, we are compelled to acknowledge the existence of other cultures . . . other faiths."

The young generation today is facing survival issues around realities of earth degradation and economic exploitation and growing chasms between haves and have-nots that are unprecedented. Is it not time for our religions to get back to their essentials—which is meant to be the teaching of spirituality—and to contribute wisdom to an increasingly despairing world? This is not a time for denominational one-upmanship. It is a time to cull wisdom from any and all of its sources and to let folly go. Even and including religious folly. One reason I depend in this book so heavily upon mystical writings is offered by Carl Jung, when he observed that "it is only the mystic who brings creativity to religion." If we are to make our faiths live again—not for their own sakes but for the survival of our species—then we had better become mystically literate again. The format of this book is an effort to further the cause of mystical literacy. The mystics are fun, and they invite us to fun; they are also outlandish, and they invite us to play at the extremities of the heart. They are also prophets who urge us to rejuvenate our systems of education, economics, and all our work worlds and professions.

Some people will raise objections to what we are doing by calling it "syncretism." Are we fusing too many religions together? they will ask. The word "syncretism" actually comes from the creating of a federation of cities in Crete. In itself, the creating of a federation of religions striving to be spiritualities in our time does not seem like such a horrible prospect. It certainly beats going to war with one another. Perhaps Father Bede Griffiths had the best response to the objection of syncretizing when he observed: "We have, of course, to guard against syncretism of any kind, but this only means that we have to learn to discriminate within each tradition between that which belongs to the universal religious tradition of mankind and that which belongs to its own limited and particular point of view." While we want to honor the differences between faiths, it is time to emphasize the likenesses, or what Griffiths calls "the universal religious tradition of mankind."

Father Bede experienced the "most profound sense of 'mystery' and 'sacrament'" as he found it in Hinduism and life in India. He marveled at the temples in whose holy place there is encountered the *garbha griba,* the center "at once of the universe and of the soul. It is the 'womb' from which all things spring and at the same time the 'cave within the heart,' the secret place where man enters into communion with the ultimate mystery." Is it wrong to want to visit such a place? Is it syncretism to say that other religions, including Catholicism, strive to create such caves of the heart? To point out that Francis of Assisi often sought out caves to pray in? That is the profound point that Griffiths is making: We need to discern *that which belongs to the universal religious tradition of mankind.*

In laying out the eighteen themes of this book we are inviting in the universal tradition of mankind. The horrible wars in Bosnia and Kosovo in our day; the Inquisitions, Crusades, pogroms, religious wars, and colonial conquests in the name of religion—haven't we seen enough of the shadow side of religious power?

It is time our species grew up. This means, among other things, that instead of relating religion to religion with our *reptilian brains* and our testesterone in high gear ("my God can beat up your God"), we ought to relate religion to religion from our deepest hearts and most creative ("mindful") minds. Reptiles, after all, do not engage in religion or pretend to, so why would we want to engage one another religiously at that level? Our deepest hearts and fullest minds are our mystical and intellectual capacities. This is what this book is trying to accomplish. A meeting of hearts and minds at a deeper place, a place of wells and watering and wisdom and mystery, not of judgment, relating heart to heart and creative mind to creative mind about issues that concern our species profoundly.

What are these issues? I propose eighteen. They constitute the chapter titles for this book. I group them into four areas: Relating to Creation; Relating to Divinity; Relating to Ourselves: Paths to Encounter and Enlightenment; and Relating to the Future: What the Divine Is Asking of Us. Within these groupings are the individual themes that can be found listed in the Table of Contents.

This book ends with a big surprise—it surprised me, I hope it surprises others. When we focus on key issues of concern such as the eighteen themes I employ, we are *de facto* involved in myth-making. This book, though I did not intend it, has proven to be a step in *remythologizing our faith lives*. By "our" I do not mean just Christians or Jewish peoples, but *all* those traditions represented here, including science. Deep Ecumenism leads us to new myth-making and ushers in a social vision that might seize the moral and spiritual imagination of our species not unlike what occurred two thousand years ago in Palestine.

It is in the deepest message of each faith, I believe, that we encounter the likenesses. But for this to happen each faith must get to its deepest essence and know its spiritual sources. In the West, discoveries of ancient and lost manuscripts in this century and new scientific methods, as well as the new cosmology from science, have contributed to a rare opportunity to reinvent both Judaism and Christianity. This return to the sources can provide a social vision and community inspiration that takes us beyond empire building and religion by institution.

Hopefully, the themes chosen here will bring ancient and needed messages up from the deep. The paths down the wells will indeed vary, and there lies the beauty and novelty of human diversity. But the path must never be confused with the source. As Meister Eckhart put it, "All paths lead to God, for God is on them all equally for the person who knows." Hopefully this book will contribute to our shared knowing and practicing so that our children's children will know ways to live peacefully on and with this earth and healthy directions to travel.

—*University of Creation Spirituality*
Oakland, California
August 4, 1999

One

RELATING

TO

CREATION

If humanity is to draw wisdom from all its wisdom traditions, then our relation to Creation will form the basis of this interchange. The reason is that we all have Creation in common, and Creation is bigger than all of us, bigger than our religions and far more ancient. At our University of Creation Spirituality, one enters by ascending a staircase. On the left wall of that staircase we have painted a history of the universe. The mural is scientifically accurate as to the proportionate distance the universe has traveled and we travel when mounting the stairs. The Milky Way appears three-quarters up the steps. When does humanity appear? Well beyond the light switch at the top of the stairs! Humanity is accurately represented by a strip one-quarter of an inch wide at the very top of the stairs. Our religions would be a speck of dust in that quarter inch and our races, too, would be merely a speck of dust.

Whatever we call the Divine, we agree that Divinity in some way is Creator or Intelligence or Wisdom or Lover of Creation. Furthermore, Creation unites us because Creation is what most suffers when we lose a sense of the sacred. The peril that earth finds herself in today is enough to motivate all of us as individuals and all of our communities of faith to lament our ways and transform our hearts and actions.

In this section we treat Creation under the following headings:

1. Deep Ecumenism and the Universality of Experience
2. Creation—All Our Relations
3. Light
4. Community and Interdependence

1.

DEEP ECUMENISM
AND THE UNIVERSALITY
OF EXPERIENCE

**It is my belief that in the Presence of God there is neither male
nor female, white nor black, Gentile nor Jew, Protestant nor
Catholic, Hindu, Buddhist, nor Moslem, but a human spirit
stripped to the literal substance of itself before God.**
—Howard Thurman, *Creative Encounter*

Religions are integral to Creation because they are themselves created, set up by humans in relationship to their stories of the Divine. In addition, religions provide us with a perspective, a lens through which we see Creation and interpret it. Therefore, it seems important to consider Deep Ecumenism even before we delve into the deep mysteries of Creation itself.

I am writing these words at the ocean in Northern California, where the waves are churning and inspired, full of energy and rushing where they will. Spirit is like that—full of energy and free to choose its own path.

My thoughts turn to the subject of our various religions. None of them is mother of the ocean, rather the ocean is mother of all things. Our religions are so recent in relation to the lifetime of the sea and to most other creatures—including humanity itself. What religions did our ancestors practice for the two million years that preceded the forms we now recognize as "world religions"? How humble our religions ought to be before all creatures. As Mechtild of Magdeburg said, **the truly wise person kneels at the feet of all creatures.**

Deep Ecumenism should be deep, it ought to demand of human religions that they imitate the depths of the sea (*la mer*) in its capacity to maintain mystery and energy, being mother (*la mère*) to all beings. Varying with the course of seasons and the topography of land and water alike, ecumenism ought to be big, accepting, magnanimous, forgiving. It ought to just be.

Our souls are meant to imitate the sea also. That is our origin. Our very life-blood imitates the saltwater of the ocean. But culture so often shrinks our souls that they fit a consumer mold or some other tribal size.

I am not alone in calling for religions themselves to practice the humility they so often demand of individual adherents. All the mystics—the truly deep ecumenists—speak as I do. Hear them out. Consider how well we are doing.

The Indian mystic Kabir sings:

> Neither a Hindu
> Nor a Muslim am I!
> A mere ensemble
> Of five elements is
> This body,
> Where the spirit
> Plays its drama
> Of joy and suffering!

Kabir is telling us how the cosmic gift of his body supersedes the claims of organized religion to his allegiance. The spirit plays within that body, it plays games of joy and games of suffering. Life is a drama when one moves beyond mere religious allegiances. Divinity cannot be locked up.

> The god of Hindus resides in a temple;
> The god of Muslims resides in a mosque.
> Who resides there
> Where there are no temples
> Nor mosques?

We are reminded of Jesus saying, **Do not look here nor there. The kingdom of God is among you.** True religion is not about institutions, be they mosques, temples, or objects of any kind. It is about relationship. It is about intersubjectivity and not objects and the objectifying of objects that we so often fall into. Creation brings us all together. As Kabir put it, **Once you experience his presence in all beings, all debate comes to naught!**

From Hinduism we hear: **Many are the paths of humans, but they all in the end come to Me.** Nikhilananda, a scholar on Hinduism, believes that **the great religions of the world are not competitive but complementary. One religion is not the enemy of the other, but all religions are faced by common enemies: skepticism, atheism, and perhaps worst of all, severe indifference. Only if the religions of the world stand together will they preserve themselves [and] help to bring about a new manifestation of the world spirit.** In the *Bhagavad Gita,* God says: **I am the thread that runs through the pearls, as in a necklace.** Nikhilananda adds to this line: **Each religion is one of the pearls.**

From the Hindu Scriptures we read: **Truth is one, sages call it by different names.** The Hindu mystic Rajjab writes:

The worship of the different religions,
which are like so many small streams,
move together to meet God, who is like the ocean.

Hindu philosopher Ramakrishna writes: **I see people who talk about religion constantly quarreling with one another. Hindus, Mussulmans, Brahmos, Saktas, Vaishnavas, Saivas all quarrel with one another. They haven't the intelligence to understand that He who is called Krishna is also Siva and the Primal Shakti, and that it is He, again, who is called Jesus and Allah. "There is only one Rama and he has a thousand names."**

Truth is one; only It is called by different names. All people are seeking the same Truth; the variance is due to climate, temperament, and name. . . . People injure and kill one another, and shed blood, in the name of religion. But this is not good. Everyone is going toward God. They will all realize him if they have sincerity and longing of heart.

Islam, too, is ecumenical in its core: **Islam considers the acceptance of anterior prophets as a necessary article of faith (iman) in Islam itself and asserts quite vigorously the universality of revelation. No other sacred text speaks as much and as openly of the universality of religion as the Quran. Islam, the last of the religions of the present humanity, here joins with Hinduism, the first and most primordial of existing religions, in envisaging religion in its universal manifestation throughout the cycles of human history.**

Following are some passages from the holy Qur'an apropos of Deep Ecumenism. **Surely, of the Believers, the Jews, the Christians and the Sabians, those who truly believe in Allah and the Last Day and act righteously, shall have their reward with their Lord and no fear shall come upon them nor shall they grieve.** Respect for Moses and the Hebrew Bible as well as for Jesus and Mary is offered in the following passages. **Indeed We gave Moses the Book and caused a number of Messengers to follow after him; and to Jesus son of Mary, we gave manifest Signs and strengthened him with the Spirit of holiness. Again, We gave Jesus son of Mary clear proofs and strengthened him with the Spirit of holiness.** The Muslim faith is clearly placed within the Jewish and Christian traditions of the prophets and of the Bible in the following passage. **We believe in Allah and in that which has been sent down to us and that which was sent down to Abraham and Ishmael and Isaac and Jacob and his children and that which was given to Moses and Jesus, and that which was given to all other Prophets from their Lord. We make no distinction between any of them and to him do we wholly submit ourselves. Again, We make no distinction between any of his Messengers; we have heard Allah's command and we have submitted ourselves wholly to him. He has sent down to thee the Book, comprising the truth, which fulfills the revelations that preceded it; and he sent down the Torah and the Gospel before this as a guidance for the people.**

The mystical tradition of Islam, the Sufi tradition, also sees all mystical traditions as one.

Rumi says:

> All religions,
> all this singing,
> is one song.
> The differences are just
> illusion and vanity.
> The sun's light looks a little different
> on this wall than it does on that wall . . .
> but it's still one light.

Rumi grounds the likeness found in every mystical tradition to the depth of the experience of the Divine one touches in a particular tradition. Love is the key.

> For those in love,
> Moslem, Christian, and Jew do not exist. . . .
> Why listen to those who see it another way?—
> if they're not in love
> their eyes do not exist.

Thirteenth-century Sufi Hafiz also addresses Deep Ecumenism. He writes:

> I have learned so much from God
> that I can no longer call myself
> a Christian, a Hindu, a Muslim, a Buddhist, a Jew.

He warns about living in the past and following a religion that lives nostalgically when he writes:

What do sad people have in common?
It seems they have all built a shrine to the past
And often go there
and do a strange wail and worship.
What is the beginning of happiness?
It is to stop being so religious like that.

Sometimes spirituality demands that we jump ship.

The great religions are the ships,
Poets the life boats.
Every sane person I know
has jumped overboard!
That is good for business, isn't it, Hafiz?

From the Buddhist tradition, Thich Nhat Hanh speaks of the centrality of going deep if we are to do ecumenism when he says: **Through the practice of deep looking and deep listening, we become free, able to see the beauty and values in our own and others' tradition.** Yet, to get to the point of seeing the beauty and value in others' traditions, one must look and listen *deeply* into one's own. One must practice some path along the journey that leads to depth. One must enter the well of mystical experience.

To meet another is to meet oneself and one's own tradition, Thich Nhat Hanh insists. **When you touch someone who authentically represents a tradition, you not only touch his or her tradition, you also touch your own.** The implication is that every tradition accomplishes like things in the soul of individuals—so alike are the things accomplished that we become *mirrors* to one another: We can see ourselves in one another. What we see emphasized by Thich Nhat Hanh is found in all mystical traditions: experience is key. The sixteenth-century Indian saint-poet Dadu once wrote:

> **All men of wisdom have one religion;**
> **They all have one caste;**
> **They all behold the face of the One!**

It has been said that Buddhism teaches that kindness and love are the universal religion.

From the African-American tradition we listen to the voice of a great mystic and prophet, Howard Thurman, who was the spiritual mentor to Dr. Martin Luther King, Jr. Howard Thurman saw what we are calling Deep Ecumenism as the central call of his vocation when he wrote: **A strange necessity has been laid upon me to devote my life to the central concern that transcends the walls that divide and would achieve in literal fact what is experienced as literal truth: human life is one and all men are members one of another. And this insight is spiritual and it is the hard core of religious experience.** He too, like Thich Nhat Hanh, Kabir, and the Dalai Lama, is calling us to experience that of which we speak. Thurman develops his Deep Ecumenism even more explicitly in another place when he writes: **It is my belief that in the Presence of God there is neither male nor female, white nor black, Gentile nor Jew, Protestant nor Catholic, Hindu, Buddhist, nor Moslem, but a human spirit stripped to the literal substance of itself before God.** Thurman had an experience of Deep vs. Theological Ecumenism when he visited India in the 1930s. He dialogued with a Hindu, Thurman speaking as a Christian, for half a day and with little result. Then they shifted gears, putting the discussion at the level of experience instead of concepts. Says Thurman: **We were thus released to communicate with each other as sharers of what each in his own way had discovered of his experience of God. We were no longer under the necessity to define anything but were free to be to each other what was most fundamental to each.**

Howard Thurman founded a church called the Church of the Fellowship of All Peoples, together with Rev. Alfred G. Fisk in San Francisco, in 1944 to bring people of all religions, races, and classes together. It was the first church in America that was interracial in its membership and leadership. This church is still vital and alive today.

We have heard in the Introduction from Christian theologians Nicholas of Cusa and Father Bede Griffiths about Deep Ecumenism, but consider also these words from Saint Thomas Aquinas of the thirteenth century who wrote:

> **Every truth without exception—and whoever may utter it—is from the Holy Spirit.**
> **The old pagan virtues were from God.**
> **Revelation has been made to many pagans.**

Imagine how different history would read if the European explorers and exploiters of the fifteenth and sixteenth centuries had approached the shores of Turtle Island and Africa and the Pacific islands with this theology instead of proposing that indigenous people have no souls and treating them as such through slavery and conscription and cultural annihilation.

Father Bede Griffiths in our own century also celebrates the commonality of mystical experience among world traditions. In the fourteenth chapter of Genesis we hear of a pagan priest named Melchizedek, who is said to pray to "the most high God, the creator of heaven and earth." The term used, *El Elyon,* is the Hebrew name for the "most high God." Comments Father Bede: **This is very important: in the beginning of the biblical tradition there was this recognition that God had revealed Himself to the Gentiles, to what were later called "pagans."** Other pagans honored in the Hebrew Scriptures as holy people include the ancient patriarchs such as Abel, Seth, and Enoch and also Noah and Job.

It is clear from these many and various examples that Deep Ecumenism will demand much of us. Religion alone will not do. Shouting that our God is better than your God will not do. Experience is what is shared in Deep Ecumenism.

The Jewish mystical work of the Middle Ages, the Kabbalah, says: **The only genuine proof of this wisdom is experience itself.** If our faith has not given us experiences to share, then we ought to spend more time with it or find another. Just as our times call for Deep Ecumenism, so Deep Ecumenism calls for 1) experience and 2) the sharing of experience. At the level of experience we are all one and we encounter the One Divinity, however he/she be named. But experience also leads to Deep Ecumenism, for when one encounters the beloved, one wants to share that encounter and one is curious about the encounters others behold. Am I alone in this experience? Have others before me shared such wonders? Will others after me? What about my community—do they, can they, share in the same glory and revelation? Many questions are aroused by love experiences. In subsequent sections of this book we will examine some of these common questions and themes. The first of these has to do with our shared existence, the reality of Creation itself.

2.
CREATION—
ALL OUR RELATIONS

Love all Creation.
The whole and every grain of sand in it.
Love every leaf,
and every ray of light.
Love the plants.
Love the animals.
Love everything.
If you love everything
you will perceive the Divine Mystery
in all things.
Once you perceive it
you will comprehend it better every day.
And you will come, at last,
to love the whole world
with an all embracing love.
—Dostoyevsky, *Brothers Karamazov*

Say what you will, whether religion or spirituality acknowledge it or not, all human experiences—including spiritual experiences—are set in the matrix of Creation itself. Our existence is totally interdependent with the existence of stars, planets, the sun, rocks, water, plants and trees, flowers, birds, supernovas, galaxies, atoms, the fireball that was the origin of this universe.

All time and space comes together in our deep selves not only at the physical level and the level of DNA but also at the level of our psychic and spiritual and emotional selves. No forest, no moon, no ocean, no field, can be labeled "Buddhist" or "Jewish" or "Muslim" or "Christian." Nature, Creation, *that which is,* is far bigger and far more ancient than any of our religious traditions. When our religions rediscover this truth, they will rediscover their own humility, their own humble place in the unfolding of things. To know that the universe is about fifteen billion years in the making and that the religions we recognize today are tens of thousands of years old (the indigenous ones) or three thousand years old (the oldest being Hinduism) is to shudder in the presence of the tenuousness of our traditions.

When I speak of "re-discovering" religion's relationship to nature and Creation, I speak consciously. It is a *re*-discovery because our religions once knew these facts well. Surely the indigenous faith traditions are all grounded in Creation and enveloped by its wonder and beauty and grace. As we shall see, all of our faith traditions of even more recent vintage share a belief in the *sacredness of the universe* and of our role in it. But this Creation-centered perspective has often taken a backseat to other agendas, including building empires in the name of religion and using religion to exclude elements of Creation, including women, slaves, homosexuals, forests, waters, the sky.

Fr. Bede Griffiths considers Hinduism to be a "cosmic religion." And the aboriginal religions were profoundly Creation centered because they "had not learned to separate man from nature and nature from God." How interesting that it takes an education to separate nature from God and man from nature! One has to learn to do this kind of unnatural disassociation. Most of us are born with a sense of awe that is expanded by our experiences in nature—expanded and called forth. So many mystics from so many traditions sing of this intimacy of the human psyche and the universe.

From the Christian tradition the thirteenth-century saint and mystic Thomas Aquinas says that **a mistake about creation results in a mistake about God.** Here Aquinas subjects our very grasp of the Divine to the accuracy of our grasp of nature itself. What greater tribute could one give to the work of scientists and others to seek out the truths of nature, the truth of Creation? Aquinas devoted his life to mixing science and faith. For science, he chose the newly translated "pagan" Greek scientist Aristotle. This was a radical move on Aquinas's part, and it got him into so much trouble that he was condemned three times by the church before it canonized him a saint. But the devotion of Aquinas to science was complete. He insisted on examining nature to find more about the maker of nature. Aquinas celebrates the wonder we experience at encountering the universe when he writes: **"They shall be drunk with the plenty of your house"—that is, the universe.** Perhaps it is the lack of cosmology in our culture that drives us to drink and to seek other ways of "getting high" that are self-defeating. Aquinas believes that **each and every creature exists for the perfection of the entire universe.**

Aquinas believed in evolution insofar as it was understood in his day, that is to say, he was explicit that Creation did not happen just in the past. Rather, it is an ongoing process, and God is deeply and intimately involved. **God's work whereby God brings things into being must not be taken as the work of a craftsman who makes a box and then leaves it. For God continues to give being. . . . God indeed "works until now" (Jn. 5.17) by preserving and providing for the creatures God has made.** Things exist for the sake of the whole, which means for Aquinas, for the good of the universe. **The ultimate end of the divine will is the divine goodness, and the nearest thing to that among created things is the good of the whole universe. . . . Thus, among created things, what God cares for most is the order of the universe.** Individuals and species serve this greater good, the order of the universe. **The principal good in things themselves is the perfection of the universe.** The diversity of Creation contributes substantially to its beauty and its purpose. **The whole universe together participates in the di-**

vine goodness more perfectly, and represents it better, than any single creature whatever.

Aquinas recognizes the divine presence in all beings. **Every creature participates in some way in the likeness of the divine essence. All things love God. All things are united according to friendship to each other and to God.**

The sacredness of creation is further celebrated by Meister Eckhart, who teaches that all beings are **words of God and books about God. My mouth expresses and reveals God but the existence of a stone does the same and people often recognize more from actions than from words.** Moreover, Eckhart assures us that **all creatures are gladly doing the best they can to express God.** For Eckhart, **God is constantly speaking only one thing. . . . In this one utterance he speaks his Son and at the same time the Holy Spirit and all creatures. . . . There where God speaks the creatures, there God is.**

This is an awareness of the Cosmic Christ or the divine nature in which all beings participate. The Christ or image of God does not exist solely in Jesus but in all of God's creation. Is that not what is praised in John's Gospel when we read that

This Word was with God in the beginning
Through it all things came to be,
not one thing had its being but through it.
All that came to be had life in it. . . .(Jn. 1.3–5)

This is what so excited the early Christians—they felt their whole universe had opened up and revealed the Divine to them. Thus, one of the earliest hymns, recalled by St. Paul in his letter to the Colossians, says: **In him all things were created, in heaven and on earth, visible and invisible, whether thrones or dominions or principalities or authorities—all things were created through him and for him. He is before all things, and in him all things hold together.** (Col. 1:16–17)

Meister Eckhart captures the full implications of this vision when he says simply, **isness is God.** To see the Divine in all things is to begin to live, to begin to be awake and aware. It is to begin to understand the meaning of *Incarnation,* the reality that God has indeed **become flesh and pitched its tent among us.** (Jn. 1:14)

The miracle that isness and Creation are is further underscored by Meister Eckhart's teaching when he tells us:

God is creating the entire universe fully and totally
in this present now.
Everything God created six thousand years ago—and even
  previous to that—as God made the world,
God creates now all at once.
Now consider this: God is in everything, but
God is nowhere as much as God is in the soul.
There, where time never enters,
where no image shines in,
in the innermost and deepest aspect of the soul
God creates the whole cosmos.
Everything which God created millions of years ago
and everything which will be created by God after millions
  of years—if the world endures until then—
God is creating all that in the innermost and deepest realms
  of the soul.
Everything of the past and everything of the present
and everything of the future
God creates in the innermost realms of the soul.

Hildegard of Bingen pictures the divine love of Creation in the following manner.

> **Creation is allowed in intimate love**
> **to speak to the Creator as if to a lover.**

The relationship of these lovers is mutual.

> **As the Creator loves his creation,**
> **so Creation loves the Creator.**
> **Creation, of course, was fashioned to be adorned,**
> **to be showered, to be gifted with the love of the Creator.**
> **The entire world has been embraced by this kiss.**
> **God has gifted Creation with everything that is necessary.**

Divinity is everywhere in Creation.

> **God's Word is in all Creation, visible and invisible.**
> **The Word is living, being, spirit, all verdant greening, all**
> **creativity. . . .**
> **This Word manifests in every creature. . . .**
> **Now this is how the spirit is in the flesh—the Word is indivisible**
> **from God.**

In the Hebrew Bible the oldest creation story is found in Psalm 104, and in that psalm we have a telling of the unfolding of Creation that celebrates the existence of the sky, the waters, the clouds, the wind, fire, the earth, the mountains, the thunder, the valleys, the wild animals, the wild donkeys, the birds, the grasses, the cattle, the plants, wine, oil, bread that come from the soil. The trees, the stork, the wild goats, the rock-badgers, the moon, the sun, the night, the forest animals, the lions all **claiming their food from God.**

> **Yahweh, what variety you have created,**
> **arranging everything so wisely!**
> **Earth is completely full of things you have made:**
> **among them vast expanse of ocean,**
> **teeming with countless creatures,**
> **creatures large and small,**
> **with the ships going to and fro. . . .**

Notice how human ingenuity, in this case ships, is included among the wonders of Creation in the psalmist's understanding of things.

In the Creation story in Genesis we are assured that creation is **good** and **very good.** The Book of Wisdom offers still another creation story, one that is evolutionary in its perspective and, like Psalm 104 and Genesis, places humankind near the end of a long unfolding of Creation and recognizes that Wisdom and Creation go together.

> **Simply I learned about Wisdom . . .**
> **the design of the universe,**
> **the force of its elements,**
> **beginning and end of time,**
> **changes in the sun's course, variation of seasons,**

cycles of years, positions of stars,
natures of animals,
tempers of beasts,
powers of winds,
thoughts of humanity,
uses of plants,
virtues of roots.
Such things as are hidden I learned,
for Wisdom, the Artisan of all, taught me.

This creation story couched in a beautiful poem is profoundly evolutionary in its message. It is not at all anthropocentric. First comes the design of the universe, followed by its powerful elements, then time, the sun, the seasons, the animals, the powers of wind—and only then come the thoughts of humanity. And the first of these is not about writing books but about the uses of plants and roots. Wisdom teaches, for she is the Artisan of all this art that we call creation.

Psalm 19 also sings of the wonder of Creation.

The heavens declare the glory of God,
the vault of heaven proclaims his handiwork;
day discourses of it to day,
night to night hands on the knowledge.
No utterance at all, no speech,
no sound that anyone can hear;
yet their voice goes out through all the earth,
and their message to the ends of the world,
high above, he pitched a tent for the sun,
who comes out of his pavilion like a bridegroom,
exulting like a hero to run his race.

Another picture of Creation emerges from Psalm 33.

By the word of Yahweh the heavens were made,
their whole array by the breath of his mouth;
he collects the ocean waters as though in a wineskin
he stores the deeps in cellars.
Let the whole world fear Yahweh,
let all who live on earth revere him!
He spoke, and it was created;
he commanded, and there it stood.

Reading and hearing these psalms one feels a sense of wonder and praise. Creation does that to the human heart. An ancient rabbinic teaching about Creation goes as follows:

Creation is the extension of God.
Creation is God encountered in time and space.
Creation is the infinite in the garb of the finite.
To attend to Creation is to attend to God.

In the Book of Daniel, we read of three young men thrown into a fire by a violent king. When, with the help of an angel, they survive, they sang this song from within the flames.

All things the Lord has made, bless the Lord:
Heavens! bless the Lord:
Waters above the heavens! bless the Lord:
Sun and moon! bless the Lord:
Stars of heaven! bless the Lord:
Showers and dews! all bless the Lord:

Winds! bless the Lord:
Fire and heat! bless the Lord:
Frost and cold! bless the Lord:
Ice and snow! bless the Lord:
Nights and days! bless the Lord:
Mountains and hills! bless the Lord:
Sea beasts and everything that lives in water! bless the Lord:
Birds of heaven! all bless the Lord:
Animals wild and tame! all bless the Lord:

This song is truly a praise of all Creation.

The Qur'an echoes this respect for God as Creator. For example, we read: **O mankind, worship your Lord Who has created you and created those who were before you, that you may be shielded against all ill; Who has spread out the earth like a bed for you and has made the heaven like a canopy, and has caused water to come down from the clouds and has therewith brought forth provision for you in the shape of fruits.** For desert people in particular, the emphasis on the earth to lie on, the water from the clouds, the fruits to eat all strike home as elements and gifts for survival itself.

The Qur'an celebrates the Creator's cosmic gifts further. **In the creation of the heavens and the earth and in the alternation of the night and the day, and in the vessels that sail in the sea carrying that which profits people, and in the water that Allah sends down from the clouds and quickens therewith the earth after its death and scatters therein all kinds of beasts, and in the course of the winds, and the clouds pressed into service between the heaven and the earth, are indeed Signs for a people who understand.** Notice how fascinated the writer is by ships and what they bring for the people and how naturally, as in the Hebrew Bible, the author wraps human creativity and technology in the form of ship-making into the overall cosmology of God's Creation. Humans are nature. What they give birth to is Creation also.

The medieval Sufi master Ibn Al-Arabi finds the Divine in all of creation: **In every abode [of being, becoming] the Unique, the Merciful has forms, whether hidden or manifest. . . . His determination applies in every abode equally. Indeed, he is [ever] unfolding his Reality to creation.**

The Bhagavad Gita, the Hindu Scriptures, address God by saying: **Although you are one, you spread throughout the sky and the planets and all space between.** Is this reality not what the biblical writer is also singing about who declares, **the Spirit of the Lord fills the whole universe**?

An ancient poem from the Hindu Scriptures tells of the primacy and the depths inherent in our relationships with the rest of Creation.

If hundreds of thousands of suns were to rise at once into the sky, their radiance might resemble the effulgence of the Supreme Person in that universal form.

O Lord of the universe, O universal form, I see in your body many, many arms, bellies, mouths and eyes, expanded everywhere, without limit. I see in you no end, no middle and no beginning.

You are the original Personality of Godhead, the oldest, the ultimate sanctuary of this manifested cosmic world. . . . O limitless form! This whole cosmic manifestation is pervaded by you!

Understand that as the mighty wind, blowing everywhere, rests always in the sky, all created beings rest in me.

O son of Kunti, at the end of the millennium all material manifestations enter into my nature, and at the beginning of another millennium, by my potency, I create them again.

There is no end to my divine manifestations. What I have spoken to you is but a mere indication of my infinite opulences.

Know that all opulent, beautiful and glorious creations spring from but a spark of my splendor. . . . With a single fragment of myself I pervade and support this entire universe.

Everywhere are his hands and legs, his eyes, heads and faces, and he has ears everywhere. In this way the Supersoul exists, pervading everything.

I enter into each planet, and by my energy they stay in orbit. I

become the moon and thereby supply the juice of life to all vegetables. It is understood that all the planets are floating in the air only by the energy of the Lord. The Lord enters into every atom, every planet, and every living being.

Hindu scholar Iyengar comments that **all creation is Brahman.** The Vedas reveal that **creation is not mechanical construction: it is a supreme spiritual act revealing divine splendor.**

Today's science is rediscovering the immensity of the awe and wonder built into the cosmic community. David Brower, for example, marvels at the **wildness within** all human beings in how our eyes operate with 120 million rods and cones that allow us to see Creation as well as pages of a book in 3-D. The human ear appears almost too complicated to work and the human body carries out 100,000 different chemical reactions—all without our having to think about it. Then there is our immune system—"You're especially impressed if you've been kept more or less intact for eighty-two years," he comments. But we are ridding the earth of its many **miracles of wildness** when we destroy species, many of which hold real medicines for our ills. The miracle of our existence did not come about from civilization. It came from wildness itself since that is all there was. **We need to tire of trashing wildness. It's not making us happy. It's not making us healthy. It is making us miserable and despairing. Killing trees, habitat, and animals, and separating ourselves from nature is making us all a bit crazy. We need to restore the earth because we need to save the wild. We need to save the wild in order to save ourselves.** Brower compares our destroying the earth with the act of burning books. The earth contains our history, our knowledge and wisdom. Why do we harm it so? We are inheritors in our genetic code of a long and beautiful history. **We all possess a little fragment of the first bit of life on earth. Consequently, everything that's alive is related—and a microscopic part of us all is three and a half billion years old.**

Intrinsic to Creation is creativity. Creativity and Creation go together. Only recently has science learned how thoroughly occupied the universe is in giving birth. We now know that the Milky Way gives birth to several stars every year. One is reminded of Meister Eckhart's inquiry: **What does God do all day long? God lies on a maternity bed giving birth.** The universe is biased in favor of birthing and generativity.

Scientist Brian Swimme writes about this bias as a *seething*. **Even where there are no atoms, and no elementary particles, and no protons, and no photons, suddenly elementary particles will emerge. . . . The base of the universe** seethes with creativity, so much so that physicists refer to the universe's ground state as "space-time foam." Swimme urges us to find ourselves in the vast creativity of the universe by meditating on how the sun is whipping the earth and all the other planets through their annual arcs. **Awaken to the fact of the Sun's gravitational power. The earth is one immense planet** [though only one millionth the size of the sun] **and it is being whipped around the Sun** *by the power of the Sun.* **This is something the Sun is** *doing* **in every instant of every day. We are held by the Sun. If the Sun released us from our bond with it, we would sail off into deep space.** Remember, too, that the entire earth is being whipped around at 180 miles per second—that is quite a velocity that is moving us and all beings on earth. We are indeed all in this together!

Thich Nhat Hanh reminds us what it is we are looking at when we look deeply at just one flower. **When we look into the heart of a flower, we see clouds, sunshine, minerals, time, the earth, and everything else in the cosmos in it. Without clouds, there could be no rain, and there would be no flower. Without time, the flower could not bloom. In fact, the flower is made entirely of non-flower elements; it has no independent, individual existence.** Of course we are the same way: Each one of us carries a fifteen-billion-year existence in us, so that when we encounter one another we ought to be awed by the experience. And when we encounter ourselves! No wonder self-knowledge is a journey that takes a lifetime. After all, every hydrogen atom in our bodies has been in existence for fourteen billion years—imagine how many stories they have to tell us alone. What a pity when culture distracts us from this deep self-awareness by its titillating bonbons.

Every day we encounter the cosmos. It is our bodies, our food, our air, our everything. **In East Asia, we speak of the human body as a mini-cosmos. The cosmos is our home, and we can touch it by being aware of our body.** This understanding is called microcosm/macrocosm in the West. We also touch the cosmos by our awareness of all other beings and their interconnected origins. **One thing is made up of all other things. One thing contains the whole cosmos. . . . A piece of bread contains sunshine. . . . Without a cloud, the wheat cannot grow. So when you eat the piece of bread, you eat the cloud, you eat the sunshine, you eat the minerals, time, space, everything.**

So important is Creation in Thich Nhat Hanh's view, that if we fail to penetrate it we will fail to find the ground of being behind it. **If you are not able to touch the phenomenal world deeply enough, it will be very difficult or impossible to touch the noumenal world—the ground of being.** Behind and within the depth of the phenomenal world there lurks the divine presence. Like Christian mysticism that sees every being as another Christ, so Thich Nhat Hanh recognizes that **all beings in the animal, plant, and mineral world are potential Buddhas.** Indeed, for a Buddhist, the supreme fullness of being human is to be awake ("Buddha" means the "awakened one.") **A Buddha is someone who is awake.** But what is more valuable than being awake to the present moment and the present place?

Existence itself is a kind of miracle and we ought to wake up to it. **Our true home is in the present moment. The miracle is not to walk on water. The miracle is to walk on the green earth in the present moment.** The more we learn about our capacity to walk, and what a gift that is, and about the green earth, and what a gift that has been and how long in the making, the more literally we can take Thich Nhat Hanh's advice. **The technique is to be in the present moment, to be aware that we are here and now, that the only moment to be alive is the present moment.** How like Jesus' teaching this is, who told us that **the reign of God is among you** and whose many parables were to underscore the simplicity and the diversity of the reign of God, which at times was like a mustard seed, at times like leaven, at times like a net, at times like a gathering of sheep and goats. An everyday thing, this kingdom/queendom of God! And yet so rare because we have eyes and do not see, ears and do not hear. Like the Buddha, Jesus taught that humanity has to wake up to see differently, to realize how close to heaven we already are. Our relationship to Creation is a kind of test of that wakefulness.

Celtic spirituality is a spirituality of Creation, an awareness of our presence in the sacred grace of Creation. St. Patrick is said to have introduced goodness or blessing as the key element to Celtic spiritual consciousness. **The difference between Patrick's magic and the magic of the druids is that in Patrick's world all beings and events come from the hand of a good God, who loves human beings and wishes them success. . . . All nature, indeed the whole of the created universe, conspires to mankind's good, teaching, succoring, and saving.** In a poem attributed to him called "The Deer Cry," or "Breastplate," Patrick repeats twice the key phrase, **The Creator of Creation.** This poem, probably birthed in the seventh or eighth century, offers **the first ringing assertion that the universe itself is the Great Sacrament.** The natural world is no longer a place of dread. It is revelatory, we can listen to it heart to heart. **This sense of the world as holy, as the Book of God—as a healing mystery fraught with divine messages—could never have risen out of Greco-Roman civilization, threaded with the profound pessimism of the ancients and their Platonic suspicion of the body as unholy.** The Celtic spirit resisted the sexual preoccupations of Jerome and Augustine and the dominant Western church, for in their view **all the world was holy, and so was all the body.** Its attitude is one of trust and expectation.

> **I arise today**
> **Through the strength of heaven:**
> **Light of the sun,**
> **Radiance of moon,**
> **Splendor of fire,**
> **Speed of lightning,**
> **Swiftness of wind,**
> **Depth of sea,**
> **Stability of earth,**
> **Firmness of rock.**

John Scotus Erigena, writing in the ninth century, says: **God is both above everything and in everything, since he, who alone truly is, is the Essence of everything; and although he is whole in everything, he does not cease being whole outside of everything; whole in the world, whole around the world, whole in sensible creation; whole in intelligible creation; whole he makes the universe; whole he is made in the universe, whole in the whole of the universe, whole in its parts.** Erigena was the first philosopher to use the term *universitas,* which played such a role in medieval thinking and indeed in the invention of the university in the twelfth century. The term *universitas* was different from "nature" or "whole" or "everything" because it included God and Creation. It bespeaks cosmology, and by it Erigena implied a belief in an infinity of universes.

African-American philosopher Dona Richards has this to say about the African experience of Creation. **The African universe is conceived as a unified spiritual totality. We speak of the universe as "cosmos" and we mean that all being within it is organically interrelated and interdependent. . . . The essence of the African cosmos is spiritual reality.** She astutely points out the difference between this ancient and holistic worldview and that of European philosophies when she writes that **both spiritual and material beings are necessary in order for there to be a meaningful reality. Enlightenment and the acquisition of wisdom and knowledge depend to a significant degree on being able to apprehend spirit in matter. This crucial difference in European and African thought helps to explain the specialness of African-Diasporic spirituality.**

In the African tradition, the universe is already sacred and its holy Creation continues to unfold. **The spiritual is the foundation of all being because the universe is sacred. The universe was created (is continually "recreated") by a divine act.**

African-American mystic and theologian Howard Thurman warns what happens when humans rupture the sacred relationship with Creation. **This we see all around us in the modern world. Our atmosphere is polluted, our streams are poisoned, our hills are denuded, wild life is increasingly exterminated, while more and more man becomes an alien on the earth and a fouler of his own nest. The price that is being exacted for this is a deep sense of isolation, of being rootless and a vagabond. Often I have surmised that this condition is more responsible for what seems to be the phenomenal increase in mental and emotional disturbances in modern life than the pressures—economic, social, and political—that abound on every hand. The collective psyche shrieks with the agony that it feels as part of the death cry of a pillaged nature.**

Other ancient spiritual teachings, those of the indigenous peoples of the Americas, take for granted the sacredness of all of Creation and how humanity relating to Creation *is* humanity facing the powers of Spirit and the Creator. Jamake Highwater writes: **The American Indian has an entirely different view of humanity and nature from that of the Greek heritage. For primal peoples, because the landscape itself is sacred it therefore embodies a divinity that it shares with everything that is part of nature, including human beings, animals, plants, rocks . . . everything.** Because humans are part of nature, so too is the architecture and creativity of human beings part of nature. The inherent sacredness of creation is attested to by Black Elk who says: **We regard all created beings as sacred and important, for everything has a *wochangi,* or influence, which can be given to us, through which we may gain a little more understanding if we are attentive. We should understand well that all things are the work of the Great Spirit. We should know that he is within all things; the trees, the grasses, the rivers, the mountains and all the four-legged animals, and the winged peoples; and even more important, we should understand that he is also above all these things and peoples.** Notice how revelation or understanding flow to humans from all beings when humans pay attention. Humans need this relationship with creation to find true peace and the center of their existence, Black Elk insists. **Peace comes within the souls of men when they realize their relationship, their oneness, with the universe and all its powers, and when they realize that at the center of the Universe dwells *Wakan-Tanka* [the Great Spirit], and that this center is really everywhere, it is within each of us.**

Given the intrinsic value and divine presence to be found in Creation, the demise of Creation's health and beauty represents an immense spiritual plight. An Old Omaha elder remembers his youth: **When I walked abroad I could see many forms of life, beautiful living creatures which *Wakanda* had placed here; and these were, after their manner, walking, flying, leaping, running, playing all about.** But changes have taken place. **Now the face of all the land is changed and sad. The living creatures are gone. I see the land desolate and I suffer an un-**

speakable sadness. **Sometimes I wake in the night and I feel as though I should suffocate from the pressure of this awful feeling of loneliness.**

Loneliness happens when humans separate from the rest of Creation and treat Creation as separate or "other." Oren Lyons, Faithkeeper of the Turtle Clan of the Onondaga Nation and spokesman for the Six Nations Iroquois Confederacy, says: **One of the Natural laws is that you've got to keep things pure. Especially the water. Keeping the water pure is one of the first laws of life. If you destroy the water, you destroy life. That's what I mean about common sense. Anybody can see that. All life on Mother Earth depends on pure water, yet we spill every kind of dirt and filth and poison into it.** The inherent sacredness of water and creation demands something from humans. That something is respect. **Another of the Natural laws is that all life is equal. That's our philosophy. You have to respect life— all life, not just your own. The key word is "respect." Unless you respect the earth, you destroy it. Unless you respect all life as much as your own life, you become a destroyer, a murderer. Man sometimes thinks he's been elevated to be the controller, the ruler. But he's not. He's only a part of the whole. Man's job is not to exploit but to oversee, to be a steward. Man has responsibility, not power.**

Matthew King, a traditionalist spokesman of the Lakota people whose Indian name is Noble Red Man, tells how Native people view nature. **We have the wind and the rain and the stars for our Bible. The world is an open Bible for us. We Indians have studied it for millions and millions of years. We've learned that God rules the universe and that everything God made is living. Even the rocks are alive. When we use them in our sweat ceremony we talk to them and they talk back to us.** This teaching is mirrored in the West by Thomas Aquinas who said that **revelation comes in two volumes: Nature and the Bible.** But the native people seem to have taken the revelation of Nature most seriously.

3.

LIGHT

Beautiful you rise, O eternal living god!
You are radiant, lovely, powerful,
Your love is great, all-encompassing.
Your rays make all radiant,
Your brightness gives life to hearts,
When you fill the Two Lands with your love.
—Praise to the Aten, Eighteenth Dynasty,
1550–1305 B.C., Kemet (Egypt)

To talk of Creation is to talk about light. This is evident in so many creation stories from that of Akhenaten in Kemet (Egypt) to that of Genesis and Psalm104 and the prologue to John's Gospel in the Bible to that of today's Creation story from science.

In today's creation story from science we learn that the universe began with a fireball that grew from a compressed light smaller than a pinprick to an expanding fire over 750,000 years. When the fireball finally burned out, it passed on its offspring of atoms that would in turn give birth to galaxies, supernovas, stars, the sun, our earth, plants that eat sunlight in the process of photosynthesis, and animals, including ourselves, who also eat, breathe, and bask in sunlight. Indeed, even our brains emit photons or light waves when we put creative ideas together.

While listening to the new storytellers about Creation's origins, one is swimming in stories about fireballs and photons and light. Thomas Berry and Brian Swimme tell the story this way.

> **Fifteen billion years ago, in a great flash,**
> **the universe flared forth into being.**
> **In each drop of existence**
> **a primordial energy blazed with an intensity**
> **never to be equaled again. . . .**
> **In the beginning the universe is a great shining**
> **that expands rapidly and then explodes into hundreds of billions of**
> **dark clouds. . . .**
> **[Later] a hundred billion galaxies light up with a splendor**
> **new to the universe.**
> **The beginning of the universe is a smooth, intense flame.**
> **A few billion years later the large-scale structure of the universe**
> **glows in great sheets of galaxies**
> **and in their intersections in long, spidery filaments of sparkling worlds.**

The originating power that brought forth a universe made reality such that stars, lizards and supernovas would all **blaze** with the same **numinous energy that flared forth at the dawn of time.** The first of the atoms, hydrogen, was special because photons or light waves could pass through them without ever being obstructed. Hydrogen becomes a special conductor for light to move through. The eventual birth of supernovas was an explosive light burst, whose intensity **outshines even a galaxy of two hundred billion stars.**

Albert Einstein said in the early part of the last century that "all I want to do is study light." As the century drew to a close, we could begin to glimpse what science is learning through light and about light. Light drives all energy systems. Plants and we eat light, breathe light, drink light and transform light into energy. Light is far more prevalent in the universe than is matter—indeed, for every molecule of matter there are one billion particles of light! The Egyptian prayers to the sun as well as the aboriginal rituals that follow the sun's path from rising to setting are seeming more and more wise every day. Part of the scientific contribution to light at this time in human history is to insist on the need to become sustainable again in human energy needs. This is the practical application of solar awareness. Only sun energies are renewable and sustainable—the time when humans ran their enterprises on fossil fuels is rapidly coming to a close. We must rediscover light or perish.

If we are to fit into creation once again instead of attempting to stand outside it and control it (and in the process killing it), then we must imitate nature's source of energy. As physicist Fritjof Capra puts it: **Ecosystems differ from individual organisms in that they are . . . open with respect to the flow of energy. The primary source for that flow of energy is the sun. Solar energy, transformed into chemical energy by the photosynthesis of green plants, drives most ecological cycles.** He draws implications for our human decision-making and the maintaining of sustainable human communities. **Solar energy in its many forms—sunlight for solar heating and photovoltaic electricity, wind and hydropower, biomass, and so on—is the only kind of energy that is renewable, economically efficient, and environmentally benign.** When our corporations and governments disregard solar energy they endanger the well-being of the planet and of generations to come.

As Capra indicates, our economic perspective, when it leaves light and the sun out, contributes to the degradation of the planet. Solar energy is economically efficient, but not if one cheats in counting the costs of energy production—and when our economists operate without a solar perspective the balance sheets lie to us. **The so-called free market does not provide consumers with proper information, because the social and environmental costs of production are not part of current economic models. These costs are labeled "external" variables by corporate and government economists, because they do not fit into their theoretical framework.**

We now know that matter is trapped light: slow-moving light; or "frozen light" as physicist David Bohm puts it. Yet, because for every particle of matter in the universe there are one billion particles of light, we are amazed to learn how special matter is, how rare matter is, what a rare gift it is to be flesh or matter, that is, slow-moving light. This is not just true of human flesh but of all flesh, the oranges we eat and the tea we drink, the grasses and the animals, the birds and the stars— all are slow-moving light. Matter *is* light. It is very special light.

Even music is light. And electricity, magnetism, and visible light are all different manifestations of radiant energy. These long, gentle undulations are what we call "radio waves." It is said that while "radio waves are at the far end of the electromagnetic spectrum and are invisible, they are a form of light." This invisible light makes music everyone can hear. Radio transmitters generate sound that has been converted into light. "Because of music's transubstantiation into light, space has contracted like an accordion, and a vast, invisible electromagnetic net has been silently cast over all of humankind."

Light is everywhere! That is today's creation story and it is a story told by many ancient traditions as well.

From Kemet or ancient Egypt the African peoples sang praises to the god Aten in the Eighteenth Dynasty, which dates from 1550 to 1305 B.C.E.

> **Beautiful you rise, O eternal living god!**
> **You are radiant, lovely, powerful,**
> **Your love is great, all-encompassing.**
> **Your rays make all radiant,**
> **Your brightness gives life to hearts,**
> **When you fill the Two Lands with your love.**

Notice how the author connects psyche and cosmos, heart and sun, in this praise of warmth and sunlight. From the same dynasty another hymn to Aten celebrates the power of the sun and its influence on daily life.

> **Beautiful you rise in heaven's horizon,**
> **O eternal, living creator! . . .**
> **You are lovely, great, radiant,**
> **High over every land;**
> **Your rays embrace the lands,**
> **To the limit of your creations. . . .**
> **Though you are far, your rays are on earth. . . .**
> **When you set in the western horizon,**
> **Earth is in darkness as if in death;. . . .**
> **Earth brightens when you rise in the eastern horizon,**
> **When you shine as Aten of daytime;**
> **As you dispel the dark,**
> **As you cast your rays,**
> **The Two Lands are in festivity.**
> **Awake they stand on their feet,**
> **You have awakened them;**

Bodies washed, clothed,
Their arms love your appearance.
The entire land sets out to work,
All beasts browse on their herbs;
Trees, herbs are sprouting.
Birds fly from their nests,
Their wings greeting your *ka*.

This Creation poem mixes light and Creation. One senses that the African peoples of Kemet did not take the sun or light for granted as we so often do in our culture. They honored its arrival each morning with outstretched hands and they understood its influence on human and other living things—giving it credit for getting them out of bed.

Another prayer from the same period also honors the Creator of light.

Primeval without equal,
Creator of men and gods,
Living flame that came from Num,
Maker of light for mankind.

The Celtic tradition also celebrates light. John O'Donohue tells us that the most venerated among the ancient gods was Lugh, the god of light and giftedness, "The Shining One." O'Donohue teaches that **the Celtic mind adored the light. . . . We desperately need a new and gentle light where the soul can shelter and reveal its ancient belonging. . . . Ultimately, light is the mother of life. Where there is no light, there can be no life. If the angle of the sun were to turn away from the earth, all human, animal, and vegetative life, as we know it, would disappear. Ice would freeze the earth again. Light is the secret presence of the divine. It keeps life awake.** In "The Deer's Cry" poem we saw earlier, the poet attributes his arising in the morning to the

> **Strength of heaven,**
> **Light of sun,**
> **Radiance of moon,**
> **Splendor of fire.**

O'Donohue believes that **light is the mother of life. The sun brings light or color. It causes grasses, crops, leaves, and flowers to grow. The sun brings forth the erotic charge of the curved earth; it awakens her wild sensuousness.** In a Gaelic poem the sun is venerated as the eye and face of God.

> **The eye of the great God,**
> **The eye of the God of glory,**
> **The eye of the king of hosts,**
> **The eye of the king of the living.**
> **Pouring upon us**
> **At each time and season,**
> **Pouring upon us**
> **gently and generously**

> Glory to thee
>> Thou glorious sun.
> Glory to thee, thou son
>> Face of the God of life.

Wisely does O'Donohue insist on the intimate and constant relation between darkness and light. **We need a light that has retained its kinship with the darkness,** he warns. Nature's cycles, the night that yields to sunrise, our own birth cycles, all these rhythms are rhythms from dark to light, winter to spring, womb to light of day. Light does not stand by its own; it stands in relation to the dark.

Among the Celts, the sense of "enlightenment" was also employed—light became a metaphor for our mind work. **In the Celtic tradition, thought has often been compared to light. In its luminosity, the intellect was deemed to be the place of the divine within us.**

Native American teachings also honor the sun as a special gift of the Creator, one that elicits gratitude from our hearts as well as a need to imitate its ways. Onondaga Chief Powless says: **The Creator gave us the sun, our elder brother. It's his duty to give us warmth and to nourish the life-giving foods that were planted on earth. And, as we see, the sun came up this morning and shines on us, keeping us warm. He's doing his duty. And for this we are very grateful. So let us put our minds together as one and thank the sun for still performing his duty. And let our minds be that way.** The moon too blesses us. **The moon will be your Grandmother. And she will have special duties also. She will give moisture to dampen the land at night. She will also move the tides. Along with the moon there will be stars. The stars help give us directions when we travel and, along with Grandmother Moon, tell us when we should begin our ceremonies.**

The Aboriginal people of Australia tell their story of the Creation of the sun. **When the world was young, everyone had to search for food in the dim light of the moon, for there was no sun. Then came the time when the emu and the brolga, both of whom were sitting on a nest of eggs, had a violent argument over the excellence of their chicks. Finally the angry brolga ran to the nest of her rival and, taking one of her eggs, hurled it into the sky, where it shattered against a pile of sticks gathered by the sky-people.**

The yolk of the egg, bursting into flame, caused such a huge fire that its light revealed, for the first time, the beauty of the world beneath. When the people in the sky saw this beauty, they decided that the inhabitants below should have day and night.

Another creation story from the Aboriginal peoples of the Dieyerie tribe teaches that all living creatures were created by the moon. When humans appeared, guided only by the moon's light, they found it dark and bitterly cold, for there was no sun. Hunting was a special problem, and hunting emu, the largest game of all, was frustrating. The emu could easily vanish into the darkness. **So the hunters held a great gathering, performed many ceremonies, and pleaded with Mooramoora (the great spirit who made all things) to make their world warmer and lighter so that they could capture the emu. And Morramoora listened to their troubles and made the sun, thus creating day and night.**

Another story tells how fire was discovered when a bolt of lightning struck a tree and set it ablaze. A couple who observed this event went to the chief of the tribe with their news, and he recognized the value of this new thing. The comfort of the blazing log convinced the chief that they **had found something that would give his people light to dispel their darkness, and heat to keep them warm.**

He gave a large torch of blazing wood to the woman and a smaller torch to the man, and so that the twin blessings of light and warmth would never be lost he sent them up into the sky to become the sun and moon. He divided the rest of the burning log amongst the tribe, and told them to place a coal in every tree so that the spirit of fire would always be available to everyone.

With fire to cook their food, keep them warm, and light their darkness, life suddenly became so much easier that the Aborigines increased in numbers and gradually spread over their new land. The use of fire not only altered man's way of life, but set him apart from the rest of Creation as nothing else could have done.

ONE RIVER, MANY WELLS

From ancient India, the Bhagavad Gita celebrates the divine origin of light. Krishna or the supreme Godhead speaks:

The splendor of the sun, which dissipates the darkness of this whole world, comes from Me. And the splendor of the moon and the splendor of fire are also from Me.

Krishna is the source of light in all luminous objects. He is beyond the darkness of matter and is unmanifested. He is knowledge, He is the object of knowledge, and He is the goal of knowledge. He is situated in everyone's heart. All light is said to derive from the light of the Lord of the Universe.

> **Your glory is unlimited.**
> **You have numberless arms,**
> **and the sun and moon are your eyes.**
> **I see you with blazing fire coming forth from your mouth,**
> **burning this entire universe by your own radiance.**

In the Mundaka Upanishad we read: **Radiant in his light, yet invisible in the secret place of the heart, the Spirit is the supreme abode wherein dwells all that moves and breathes and sees. . . . He is self-luminous and more subtle than the smallest; From the Light of the Spirit, the sun, moon and stars give light; and his radiance illumines all Creation.**

In the Vedas, Brahman is celebrated as Light.

> **The cosmic waters glow. I am Light!**
> **The light glows. I am Brahman!**

But this great light also glows within humans. Atman is a great light residing inside of us. **There is a Light that shines above this heaven, above all worlds, above everything that exits in the highest worlds beyond which there are no higher—this is the Light that shines within man.**

God's light illumines all being.

In the highest golden sheath is the Godhead,
unsullied, indivisible; pure is it,
the Light of lights. He who knows the self knows it. . . .
With the radiance of that Light alone all things shine.
That radiance illumines all this world.

Nikhilananda says that *chit*, or awareness, remains even when we are sleeping and even when one's body and mind are dead. This knowing subject within us is self-luminous and needs no other light to illuminate itself. **The light that illumi-nates the sun is the light of Brahman; when Brahman shines everything shines, by Brahman's light everything is lighted.** Light is the supreme image of both the Atman and the Brahman. We touch this light when we understand our own Self. **Since Vedic times light has been regarded as an epiphany of Being, of Spirit.** It is where cosmos and psyche come together. **The light that shines beyond this Heaven, beyond all, in the highest worlds beyond which there are none higher, is truly the same light that shines within the person.** The light is in the human heart. The Atman is the Self that is in the heart of a human being, in the form of a **light in the heart.**

To approach Divinity is difficult because of the immense radiance that is there. **Your form is difficult to see because of its glaring effulgence, spreading on all sides, like blazing fire or the immeasurable radiance of the sun. Yet I see this glowing form everywhere, adorned with various crowns, clubs, and discs.**

Parallels between the African, Celtic, Native, and Hindu teachings and the Jewish Scriptures around this theme of light abound. In Genesis we learn that the first thing created was light. **God said, "Let there be light," and there was light. God saw that light was good, and God divided light from darkness. God called light "day," and darkness he called "night." Evening came and morning came: the first day.** The psalmist sings of how Divinity itself comes robed in light.

> **Yahweh my God, how great you are!**
> **Clothed in majesty and glory,**
> **wrapped in a robe of light!**

The word *glory (doxa* in Greek) bespeaks light, radiance, and splendor. Nature is filled with the glory of God, who is **king of glory** and has poured out the divine radiance into Creation. We hear that **the heavens declare the glory of God, and the firmament proclaims His handiwork.**

One of the great mystical works in Judaism is named *Zohar.* This medieval mystical text has been called the magnum opus of Spanish Jewish Kabbalah in the late thirteenth century. The very meaning of the word *Zohar* is **radiance, splendor,** or **brilliance.** It is a word like glory. In the *Zohar* we are instructed that the **radiance of Shekinah shined in Moses and when he was born the whole house was filled with light!** Shekinah is said to rest on the heads (the seventh chakra?) of those who do good deeds. Indeed, **the human body is a wick, and a light is kindled above. . . . The light on one's head needs oil, the oil of good deeds!**

In the *Zohar,* Creation began as **a blinding spark flashed within the Concealed of the Concealed from the mystery of the Infinite.** Sparks were everywhere, dancing and whirling about.

> **Sparks burst into flashes, up high and down below**
> **then quieted down and rose up high, beyond, beyond. . . .**
> **The spark expanded, whirling round and round.**

Sparks burst into flash and rose high above.
The heavens blazed with all their powers;
everything flashed and sparkled as one.
Then the spark turned from the side of the South
and outlined a curve from there to the East
and from the East to the North
until it had circled back to the South, as before.
Then the spark swirled, disappearing;
comets and flashes dimmed.

Notice how the four directions are invoked to depict the cosmic nature of the sparkling of the universe.

In the great Jewish mystical work, the *Kabbalah,* sparks are frequently invoked. The creation of human beings is attributed to sparks gathering. **In our case, a few sparks of light adhered. . . . They were transformed into the four elements— fire, air, water, and earth—from which evolved the stages of mineral, vegetable, animal, and human. When these materialized, some of the sparks remained hidden within the varieties of existence. You should aim to raise those sparks hidden throughout the world, elevating them to holiness by the power of your soul.** Our interaction with other creatures is an exchange of light and sparks. **Sparks of holiness intermingle with everything in the world, even inanimate objects. Even by eating, you bring forth sparks that cleave to your soul.**

All pleasure is due to sparks meeting sparks. **When you eat and drink, you experience enjoyment and pleasure from the food and drink. Arouse yourself every moment to ask in wonder, "What is this enjoyment and pleasure? What is it that I am tasting?" Answer yourself, "This is nothing but the holy sparks from the sublime, holy worlds that are within the food and drink."**

Holiness is an educing of the spark from within. **When you desire to eat or drink, or to fulfill other worldly desires, and you focus your awareness on the love of God, then you elevate that physical desire to spiritual desire.**

Thereby you draw out the holy spark that dwells within. You bring forth holy sparks from the natural world. There is no path greater than this. For wherever you go and whatever you do—even mundane activities—you serve God. Our task in life is to awaken the sparks in one another. We constantly aspire to raise the holy sparks. We know that the potent energy of the divine ideal—the splendor at the root of existence—has not yet been revealed and actualized in the world around us. Yet the entire momentum of being approaches that ideal. . . . In proportion to the sparks we raise, our lives are enriched. It is from the heart that our sparks fly. Love and sparks from the flame of our heart will escort you.

Two stories concerning Divinity and fire stand out in the Jewish Scriptures and receive imaginative interpretations in the *Zohar*. One concerns the experience Moses had with Divinity in the burning bush; and the second concerns the first act of Creation, the making of light.

> "The angel of YHVH appeared to him in a flame of fire."
> To Moses in a flame of fire, unlike other prophets.
> Why?
> Rabbi Judah said,
> "Moses was not like other prophets.
> We have learned:
> One who comes close to fire is burned.
> Yet Moses came close to fire and was not burned,
> as it is written."

Commenting on the story of Creation, **God said, "Let there be light!" And there was light,** the *Zohar* teaches:

> This is the light that the Blessed Holy One created at first.
> It is the light of the eye.

It is the light that the Blessed Holy One showed the first Adam;
with it he saw from one end of the world to the other. . . .
It is the light that the Blessed Holy One showed David;
he sang its praise:
"How great is Your good that You have concealed for those who fear
You!"
It is the light that the Blessed Holy One showed Moses. . . .

It is said that God hid the light away so that evil ones could not make use of it.
Then God gave it to Moses.

Rabbi Isaac said,
"the light created by the Blessed Holy One in the act of Creation
flared from one end of the world to the other
and was hidden away.
Why was it hidden away?
So the wicked of the world would not enjoy it . . ."
Rabbi Judah said,
"If it were completely hidden
the world would not exist for even a moment!
Rather, it is hidden and sown like a seed
that gives birth to seeds and fruit.
Thereby the world is sustained.
Every single day, a ray of that light shines into the world
and keeps everything alive,
and with that ray the Blessed Holy One feeds the world. . . .
Since the first day, it has never been fully revealed,
but it plays a vital role in the world,
renewing every day the act of Creation!"

The Christian Scriptures take up the theme of connection between the Divine and light. Much of this derives from comparing the Christ experience to Wisdom, who is called **a reflection of light, a spotless mirror of the working of God, and an image of his goodness.** In John's Gospel we read:

All that came to be had life in him
and that life was the light of people,
a light that shines in the dark,
a light that darkness could not overpower.

The Christ in John's Gospel is continually discoursing on the theme of light.

I am the light of the world;
anyone who follows me will not be walking in the dark;
he will have the light of life.

And when he was preparing to cure the man born blind who would receive his sight back (i.e., light), the Christ is reported to say:

As long as I am in the world
I am the light of the world.

This idea that Christ brings light to the world or enlightenment is spoken of in the prologue to John's Gospel:

The Word was the true light
that enlightens all men;
and he was coming into the world.

The Gospel of Thomas relays the following teaching from Jesus. **Jesus said: If they say to you: "Where are you from?" say to them: "We came from the light** there, where the light was, by itself. It stood boldly and manifested itself in their image." Jesus speaks in that gospel as he does in John's about his relationship to light. **I am the light that is over all things. I am all: from me all came forth, and to me all attained.** Clearly these are not words of the historical Jesus but of the Cosmic Christ, which the community put into the mouth of Jesus.

The Christian Scriptures also employ the term *doxa* or *glory* or radiance to speak of Christ's relationship to light. This is often used of theophanies in the Scriptures and in the gospels. For example, in John's Gospel we read:

> **The Word was made flesh,**
> **he lived among us,**
> **and we saw his glory [doxa],**
> **the glory that is his as the only Son of the Father,**
> **full of grace and truth.**

The word *doxa* relates to the *Shekinah* of Judaism, the divine light that dwells among us everywhere. Glory bespeaks brightness and radiance, magnificence and splendor in the New Testament literature. Mark's Gospel depicts the transfiguration as a scene of brightness and dazzlement. In this scene, Jesus is seen in all his glory or *doxa*. The glory of humanity is to be a brilliant mirror or image of Divinity. As St. Paul put it: **We all, with faces unveiled, reflecting as in a mirror the glory of the Lord, are being transformed into His very image from glory to glory, as through the Spirit of the Lord.** The risen Christ, whom we are to emulate, is called **the Lord of glory.** Yet Christ's glory in Jesus did not come as a privilege but through the suffering of his death and crucifixion.

Fire is also an important theme and a sign of Spirit. At the Pentecost event, disciples are said to have experienced fire. At the Easter liturgy, the Resurrection event is celebrated with a newly kindled fire and a Paschal candle. Fire is a numinous presence in Moses' experience on the mountaintop with Divinity. Spirit brings fire, as Mechtild of Magdeburg celebrates:

Lie down in the Fire.
See and taste the flowing Godhead
    through your being.
Feel the Holy Spirit moving and compelling you
    within the flowing Fire and Light of God.

Thomas Aquinas says that **God is light; and one who approaches this light is illuminated, as Isaiah says: "Rise, in love, and be enlightened."** To understand the image of God in the human is to approach the divine light. We possess reason, which is **nothing other than the light of divine brightness reflected in the soul. It is because of this brightness that the soul is close to the image of God, as the psalmist says: "Lord, the light of your face has shown upon us."** Aquinas teaches that God has planted a divine radiance in every creature. **God puts into creatures, along with a kind of "sheen," a reflection of God's own luminous "ray," which is the fountain of all light . . . Shining reflections of the divine radiance must be understood as the sharing of God's likeness and constitute those "beautifying" reflections that make beauty in things.** Like today's science, Aquinas sees light as being at the heart of every creation. **The being of things is itself their light and the measure of the being of a thing is the measure of its light.**

Hildegard of Bingen celebrates the presence of the divine light on numerous occasions. **There is no Creation that does not have a radiance. Be it greenness or seed, blossom or beauty. It could not be creation without it.** The divine radiance or glory (*doxa*) is everywhere among us. **All Creation is gifted with the ecstasy of God's light**, Hildegard observes. Indeed, every creature is a glittering, glistening **mirror of divinity.** To be an image is to mirror something. And the Divinity we image is a light-filled, light-making, enlightening, warm, radiant, glorious face. We mirror light because God is light. **God says: I am the day unto myself, not formed by the sun, but rather, forming the sun, igniting it.** Creation, light, and Divinity go together for Hildegard. **I, God, remain hidden in every kind of reality as a fiery power. Everything burns because of me.** Wisdom is said to reside in Creation as light.

> **I, the fiery life of divine wisdom,**
> **I ignite the beauty of the plains,**
> **I sparkle the waters,**
> **I burn in the sun, and the moon, and the stars.**

God is the fire in all things.

> **God says: I am the supreme fire;**
> **not deadly, but rather, enkindling every spark of life.**

But the light of which Hildegard sings burns also in human consciousness—indeed it is the light of the Holy Spirit.

> **Who is the Holy Spirit?**
> **The Holy Spirit is a Burning Spirit.**
> **It kindles the hearts of humankind.**

Like tympanum and lyre it plays them,
gathering volume in the temple of the soul.

She describes her own awakening at forty-two years old as a **burning light of tremendous brightness coming from heaven pour[ing] into my entire mind. Like a flame that does not burn but enkindles, it enflamed my entire heart and my entire breast, just like the sun that warms an object with its rays.** The paintings that she drew from her visions that followed on this experience she called **Illuminations.** She paints her awakening experience in the image of the Pentecost event, with flames of fire descending on her head just as they were said to have descended on the first apostles. In calling on the image of the "spark of life," Hildegard is invoking the tradition of the "ancilla animae" or spark of the soul that was developed so richly in Jewish mysticism.

Meister Eckhart develops the tradition of the *ancilla animae* when he says: **God glows and burns with all the divine wealth and all the divine bliss in the spark of the soul.** Indeed, God is birthed there in the spark of the soul. It is a kind of manger. This spark is **never extinguished** and contains a knowledge that sees **all in all and all in all**—a mystical knowledge. The spark is **a simple power that knows God** and within it **is hidden something like the original outbreak of all goodness, something like a brilliant light that glows incessantly and something like a burning fire which burns incessantly. This fire is nothing other than the Holy Spirit.** Furthermore, this spark names the image of God in us. **In the soul there is something like a spark of divine nature, a divine light, a ray, an imprinted picture of the divine nature. . . . Here is located the image of God that the mind is.** Indeed, the term "spark" becomes an intimate and personalized term for the divine light that bathes all being.

St. John of the Cross, the sixteenth-century Spanish Carmelite mystic and poet who was imprisoned and beaten daily by his Carmelite brothers for trying to reform his order in a time of corruption, wrote a poem about his escape from that prison. It was a daring escape, for had he been captured he would have been killed; but also had he not escaped, he would have died from his rapidly declining health. Where did he get the courage for his decision? He tells us.

> **There in the lucky dark,**
> **none to observe me, darkness far and wide;**
> **no sign for me to mark,**
> **no other light, no guide**
> **except for my heart—the fire, the fire inside!**
> **That led me on**
> **true as the very noon is—truer too!—**
> **to where there waited one**
> **I knew—how well I knew!—**
> **in a place where no one was in view.**

It was from the fire in his heart, the sparks in his heart, his desire to live that he acquired the courage to risk everything. And this fire was as bright as the noonday sun even though the night, happily, was a moonless one that made the escape successful.

John of the Cross writes a poem called "The Living Flame of Love," which is about the "total transformation of the soul in the Beloved." To read it and his commentary is to recognize the fullness of sparks that mature into flame. The soul not only unites to the fire that God is but also **produces within a living flame.** Thus, for John, true love is creative and fruitful. **This flame of love is the Holy Spirit. . . . And that flame, every time it flares up, bathes the soul in glory and refreshes it with the quality of divine life. Such is the activity of the Holy Spirit in the soul transformed in love: the interior acts he produces shoot up flames,** for they are acts of inflamed love, in which the will of the soul united with that flame, made one with it, loves most sublimely.

John believes that because the Holy Spirit is so fully at work, **all the acts of the soul are divine. . . . Hence it seems to a person that every time this flame shoots up, making him love with delight and divine quality, it is giving him eternal life, since it raises him up to the activity of God in God.** Love takes on the characteristics of fire; it is highly active. **Since love is never idle, but in continual motion, it is always emitting flames everywhere like a blazing fire. . . .** The soul is affected **in its deepest center,** for **God does his work in the soul's depths.** And **the soul's center is God.** The soul can always go deeper into the center, deeper into God.

Taoist poet Liu I-Ming calls us to inner and outer illumination, which culminates in our **round luminosity.**

> **When the inward and the outward are illuminated,**
> **and all is clear,**
> **you are one with the light of sun and moon.**
> **When developed to its ultimate state,**
> **this is a round luminosity**
> **which nothing can deceive. . . .**

Buddhism honors the *enlightenment* that can befall every human being. We all share the potential for luminosity. Buddhism understands the nature of the mind to be luminous. **Buddha said, "Be you lamps unto yourselves."**

Just as the Cosmic Christ is understood by Christians to be the light in all beings in the universe (a fact now scientifically spoken of as the photons or light waves in every atom in the universe), so in Buddhism the Living Buddha is **always shining, always enlightening trees, grass, birds, human beings, and so on, always emitting light. It is this Buddha who is preaching now and not just 2,500 years ago.** In Buddhism, the word for ignorance is *avidya* and this means literally "the lack of light." *Vidya* or understanding means "made of light." Because light exists in all things, all things preach of the Buddha (is this not an insight from St. Francis of Assisi also?). Thich Nhat Hanh says: **The trees, the birds, the violet bamboo, and the yellow chrysanthemums are all preaching the Dharma that Shakyamuni** (the historical Buddha) **preached 2,500 years ago. We can be in touch with him through any of these. He is a living Buddha, always available.** All are invited to find the Buddha within. **The road to Buddhahood is open to all. At all times all living beings have the Germ of Buddhahood in them. If the element of the Buddha did not exist in everyone, there could be no disgust with suffering, nor could there be a wish for Nirvana.**

This teaching about the living Buddha found in light beings and bringing enlightenment to human beings seems identical to the teaching of the Cosmic Christ, who is present in all beings as light and brings enlightenment to humans. Perhaps we can, borrowing from today's science, distinguish between *light as wave* and *light as particle. As wave,* both the Cosmic Christ and the Buddha Nature extend everywhere and permeate all beings. *As particles,* the historical Buddha and the historical Jesus were particular people from particular cultures operating in a particular time period. Thus the light of the Buddha and the light of the Christ have both wave and particle elements to them. As do we who share in their light.

The Qur'an celebrates the divine light and the light of Creation.

> God is the light of the Heavens and the earth.
> The likeness of his Light is as a niche wherein is a lamp,
> the lamp in a glass
> the glass as it were a glittering star,
> kindled from a Blessed Tree,
> an olive that is neither of the East nor of the West
> whole oil well nigh would shine, even if no fire touched it:
> Light up on Light;
> God guides to his Light whom he will.
> And strikes similitudes for men,
> and God has knowledge of everything.

Sufi poet Rumi celebrates the spark of the Divine in all our hearts.

Ah, once more he put a fire in me,
And once more this crazy heart
    is craving the open plains.
This ocean of love breaks into another wave
And blood pours from my heart
    in all directions.

Ah, one spark flew
    and burned the house of my heart.
Smoke filled the sky.
The flames grew fierce in the wind.

The fire of the heart is not easily lit.
So don't cry out: "O Lord, rescue me
    from the burning flames!"

Sufi poet Hafiz sees light permeating nature.

The sun's eyes are painting fields again.
Its lashes with expert strokes
are sweeping across the land.
A great palette of light has embraced this earth.

Sun and moon both teach us to become light and be transformed into our true, light beings.

The moon came to me last night
with a sweet question.

She said:
"The sun has been my faithful lover
for millions of years.
Whenever I offer my body to him
Brilliant light pours from his heart.
Thousands then notice my happiness
And delight in pointing
Toward my beauty.
Hafiz, is it true that our destiny
Is to turn into Light Itself?"

The sun's source is nothing other than Divinity itself and this has implications
for all of us.

The sun once glimpsed God's true nature
    And has never been the same.
Thus that radiant sphere
Constantly pours its energy
    Upon this earth.
As does he from behind the veil.
With a wonderful God like that
Why isn't everyone a screaming drunk?

We have considered the theme of *light*. One cannot talk about creation or its
manifold periods of light and dark without talking about light. Nor can one talk
about consciousness without alluding to light. Nor can we talk about love without
recalling sparks and fire and flame. Thomas Aquinas observes that **the first effect of
love is melting.** Perhaps our reintroducing awareness of light will allow us to revisit
the warmth and melting of frozen hearts that occurs when we are less than enlightened.

4.

COMMUNITY AND
INTERDEPENDENCE

> **In tribal religions there is no salvation apart from the
> continuance of the tribe itself because the existence
> of the individual presupposes the existence of
> the community. . . . Life does not exist without the tribe
> which gives animation to its members.**
> **—Jamake Highwater, *The Primal Mind***

Having considered spiritual teachings around creation and light, it seems appropriate to consider teachings around *community*. Community is another word for *Creation*. If all Creation is made up of light, then all community is in some way the gathering of light, the relationship of light beings to each other.

Community is the basis of much spirituality around the world, as we shall see. And yet so much sense of community has been lost in the modern world. Loneliness in its many guises replaces community. Loneliness often speaks it sad story through addictions of alcohol, drugs, shopping, food, sex. For the human heart was not meant to be cut off from other hearts, either human or other than human. But modern science taught us that we humans were accidents in the universe, having arrived by blind chance, and that the universe itself was cold and hard and indifferent like a machine—such a story from our scientific elders did not make for community. In addition, we were instructed that the building blocks of matter were impenetrable objects fighting each other for space—this, too, did not create a model for community to happen.

Post-modern science, however, has taken us back to more ancient notions that are conducive to and supportive of community. Today we are told that atoms are not impenetrable—they are more like bubbles than like billiard balls and their linking up is what forms molecules, whose linking up forms cells, whose linking up forms organisms, whose linking up forms communities. Behold! Now we have a basis in physics once again to honor community.

Communities exist everywhere in nature. One example comes from Wes Jackson, director of the Land Institute in Salina, Kansas, who points to the relationship between soil and the human. "Soil is a placenta or matrix, a living organism which is larger than the life it supports, a tough elastic membrane which has given rise to many life forms. . . ." But soil is not being acknowledged for what it is. "It is itself now dying. It is a death that is utterly senseless, and portends our own." The split in the natural community between the human and the soil is responsible for this killing. What is good for the hive is good for the bee. What is good for the community is good for the individuals in it. As we humans get over our anthropocentrism and return to a sense of our rightful place in nature and in Creation, we can put our curiosity and talent into learning from nature instead of trying to conquer it and lord over it.

To hear the new Creation story from scientists is to hear of the **bonding** that exists between the sun and its planets and between all beings, for we all share a common origin. Another way to say this is that **reality is a universe and not a pluriverse.** In this reality all things are indeed connected. Hundreds of billions of stars in our Milky Way galaxy spin about **in a bonded relationship with every other one.** At the same time, the Milky Way itself is in a bonded relationship with all one hundred billion galaxies of the universe, **for instant by instant the universe creates itself as a bonded community.** To hear how omnipresent community is in the universe is to encourage our own difficult steps in community-building. The effort at community is an effort to imitate the universe. Therefore, it is a good effort. Therefore, it cannot fail.

The interdependence of earth and sun is demonstrated by the following fact. German researchers have found that the Sahara desert, which less than seven thousand years ago was rich with vegetation, grass, and shrubs, was created by an alteration in the Earth's tilt, which went from 24.14 degrees to 23.34 degrees. The point in orbit closest to the sun was affected enough to render the Sahara the desert it is today. This is truly a lesson in interconnectivity.

Swimme points out that our traditional notions of sunlight bouncing off the moon to make moonlight are illusory. In fact, there is so much interaction between the photons of the sun and the particles of the moon that *a whole new set of particles are created*—thus the particles created by sun and moon together are new and different particles. It can and must be said that **moonlight is *created* by the moon.** The moon, like every other being in the universe, has its creative role to play.

Far from being dead and inert objects, the universe is indeed a community. In Swimme's words, **The universe is not a collection of dead objects but is, rather, a seamless whole community made up of cosmos-related subjects.** This becomes clearer and clearer in our own local home, the earth planet.

Phrases like "the Earth community" are coming home to us again. **Through this story we learn that we have a common genetic line of development. Every living being of earth is cousin to every other living being. Even beyond the** realm of the living we have a common origin in the primordial Flaring Forth of the energies from which the universe in all its aspects is derived. In the new cosmology, community is seen to be happening at all levels of existence including the most minute. **Each particle is in some way intimately present to every other particle in the universe. . . . Hydrogen [was] a new identity that has the power to seal a proton and an electron into a seamless community.** We seek out a deeper remembrance of this "seamless community." The importance of interconnectivity and its omnipresence is confirmed by what Swimme calls **the great news of our time [which] is the evolutionary story in which we come to realize that we humans are all embedded in a living, developing universe, and that we are therefore cousins to everything in the universe.** If we are cousins, we are already community. It follows that Creation is not a box in which we find ourselves, it is not a container. Creation is more of a verb than that; it is an ongoing drama wherein all the players are sacred, interacting with one another and creating anew their roles and relationships.

Ecosystems are, as scientist Fritjof Capra points out, **sustainable communities of plants, animals, and microorganisms.** Our own human communities can be reinvented by learning how these more-than-human communities operate successfully in creation. The principles for living systems that Capra explicates include the following:

1. Interdependence—**all members of an ecological community are interconnected in a vast and intricate network of relationships, the web of life. . . . The success of the whole community depends on the success of its individual members, while the success of each member depends on the success of the community as a whole.**

2. Non-linear relationships. The network pattern that characterizes basic patterns of life involves not so much cause and effect relations as **multiple feedback loops.**

3. Cyclical processes of feedback loops lead to recycling. What one species produces as waste, another takes in as food, **so that the ecosystem as a whole remains without waste. Communities of organisms have evolved in this way over billions of years, continually using and recycling the same molecules of minerals, water, and air.** In contrast, the industrial systems we now operate under are linear and waste becomes endless.
4. Ecosystems run on solar energy. So ought we.
5. Partnership or **pervasive cooperation** is what has made the ecosystem work over two billion years. **Since the creation of the first nucleated cells over two billion years ago, life on earth has proceeded through ever more intricate arrangements of cooperation and coevolution.** Partnership is **one of the hallmarks of life.**
6. Flexibility. Fluctuation is found everywhere in an ecosystem. **The web of life is a flexible, ever-fluctuating network.** Adapting to changing circumstances is the key to the dynamic feedback looping that goes on. Paradox and dialectic are key to maintaining a community of any kind. There are tolerance limits as well as tolerance, stability as well as change, tradition as well as innovation.
7. Diversity. Biodiversity makes a community resilient. Human communities can imitate this resilience through honoring diversity.

According to Capra, these seven patterns of organization we witness in nature explain how Creation operates as efficiently and elegantly as it does. Why should the human not follow suit?

When we examine the depths of our wisdom traditions we will find such principles called for throughout our spiritual history.

African-American mystic and theologian Howard Thurman speaks often and eloquently of the primacy of community. He perceives the struggle between good and evil as being very much a struggle between community and lack of it. **The loneliness of the seeker for community is sometimes unendurable,** he warns us. Thurman explains Adam's fall as being his loss of a **sense of community with the rest of creation.** The fall is a fall away from the community of all Creation with one another. Thurman believes that both the Genesis Creation story and the Creation story of the Hopi people tell the story of the **climate of community** in which our species began and to which we yearn to return. We are always seeking a return to our beginnings, a healing and redemptive community. But the community which we yearn for is a full community, one that includes all God's creation, not just a segregated one of human dwellers alone. When this community is torn asunder, awful things happen to the human psyche.

Thurman actually defines sin as our being outside community. In community, the citizen receives **an integrated basis for his behavior so that there is always at hand a socially accepted judgment that can determine for him when he is lost, when he has missed the way—that is, when he is out of community.** Humanity, he says, **would never accept the absence of community as his destiny. . . . Man has lost this dimension in his journey; he has sinned and missed the way.** Community by definition includes all our kin; therefore it embraces the cosmic relationships of all Creation. We seek to *belong,* we *long to be with others* and to be part of their work, their drama. Thurman saw this when he warned us that **the community cannot feed for long on itself; it can only flourish where always the boundaries are giving way to the coming of others from beyond them—unknown and undiscovered brothers. . . . What we have sought we have found, our own sense of identity. We have committed to heart and to nervous system a feeling of belonging and our spirits are no longer isolated and afraid. . . . [We need to resist the] "will to quarantine" and to separate ourselves behind self-imposed walls. For this is why we were born: Men, all men, belong to each** other, and he who shuts himself away diminishes himself, and he who shuts another away from him destroys himself.

Thurman rightly observed that it is the Native American's sense of belonging to the land that is primal. This cosmic relation cannot be broken without impunity. As the native peoples' land was desecrated the self was also, and a **unique form of torture, a long, slow, anguished dying** took place. One result of this rupture of community between the original Americans and the European Americans was a deep sense of unconscious guilt which touches the very **fiber of the American character and there is no catharsis to be found.** Once again, we are struck by the price our species pays for resisting community or destroying those that have it. In contrast, to relate to the land and its creatures is to **greatly enlarge** a person's own sense of self.

In a study on the ideal of community in Howard Thurman and Dr. Martin Luther King, Jr., scholar Walter E. Fluker concludes that "for both thinkers, the nature of community is rooted in the interrelatedness of all life, which is teleological." In other words, community is a cosmic principle with them both. "For Thurman, community or 'common ground' refers to wholeness, integration, and harmony. All life is interrelated and involved in goal-seeking. . . . There is, for him, a fundamental structure of interrelatedness and interdependability inherent in all living things, at microscopic levels of existence and in human society. . . . The origin and goal of community, therefore, is in the Mind of God, which is coming to Itself in time."

As for Dr. King, "like Thurman, community is the single, organizing principle of King's life and thought." Dr. King talked often of **the beloved community.** What did he mean by that phrase? The beloved community, "is rooted in the interrelatedness of all life and in the unity of human existence under the guidance of a personal God of love and reason who works for universal wholeness." King developed what has been called a philosophy of personalism into a call for community, for in his understanding a person becomes a person only in community. Said King: **An individual reaches the level of personhood only in social relations, a person grows and develops through social relations with other persons.**

King differs from Thurman insofar as his teaching is more Christocentric than Thurman's. For King, Christ is the source of the beloved community. "The redemptive love of God, revealed in the cross of Christ, is King's answer to the possibility of achieving community within history." King believed that **Jesus eloquently affirmed from the cross a higher law [the law of love which transcended] the old eye-for-an-eye philosophy.** In fact, **self-sacrificing and forgiving compassion are the ultimate fulfillment of person-in-community and the ultimate revelation of the character of God.** For Thurman, Jesus is more an exemplar, "an expression of the inherent potentially of human nature to achieve the highest goal of the moral life, love." The cross was not an abstraction for King but a concrete shift in human history from revenge to compassion.

What is the beloved community for King? It involves a change in people's souls, an end to hatred. A commitment to non-violence, a refusal to live with fear. **Only a refusal to hate or kill can put an end to the chain of violence in the world and lead us toward a community where men live together without fear. Our goal is to create a beloved community and this will require a qualitative change in our souls as well as quantitative change in our lives.**

Much of Thurman's and King's deep commitment to and analysis of community comes from their African roots. Scholars of African philosophies point out that **prior to the interaction with the European and Arab populations that invaded Africa, the idea of race was nearly nonexistent; however, the concepts of community group, clan, family, and ethnicity did exist.** It is in community that values were based, including ancient beliefs in resurrection and life, reincarnation, matrilineality, the value of children, **and the ultimate goodness of the earth.**

Dr. Asante recognizes community as being at the core of African belief systems. We are in the universe and it is in us; there is no separation between us and nature, between life and spirituality or spirituality and religion. Asanti sees the deep teaching of community among African people as connecting to the principle of *harmony*. **Among the Yoruba, the goal is always to restore harmony. . . . Harmony and peace, societal and individual, come from the right ordering of the earth through an appeal to Ifa** (sacred texts). Community embraces the ancestors—not only those from the past who are present as spirit but also those not yet born who are to come on the scene in the future. All ritual begins with libations to these ancestors. They are part of any prayer service. (Is this unlike the prayer to "all our relations" that Lakota people pray whenever they pray?) There is a *personal harmony* that must be developed **because an undisciplined person creates disharmony within the society.** Becoming human is the task at hand, and **one becomes human only in the midst of others,** that is, in community. The development of personal powers that are inherent in us means our harmonizing with the universe, becoming **in tune with the rhythm of the universe.** This happens, among other places, at community rituals and celebrations. **I am most healthy when I am harmonized with others. I am most in touch with transcendence when I am moving in time to others.**

Asante names the *secret* of African-American spirituality to be the following: **While we recognize the individuality of the responsibility, we know that it cannot be carried out without others. We can reach our *own* transcendence, but never without the help of others.** It is in joining in collective expression of power that true spirituality is manifested. **This is one of the supreme legacies we have given to the United States. I am no longer myself, I am a transpersonal being at this moment. . . . It is joy ineffable, because I am in tune with the feelings of others. I experience *nommo* [the "word magic" that through the generation and transformation of sounds contributes to a speaker's power].**

The seven principles that form the basis of Kwanza celebration all center around community. They include the following: self-determination for the community; collective work and responsibility; cooperative economics; the collective vocation of building the community; and creativity whose purpose is "to leave our community more beautiful and beneficial than we inherited it."

The primary community is that of the universe itself. Psyche and cosmos connect and come together in community celebration, music, and dance. The microcosm of the human community gets energized by the macrocosm of the spirit community and the cosmos. As Dona Marimba Richards puts it in her book *Let the Circle Be Unbroken: The Implications of African Spirituality in the Diaspora:* **The relationship between the human and the divine; the heavenly and earthly spheres, is one of interdependence. The spirits "need" us, just as we "need" them; just as spirit "needs" matter to give it form, and matter "needs" spirit to give it force, being and reality.**

Life, events, and phenomena derive meaning, value, or significance through relationship to an organic whole. The family or community is understood as just such a "whole." Indeed, the theme of *ongoing creation* is explicitly honored and entered into through ritual. The Spirit still creates. Creation is not in the past. Like the Aboriginals of Australia, there is a "Dreamtime" that persists; in Jesus' words, a divine kingdom or realm that is very much alive and active. We tap into this ongoing creation through our ritual times. **The universe was created (is continually "recreated") by a divine act. We participate in that act as we perform rituals in imitation of the Creator and aspects of the Creator. . . . Through association with this sacred universe, divinely created, life itself becomes sacred and a most precious gift to be cherished, preserved, passed on and revitalized. It is to be lived to its fullest.**

African spiritual teacher Malidoma Somé says that there is no community without ritual. It is in community that the rituals of birth and marriage, rites of passage and death, are remembered and practiced. These rituals make us worthy and ready to join the greater community of Creation itself. They connect the inner community with the outer community, the microcosm with the macrocosm. They also allow the community as a single organism to wake up, stretch, connect, celebrate, let go, heal, grieve, forgive, remember. Just as there is no community without ritual, so there is no ritual without community. Even if we do ritual in a private place, our ancestors are there, all spirits and angels are there.

Among Native peoples in America the community holds primacy over notions of individualism. Identity is not an issue of *I think therefore I am,* as philosopher Descartes saw things. Rather, identity comes from one's relation to the whole. To cosmos. To the tribe. To the whole community, local and distant. As Vine Deloria puts it, "the possibility of conceiving of an individual alone in a tribal religious sense is ridiculous. The very complexity of tribal life and the interdependence of people on one another makes this conception improbable at best, a terrifying loss of identity at worst." Jamake Highwater comments: "In tribal religions there is no salvation apart from the continuance of the tribe itself because the existence of the individual presupposes the existence of the community. . . . Life does not exist without the tribe which gives animation to its members."

As in African tradition, ceremonies unite people to each other but also people to the community of Creation itself. Dance and sacred rituals accomplish this. Indigenous people have been living out of the context of interdependence and drawing lessons for living from it for countless centuries. Their ceremonies and rituals attest to that. A commentator on the Hopi way of life says: **In the Hopi world all life is cyclical. The ceremonial year follows a ritualistic pattern of fertilization, germination, growth, fruition, and regeneration which mirrors the life cycle of the crops and particularly the life cycle of corn. The Hopis believe that [the human] cannot prosper on Earth unless his life is in harmony with the fixed order of the universe.**

In the Kabbalah, the Jewish tradition encourages community linked to celebration and holy sounding. First, we learn that community is happening among all beings. **Everything teems with richness, everything aspires to ascend and be purified. Everything sings, celebrates, serves, develops, evolves, uplifts, aspires to be arranged in oneness.** Then we are instructed in how humans do community. **There is one who sings the song of his soul . . . who sings the song of his people. . . . Together with her, he sings her song, feels her anguish, delights in her hopes. . . . There is one whose soul expands until it extends beyond the border of Israel, singing the song of humanity. . . . further until he unites with all of existence, with all creatures, with all worlds, singing a song with them all. There is one who ascends with all these songs in unison—the song of the soul, the song of the nation, the song of humanity, the song of the cosmos—re-sounding together, blending in harmony, circulating the sap of life, the sound of holy joy.**

Rabbi Abraham Heschel develops an understanding of community in the Jewish tradition when he insists that spirit requires both learning from the past and pioneering into the future. **Only he who is an heir is qualified to be a pioneer [and] in the realm of spirit only he who is a pioneer is able to be an heir.** He calls his people to be pioneers and know the past not to slavishly imitate it but to recreate it. **We should be pioneers as were our fathers three thousand years ago.** A true pioneer creates anew. **To have faith does not mean . . . to dwell in the shadow of old ideas conceived by prophets and sages, to live off an inherited estate of doctrines and dogmas. . . . Authentic faith is more than an echo of a tradition. It is a creative situation, an event.** True community and being true to communal tradition take courage. Faith **requires bold initiative rather than continuity. Faith is forever contingent on the courage of the believer.** For this, the tradition of the past is helpful but never merely repeatable. **The endeavor to integrate the abiding teachings and aspirations of the past into our own thinking will enable us to be creative and expand, not to imitate or to repeat.** Heschel calls for a living tradition, a living community, not one pining nostalgically for past heroics. While we inherit a **legacy of wonder** from our community's past, and while we apprentice from elders who know that legacy, still we apprentice in order to move beyond and make the community live. Religious living is not only a private concern [for] our own life **is a movement in the symphony of ages.**

In the spirit of this "sound of holy joy," Heschel relates community to worship. **A Jew never worships as an isolated individual but *as a part of the Community of Israel.* Yet it is within the heart of every individual that prayer takes place.** He is underscoring the tension between the individual and the group—how deeply they need one another. But worship is very much an ancestral thing for the Jew as it is for the African, for **every act of worship is an act of participating in an eternal service, in the service of all souls of all ages.** Nor is community praise only a human thing—quite the opposite. **Our kinship with nature is a kinship of praise. All beings praise God. We live in a community of praise.** It is the task of the human to lead the **silent worship** of the rest of creation. We are its cantors. **The cosmos is a congregation in need of a Cantor. . . . It is man who is the Cantor of the universe, and in whose life the secret of cosmic prayer is disclosed. And when we sing we sing for all things. . . . The universe is a score of eternal music, and we are the cry, we are the voice.**

Buddhism speaks of community as one of the three "Jewels," "Gems" or "Refuges." The three jewels are Buddha, Dharma (teachings), and Sangha or community. The Sangha or community is meant to be the place where the teachings of the Buddha are practiced. It is comprised of monks, nuns, and lay persons who practice mindfulness. It is, as Thich Nhat Hanh puts it, **the community that lives in harmony and awareness.** It is in community that everyday activities become the sacred events that they truly are. They are a kind of coming home. **The Sangha members practice going home all day, through walking, breathing, cooking, and doing their daily activities mindfully.** The Sangha is also a kind of refuge, a place to be safe and free. **In the Buddhist tradition, we practice taking refuge instead of receiving baptism. With a teacher and Sangha, or spiritual community, surrounding you, you join your palms and say, "I take refuge in the Buddha. I take refuge in the Dharma. I take refuge in the Sangha." That also is the practice of going home. Your home is the Buddha, the Dharma and the Sangha. . . .**

However, Thich Nhat Hanh also recognizes the greater community that we all belong to, that of Creation itself. **Your greater Sangha is society and other living beings because your practice not only profits the society of man and woman, but it will profit trees, animals, and minerals. That is your larger Sangha. And you know that the Sangha is also an agent of protection.** Thich Nhat Hanh is so taken by the truth of our common interdependence that he has felt driven to invent a new word for it: **interbeing.** It forms the basis for compassion, as we will see in chapter seventeen.

The Dalai Lama laments the loss of community in modern life, a sense of community that rural and less consumer-driven societies cherished. **We have, in my view, created a society in which people find it harder and harder to show one another basic affection. In place of the sense of community and belonging, which we find such a reassuring feature of less wealthy (and generally rural) societies, we find a high degree of loneliness and alienation. Despite the fact that millions live in close proximity to one another, it seems that many people, especially among the old, have no one to talk to but their pets.** He calls us to the challenge of creating **the same degree of harmony and tranquillity as those more traditional communities while benefiting fully from the material developments of the world as we find it today.** Because of the truth of interdependence among all beings, **we come to see that the habitual sharp distinction we make between "self" and "others" is an exaggeration.** We come to see that **there is no self-interest completely unrelated to others' interests. Due to the fundamental interconnectedness which lies at the heart of reality, your interest is also my interest.** In other words, community already is. We need to remove the obstacles in us that prevent it from happening.

The ancient teaching of humanity's interdependence with all of Creation is announced by numerous Christian mystics. Consider Hildegard of Bingen, the twelfth-century Benedictine abbess and musician, artist and healer. **God has arranged all things in the world in consideration of everything else. . . . Every thing that is in the heavens, on the earth, and under the earth, is penetrated with connectedness, is penetrated with relatedness.** Is this awareness not the same as that of the Lakota people who pray with the sacred pipe for **all our relations**? Relationship lies at the center of existence and Creation in all of it its myriad expressions. As Meister Eckhart put it, **relation is the essence of everything that exists.** Relationship is at the heart of all existence, all community. Community is relation and relation is community. Therefore life itself requires what Eckhart calls an **equality of being.**

The Muslim community is called the *umma*. This word derives from the word for "mother," which is *umm*. Muhammad said that **paradise lies under the feet of mothers.** Followers of Islam are urged to form one community no matter what their class, race, language, or national origin. Malcolm X had such an experience of community when he visited Mecca and it changed him forever. He saw an integrated experience of race and faith. The Qur'an and the sayings of Muhammad lay down attitudes of community both between humans and between humans and other species. **All believers are brothers; so make peace between your brothers, and be mindful of your duty to Allah that you may be shown mercy.**

The Believers are like a single man; if his eye is affected, all of him is affected, and if his head is affected all of him is affected. . . . None of you has believed until he loves for his brother what he loves for himself. . . . All creatures are God's children, and those dearest to God are the ones who treat His children kindly. Community consciousness requires action on behalf of those who need it, especially the old and the young.

He from whose injurious conduct his neighbor is not safe will not enter Paradise. And who is one's neighbor? "To the Muslim all human beings are brothers- and sisters-in-humanity, and the same obligation of kindness, fairness and consideration are due to them all." Christians and Jews are meant to be especially close to the Muslim because they too are "People of the Scripture." For that reason intermarriage is allowed between Muslims, Jews, and Christians. The Prophet lived respect and neighborliness with non-Muslims and Muslims are to follow his lead.

As we shall see in chapter eleven below, the ritual practices and dervish dances of the Sufi order are all about experiencing our oneness with the sun, the planets, the universe, and the Source behind and permeating all our relationships.

Two

RELATING

TO

DIVINITY

Divinity comes by many names. We live in a time when we can hear many ancient and many new-sounding names for God.

That is a good thing, for it can open our own souls up to greater possibilities. As Meister Eckhart puts it, **All the names which the soul gives God it receives from the knowledge of itself.** In each spiritual tradition, there are numerous, indeed infinite ways by which we can name God. There are also severe warnings not to name God in any definitive way.

In this section we name the multiple faces of God in the following ways:

5. Names for God: the Multiple Faces of Divinity
6. The Feminine Face of Divinity
7. Wisdom, Another Feminine Face of the Divine
8. Form, Formlessness, Nothingness
9. The Divine "I Am": Humanity's Share in Divinity

5.

NAMES FOR GOD

God has a million faces.
—Baghavad Gita

The one Being the wise call by many names.
—Ṛg Veda

We call Divinity by many names. We might call Divinity God or Allah or Yahweh or Buddha or Christ or Tao or the Goddess or the Great Spirit or Creator or Redeemer or Liberator or Supreme Being or Rama, or Ground of All Being or Ra or Aten or Vishnu or Brahmin or Godhead or Nothingness or Mooramoora or Mystery or Beauty or Justice or Goodness or Wisdom and many more. The Hindu tradition says that **there is only one Rama and he has a thousand names.** Still others say that there are an infinite number of names for God. We shall explore some of those names here, for they reveal, as Eckhart says, something of our own souls. And they make it possible to reimagine ourselves and to let Divinity continue to evolve and cease making Divinity into our own projections.

The Muslim tradition provides a practice in which the practitioner recites and meditates on ninety-nine of "the most beautiful names for God." These names follow.

The Fashioner (Al-Musawwir)
The Maker (Al-Bari)
The Creator (Al-Khaliq)
The Majestic (Al-Mutakabbir)
The Compeller (Al-Jabbar)
The Mighty (Al-Aziz)
The Protector (Al-Muhaimin)
The Giver of Peace (Al-Mu'min)
The Author of Safety (Al-Salam)
The Holy (Al-Quddus)
The Sovereign (Al-Malik)
The Merciful (Al-Rahim)
The Compassionate (Al-Rahman)
The All-Hearing (Al-Sami')
The Dishonorer (Al-muzi'l)
The Honorer (Al-Mu'izz)
The Exalter (Al-Rafeh)
The Abaser (Al-Khafid)
The Expander (Al-Basit)
The Constrictor (Al-Qabiz)
The All-Knower (Al-'Alim)
The Judge (Al-Fattah)
The Provider (Al-Razzaq)
The Bestower (Al-Wahhab)
The Dominant (Al-Qahhar)
The Forgiver (Al-Gaffar)

The Maintainer (Al-Muqit)

The Preserver (Al-Hafiz)

The Most Great (Al-Kabir)

The Sublime (Al-Aliyy)

The Appreciative (Al-Shakur)

The All-Forgiving (Al-Ghafoor)

The Great One (Al-Azim)

The Patient (Al-Halim)

The Aware (Al-Khabir)

The Subtle One (Al-Latif)

The Just (Al-Adl)

The Judge (Al-Hakam)

The All-Seeing (Al-Basir)

The Trustee (Al-Wakil)

The Truth (Al-Haqq)

The Witness (Al-Shahid)

The Awakener (Al-Ba'ith)

The Noble (Al-Maajid)

The Loving (Al-Wadud)

The Wise One (Al-Hakim)

The All-Embracing (Al-Wase')

The Responsive (Al-Mujib)

The Watchful (Al-Raqib)

The Generous One (Al-Karim)

The Glorious (Al-Jalil)

The Reckoner (Al-Hasib)

The Noble (Al-Maajid)

The Finder (Al-Wajid)

The Self-Subsisting (Al-Qayyum)

The Alive (Al-Hayy)

The Giver of Death (Al-Mumit)
The Giver of Life (Al-Mohyi)
The Restorer (Al-Muid)
The Beginner (Al-Mubdi)
The Counter (Al-Muhsi)
The Praiseworthy (Al-Hamid)
The Protecting Friend (Al-Wali)
The Firm One (Al-Matin)
The Most Strong (Al-Qawi)
The Source of All Goodness (Al-Barr)
The Most Exalted (Al-Muta'ali)
The Governor (Al-Waali)
The Hidden (Al-Batin)
The Manifest (Al-Zahir)
The Last (Al-Akhir)
The First (Al-Awwal)
The Deferrer (Al-Mu'akhir)
The Forward Bringer (Al-Muqaddam)
The Powerful (Al-Muqtadir)
The Able (Al-Qadir)
The Eternal (As-Samad)
The One (Al-Wahid)
The Withholder (Al-Mane')
The Enricher (Al-Mughni)
The Self-Sufficient (Al-Ghani)
The Gatherer (Al-Jame)
The Equitable (Al-Muqsit)
The Lord of Majesty and Bounty (Dhul-Jalal-Wal Ikraam)
The Lord of the Kingdom (Malikul-Mulk)
The Compassionate (Ar-Ra'uf)

The Pardoner (Al-Afuw)
The Avenger (Al-Muntaqim)
The Acceptor of Repentance (Al-Tawwab)
The Patient (Al-Saboor)
The Guide (Al-Rashid)
The Inheritor (Al-Warith)
The Everlasting (Al-Baqi)
The Originator (Al-Badi')
The Guide (Al-Haadi)
The Light (Al-Nur)
The Profiter (An-Nafe)
The Distresser (Ad-Darr)

A peace and deep insight are gained from praying these names and reciting them as a litany or list, on the one hand, or just settling on meditating on one of them at a time. It expands the mind and soul to grant Divinity a diversity of names. It is a way into understanding our own depths and of expanding ourselves to let God be known—and ourselves be known—by a myriad of names. We too can recognize ourselves as **fashioners, makers, creators, majestic, compellers, mighty, protectors, givers of peace, authors of safety, holy, sovereign, merciful, compassionate, all-hearing, dishonoring, honoring, exalting, abasing, expanding, constricting, all-knowing, judging, providing, bestowing, dominant, forgivers, maintainers, preservers, great, sublime, appreciative, patient, aware, subtle, just, all-seeing, trustworthy, truth, witness, awakeners, noble, loving, wise, all embracing, responsive, watchful, generous, glorious, reckoning, noble, finding, self-subsisting, alive, giver of death, giver of life, restoring, beginning, counting, praiseworthy, a protecting friend, firm, strong, a source of goodness, most exalted, governing, hidden, manifest, last, first, deferring, forward-bringing, powerful, able, eternal, one, withholding, enriching, self-sufficient, gathering, equitable, lords of majesty and bounty, lords of the kingdom,**

pardoning, avenging, accepting repentance, patient, guiding, inheriting, ever-lasting, originating, light, profiting, distressing.

It is interesting how many of these names do indeed apply to our own experience—or do they? It is equally telling which ones do not yet apply.

Sufi teacher Hafiz offers more names for God including: **Sweet Uncle, the Generous Merchant, the Problem Giver, the Problem Solver, the Friend, the Beloved, Ocean, Sky, Sun, Moon, Love.** He warns us that, whatever our names for God, we ought not to settle for too small a god.

> **Dear ones,**
> **Beware of the tiny gods frightened men create**
> **To bring an anesthetic relief**
> **to their sad days.**

In the Christian mystical tradition, Meister Eckhart offers the following prayer: **I pray God to rid me of God.** What images and projections of Divinity do we need to move beyond and let go of?

St. Thomas Aquinas offers a litany of names for God, all of which are taken from the Scriptures. To read and pray this list and meditate upon it does indeed offer liberation for ourselves and our God-understanding. It is one way of responding to Eckhart's and Hafiz' challenges to move beyond too small a naming of Divinity. How might the following names, all taken from Scriptures, give us imagination and freedom to move on in our naming of divine experiences?

Even the very ones who were experienced concerning Divinity, such as the apostles and prophets, praise God as

> **as the Cause of all things**
> **as good**
> **as beautiful**
> **as wise**
> **as beloved**
> **as God of gods**
> **as holy of holies**
> **as eternal**
> **as manifest**
> **as the cause of the ages**
> **as the bestower of life**
> **as wisdom**
> **as mind or intellect**
> **as reason**
> **as the knower**
> **as the one possessing in advance all the treasures of universal knowledge**
> **as virtue**

as the powerful
as King of kings
as the Ancient of days
as without age and unchanging
as salvation
as justice
as deliverance or redemption
as magnitude exceeding all things
as in the light breeze
as in minds or hearts
as in spirits
as in bodies
as in heaven and on earth
at the same time in the same place
in the world
involved in the world
above the world
supercelestial or above the heavens
supersubstantial
as the sun
as a constellation, that is, a star
as fire
as water
as air
as dew
as cloud
as stone
as rock
and all the other beings attributed to God as cause.

Such a litany! And these are only names of God from the Scriptures.

But Aquinas adds another and very powerful caveat: **And the Divine One is none of these beings insofar as God surpasses all things.** Thus, in Aquinas's view, God can be named by *any being in the universe* because God is the cause of every being in the universe. But Aquinas also warns us to live with this dialectic—that God is named by all beings and by no beings. To live this way is to dance the dance of truth. No name, absolutely no name, suffices for Divinity. Which is also to say that *all names suffice for Divinity*—but on a limited scale only.

How this truth puts to rest the religious wars and strife over the centuries that have been waged over My God vs. Your God! None of us controls God. Not even God's name. To attempt to control God by controlling a name of God is an act of idolatry, an act of freezing Divinity. Surely this lies behind Meister Eckhart's radical prayer to rid himself of God. It may also lie behind the Jewish tradition that refuses to pronounce the divine name or to write it out in its entirety. YHWH as a name for God is unfinished, it is in a state of becoming, as Divinity and all of Creation is in a state of becoming. Indeed, Meister Eckhart says that **God becomes and ceases to become** and that creatures bring about this becoming in God. This means that Divinity itself is not finished but awaits the unfolding of all the divine words and names that every creature represents and utters. God is not yet finished.

John of the Cross speaks in a similar way when he says:

> My Beloved is the mountains,
> And lonely wooded valleys,
> Strange islands,
> And resounding rivers,
> The whistling of love-stirring breezes,
>
> The tranquil night
> At the time of the rising dawn,
> Silent music.
> Sounding solitude,
> The supper that refreshes, and deepens love.

John of the Cross elaborates on the meaning of his poetry: **Inasmuch as the soul in this case is united with God, she feels that all things are God, as St. John experienced when he said: "That which was made, had life in him." It should not be thought that what the soul is said to feel here is comparable to seeing things by means of the light, or creatures by means of God; rather in this possession the soul feels that God is all things for her. Neither must it be thought that, because the soul has so sublime an experience of God, we are asserting that she has essential and clear vision of him. This experience is nothing but a strong and overflowing communication and glimpse of what God is in himself, in which the soul feels the goodness of the things mentioned in these verses.**

What follows can be understood as an elaboration of what John means by calling God the **Beloved.** He writes:

"My Beloved is the mountains":
Mountains have heights and they are affluent, vast, beautiful, grace-

ful, bright, and fragrant. These mountains are what my Beloved is to me.

"And lonely wooded valleys":

Lonely valleys are quiet, pleasant, cool, shady, and flowing with fresh waters; in the variety of their groves and in the sweet song of the birds, they afford abundant recreation and delight to the senses, and in their solitude and silence they refresh and give rest. These valleys are what my Beloved is to me.

"Strange islands":

Strange islands are surrounded by water and situated across the sea, far withdrawn and cut off from communication with other men. Many things very different from what we have here are born and nurtured in these islands; they are of many strange kinds and powers never before seen by men, and they cause surprise and wonder in anyone who sees them. Thus, because of the wonderful new things and the strange knowledge (far removed from common knowledge) which the soul sees in God, she calls Him "strange islands."

The soul calls God "strange" for these two reasons. Not only is he all the strangeness of islands never seen before, but also his ways, counsels, and works are very strange and new and wonderful to man.

"And resounding rivers":

Rivers have three properties: first, they besiege and inundate everything they encounter; second, they fill up all the low and empty spots found along their path; third, they are so loud that they muffle and suppress every other sound. Since in this communication the soul has in God a delightful experience of these three properties, she says that her Beloved is resounding rivers. . . . This divine onslaught God causes in the soul is like a resounding river which fills everything with peace and glory. . . .

This clamor or resounding of these rivers which the soul refers to here is such an abundant plenitude that she is filled with goods, and it is so powerful a force that she is possessed by it, for it seems to be not merely the sound of rivers but the sound of roaring thunder. . . .

Hence it should be known that God is an infinite voice, and by communicating himself to the soul in this way he produces the effect of an immense voice.

"The whistling of love-stirring breezes":

By "love-stirring breezes" is understood the attributes and graces of the Beloved which by means of this union assail the soul and lovingly touch it in its substance. . . . This is the most exalted delight of all the soul here enjoys. . . . Two things are experienced: knowledge and a feeling of delight.

"Silent music":

In that nocturnal tranquillity and silence and in that knowledge of the divine light the soul becomes aware of Wisdom's wonderful harmony and sequence in the variety of his creatures and works. Each of them is endowed with a certain likeness of God and in its own way gives voice to what God is in it. So creatures will be for the soul a harmonious symphony of sublime music surpassing all concerts and melodies of the world. . . . She says that her Beloved is silent music because in him she knows and enjoys this symphony of spiritual music. Not only is he silent music, but he is also

"Sounding solitude":

The soul perceives in that tranquil wisdom that all creatures, higher and lower ones alike, according to what each in itself has received from God, raise their voice in testimony to what God is. She beholds that each in its own way, bearing God within itself according to its capacity, magnifies God. And thus all these voices form one voice of music praising the grandeur, wisdom, and wonderful knowledge of God. This is the meaning of the Holy Spirit in the Book of Wisdom when he said: "The spirit of the Lord filled the whole earth, and this world which contains all things has knowledge of the voice." This voice is the sonorous solitude the soul knows here, that is, the testimony to God which, in themselves, all things give.

In Hinduism, the Vedas celebrate the diversity of Divinity when they declare: **The One Existence the wise call by many names.** God has so many names because God is found in so many places, indeed at the heart of all Creation. Father Bede Griffiths says that if you ask "Where does God dwell?" of Catholic children, they will point to the sky; if you ask it of Hindu children they point to their breasts. God is in the heart. The Upanishads say: **to that God who is in the plants, to the God who is in the trees, to the God who is in the earth, to that God who is in everything, adoration to him, adoration to him.**

God's manifestation in the world of creation is commonly attributed to Brahma, Vishnu and Shiva. Brahma is the Creator, Vishnu the preserver, and Shiva the destroyer. Father Bede comments: **It can be called panentheism. God is in everything. . . . First of all God is in the whole creation by his power, because he sustains everything by his power. . . . shakti, the "Power of God." He is in everything by his Presence. God is present in everything. . . . (Brahman) is the source from which everything comes. . . . Brahman pervades the universe . . . which is woven in the Creator.**

Examples of the panentheism—God in all things and all things in God—that is explicit in the Bhagavad Gita follow:

> **A true yogi observes me in all beings and also sees every being in me. Indeed, the self-realized person sees me, the same Supreme Lord, everywhere.**
> **For one who sees me everywhere and sees everything in me, I am never lost, nor is he ever lost to me.**
> **Such a yogi, who engages in the worshipful service of the Supersoul, knowing that I and the Supersoul are one, remains always in me in all circumstances.**
> **And of all yogis, the one with great faith who always abides in me, thinks of me within himself, and renders transcendental loving ser-**

vice to me—he is the most intimately united with me in yoga and is
the highest of all.

Many superlative names for Divinity are sprinkled throughout the Vedas.
Among them are:

the supreme giver of treasure
the greatest leader of heroes
fullest among the full
most youthful
most liberal
most adored
the wisest
destroyer of darkness and evil
the best of guardians
most beloved and manliest
best praised
mightiest
most victorious
most mighty
kindest, most blissful
strongest
readiest to hear
most skillful among the skilled
most gentle-hearted
most wonderful
most beloved
most splendid one
best of physicians

motherliest
best of poets
most zealous
most victorious
the kindest
most fatherly of fathers
most heroic
greatest bestower of bliss
most joyous

How else might one understand God? **One should meditate upon the Supreme Person as the one who knows everything, as he who is the oldest, who is the controller, who is smaller than the smallest, who is the maintainer of everything, who is beyond all material conception, who is inconceivable, and who is always a person. He is luminous like the sun, and he is transcendental, beyond this material nature.**

We have touched in this section on the thousands of faces of Divinity. And it is just a beginning—our touching on these holy visages, our calling them forth from our own experience and that of our ancestors. How richly our ancestors went about naming the divine personality, how diverse was that personality, how many layers of work and accomplishment, of feeling and passion lie behind each of these names. But there are many more to come.

6.

THE FEMININE FACE
OF DIVINITY

**The Goddess in all her manifestations was a
symbol of the unity of all life in Nature.
—Marija Gimbutas, *The Language of the Goddess***

Patriarchy has so swamped our civilizations, East and West, over the past forty-five
hundred years that we have almost blotted out an entire side to Divinity: the Feminine side. This was not always the case, this ignoring of the Divine Feminine, but
it has served political interests and gender interests (which can be highly political)
to limit our God-language to the masculine and to exclude the feminine in our collective imagination no less than in our religious leadership. Women and male fem-
inists have been chipping away at this distortion with the ordaining of women and
with women achieving significant achievements in areas of theology and spiritual
leadership. But much still needs to be done and much needs to be learned about the
wisdom of the past when the feminine was honored as integral to the Godhead. If
Meister Eckhart is correct that "all the names we give to God come from an under-

standing of our own souls," then we clearly distort ourselves, our souls, our culture, and our God by insisting on calling God masculine and avoiding the feminine. By praying to God as "Father" and never as "Mother." By repressing the Wisdom and Sophia traditions of the Bible in exclusive favor of the God of judgment and revenge and war. The traditions of God as female and Divinity as Mother are deep among all world religions as we shall see. There is liberation in this insight and awareness. "The truth shall make you free." We liberate God as we liberate ourselves. The feminine insists on being heard today. Again.

One expression of the Feminine side of Divinity is the ancient tradition of the Goddess. Marija Gimbutas, who spent her life as archeologist researching the era of the Goddess, summarizes what she learned. **The Goddess in all her manifestations was a symbol of the unity of all life in Nature. Her power was in water and stone, in tomb and cave, in animals and birds, snakes and fish, hills, trees, and flowers. Hence the holistic and mythopoeic perception of the sacredness and mystery of all there is on Earth.** When the Goddess-based cultures were overthrown by warlike invaders, there was a great effort to discredit the Goddess. Thus the Babylonian creation myth, the *Enuma Elish* (c. 668–626 B.C.E.) tells the story of Tiamet, the Goddess of the Salty Sea, who is slain by the new God Marduk. The Goddess is vilified for having brought a race of evil monsters into the world. The story told is very violent—Marduk cuts open the belly of Tiamet. The warrior was celebrated as a hero and rituals were enacted annually to celebrate this killing of the Goddess.

In Greece, too, stories circulate of Apollo's conquering Delphi by slaying a female dragon, who guards the shrine of Mother Earth. This female dragon is portrayed as the source of evil. Also, we are told that Zeus kills the Goddess Metis (Wisdom) by swallowing her whole. He goes on to rape Goddesses, nymphs, and human women.

The Bible does not follow so violent a path of destruction, but it does carry underlying hints of killing off the Goddess by implying that Eve, the snake, and the tree are responsible for bringing evil into the world. In the Christian tradition, this is carried further when Eve is blamed for what St. Augustine would later call "original sin." According to theologian Carol Christ, "Christian tradition thus identifies woman with sexuality and death and views her as the origin of sin and evil. In Christian myth, woman is the chaos monster who is not slain and therefore leads all humanity into sin and death. According to Tertullian woman is 'the Devil's gateway.' Her sin causes the death of the savior."

The goddess was alive and well among the Celtic peoples. Among the Celts, gender justice was real—strong women held leadership roles. Irish women held their own in the struggle for existence and real influence in the community. Sacred wells play an important role in Celtic spirituality. **The land of Ireland was understood in ancient times as the body of the goddess. Wells were reverenced as special apertures through which divinity flowed forth. . . . Wells were sacred places. Wells were seen as threshold places between the deeper, dark, unknown subterranean world and the outer world of light and form.**

Celtic myths abound with powerful goddesses. One scholar has written: **Irish mythology points to the early preeminence of goddesses. As agriculture and many of the arts were first in the hands of women, goddesses of fertility and culture preceded gods, and still held their place when gods were evolved. Even war goddesses are prominent in Ireland.** The goddess Brigid, who was later taken over as a Christian saint and kept the same feast day as the ancient goddess (February 1), had three roles: as a healer, as protector of smiths, and as goddess of fertility and poetry. The latter was her most important role. When the great Celtic chieftain Viridomar attacked Rome in 222 B.C.E., he called himself a "son of the Rhine," meaning a son of the goddess of the Rhine. The Celts all considered themselves **children of a Great Mother Goddess.**

A matricentered society survived for a long time among the Celts. "Throughout Irish mythology, relationships to the mother are emphasized. The Tuatha De Danaan were 'children of the goddess Dana.' " Creativity lay at the heart of the universe, as the Celts saw things. "For the pagan Celt, the essence of the universe and all its creativity was female. The mother goddess, and all her personifications of fertility, sovranty, love and healing, was an essential basis of their very role in the world. Therefore, when the Christian movement, at the Council of Ephesus in C.E. 431, made Mary officially the 'Mother of God,' the Celts turned to her enthusiastically as the replacement 'mother goddess', seeing in her the goddesses of fertility, love and healing." Women played prominent roles in preaching the new faith among the Celts. Some were ordained as priests and others even as bishops, it appears.

In *The Heart of the Goddess*, a rich collection of stories and artifacts of the Goddess from religious traditions around the world, the author, Hallie Iglehart Austen, describes three categories around which the goddess gathers: "Creation, including birth, nurturance, and the abundance of the natural world; transformation, meaning physical death and rebirth as well as the metaphorical deaths and rebirths of trance and descent to the underworld; and celebration, encompassing sexuality, sensuality and creativity. The unity of birth, growth, death and rebirth is the basis of the Goddess's teachings. We see them daily in the cycles of night and day, waking and sleeping, creating and letting go." This naming of the work of the Goddess almost names the structure of this book—clearly the Goddess is integral to all that we are sharing around creation, light, community, and more.

Austen goes on to describe the work of the Goddess. "The Goddess is she who gives life and, when the form is no longer viable, transforms it through death. And then, through the exquisite pleasures of creativity and sexuality, she brings forth new life. All of us experience these cycles. They are what unite us in our human existence . . ." We are instructed that "in most primal cultures the sun is female." Among the cultures that worship the sun goddess are the following: the Cherokee people of North America call her Igaehindvo; the Celts call Brigit the Fire Goddess; the Sun Woman is honored among the Australian Arunta; Akewa of the Toba people in Argentina is the Sun Goddess there. Among the Inuit peoples in the Arctic there is Sun Sister; and the Arab people revere Allat; and the most ancient Japanese deity is Amaterasu Omikami, the Great-Goddess-Spirit-Shining-in-heaven, Creatrix Goddess of the sun, weaving, and agriculture. She is honored even today at Shinto shrines throughout Japan where people take offerings to her each morning when the sun rises.

Among the Maori people of New Zealand, it is believed the Mahuika brought the people to those islands and that she also discovered the art of making fire. The Egyptian Goddess Nut, who is an ancient African Goddess of the Cosmos dating back to at least 3000 B.C.E., was thought to give birth to the Sun each morning. "As genetrix of the sun, Nut is the Mother of Life" but also the promise that death brings rebirth. The Aztec Goddess Tlazolteotl is also honored for giving birth to the sun, "while numerous legends say that women keep fire in their genitals."

"Myths around the world describe the Goddess as the keeper of the flame, for woman is the custodian of the hearth and spiritual power." It is interesting that, as we have seen, both Hildegard of Bingen's self-portrait and the early Christian story of Pentecost are about flames coming over the apostles—this may well be a reference to the goddess dimension of the Christ power that early Christians recognized. A hint of the Holy Spirit as Feminine.

If it is true that so many ancient teachings associate the Sun with the Goddess, then a return to awareness about light and enlightenment that we treated in chapter three bespeaks a return to the Goddess. The era of light-awareness that Einstein ushered in early in this century includes the return of the Goddess.

Queen Maya is the mother of the historical Buddha, Prince Siddhartha, who became the Buddha. The Goddess Prajnaparamita, which means "highest perfect wisdom," is called the Spiritual Mother of all the Buddhas, the source of enlightenment itself. Many works celebrate Queen Maya and underscore the female origins of Buddhism.

In China, the most universally admired deity is Guanyin or Kuan Yin, the Bodhisattva of Compassion. She listens to and responds to the cries of all beings. Like Mary and Artemis, she is a virgin Goddess who "protects women, offers them a religious life as an alternative to marriage, and grants children to those who want them." We are invited to meditate on her attributes of compassion in particular in order to bring them into our lives of service.

In the lands of the universe there is no place
Where She does not manifest herself . . .
Compassion wondrous as a great cloud,
Pouring spiritual rain like nectar,
Quenching the flames of distress!

In Tibet, the primordial Great Goddess of Central Asia is known as Tara, which can be translated as "Star and She Who Leads Across." Like Prajnaparamita, she is the spiritual mother of all the Buddhas, and she supports those who resist the great dangers that Buddhism names as pride, delusion, anger, envy, wrong views, avarice, attachment, and doubt. Buddhism adopted her as a bodhisattva, an enlightened being who chooses to remain in the world until all beings are liberated. She vowed to always reincarnate as a woman. Tara is an aspect of the Buddha of Compassion.

Tara means tear as well as star. It is said that she was born out of one of the tears of the Buddha of compassion that fell to the earth. She who saves and restores was born from that tear. Mahayan Buddhism worships the Divine Mother as Tara. She offers final liberation and illumination, instructing how everyday life in the world and nirvana are one. Enlightenment is available to all.

Her original roots are as the Great Mother of India and Tibet, the fierce Goddess of the Underworld, of plants, animals, and human beings and the heavenly Goddess of wisdom and spiritual transformation. She has been given thirty-two names of praise:

Buddha!
Emanator!
Chief Guide!
You of noble morals!
Superior One!
Sole Mother!
Saviour!
Leader!
Doctor!
Jewel!
Bearer of knowledge!
Heroine!
Turner of the wheel of healthy Dharma!
Sun!
Full moon!
Lotus!
Fearless one!
Very firm one!
Thoroughbred!
Peahen!
Cuckoo!
Lamp!
Clear revealer of beauty!
Liberator!
Great-voiced one!

Ambrosia!
Guarding life-giver!
Life-giver healing the world!
Sole friend!
Dakini!
Way-shower!
Friendly minded one!

A traditional Tibetan prayer to Tara follows:

Homage to Tara our mother: great compassion!
Homage to Tara our mother: a thousand hands, a thousand eyes!
Homage to Tara our mother: queen of physicians!
Homage to Tara our mother: conquering disease like medicine!
Homage to Tara our mother: knowing the means of compassion!
Homage to Tara our mother: a foundation like the earth!
Homage to Tara our mother: cooling like water!
Homage to Tara our mother: ripening like fire!
Homage to Tara our mother: spreading like wind!
Homage to Tara our mother: pervading like space!

Tantra and Tibetan Buddhism still honor the Sacred Feminine. Some of the movements within that tradition were founded by women, and what they have in common is that "they emphasize immanence and a delight in the world rather than transcendence and a belief that the world is evil. Instead of encouraging harsh asceticism, they teach that we are already enlightened and need only to allow our original natures to shine through." This sounds a lot like Creation spirituality.

Also in China, the Tao is recognized as female. She is **The Great Mother, Mother of the universe** She is immanent and deeply personal—she is **always present within** you—yet she is deeply cosmic as well. For she

> **flows through all things,**
> **inside and outside, and returns**
> **to the origin of all things.**

> All things obey her.

> **The Tao is great**
> **The universe is great**
> **The earth is great**
> **Man is great.**
> **These are the four great powers.**

> **Man follows the earth.**
> **Earth follows the universe.**
> **The universe follows the Tao.**
> **The Tao follows only itself.**

> She is the source of all things and all things are representative of her.

> **Every being in the universe**
> **is an expression of the Tao. . . .**
> **That is why every being**
> **spontaneously honors the Tao.**

> She is like a mother to all beings and she is beloved by them all.

The Tao gives birth to all beings,
nourishes them, maintains them,
cares for them, comforts them, protects them,
takes them back to herself,
creating without possessing,
acting without expecting,
guiding without interfering.
That is why love of the Tao
is in the very nature of things.

Among the Yoruba people of West Africa, Orisha or Ochun or Oshun is honored as the deity of the river, love, sensuality, and creativity. Myth has it that women learned to move and sway sensuously by imitating Ochun, the River Goddess. She is a kind of celestial mermaid about whom it has been said:

She presides over the arts, healing, gold, love and all things beautiful.
She rests, full of self-awareness and self-love, glowing in the silver
light of the moon, symbol of the feminine principle. Ochun is Mama
of All Waters, on Earth and in the heavens. Her cooling waters are
believed to soothe any person, emotion or situation, and she will
send them to those in need.

Isis is the primordial Great Goddess of Africa in Egypt; she is mother of the deities, the sun, and the world. Her name means "throne," and both the female and male pharaohs claimed to be descended from her. She guaranteed the fertility of the land and guarded over the dead. An ancient prayer is said of her.

I am Nature, the universal Mother,
Mistress of all the elements,
primordial child of time,
sovereign of all things spiritual,
queen of the dead,
queen also of the immortals,
the single manifestation of all gods and goddesses that are. . . .
Both races of Aethiopians, whose lands the morning sun first shines
upon, and the Egyptians who excel in ancient learning
and worship me with ceremonies proper to my godhead,
call me by my true name,
namely Queen Isis.

Tassili rock paintings in today's Algeria contain marvelous paintings of the Dancing or Horned Goddess, accompanied by images of many animals. These painting were executed about 6000 B.C.E., when the area was green and not the desert it is today. The Goddess is wearing horns, which indicate a crescent moon. It may be that these frescoes are depicting Isis as an agricultural deity. To this day the Taureg women of the area are strongly independent while the men appear in public veiled.

In a hymn by Christian theologian Alan de Lille in the twelfth century, Nature is exalted as a goddess.

> **O Child of God and Mother of things,**
> **Bond of the world, its firm-tied knot,**
> **Jewel set among things of earth, and**
>   **mirror to all that passes away,**
>   **Morning star of our sphere;**
> **Peace, love, power, regimen and strength,**
> **Order, law, end, pathway, captain and source,**
> **Life, light, glory, beauty and shape,**
>   **O Rule of our world!**

In medieval Christianity Mary has much in common with Isis. Joseph, Mary, and Jesus make a divine family and so do Osiris, Horus, and Isis. Like Isis, Mary is often depicted sitting on a throne with a small son on her lap. The Cathedral movement, indeed revolution, of the Middle Ages was a *throne* movement for *cathedra* means throne. It was a rethroning of the Goddess, this time in the center of the newly burgeoning cities. It was also a *de*throning of the patriarchal God that still ruled the feudal countryside and the privileged monastic establishment. In a mere one hundred fifty years over five hundred Gothic temples were built in Europe and every one was dedicated to Mary.

At times Isis is depicted with a headdress in the shape of a throne. Erich Neumann interprets this. "As mother and earth woman, the Great Mother is the 'throne' pure and simple. . . . To be taken on the lap, is like being taken to the breast, a symbolic expression for adoption of the child, and also of the man, by the Feminine. It is no accident that the greatest Mother Goddess of the early cults was named Isis, 'the seat,' 'the throne,' the symbol of which she bears on her head; and the king who 'takes possession' of the earth, the Mother Goddess, does so by sitting on her in the literal sense of the word." Like Isis, whose tears are said to have launched the Nile river, Mary weeps. Osiris, Isis' son, is the first of many resurrected gods. Mary's son, too, is said to have resurrected. Isis is called "Lady of Heaven"; Mary is called "Queen of Heaven."

The tradition of the Black Madonna in Catholicism is an offshoot of the honoring of Isis. China Galland is a pilgrim who set out on a journey in search of the Black Madonna and her relationship to other Goddesses. In her book *Longing for Darkness: Tara and the Black Madonna,* she writes about the connection between Isis of Africa and Mary as the Black Madonna in Europe. "Isis, out of the Nile Valley, bringing the influence of Africa and Egypt to the West throughout the Mediterranean into Italy, Spain, and France and as far north as Germany, Switzerland, even England, some say. Called 'the Star of the Sea' and 'Queen of Heaven,' Isis, like the Black Madonnas, was renowned as a miracle worker and healer. Some scholars claim that some of the early statues of the Madonna and Child were actually Isis and Horus, renamed as Mary and Jesus." What is the Black Madonna about? She "presents us not with an issue of sex or gender, but of life, life with all its teeming diversity of peoples, our different colors, our fullness."

Hildegard of Bingen, whose lifetime spans the time when Chartres Cathedral was for the most part constructed, wrote many songs to Mary. She calls Mary "ground of all being."

> **Mary, ground of all being,**
> **Greetings!**

In Mary is the "fullness of all joy."

> **Mary, the heavens gift the grass with moist dew.**
> **The entire earth rejoices.**
> **From your womb the seed sprouted forth.**
> **The birds of the air nest in this tree.**
> **Blessed is the fruit of your womb!**
> **Your womb's fruitfulness is food for humankind.**
> **Great is the joy at this delicious banquet!**
> **In you, mild virgin, is the fullness of all joy.**

Mary is a "healing art" who has "conquered death and established life."

> **Mary, O luminous mother,**
> **holy, healing art! . . .**
> **You have indeed conquered death!**
> **You have established life!**
> **Ask for us life.**
> **Ask for us radiant joy.**
> **Ask for us the sweet, delicious ecstasy that is forever yours.**

> **Mary, your womb exalts**
> **It exalts like the grass,**

grass the dew has nestled on,
grass the dew has infused with verdant strength.

She is the "mother of all joy" who is green and full of creativity.

That is how it is with you, Mother of all joy. . . .
You glowing, most green, verdant sprout,
in the movement of the spirit,
in the midst of wise and holy seekers,
you bud forth into light.

A profound parallel with the goddess tradition can be found in the role that Mary plays in Christianity, first with the birth narratives which, while not being historical, are nevertheless powerful at every cosmic and spiritual level. In addition, in the role Mary played in the twelfth-century renaissance and the building of the great Gothic cathedrals, cathedrals of *light and color and space* and beauty. All of these cathedrals were inspired by her.

What was behind that inspiration? Historian Henry Adams believes that Mary's role in the Middle Ages renaissance was so strong because she alone was Mother who was "human, imperfect, and could love." She represented a refuge for "whatever was irregular, exceptional, outlawed; and this was the whole human race." She represented the Unity that encompassed all—"Duality, Diversity, Infinity—Sex!" She also oversaw the intellectual awakening. "The Virgin of the twelfth and thirteenth centuries had not only the powers of Eve and Demeter and Venus; she was also the mistress of all the arts and sciences, was afraid of none of them, and did nothing, ever, to stunt any of them." Protestantism would banish her along with sex and imagination and Catholicism would distort her.

But she persisted because she represented "the whole rebellion of man against fate; the whole protest against divine law. . . . She was above law" and her attraction "was due much less to her power of saving soul or body than to her sympathy with people who suffered under law—justly or unjustly, by accident or design, by decree of God or by guile of Devil." Her key was "positive compassion; she was what might be called the Buddhist element in Christianity, for with her as with Buddha compassion is [primary]. To Kwannon the Compassionate One and to Mary the Mother of God, compassion included the idea of sorrowful contemplation."

Mary still plays a powerful role in her many forms, including that of the Black Madonna and in the story of Our Lady of Guadalupe in Mexico. In the sixteenth century, shortly after the Spanish invaders took over most of Mexico, a young Indian named Juan Diego visited Tepeyac Hill where Tonantsi, the Goddess of Earth and Corn, had enjoyed a major temple in her honor before the European invasions. The Lady of Guadalupe appeared to Juan Diego and promised to protect him and his people. Asking for a sign, roses suddenly grew among the cactuses. When telling his story to the bishop of the diocese, there appeared on Juan's cloak an image of the Virgin as a pregnant, dark-skinned Indian woman with stars on her cloak and a crown on her head and the moon supporting her and the rays of the sun surrounding her. She was the Queen of heaven, and to this day she symbolizes freedom from the early European invaders. She is the compassionate Goddess. She stirs controversy still.

Artist and writer Guillermo Gomez-Pena confesses that the Lady of Guadalupe was often employed "as a demagogic tool of control" supporting a "fundamentalist Catholic movement operating out of fear of modernity and change." However, on moving from Mexico to the United States, he learned that the icon could be deconstructed and reconstructed, thus transforming it "into symbols of contestation against the dominant Anglo culture." Now she became a symbol of resistance. "In the Chicano movement, *la Virgen* was no longer the contemplative mestiza Mother of all Mexicans, but a warrior goddess who blessed the cultural and political weapons of activists and artists. She was against racism, the border patrol cops, and supremacist politicians." And she stood with other strong women such as Frida and Sor Juana on behalf of women's rights.

Writer Sandra Cisneros concurs. She writes about finding the Lady of

Guadalupe outside the Roman Catholic Church and about finding her as the Sex Goddess who endorsed her own womanhood in all its dimensions. "My *Virgen de Guadalupe* is not the mother of God. She is God. She is a face for a god without a face, an *indigena* for a god without ethnicity, a female deity for a god who is genderless, but I also understand that for her to approach me, for me to finally open the door and accept her, she had to be a woman like me." And what kind of a woman is that? "She is not neuter like Barbie. She gave birth. She has a womb. *Blessed art thou and blessed is the fruit of thy womb* . . . Blessed art thou, Lupe, and therefore, blessed am I."

God is understood as mother in the medieval Christian tradition. Mechtild of Magdeburg said: **God is not only fatherly. God is also mother who lifts her loved child from the ground to her knee.** And as for the Trinity, it is **like a mother's cloak wherein the child finds a home and lays its head on the maternal breast.** Hildegard of Bingen offers images of a curved Divinity. We are **surrounded with the roundness of divine compassion,** she writes. **Divinity is like a wheel, a circle, a whole.** Meister Eckhart describes God as mother when he says: **From all eternity God lies on a maternity bed giving birth.** And, **What does God do all day long? God gives birth.** Acknowledging and desentimentalizing the work of Mary at the same time, he declares that **we are all meant to be mothers of God.**

English mystic of the late fourteenth century Julian of Norwich most developed the theme of God as mother.

> **Just as God is truly our Father, so also is God truly our Mother. . . .**
> **The deep Wisdom of the Trinity is our Mother. In her we are all enclosed. . . .**
> **[God is] our true Mother in whom we are endlessly carried and out of whom we will never come.**
> **God is the true Father and Mother of Nature, and all natures that are made to flow out of God to work the divine will will be restored and brought again into God.**
> **God feels great delight to be our Mother.**

Among the Native American people there is special honor given the Goddesses of food. The Iroquois people honor the Three Sisters who are Corn, Bean, and Squash. The Hopi honor the Corn Mother. Corn represents the source of life, the gift from the underworld of nourishing food. A Hopi baby is given a perfect ear of white corn at birth as a symbol of its mother. The corn rises each season and stands tall like a human being. She reminds us of the cycles of life, death, and rebirth, and she tells of our connection to the earth at our feet and the sky and sun at our top.

Among the Inuit peoples of the Arctic lands there is the Sea Goddess known as Sedna or the "woman of the depths of the sea." She controls the food supply of many Arctic lands and also reigns over the land of the dead. She brings equilibrium and balance to those who live on land and sea, balance between the human and the other-than-human species.

Pele, the Goddess of the volcanoes in the Hawaiian islands, personifies the life force. She created the land out of the ocean with her red-hot flow of lava, an act of Creation that is still taking place since the islands are still being formed by this active volcano.

Among the Kagaba people, an indigenous tribe in Brazil, there is the following hymn:

The mother of our songs, the mother of all our seed,
bore us in the beginning of things
and so she is the mother of all types of men, the mother of all
nations. . . .
She alone is the mother of the fire and the Sun and the Milky Way. . . .
She is the mother of the rain and the only mother we possess.
And she has left us a token in all temples . . .
a token in the form of songs and dances.

In Hinduism, we have an ancient honoring of Shakti, the mother who is the creative life-force of the universe, who also dwells within every human being. She is the creative power of Brahman, the divine Source. She creates, sustains, destroys, and remakes all things. Yet she is intimate as well. She is terrible as well as tender, Destroyer as well as Preserver. She is God the Mother. She unwinds like a coiled serpent through the lotuses of the body as well as through the lotus chakras of the universe itself.

Ramakrishna teaches about the Divine Mother when he says: **Whatever we see or think about is the manifestation of the Mother, of the Primordial Energy, the Primal Consciousness. . . . The Primordial Power is ever at play. She is creating, preserving, and destroying in play, as it were. This power is called Kali.** He counsels us to pray to her. **Pray to the Divine Mother with a longing heart. Her vision dries up all craving . . . and completely destroys all attachment.** Another spiritual teacher, Aurobindo, describes the Divine Mother in the following fashion: **Transcendent, the original supreme Shakti, she stands above the worlds and links the Creation to the ever unmanifest mystery of the Supreme. . . . All is her play with the Supreme; all is her manifestation of the mysteries of the Eternal, the miracles of the Infinite. . . . That which we call Nature or Prakriti is only her most outward executive aspect.** He, too, advises devotion and attachment to this Mother. **[Become] completely identified with the Divine Mother and feel yourself to be no longer another and separate being, instrument, servant or worker but truly a child and eternal portion of her consciousness and force. Always she will be in you and you in her.**

In the Vedas, the mother is called the **Mighty Mother. The Divinity is the underlying Spirit in Nature, in human relations. . . . The Divinity as the Feminine Power or Spirit became the object of worship in Tantra.** A Vedic hymn sings:

**The Goddess who exists in all beings as Mother,
obeisance to her! Obeisance to her!**

Another hymn sings:

> O God (Brahman): Thou art woman, Thou art man;
> Thou art boy, Thou maiden.
> Thou existest in all forms.

The goddess Usas is celebrated in the Vedas. She is **the Daughter of Heaven, who was born in the sky. She is the Lady of Light, the mistress and wife of the sun. He follows her as a young man follows a maiden.** [The Goddess of hope, the elder sister of Night, is mentioned more than three hundred times in the Rg Veda.] To be the "Lady of Light" is especially significant, since in the Upanishads, the Spirit is named Light. Philosopher Raimundo Panikkar comments: **The poetry of these hymns is imbued with intense luminosity. The yearning for light, the deep longing for the sun, and, by contrast, the fear of shadows and of darkness are strongly marked characteristics of the soul-strivings of the Vedic people. . . .**

Ancient Vedas sing to Usas, the "friendly lady" who brings on the dawn.

> **See now, the shining Daughter of Heaven approaches,**
> **dispelling gloom of night that we may see.**
> **The friendly lady ushers in the light. . . .**
> **O Dawn, at your arising and the Sun's,**
> **grant us, we pray, our portion in your light. . . .**
> **O shining Dawn, you who inspire the generous**
> **and are full of grace, drive from us all our foes.**

Notice that this lady is honored as being "full of grace." Another hymn follows.

> **Dawn comes shining**
> **like a Lady of Light,**

stirring to life all creatures. . . .
Our Lady of Light
brings the Eye of the Gods,
as she rides her white, beautiful steed. . . .
Beam forth your light
to guide and sustain us,
prolonging, O Goddess, our days.
Give to us food,
grant to us joy,
chariots and cattle and horses.

Kali is also called Devi. She takes on many forms. The following prayer is dedicated to her.

By you this universe is born, by you this world is created.
By you it is protected, O Devi. By you it is consumed at the end.
You who are eternally the form of the whole world,
at the time of creation you are the form of the creative force,
at the time of preservation you are the form of the protective
    power,
and at the time of the dissolution of the world
    you are the form of the destructive power.

In the Hindu Scriptures there is a whole book dedicated to the Divine Mother known as *Chandi*. It is a promise of liberation against forces of oppression. In it the Universal Mother says: **Wherever there is oppression in the world, I shall descend and destroy it.** There is a warriorlike energy associated with the Divine Mother that is anything but passive or ladylike. It represents a prophetic energy.

Vivekenanda, a Hindu leader of our century, said: **One vision I see clear as life before me, that the ancient Mother has awakened once more, sitting on her**

throne rejuvenating more glorious than ever. Proclaim her to all the world with a voice of Peace and Blessing.

The Mother Goddess is found in India long before Hinduism began. She was central to the urban and agricultural civilization dating from at least 3000 B.C.E., which preceded the Aryan invasions. She represented the fertility of nature, the giving and sustaining of life. This civilization closely paralleled that of Sumeria. The role of the Mother Goddess was carried over into Hinduism. The Aryan invasion of the Greek, Roman, and Iranian empires began around 1500 B.C.E.

Inanna or Ishtar was the most important deity worshipped in ancient Sumeria thirty-five hundred years ago. She was Goddess of the earth, of fertility, and of Eros and was Queen of Heaven and a Goddess of death and rebirth. A story about her concerns her journey into the Underworld to visit her sister, who is queen there. She is stripped of her powers and is killed and hung from a hook, but after three days she is revived by spirit helpers and reborn. Inanna's story of resurrection precedes that of Persephone, Orpheus, and Jesus. Like Jesus, she lies buried for three days and three nights—perhaps this symbolizes the three nights of the month when the moon disappears from her monthly cycle.

A prayer to Inanna composed by the priestess Enheduanna survives from about 2300 B.C.E.

> Lady of all the essences, full of light,
> good woman clothed in radiance
> whom heaven and earth love . . .
> You are a flood descending from a mountain,
> O primary one,
> moon goddess Inanna of heaven and earth!

This rich but brief excursion through the Goddess traditions makes clear that Divinity does indeed boast many faces. The implications of our having lost these faces of the Divine are very great. Our souls have shrunk and our relationship to the rest of nature has been practically choked off. For without the Goddess it is very easy to neglect the sacred in nature. Joseph Campbell put it this way: "When you have a Goddess as the Creator, it's her own body that is the universe. She is identical with the universe. Myths of the Great Goddess teach compassion for all living beings. There you come to appreciate the real sanctity of the earth itself, because it is the body of the Goddess."

Now we shall turn to another Goddess tradition, that of Wisdom, or Chokmah in Hebrew, as well as Shekinah. It has been said that all the aspects of the Divine Feminine which we find in Judaism and Christianity come from the original Great Goddess of the Semitic people.

7.

WISDOM:
ANOTHER FEMININE FACE
OF THE DIVINE

Sophia (Wisdom) I loved;
I sought her out in my youth,
I fell in love with her beauty,
and I longed to make her my bride. . . .
Once you have grasped her, never let her go.
In the end, she will transform herself into pure joy.
—Book of Wisdom; Sirach

The Feminine face of God was not altogether wiped out by patriarchy. She returned as Wisdom and as Shekinah, in the Hebrew Scriptures. And she returned as Christ-Sophia in the Christian writings. The experience that Wisdom is Feminine is an old idea and a transcultural one as we shall see.

In the Hebrew Scriptures, Wisdom is celebrated for her cosmic oversight. She comes wrapped in cosmology, as we saw in chapter two. She has a universal perspective, a cosmic sense. **She is fairer than the sun, greater than every constellation . . . and the source of all treasure in the universe.** There is nothing petty or sectarian about Wisdom—she is truly universal dwelling in the cosmos itself.

> **My dwelling place was in high heaven,**
> **my throne was in a pillar of cloud.**
> **Alone I made a circuit of the sky**
> **and traversed the depth of the abyss.**
> **Over the waves of the sea and over the whole earth,**
> **and over every people and nation I have held sway . . .**
> **From eternity, in the beginning, he created me,**
> **and for eternity I shall remain . . .**
> **Approach me, you who desire me,**
> **and take your fill of my fruits.**

She undergirds all things and permeates them, bringing order from chaos while she plays with God from before the beginning of the world. She is the object of our pursuit of truth at the same time that she is accessible as the fruit of awe and wonder. Indeed, **awe is the beginning of wisdom.** In her is found rest and repose, delight and joy. She is the source of all eros, all love of life. **Whoever loves her loves life.** Hers is the way of true justice and she is a **friend of the prophets. She deploys her strength from one end of the earth to the other, ordering all things for good.**

She entices us with her fruits and attractions for **she is an inexhaustible treasure for humankind, she blesses the world with Supreme wisdom and allows all people to realize their unity with God.** Notice how ecumenical Wisdom is—she brings *all people* to unity with God. (This same sense of ecumenism is echoed in the story of Christ's birth in Bethlehem when the angels sing out to the shepherds:

Glory [Doxa, Radiance] to God in the highest and peace to *all* people of good will.)

We are told that she is **the mother of all good things,** who **age after age enters into holy souls.** She also **makes all things new** and **to love her is to love life.** Indeed, **a desire to know her brings one to love her,** we are assured.

Where will we find her? The Wisdom of Solomon says you **will find her seated in your own heart.** Thus our hearts become a throne where holy Wisdom sits, that is how near and intimate she is to us. The author of the Book of Wisdom tells of his experience with her.

> **Sophia I loved;**
> **I sought her out in my youth,**
> **I fell in love with her beauty,**
> **and I longed to make her my bride.**

We are advised:

> **Once you have grasped her, never let her go.**
> **In the end, she will transform herself into pure joy.**

This is quite a promise—that pure joy comes our way by way of Wisdom. Furthermore, it is not just our pursuit of her that makes up this holy relationship, but her pursuit of us. **Sophia goes about in search of those who are worthy of her. With every step she comes to guide them; in every thought she comes to meet them.** This teaching is about *grace*—Sophia operates gracefully, generously. She is as much in pursuit of us as we are in pursuit of her.

Wisdom is present at creation and involved in all creative processes. The Book of Proverbs tells her story this way:

> **Yahweh created me when his purpose first unfolded,**
> **before the oldest of his works.**

From everlasting I was firmly set,
  from the beginning, before earth came into being.
The deep was not, when I was born,
  there were no springs to gush with water.
Before the mountains were settled,
  before the hills, I came to birth;
before he made the earth, the countryside
  or the first grains of the world's dust.
When he fixed the heavens firm, I was there,
  when he drew a ring on the surface of the deep,
when he thickened the clouds above,
  when he fixed fast the springs of the deep,
when he assigned the sea its boundaries
  —and the waters will not invade the shore—
  when he laid down the foundations of the earth,
I was by his side, a master craftsman,
  delighting him day after day,
  ever at play in his presence,
at play everywhere in his world,
  delighting to be with the sons and daughters of the human race.

Sophia or Wisdom has often been presented as a minor figure in Jewish theology. However, a serious look at the Hebrew Scriptures reveals that "there is more material on Sophia in the Hebrew Scriptures than there is about almost any other figure. . . . Only God (under various titles), Job, Moses, and David are treated in more depth." There is more written about Sophia than about "Abraham, Isaac, Jacob, Solomon, Isaiah, Sarah, Miriam, Adam, or Noah. But we do not know her. . . . Sophia, who stands taller than any of them, is ignored."

We are told that Sophia is a late development in Israel's interest in Wisdom. Yet she is an "organic part of the social drama in later Israel," as one scholar puts it. She came along at a time of turmoil in the consciousness of Israel, that is during the Hellenistic age when Greek philosophy and science were having an impact on Israel. A diversity of religious beliefs was very much in the air at the time. "The figure of Sophia was a response to the increasingly complex social world the people of Israel were experiencing. She was herself understanding. She was also above, beyond, and in all that is. She was creator of more than Israel. She was, in fact, the symbol which represented the Hebrew people's attempt to relate to a new and larger world."

In Jewish mysticism the Divine Mother is spoken of as *Binah*. She flows and engenders the coming to be of the seven lower *sefirots* or attributes of Divinity. Wisdom or *Hokhmah* lies in the depths of *Binah*. Wisdom cannot be grasped consciously, only absorbed. As an early kabbalist put it: **No creature can contemplate the wondrous paths of Wisdom except one who sucks from It. This is meditation through sucking, not through knowing.**

Indeed, Sophia's presence on the scene during the Hellenistic era of Israel does not seem that different from our own times. With patriarchal versions of Christianity having taken over so much of the mindset of Western religion, and with new explosions of scientific discovery and even scientific wisdom, and with the mixing of religions occurring on an unprecedented scale, and with the Goddess returning in many new and old forms, and with nature so endangered by human folly, it seems all the more timely that Wisdom and our appreciation of it is reentering our hearts and minds and awarenesses.

The Christian appropriation of the Sophia tradition was profound and pervasive. When the first generations of Christians started reflecting on Jesus and his teachings, time and again they compared him to Sophia. Indeed, he was, like Sophia herself, both teacher and subject taught. We should not underestimate what a surprise this was, that Wisdom returned in the form of a male sage in first-century Palestine. But that is the best interpretation of the Jesus event that we can surmise today: Jesus was a teaching sage, a member of the Wisdom movement of his day, and the people whose hearts he touched by his teaching and his life, who experienced him as a Christ, did so in the name of Sophia or Lady Wisdom. They scoured the Hebrew Bible for texts about Jesus, and they found the Wisdom Scriptures best named their experience of the man, his teaching, and his story. The Goddess, then, Wisdom, took flesh in Israel and in the person of Jesus. That is what the earliest Christians believed. That is what so upset the patriarchal culture of the Roman Empire and of Jesus' own Jewish community. The historical Jesus reveals the feminine side of Divinity, though not exclusively.

Time and again Paul calls Jesus Sophia. **We are preaching a crucified Christ . . . a Christ who is the power and the Sophia of God. . . . By God's action Jesus Christ has become our Sophia. . . . But still we have a Sophia to offer those who have reached maturity: not a philosophy of our age, it is true, still less of the masters of our age, which are coming to their end. The hidden Sophia of God which we teach in our mysteries is the Sophia that God predestined to be for our glory before the ages began. She is a Sophia that none of the masters of this age have ever known.** Furthermore, Paul's teaching of the **new creation** in Christ is based on the secret presence of Sophia in all things.

But it is not only Paul who interpreted Jesus as Sophia; John's Gospel is built around the entire motif of Sophia **setting up her tent in Israel** and Jesus being that Sophia (albeit with a new name, Logos or Word). In Sirach we read:

> **The Creator of all things instructed me . . .**
> **"Pitch your tent in Jacob,**
> **make Israel your inheritance."**

In John we read:

The Word was made flesh,
and pitched his tent among us.

Jesus' many discourses in John's Gospel resemble discourses Wisdom makes about herself. "Jesus in John takes his character from Sophia. The picture of Jesus in John as self-proclaiming teacher sent from heaven by God with whom he creates and communicates is the picture of Sophia."

The Gospels of Luke, Matthew, and Thomas also present Jesus as speaking the words of Sophia. Today many believe, since the discovery of further Gnostic literature in this century, that the gospel writers were a bit skittish about acknowledging the relation of Jesus and Sophia in order to distance themeselves from Gnostic ideas. Because some Gnostics were reluctant to admit the crucifixion of Jesus and his humanity, their writings were not included in the official "canon" of the Christian Scriptures. It also is a reason why the Sophia connection, while strong in the gospels and in the early hymns of the Christian church, was not made more explicit. To have done so would have invited some doubting of the full humanness of Jesus—or at least that was the concern of early Christians who were resisting the Gnostic wing of Christianity. In any case, it is certain that the insight that Jesus, a male, was connected in some deep and profound way with Sophia, who is female, was revelatory to the world. It also made early Christianity what Otto Rank claims it was: a Goddess religion.

Hildegard of Bingen picks up on the Sophia relationship when she urges us to **dwell in the house of wisdom** and that wisdom **arouses every soul for living.** Furthermore, wisdom will **fill your whole house with heavenly desire,** for **wisdom resides wonderfully in the Godhead's heart.** The Godhead's heart houses Wisdom *and* our hearts house Wisdom.

In the mystical tradition of Sufiism there were many women who were spiritual guides and teachers. Women participate in the same ceremonies with men on an equal basis and they undergo the same initiations. Ibn Al-Arabi, a thirteenth-century mystic, proclaimed: **One obtains the highest theophanic vision in contemplating the Image of the Feminine being, because it is in the Image of the Creative Feminine that contemplation can apprehend the highest manifestation of God, namely creative divinity.**

One contemplates Feminine Being as the Image of Wisdom or Creative Sophia. The Creative Sophia is the mediatrix of creation and is called the Active Intelligence. One Commentator on Ibn Al-Arabi's writings concludes: **The spirituality of our Islamic mystics is led to the apparition of the Eternal Woman as an Image of the Godhead because in her it contemplates the secret of the compassionate God, whose creative act is a liberation of beings. This is called recollection of Sophia in which the Feminine is not opposed to the Masculine but encompasses and combines it.** Rumi sees women as the image of the divine Beloved.

> **Woman is a beam of the divine Light.**
> **She is not the being whom sensual desire takes as its object.**
> **She is Creator, it should be said.**
> **She is not a creature.**

Muhammad is acknowledged historically as a foremost advocate of women's rights for his time. In a rabidly patriarchal society he pronounced in favor of choice and rights for women, a position that flew in the face of the prevailing abuse of women in the tribal society of his time and place. Muhammad said:

> **All people are equal, as equal as the teeth of a comb. There is no**
> **claim of merit of an Arab over a non-Arab, or of a white over a black**
> **person, or of a male over a female.**
> **He who honors women is honorable, he who insults them is lowly**
> **and mean.**

**He who has a female child and does not insult her and does not
prefer his sons over her, will be ushered by God into paradise.**

And on his deathbed the Prophet uttered as almost his last word,

**I urge you to treat women kindly. They are a trust. Be in awe of
God's trust.**

In the Islamic telling of the Fall, Eve plays no part as an instrument of Adam's
transgression. Rather, the satanic force is responsible for the downfall of both Adam
and Eve. The Qur'an gives full equality to women in education, voting, and vocation. (Many Muslim cultures have not caught up with the Qur'an in this regard,
which demonstrates how entrenched patriarchy can make itself. Yet, also, though
Jesus also supported women and broke taboos against them, the Christian church
in many of its manifestations in no way mirrors his beliefs. The Vatican is one obvious example.)

In Muhammad's time and culture the constant tribal wars separated men from
women. The deaths of men in battle resulted in there being more women than men
in the society. Women and children were deprived of livelihood and prostitution
was rampant. But the Qur'an stated that marriage was to be the only place for sex.
This dictate created a substratum of security for women and children and it established the link between sex, love, and commitment. Prostitution became a thing of
the past thanks to Muhammad's influence. The ideal relationship held up in the
Qur'an was monogamy. Yet polygamy was allowed provided the husband treated
each wife equally because there were more women than men in the society. Before
Islam, women were treated as property subject to the will of their father or hus-
bands, but with Islam rules were established that granted women the right to initi-
ate divorce, and a trust fund established before the marriage was in the woman's
name so that if she were divorced that fund would go to her.

In Islam, women were allowed to inherit whereas previously they were forbidden inheritances. Women were no longer to be part of an inheritance, nor could they be taken as prisoners or booty in war. Islam established the right of women to own property a full thirteen hundred years before Western culture established it as a right. Islam established the right and duty of women as well as men to learn. Muhammad's wife was herself a prominent merchant. After her husband's death, Aisha became a significant authority and leader in the Islam movement, giving, among other things, a model to future generations of women of their capacity and right to lead. The Prophet's daughter, Fatima, is venerated to this day in Shiite movement, and the first real saint of Islam was a woman named Rabia. The Qur'an proclaims that **the believers, men and women, are friends one of another.** Surely this is a call to equality between sexes. In the Islamic tradition, Mary the mother of Jesus is held in high regard. Ibn Al-Arabi writes that God **is seen more perfectly in woman than in man. . . . To see God in woman is to see him in both these aspects [as agent and as patient], and such vision is more perfect than seeing him in all the forms in which he manifests himself.**

In her essay "The Feminine Element in Sufism," Annemarie Schimmel tells the story of Layla and Majnun in Persian literature. Layla is a woman whose name means "night" and she becomes a symbol of the divine Beloved present in every single being. Majnun sees only beauty because he sees only with the eye of love. He becomes a mystical lover who sees God everywhere, including in the innermost core of his own heart. In contrast, one who sees only with the eye of intellect will not be able to perceive divine beauty in all its forms.

Ana Matt comments on how Islam seems to have strayed from Muhammad's very prophetic stand on behalf of women. Because of the long-standing patriarchal attitudes of the Middle East, "patriarchy was able to devour Islam and quickly make it its own after the death of Muhammad. There was a decline of the huge Arab empire and civilization, which paved the way for western colonization and subjugation. Oppression of men tends to create double oppression of women."

Buddhism honors Wisdom as Feminine in its tradition of Prajna. Prajna or Wisdom lies at the core of all forms of Buddhism because it names the essence of the enlightenment experience, namely the elimination of all dualities. Prajna is often conceived of as a goddess, especially in the Tantric tradition, and is frequently called the Mother of all the Buddhas. Tantric Buddhism further emphasizes the need for the union of wisdom with compassion.

Sariputra, a leading disciple of the historical Buddha, speaks to Lady Wisdom in this text from the Mahayan school of Buddhism. **The perfection of wisdom gives light, O Lord. I pay homage to the perfection of wisdom! . . . She is a source of light, and from everyone in the triple world she removes darkness, and leads them away from the blinding darkness caused by defilements and wrong views. In her we can find shelter. Most excellent are her works. She makes us seek the safety of the wings of enlightenment. She brings light to the blind, so that all fear and distress may be forsaken. . . . She cannot be crushed. She protects the unprotected, with the help of the four grounds of self-confidence. She is the antidote to birth and death.**

Wisdom is praised for her cosmic dimension and her compassion in the following hymn.

Spotless, unobstructed, silent,
Like the vast expanse of space. . . .
As the moonlight does not differ
From the moon, so also Thou
Who aboundst in holy virtues,
And the Teacher of the world. . . .
Thou a mother who does nourish,
Who gives birth, and who gives love.
Teachers of the world, the Buddhas
Are Thine own compassionate sons.

It is evident that in all teachings of Wisdom, Wisdom includes the universe and Wisdom passes through the heart. Wisdom is knowledge and awareness and experience of the whole that touches the heart. Many traditions honor the special place where heart and universe, microcosm and macrocosm, meet. In the Hindu tradition, the *Gita* teaches that **the Lord dwells in the hearts of all creatures, and he whirls them round on the wheel of time.** In addition, the Upanishads teach that **there is a Light that shines beyond all things on earth, beyond us all, beyond the heavens. . . . This is the Light that shines in our heart.** The Upanishads also teach the following: **In the center of the castle of Brahman, our own body, there is a small shrine in the form of a lotus-flower, and within can be found a small space. We should find who dwells there, and we should want to know him.** Who dwells there? **The little space within the heart is as great as this vast universe. The heavens and the earth are there, and the sun, and the moon, and the stars; fire and lightning and winds are there; and all that now is and all that is not: for the whole universe is in him and he dwells within our heart.**

From the Native American tradition Black Elk teaches: **The heart is a sanctuary at the center of which there is a little space, wherein the Great Spirit dwells, and this is the Eye. This is the Eye of the Great Spirit by which he sees all things, and through which we see him.** It is from this center that true peace derives. It is the peace that comes when cosmos and heart are reunited. **The first peace, which is the most important, is that which comes within the souls of men when they realize their relationship, their oneness, with the universe and all its powers, and when they realize that at the center of the universe dwells Wakan-Tanka, and that this center is really everywhere, it is within each of us. This is the real peace, and the others are but reflections of this.**

In the Islamic tradition, Ibn Al-Arabi teaches the folllowing:

"You thought yourself a part, small;
Whereas in you there is a universe, the greatest."

That is to say, you think of yourself as a small thing, whereas in you there is hidden the biggest of the universes. . . . The meaning of the Qur'anic verse becomes clear to the gnostic: "Wherever way you turn, there is the face of God."

All this teaching honors Wisdom and honors the universe and honors humans who are capable of wisdom, love, and reconnecting to the whole.

8.

FORM, FORMLESSNESS, NOTHINGNESS

> Love God as God is a not-God, a not-mind,
> a not-person, a not-image.
> —Meister Eckhart, *Sermon 12*

The Divine is not only the images we carry and wonder at and imagine about the Divine. The Divine is also without image and without form. We heard Thomas Aquinas say this earlier when, on telling us that we could understand God as imaged by every being of which he is the cause—**and all the other beings attributed to God as cause**—he also said: **And the Divine One is none of these beings insofar as God surpasses all things.**

This is a common teaching, East and West, that God is both manifest and unmanifest; with form and formless. Yet it is difficult for modern Westerners to grasp this common theme of form and formlessness because modern science actually instructed us that form is absolute and eternal—indeed it was immutable law. That is the language that Francis Bacon used when he advised people in his *Novum Organum* to replace the term "form" with "law." Bacon writes: "It may be that nothing really exists except individual bodies, which produce real motion according to law; in science it is just that law, and the inquiry, discovery and explanation of it, which are the fundamental requisite both for the knowledge and for the control of Nature. And it is that law and its 'clauses' which *I* mean when I use (chiefly because of its current prevalence and familarity) the word 'forms.'"

Law in the eighteenth century was mechanical, unchanging, unchangeable. The modern mindset *froze form* and made an idol of it, calling it "Law." Machines took over. And obedience to them. Chaos was banished (or so they thought and tried). Notice that it was modern science's desire to "control Nature" (Bacon's words) that was behind the drive to deprive form of its flexibility and replace it with law.

Fortunately, today's science is quite opposite to Bacon's—we see form as itself evolving—or in Rupert Sheldrake's words, what we have understood to be "laws of the universe" we should now understand as *habits*. Even these so-called laws themselves evolve. How much more so form itself!

As we saw in chapter four, science is rediscovering respect for emptiness and nothingness. As Brian Swimme puts it, **The ground of the universe . . . is an empty fullness, a fecund nothingness.** Nothingness is returning as an operative category in scientific understanding.

The ancient Chinese Scriptures speak this way:

> **There was something formless and perfect**
> **before the universe was born.**
> **It is serene. Empty.**
> **Solitary. Unchanging.**
> **Infinite. Eternally present.**
> **It is the mother of the universe.**
> **For lack of a better name,**
> **I call it the Tao.**

Nor is this formless Tao so transcendent that it is not immanent to us. Quite the contrary,

> **It flows through all things,**
> **inside and outside, and returns**
> **to the origin of all things.**

Practical ramifications follow from our recognition of the formless side of the Tao and of all things.

> **When you have names and forms,**
> **know that they are provisional.**
> **When you have institutions,**
> **know where their functions should end.**
> **Knowing when to stop,**
> **you can avoid any danger.**

It is easier to let go when one responds to the formless side of the Tao. It also cuts into our desire to grasp and control.

Look, and it can't be seen.
Listen, and it can't be heard.
Reach, and it can't be grasped. . . .
Seamless, unnamable,
it returns to the realm of nothing.
Form that includes all forms,
image without an image,
subtle, beyond all conception.

In Hinduism, Brahman can be looked at two ways. There is Saguna Brahman, who is God with attributes understood as Creator, Lord, Savior; and there is Nirguna Brahman, who is without qualities or attributes and is beyond everything which we can conceive of. This side of Brahman is unnameable. Father Bede Griffiths puts it this way: **There is nothing higher than this, than if one says, "not this, not this." This is negative theology. We cannot name Brahman. It is "not this, not this." Whatever word we use, whatever image, whatever concept, we have always to go beyond. . . . One cannot stop with any name of God. . . . We are all seeking that inexpressible mystery beyond, and that is Brahman, which is neti, neti, "not this, not this."**

In this understanding, Brahman is a mystery that cannot be named and ought not be named. **It is without name or form.**

The Godhead called Brahman not only sustains all phenomena as the ground of being and foundation of the world at large. It is also **the core of human consciousness.** We make contact with this groundless being, and when we do Brahman is known as "Atman."

There is no contradiction between these two aspects of Brahman. The Upanishads teach that there is no conflict between what Eckhart would call "God" and the "Godhead," between Divinity as form and Divinity as formless. Iyengar writes: **From the lowliest insect to the most perfect sage, there breathes the same Universal Spirit, which assumes innumerable forms. He knows that the highest form is that of the Formless. He finds unity in universality.** The Vedas sing:

Such is thy greatness, O Liberal Lord!
A hundred bodily forms are thine.
Millions are in thy million.
For every form he has been the model,
that form of his is the one to look on everywhere.

A scholar comments: **God is one, his glory multiplying in many forms.** The Vedas teach that **there are two forms of Brahman: the embodied and the bodiless, the mortal and the immortal, the stable and the moving, the tangible and the intangible.** A tension is acknowledged between the God of forms and the God beyond forms. **The problem of the relationship between the unconditioned Brahman and the phenomenal universe can never be completely solved.**

Meister Eckhart speaks of the distinction between God and Godhead. God acts in history and in creation, but the Godhead does not act. The Godhead is being, mystery, silence; while God is action, history, and word. God becomes as creatures—who are words of God—express God. But the Godhead does not become. Yet we flow from the Godhead when we are born and we return to it when we die and we experience it in this lifetime as well. Eckhart says Divinity **is nameless, for no one can know or articulate anything about God. . . . God is a being beyond being and a nothingness beyond being** who consists of a **changeless existence and a nameless nothingness.** Eckhart attempts to name the nothingness of God. **God is nothing. It is not, however, as if he were without being. He is rather neither this thing nor that thing that we might express, He is a being above all being. He is a beingless being. . . . God is nothingness, and yet God is something.**

Mystery lies behind Divinity. **The mystery of the darkness of the eternal Godhead is unknown and never was known and never will be known. God dwells therein, unknown to himself/herself.** The Godhead is nameless:

The naked God is without a name
and is the denial of all names
and has never been given a name
and so remains a truly hidden God.

He advises persons to let go of talk about God. **Be silent and quit flapping your gums about God. . . . The most beautiful thing which a person can say about God would be for that person to remain silent from the wisdom of an inner wealth.** Eckhart is encouraging us to imitate the Godhead's silence and thereby touch the Godhead. He says it another way as well.

How should you love God?
Love God as God is—
    a not-God,

> not-mind,
> not-person,
> not-image—
> even more, as God is a pure, clear One
> who is separate from all twoness.

Furthermore, **the Divine One is a negation of negation and a denial of denials.**

Jan van Ruysbroeck, also of the Christian tradition, writes that **the Godhead is, a simple essence, without activity; Eternal Rest, Unconditioned Dark, the Nameless Being, the Superessence of all created things.**

Thomas Aquinas also writes of the Godhead experience, the experience of the formless side of Divinity. He recognizes the paradox involved in saying God is known in all creatures when he observes: **Through creatures God is both hidden from us and made manifest to us.** And this is why **every name imposed by us onto God falls short of God. . . . God is inaccessible light, surpassing every light that can be seen by us either through sense or through intellect.** Our intellect cannot grasp the Divine. **Concerning God all things can be affirmed and denied. Yet the Divine One is above all affirmation and denial, for God is beyond our entire intellect, which composes affirmations and denials.**

Mystery and wonder overwhelm cause and effect. **The cause at which we wonder is hidden from us.** Ultimately, God is mystery and unknowable. **We are united to God as to One Unknown. . . . God alone knows the depths and riches of the Godhead, and divine wisdom alone can declare its secrets. The mind's greatest achievement is to realize that God is far beyond anything we think. This is the ultimate in human knowledge: to know that we do not know God. . . . By its immensity the divine essence transcends every form attained by the human intellect.**

Divinity is without a name. **Divinity is incomprehensible. It can be neither embraced nor designated by a name.** Even the name "being" fails in regard to God. Thus Nothingness can be an appropriate naming. **God is said to be nonbeing (*non-existens*) not because God is lacking in being but because God is beyond all beings.**

Thich Nhat Hanh echoes Meister Eckhart when he says: **We have to rid ourselves of all notions of God in order for God to be there. The Holy Spirit, the energy of God in us, is the true door. We know the Holy Spirit as energy and not as notions and words.** Like Aquinas and Eckhart, he sees concepts falling short of who the Divine is and prefers silence. **It is impossible to use our concepts and words to describe God. . . . It's very wise not to say anything about God. To me the best theologian is the one who never speaks about God.** When Thich Nhat Hanh talks about Nirvana, he sounds like Eckhart talking about the Godhead. **In the phenomenal world, we see that there is birth and death. There is coming and going, being and non-being. But in nirvana, which is the ground of being equivalent to God, there is no birth, no death, no coming, no going, no being, no non-being. All these concepts are transcended.**

North American Buddhist nun Pema Chodron discusses the need to move from theism to "nontheism." She sees theism as an addiction. This is how she puts it: **The difference between theism and nontheism is not whether one does or does not believe in God. It is an issue that applies to everyone, including both Buddhists and non-Buddhists. Theism is a deep-seated conviction that there's some hand to hold: if we just do the right things, someone will appreciate us and take care of us. It means thinking there's always going to be a baby-sitter available when we need one.** The problem with theism is that it invites projections. **We all are inclined to abdicate responsibilities and delegate our authority to something outside ourselves. Nontheism is relaxing with the ambiguity and uncertainty of the present moment without reaching for anything to protect ourselves.**

What is at issue is the nature of reality itself—and our relation to it. Will we manipulate or will we trust? **Nontheism is finally realizing that there's no baby-sitter that you can count on. You just get a good one and then he or she is gone. Nontheism is realizing that it's not just baby-sitters that come and go. The whole of life is like that. This is the truth, and the truth is inconvenient. The-**

ism is an addiction. Perhaps this is what Meister Eckhart had in mind when he prayed: **I pray God to rid me of God.** If we do not let go of theism, of a "God outside," then we may never allow ourselves to be broken through by the Godhead.

I have a Buddhist friend who said to me recently: "Don't use the word soul. I hate the word soul. Buddhists don't talk of soul." The main objection Buddhists have to our Western soul-talk is that they see us making a permanent, immutable, and immortal *thing* or substance of the soul and this makes them nervous because they see all reality as evolving and changing. *Sunyata* is the understanding of the interrelatedness of the soul and all things. "Sunyata is relative or contingent. This emptiness means that nothing exists in and of itself but only in relation to other things which are themselves interrelated and thus empty of independent existence. There is no such thing as self-substantiated reality."

I believe that Eckhart was teaching the same thing when he said: **the essence of everything is relation.** If we Westerners would take Eckhart up on his statement—an observation very much buttressed by today's science—then we would, I believe, be sharing *concepts* if not always *terms* that Buddhists would agree with. To say the essence of the soul is relation is to say that soul is *not* an object or straight substance but a relation, an ongoing relation of many relations.

Buddhist scientist Wes Nisker puts this teaching in the context of today's evolutionary thought and with good reason. **There is no independently existing self apart from all of biological and cosmic evolution. The Buddha realized that by experiencing this truth inside us, we can weaken our inordinate attachment to our individual drama, relieve our suffering, and increase our compassion for all life.** The "self" is not permanent. Self **refers to something that is singular or "uncompounded," which means that its existence does not depend on the coming together of any two separate elements and, furthermore, that it will be able to sustain itself independently from all other things . . . all things, including human beings, can be said to be without self. In fact, all things can be said to be without ultimate "thingness." This is the basis for the common Bud-**

dhist notion of the emptiness of the world. There is a very positive side to experiencing our emptiness and that is the contact we make with fullness. **We begin to realize that we exist only in relationship, and that rather than being nothing, we could more accurately say that we are everything. [We] become one with all the things of the world.** Emptiness and fullness, nothing and everything, come together.

In Judaism, the *Kabbalah* God is referred to as **Ein Sof,** which means literally "there is no end," "Endless," "Infinity." Thus Ein Sof "is the designation of the Absolute, God as infinite being, beyond the specific qualities of the sefirot" or attributes of God. It is also called "that which thought cannot comprehend" and "the annihilation of thought." And it is also called Nothingness or *Ayin:* Mystical Nothingness.

> **Ayin, Nothingness, is more existent than all the being of the world....**
> **The Depth of primordial being is called Boundless. Because of its concealment from all creatures above and below, it is also called Nothingness. . . .**
> **All is one in the simplicity of absolute undifferentiation. Our limited mind cannot grasp or fathom this, for it joins infinity. . . .**
> **God is the annihilation of all thoughts, uncontainable by any concept. Indeed, since no one can contain God at all, it is called Nothingness, Ayin.**

Nothingness is named in the Kabbalah as *Keter* which is the annihilation of thought by which "human consciousness expands, dissolves into Infinity." Thus we see that Jewish mystics also honor the formlessness and nothingness of the Godhead. And, like the other traditions, there are practical ramifications when we experience the Divine Nothingness. We become more ample channels for grace to pour through, less self-conscious and more trusting and certainly less in control. **The essence of serving God and of all the *mitsvot* is to attain the state of humility, that is, to understand that all your physical and mental powers and your essential being depend on the divine elements within. You are simply a channel for the divine attributes . . . Then you come to the state of Ayin, the state of humility.**

In the *Zohar* we also learn about the hiddenness of Divinity. We read:

The Blessed Holy One too is known and unknown.
For he is *Neshamah* of *neshamah*, Pneuma of pneuma,
completely hidden away.

A dialogue proceeds as to how to find Divinity in spite of its great hiddenness.
The dialogue transpires around the text from Proverbs 31:23:

Her husband is known in the gates
when he sits among the elders of the land.

Rabbi Judah comments:

The Blessed Holy One. . . . is hidden, concealed, far beyond.
There is no one in the world, nor has there ever been,
who can understand his wisdom or withstand him.
He is hidden, concealed, transcendent, beyond, beyond. . . .
He is unknowable.
No one has ever been able to identify him.

9.

THE DIVINE "I AM":
HUMANITY'S SHARE IN DIVINITY

**Moses asked: "But if they ask me what his [God's] name is,
what am I to tell them?" And God said to Moses, "I Am
who I Am. . . . I Am has sent me to you."
—Exodus 3:13–14**

In many traditions around the world, the term "I am" is employed of Divinity. Recently I was leading a group of young adults in an evening of discussion about Urban Spirituality, and I led the group in a simple circle dance that included the Wikka chant that says, "Earth I am, Fire I am, Water, Air and Spirit I am," and I was amazed at the response. A tough, inner city African-American young man insisted that we end the evening with the same song. "I love to sing **I AM**," he said, "I can't get enough of it." Maybe we all need to sing this sacred name more often and in more ways. Perhaps this young African American was tapping into an echo of his African spiritual awareness, for Dona Richards says that in Africa **the human is divine.**

The Goddess Isis speaks in a poem by Lucius in the second century C.E.

I am she that is the natural mother of all things,
mistress and governess of all the elements,
the initial progeny of worlds,
chief of the powers divine,
queen of all that are in Hell,
the principal of them all that dwell in Heaven,
manifested alone and under one form of all the gods and goddesses.
At my will the planets of the sky,
the wholesome winds of the seas,
and the lamentable silences of Hell
be disposed;
my name, my divinity is adored throughout the world,
in divers manners,
in variable customs,
and by many names.

The "Zulu Personal Declaration," composed in South Africa in 1825, begins thus:

I;
I am;
I am alive;
I am conscious and aware;
I am unique;
I am who I say I am; I am the value UQOBO [essence]
I forever evolve inwardly and outwardly in response to the challenge
   of my nature;
I am the face of humanity;
The face of humanity is my face.

The Hindu faith recognizes a litany of "I am" sayings attributable to Divinity.

> I am the Father and Mother of the world.
> In ancient days I established it.
> I am what needs be known, what purifies.
> Your way and goal, upholder, friend, witness, dwelling, refuge,
>   friend.
> The world's origin, continuance and dissolution, abiding essence,
>   seed.
> I am deathlessness and death.
> I am the entire world.
> I am the beginningless, unborn, the Spirit of the world.
> I am the soul which dwells in the heart of all things.

An additional "I am" poem is offered in the Gita.

> O son of Kunti, I am the taste of water, the light of the sun and the
> moon, the syllable om in the Vedic mantras; I am the sound in ether
> and ability in man.
>   I am the original fragrance of the earth, and I am the heat in fire.
> I am the life of all that lives, and I am the penances of all ascetics.
>   O son of Prtha, know that I am the original seed of all existences,
> the intelligence of the intelligent, and the powers of all powerful
> men.
>   I am the strength of the strong, devoid of passion and desire. I
> am sex life which is not contrary to religious principles, O lord of the
> Bharatas [Arjuna]. . . . Know that all states of being—be they of
> goodness, passion or ignorance—are manifested by my energy. I am,
> in one sense, everything, but I am independent. I am not under the
> modes of material nature, for they, on the contrary, are within me.

I am the goal, the sustainer, the master, the witness, the abode, the refuge and place and the eternal seed.

I give heat, and I withhold and send forth the rain. I am immortality, and I am also death personified. Both spirit and matter are in me.

I am the Supersoul, O Arjuna, seated in the hearts of all living entities. I am the beginning, the middle and the end of all beings.

Of the senses I am the mind; and in living beings I am the living force [consciousness]. . . . Of purifiers I am the wind, of the wielders of weapons I am Rama, of fishes I am the shark, and of flowing rivers I am the Ganges. . . . Of all creations I am the beginning and the end and also the middle, O Arjuna. Of all sciences I am the spiritual science of the self, and among logicians I am the conclusive truth.

I am all-devouring death, and I am the generating principle of all that is yet to be. Among women I am fame, fortune, fine speech, memory, intelligence, steadfastness and patience. . . .

Among all means of suppressing lawlessness I am punishment, and of those who seek victory I am morality. Of secret things I am silence, and of the wise I am the wisdom. . . . Furthermore, O Arjuna, I am the generating seed of all existences. There is no being—moving or nonmoving—that can exist without me.

The Celtic tradition also celebrates "I am" namings of Divinity. In what John O'Donohue calls "the first poem ever composed in Ireland," we hear the following.

> I am the wind which breathes upon the sea,
> I am the wave of the ocean,
> I am the murmur of the billows,
> I am the ox of the seven combats,
> I am the vulture upon the rocks,
> I am a beam of the sun,
> I am the wild boar in valour,
> I am the salmon in the water,
> I am a lake in the plain,
> I am a world of knowledge,
> I am the point of the lance of battle,
> I am the God who created the fire in the head.

As O'Donohue wisely points out, this spirituality is light years beyond Descartes's dictum, "I think therefore I am." This is about community, the community of all things with one another and in God and God in all things. **I am because everything else is. I am in everything and everything is in me.** The Divine "I am" is omnipresent if we allow it to be.

An example of the nearness of the Christ who is the "I am" present in all things is found in the ancient poem called "The Deer Cry." In it we hear the following prayer.

> Christ with me, Christ before me, Christ behind me,
> Christ in me, Christ beneath me, Christ above me,
> Christ when I lie down, Christ when I sit down, Christ when I arise,
> Christ in the heart of every one who thinks of me,
> Christ in the mouth of every one who speaks of me,

Christ in every eye that sees me
Christ in every ear that hears me.

Celtic Christianity addresses the suffering Christ as well in the following poem attributed to St. Patrick.

> **I see his blood upon the rose**
> **And in the stars the glory of his eyes,**
> **His body gleams and eternal snows,**
> **His tears fall from the skies.**

> **I see his face in every flower;**
> **The thunder and the singing of the birds**
> **Are but his voice—and carven by his power**
> **Rocks are his written words.**

> **All pathways by his feet are worn,**
> **His strong heart stirs the ever-beating sea,**
> **His crown of thorns is twined with every thorn,**
> **His cross is every tree.**

Notice that the poet does not dwell exclusively or in an isolated fashion on the pain and suffering of the Cosmic Christ but alternates between the glory and the suffering. This is not unlike the writers of John's Gospel who also understood Jesus' death as his hour of glory.

In the Gospel of John, the Christ says:

> **I am the true vine.**
> **I am the resurrection.**
> **I am the gate.**

I am the good shepherd.
I am the light of the world.
Before Abraham ever was, I am.
I am the bread of life.
I am the bread that came down from heaven.

While scholars have established that these sayings and much else in John's Gospel are not from the lips of the historical Jesus, they certainly are from the heart of the Christian community. They bespeak the power of the Jesus event as it touched on the lives of his disciples. And they also bespeak the ancient name of Divinity as the "I am."

Aramaic scholar Neil Douglas Klotz points out that "in a culture where the word for 'God' means Unity, the sense of the individual cannot be ultimately separated from the Divine. Only one 'I Am' exists, which is Alaha (or God)." Indeed, the theology of the Cosmic Christ is a theology of the "I am" names of Divinity, for that tradition says that every creature is an expression of the Divine from its essence, from its "I am-ness." To cite just one theologian on this topic, Thomas Aquinas says: **The Incarnation accomplished the following: that God became human and that human beings became God and sharers in the divine nature. The only-begotten Son of God intended to make us "partakers of his divine nature." For this reason the Godhead did take our nature on itself and became human in order to make humans gods.**

The "I am" emerges in a translation from the original Aramaic that Jesus spoke. Matthew 18:20, usually translated, **where two or three are gathered together in my name, there am I in the midst of them,** takes on new meaning in this context.

Wherever two or three gather
in my name and light,
in my experience of
the vibrating, shining cosmos—

**then the 'I Am' is already there
around, among and inside them.**

In Christianity, the divine "I am" is not just the light in all things but also the suffering in all things. This is one of the deep dimensions of the crucifixion story—that Divinity as it passes into our world also suffers with the rest of Creation. This is told in stories about the Christ's death in Jesus and how the cosmos was affected—darkness at high noon, the veil of the temple torn in two, the breaking out of tombs by the dead. While these are Christ stories and not historical Jesus stories, nevertheless they tell a great myth and teach a great lesson: how suffering is universal.

Hildegard of Bingen, who lived in a Celtic monastery along the Rhine river in Germany, also composed "I am" poems.

> **God says: I am the day unto myself,**
> **not formed by the sun, but rather, forming the sun,**
> > **igniting it.**
> **I am the understanding not understood, but rather,**
> > **allowing all understanding, illuminating it.**
>
> **I am the one whose praise echoes on high.**
> **I adorn all the earth.**
> **I am the breeze that nurtures all things green.**
> **I encourage blossoms to flourish with ripening fruits.**
> **I am led by the spirit to feed the purest streams.**
> **I am the rain coming from the dew**
> > **that causes the grasses to laugh with the joy of life.**
> **I call forth tears, the aroma of holy work.**
> **I am the yearning for good.**

Julian of Norwich also offers an "I am" poem around Jesus.

> **Our Lord Jesus oftentimes said:**
> **"This I am.**
> **This I am.**
> **I am what you love.**
> **I am what you enjoy.**
> **I am what you serve.**
> **I am what you long for.**
> **I am what you desire.**
> **I am what you intend.**
> **I am all that is."**

And again,

> **God said:**
> **"This I am—the capability and goodness of the Fatherhood.**
> **This I am—the wisdom of the Motherhood.**
> **This I am—the light and the grace that is all love.**
> **This I am—the Trinity.**
> **This I am—the Unity**
> **I am the sovereign goodness of all things.**
> **I am what makes you love.**
> **I am what makes you long and desire.**
> **This I am—the endless fulfilling of all desires."**

Two contemporary Aboriginal poets in Australia have written their own "I am" poems. This one by Hyllus Maris honors the relationship to the land.

> I am a child of the Dreamtime People
> Part of the Land, like the gnarled gumtree
> I am the river, softly singing
> Chanting our songs on my way to the sea
> My spirit is the dust-devils
> Mirages, that dance on the plain
> I'm the snow, the wind and the falling rain
> I'm part of the rocks and the red desert earth
> Red as the blood that flows in my veins
> I am eagle, crow and snake that glides
> Through the rain-forest that clings to the mountainside
> I awakened there when the earth was new
> There was emu, wombat, kangaroo
> No other man of a different hue
> I am this land
> And this land is me
> I am Australia.

Aboriginal poet Kevin Gilbert also speaks an "I am" poem called "Tree."

> I am the tree
> the lean hard hungry land
> the crow and eagle
> sun and moon and sea
> I am the sacred clay
> which forms the base
> the grasses vines and man

I am all things created
I am you and
you are nothing
but through me the tree
you are
and nothing comes to me
except through that one living gateway
to be free
and you are nothing yet
for all creation
earth and God and man
is nothing
until they fuse
and become a total sum of something
together fuse to consciousness of all
and every sacred part aware
alive in true affinity.

When we honor all creation as housing the Divine Source we include, of course, human Creation. Humanity is made, as the Hebrew Scriptures put it, **in the image and likeness of God the Creator.** This tradition is named in Christianity as the Cosmic Christ that is in all of us and in Buddhism as the **living Buddha, who is within ourselves and who transcends space and time.** Why should we be so startled to learn of our divine ancestry? Why, indeed, except that we have lost all contact with our origins and Creation's divine ancestry.

Thich Nhat Hanh declares: **From a Buddhist perspective, who is not the son or daughter of God? . . . When we are in touch with the highest spirit in ourselves, we too are a Buddha, filled with the Holy Spirit, and we become very tolerant, very open, very deep. And very understanding. . . . We do not have to die to arrive at the gates of Heaven. In fact, we have to be truly alive.**

Pema Chodron believes that the deep encounter that occurs in meditation is nothing less than an encounter with the Buddha Nature in us. **When we look into our own hearts and begin to discover what is confused and what is brilliant, what is bitter and what is sweet, it isn't just ourselves that we're discovering. We're discovering the universe. When we discover the Buddha that we are, we realize that everything and everyone is Buddha.**

Yes, here is where psyche and cosmos come together, and with them the maker or the holder of the two. Cosmic Buddha, Buddha Nature, Cosmic Christ, Christ Nature—maybe that is why the spiritual practice is called *mind-ful-ness*—it is about filling the mind with something we richly deserve to be filled with: the universe in all its sacred radiance. But that is also why mind-emptying is so necessary—because the mind is *already* so filled—it's just that we are so busy with other matters that we forget.

It takes a lot of trust to recognize humanity's divinity. At first blush, humanity seems to be anything but divine. We almost appear to be demonic in our capacity for rapaciousness and destruction. But our powers of creativity are so magnificent and so Godlike that, in fact, we dance a dance between the Divine and the demonic, between power-with and power-over. It is this dance that urges us to make decisions that are Godlike in preference to choices that are destructive. **I set before you life and death; choose life** (Dt. 30:19). To choose life is to choose God, for **God is life, per se life.**

Once, on conducting a workshop in the Philippines, I encouraged the group of two hundred and fifty participants to create an "I am" poem appropriate to the Filipino experience. Following is a portion of their group poem.

> **I am the sunrise that brightens up the sky in the early morning.**
> **I am the rays of the sun that give radiance to every creature during**
> **the sunrise at Manila Bay.**
> **I am the fire that kindles the stars, and the stars in your eyes.**
> **I am the white sand kissed by the bubbling waves of the blue seas.**
> **I am the fresh smell of the rice fields.**
> **I am the trunk of a talisay tree standing amidst the polluted and**
> **overpopulated areas.**
> **I am the sturdy bamboo that sways unbroken by strong winds.**
> **I am the sweat of an oppressed people.**
> **I am the smile on the lips of a fallen comrade.**
> **I am the tears of a mother in pain.**
> **I am the color of the rainbow that gives hope.**
> **I am the forlorn trees resisting extinction.**
> **I am the Filipino soul struggling to be free.**
> **I am what I am—the Holy God of the universe who is of all, in all,**
> **under all, over all, all.**

Three

RELATING TO

OURSELVES: PATHS

TO ENCOUNTER AND

ENLIGHTENMENT

We have seen how widespread the sense of the transcendence, mystery, unknowability of the Godhead, Brahman, Ayin is in many spiritual traditions. We have also seen how common the tradition is of the Divine as the "I am" in every creature. The question arises: How do we make contact with Divinity and the Godhead in all its mystery and beauty? How do we overcome obstacles to this union? Creation is one way the Divine reaches out to us. But other ways also are open to us. Now we shall explore the human side to this relationship, paths other than direct encounter with Creation, by which we enter into the divine life.

Among the paths we will travel are the following:

10. Meditation and Mindfulness
11. Holy Imagination: Art and Ritual as Paths to Mindfulness
12. Joy
13. Suffering
14. Beauty
15. Sacred Sexuality
16. Dying, Resurrection, Reincarnation

10.

MEDITATION AND
MINDFULNESS

Meditation is stopping, calming, and looking deeply.
—**Thich Nhat Hanh,** *Living Buddha, Living Christ*

There are many kinds of meditation or ways to train the mind that spiritual traditions the world over have developed. I distinguish them into two basic categories: the emptying kind and the filling kind. They are not at all exclusive one of the other. Quite the contrary, one serves the other. When one is very filled, for example, with the beauty of the ocean, one is often put into a state of silent appreciation. Filling turns to emptying. In contrast, when one fasts for a while or meditates by letting go of all images and distractions and goals, thereby emptying the mind, then the return to simple joys like eating a tomato or smiling with a friend take on all new levels of depth and delight.

The two kinds of meditation correspond to the two aspects of Divinity that we have discussed: form and formlessness. In this chapter we will be considering the emptying kind of meditation and in the following chapter the filling kind.

We humans carry enough of the "image of God" in us that we, too, are form and formless; we have access to the God of form and Creation and the Godhead of nothingness. Meister Eckhart puts it this way: **In that respect in which the soul is an image of God and is, like God, nameless, there the soul knows no renewal but only eternity, like God.** The Hindu teaching that the eternal Godhead, Brahman, is known through human consciousness as Atman, is also saying what great things are before the human when we learn to perceive correctly.

That is why each of these meditation ways is appropriate and useful for us. At different times and episodes in one's life, we may need one more than the other. In general, I would say that Westerners today, so swamped in media-driven cultures of consumerism and affluence, and so distant from nature and her secrets and beauties, and so driven by busyness, will find themselves more and more drawn to the emptying kinds of meditation. Then we can return to creation itself with a clearer mind and calmer heart.

The goal of each kind of meditation is the same: To see reality as it is in all its clarity and radiance and truth. Jesus called it **recognizing that the domain of God is among us.** Thich Nhat Hanh describes it as developing our capacities for deep looking, listening, and awareness of the present state of things beginning with ourselves. In his own words: Meditation is **stopping, calming, and looking deeply. When we are mindful, touching deeply the present moment, we can see and listen deeply, and the fruits are always understanding, acceptance, love, and the desire to relieve suffering and bring joy.**

Authentic meditation practice does not force one to withdraw from everyday existence but to stay there with new eyes and fuller heart and not to run away from things. It is about being fully present to what is. **The technique is to be in the present moment, to be aware that we are here and now, that the only moment to be alive is the present moment.**

To arrive at the inner self where this God-birth really takes place, we need to let go of some of the soul's busyness. The soul is sometimes like a monkey cage, full of busy, busy monkeys. The soul gets to be very busy—it responds to everything about it not only during waking hours but in sleep as well. It wanders, it looks, it feels, it imagines, it hopes, it remembers, it regrets, it rejoices, it longs. So much goes on in the soul that, at times, it needs slowing down, resting and repose, forgetting and emptying, letting go and just *being*, returning to its source. It needs a vacation. Recreation. Refreshment. Meditation is another word for that vacationing time, time-off for the soul.

When we do meditation we are changing our relationship to *space and time*. Meditation affects the realities we discussed in Part I of this book—Creation and our perception of it. If Creation is so full of Divinity, a temple of the Divine, do we perceive it as such? We are talking about perception, clearing ours out and cleaning ours up. Says Eckhart: **Every angel is with his whole joy and his whole bliss inside me and God himself with his whole bliss. Yet I do not perceive this.** Eckhart said above in chapter two that everything of the past and the future is present now in our soul—but do we perceive this?

The great gift of Buddhism is not to offer us a new religion but to give us practices that anyone can develop, no matter what his or her spiritual tradition. **It is not a matter of faith; it is a matter of practice,** Thich Nhat Hanh points out. To undergo authentic Buddhist teaching is not so much to read texts as to practice meditation and ways to mindfulness. **The living Dharma is not a library of scriptures. . . . It is mindfulness manifested in your daily life.** When we do this we become agents for transformation and we become gentler people. That is Thich Nhat Hanh's point: There are ways to come to perceive the bigger reality in which we swim, the true depths of the space and time that we inhabit and that inhabit us. This is what it means to be awake. **A Buddha is someone who is awake. . . . Our true home is in the present moment. The miracle is not to walk on water. The miracle is to walk on the green earth in the present moment.**

Our species learns the better part about itself, that we are capable of forgiveness and nonviolence. We can, Thich Nhat Hanh promises, choose to **live in a way that reduces the world's suffering.** The primary practice is that of stilling the busy mind. **Meditation means to look deeply. Meditation is to be still: to sit still, to stand still, and to walk with stillness.** The goal is mindfulness. What is mindfulness? **Mindfulness is the energy of the Buddha.** In meditation we are emptied— not only of busyness but of concepts. **Emptiness means the emptiness of a separate existence, the emptiness of a permanent entity, emptiness of all concepts. . . . The practice is to transcend both notions of being and non-being.** In this stilling of our mind and its busyness we return home. We return to our true selves, our primal nature. What is that?

In Buddhism, our true nature is called variously the " 'essence of mind,' or our 'original mind,' 'original face,' 'Buddha nature,' 'emptiness.' " Buddhism describes the "universal Mind" as **"luminous," "immaculate," "lucid," "unstained," and "ineffable." Over the centuries, the universal Mind has been given many wondrous names, including the unborn, the source, the predicateless primordial essence, the weaver of the web of appearances, and—a breathless Tibetan Buddhist appellation—the outbreather and the inbreather of infinite universes throughout** the endless duration of time. For some, the universal Mind has god-like attributes: it is the great mystery itself, the creator and destroyer, all-knowing and all-powerful.

North American Buddhist Wes Nisker writes about what he has derived from meditation. He points out that our "thinking minds"—what Aquinas calls the "discursive intellect"—have taken over too much of our mind's activities. Meditation can bring back the balance.

I believe that my years of meditation practice have brought me a new degree of intimacy with my moment-to-moment experience. I am not in some altered state of consciousness, feeling a mystical unification with the sidewalk and the bird songs, and I don't feel totally present at all times by any means. But I do believe that meditation has brought me more awareness of whatever physical activity I am engaged in, which in turn has led me to a new sense of ease and connection with my environment.

One lesson Nisker learns from Buddhist practice is to distinguish between "mind-states" of pleasant or unpleasant, grasping or averting, and the "self." **We mistake each emotion as "I" or "self," and become completely identified and lost in it. We fail to see that emotions come with being human; that they have biological origins and important survival functions. We don't realize that they are evolution's emotions.**

Meditation can assist us in freeing ourselves from our excessive attachment to certain states of the mind or emotions. An amazing achievement of Buddhist practitioners who followed after the Buddha was to recognize 121 classes of consciousness and 89 different mind-states. In meditation, one does not judge. Mind-states are not praiseworthy or condemned. "They are first of all to be understood as natural occurrences, arising as a condition of being human—having a body, contact with the world, the feelings of pleasant, unpleasant, and neutral, and self-consciousness."

The Mahasatipatthana Sutra instructs the meditator in this way: **A meditator knows a lustful mind as lustful, a mind free from lust as free from lust; a hating mind as hating, a mind free from hate as free from hate. . . . [Notice] a distracted mind as distracted, a concentrated mind as concentrated, a deluded mind as deluded.**

The Buddha put it this way:

> **Thus any feeling whatsoever—past, future or present; internal or eternal; blatant or subtle, common or sublime, far or near; every feeling—is to be seen as it actually is with right understanding: "this is not mine. This is not my self. This is not what I am."**

Meditation is about not taking the ordinary for granted. Like breathing. Thich Nhat Hanh teaches about the simple power that breathing meditation affords.

> **You should know how to breathe to maintain mindfulness, as breathing is a natural and extremely effective tool which can prevent dispersion. Breath is the bridge which connects life to consciousness, which unites your body to your thoughts. Whenever your mind becomes scattered, use your breath as the means to take hold of your mind again.**

Thich Nhat Hanh offers a practical guide to meditation. He cites the rule in a Buddhist community which says: **One should not lose oneself in mind-dispersion or in one's surroundings. Learn to practice breathing in order to regain control of body and mind, to practice mindfulness, and to develop concentration and wisdom.** Thich Nhat Hanh is convinced that because of the link between breath, body, and mind, **it alone is the tool which can bring them both together, illuminating both and bringing both peace and calm.** Meditation is not just about sitting still for an hour a day; it is a way of breathing and staying attentive all day whether we are walking, sitting, working, or lying down. It is about being present fully to self and others. It is about breathing.

Pema Chodron also teaches meditation practices. She recognizes that the mind has **more projections than there are dust motes in a sunbeam** so we ought not to fight it. Just learn to let it go. **As meditators we might as well stop struggling against our thoughts and realize that honesty and humor are far more inspiring and helpful than any kind of solemn religious striving for or against anything. In any case, the point is not to try to get rid of thoughts, but rather to see their true nature. Thoughts will run us around in circles if we buy into them, but really they are like dream images. They are like an illusion—not really all that solid. They are, as we say, just thinking.** When distracted while meditating, she recommends simply saying to oneself, "thinking" and then returning to openness and relaxing on the out-breath. Return to one's breath.

Chodron believes that healthy meditation can both put us in touch with the deep joy of our existence and prepare us to face the darkness in our existence. **Through practice, we realize that we don't have to obscure the joy and openness that is present in every moment of our existence. We can awaken to basic goodness, our birthright. When we are able to do this, we no longer feel burdened by depression, worry, or resentment.** Meditation is a way to return to the sense of what I call original blessing, and what Hildegard of Bingen called **original wisdom** that, as Chodron points out, is *our birthright*. Buddhist writer Pahmasambhava has written: **In its true state, the mind is self-radiant, immaculate, transparent, timeless, unimpeded; not realizable as a separate thing, but as the unity of all things, yet not composed of them. Your own Mind shines forth, unobscured, for all living beings. Your own Mind is originally as pure and clear as the sky. Your original wisdom is as continuous and unstoppable as the current of a mighty river. To know whether or not this is true, look inside your own Mind.** Our minds expand. Another way to name this return to our origin is "Big mind." Big mind is called Buddha-Mind and it is our basic original nature.

In dealing with pain and negative experience, meditation helps us also. When it comes to fear, for example, I recommend people talking to fear as if it were a being (which it can be). Ask it questions: "Mister Fear, why are you here today? What are you here to teach me?" If we don't befriend fear (Jesus said, "love your enemies"), fear might take us over. It might become a demon or a boogie man in our psyche. Chodron recommends approaching **what you find repulsive, help the one thing you cannot help, and go to places that scare you. This begins when we sit down to meditate and practice not struggling with our own mind.**

Another method is to breathe in what is distasteful: **Breathe it in—not just the anger, resentment, or loneliness that we might be feeling, but the identical pain of others who in this very moment are also feeling rage, bitterness, or isolation.** Just like air, pain belongs to everybody. When we breathe, we are breathing one another's molecules; the same is true of pain which is so shareable an experience. **We breathe in for everybody. This poison is not just our personal misfortune, our fault, our blemish, our shame—it's part of the human condition.** Accompanying our breathing is a wish that all may be free of this suffering.

One form of Buddhist meditation is called *Vipassana* meditation. Five years ago a newly appointed warden in the largest and most violent prison in India named Kiran Bedi was desperate for new directions for the prison. She introduced Vipassana meditation practice at first gradually and then to all the inmates. The result? After the ten-day course, which included total silence, violent prisoners became people whose hearts overflowed with joy and tears. Staff were also included in the meditation practice. A film, *Doing Time, Doing Vipassana,* has been made about that experience. What an ennobling thing it would be to introduce Vipassana to American prisons where so many young people—an inordinate percentage of whom are people of color—with great potential as leaders and creative minds are being warehoused.

Christian theologian Thomas Aquinas offers a meditation method. **The first requirement, then, for the contemplation of wisdom is that we should take complete possession of our minds before anything else does, so that we can fill the whole house with the contemplation of wisdom. It is also necessary that we be fully present there, concentrating in such a way that our aim is not diverted to other matters.** Thus Scripture says: "Return home quickly and gather yourself together there and play there and pursue your thoughts" (Eccles. 32.15–16). To "gather yourself together there" is to draw together your whole intention. He goes on to recommend returning to oneself. **Return from external things to your own mind, before anything else gets hold of it and any other anxiety distracts it. . . . When our interior house is entirely emptied like this and we are fully present there in our intention,** the text tells us what to do next: "And play there."

Aquinas compares play to contemplation (what the East calls meditation) because first it is enjoyable and secondly, **playing has no purpose beyond itself; what we do in play is done for its own sake. And the same applies to the pleasure of wisdom.** He recommends complete focusing and concentration. **Abandon discursive reasoning and fix . . . the soul's gaze in the contemplation of one unified truth. After these two steps, a third act of oneness occurs which is like that of the angels. In it the soul ignores everything else and settles down to the sheer contemplation of God. . . . Becoming calm means calming our intellectual activities.** He also encourages calming our appetites. He sees our return to our center as a return to God, who is at our center. **The heart is said to be in the midst of the person. Since God dwells in our hearts, God is said to be in the midst.** There, in the depths of the heart, one hears the divine words as Hosea put it: **I will lead her into solitude, and speak to her heart to heart (Hos. 2).** We begin to experience the divine silence which is a **chaste silence and through it we reverence ineffable things.**

Like Buddhist teachers, Meister Eckhart constantly advises to let go and let be (*Abgeschindenheit* and *Gelassenheit*). Let your thoughts be your thoughts, don't judge them in meditation but do recognize them. Eckhart talks about people letting go of willing, knowing, and having—this he calls "radical poverty." **He is a poor person who wills nothing and knows nothing and has nothing.** To undergo this letting go, one becomes empty of all experience. **For a human being to possess true poverty, he or she must be as free of his or her created will as they were when they did not yet exist. . . . People should stand empty.** He encourages us to **follow the way of your unborn being**, a return to origins.

Eckhart is very loath to encourage people to get attached to a practice, for he feels the practice can readily become an attachment and be confused with a goal. Yet he describes a meditative practice in the following manner: **How then should one love God? You should love God mindlessly, that is, so that your soul is without mind and free from all mental activities, for as long as your soul is operating like a mind, so long does it have images and representations. But as long as it has images, it has intermediaries, and as long as it has intermediaries, it has neither oneness nor simplicity. And therefore your soul should be bare of all mind and should stay there without mind.**

Eckhart recognizes that this path of emptying of the mind connects to the *formless* side of Divinity. **When all the images of the soul are taken away and the soul can see only the single One, then the pure being of the soul finds passively resting in itself the pure, form-free being of divine unity, when the being of the soul can bear nothing else than the pure unity of God.** Divinity was there all along—but we hardly knew it!

Eckhart addresses the human temptation to fill in the void and the silence of the mind in meditation when he asks: **If people find themselves in this way in pure nothingness, is it not better for them to do something to drive away the darkness and the abandonment? Should such people not somehow pray, read, listen to a sermon, or carry out other works that are virtuous so as to help themselves? No! Understand this truly that remaining quite still and for as**

long at a time as possible is the best thing you can do! Important gifts come one's way in these times of emptiness. **It would be a great deficiency in God if he did not accomplish great deeds in you and infuse a great blessing into you, provided he finds you unencumbered and bare.** In fact, this time of infusion is the moment of grace. **It is a single moment: readiness and the infusion. If nature attains its highest point, God will give grace. At the same moment that a spirit is ready, God enters into it without delay and hesitation. . . . Opening up and entering in are but a single moment.** He gives practical advice. **Therefore, be still and do not flinch from this emptiness. For you can indeed turn away from this moment, but you will never again return to it.**

Meditation is about returning home, returning home and finding the greatness that was there all along. As Eckhart put it, **God is at home; it is we who have gone out for a walk.**

A new translation from Jesus' Aramaic reveals more of his teaching about meditation than previous versions. From Matthew 6:6, usually translated **But when you pray enter into your closet,** we can now understand the following advice as an instruction in meditation.

> **When you want to lay yourself open for the divine,**
> **like a snare that is hollowed out to its depth,**
> **like a canopy that projects a shadow**
> **from the divine heat and light**
> **into your soul,**
> **then go into your inner place physically,**
> **or to that story or symbol that reminds you of the sacred.**
> **Close the door of your awareness to**
> **the public person you think yourself to be.**
> **Pray to the parent of creation, with your inner sense,**
> **the outer senses turned within.**
> **Veiling yourself, the mystery may be unveiled through you.**
> **By opening yourself to the flow of the sacred,**
> **somewhere, resounding in some inner form,**
> **the swell of the divine ocean can move through you.**
> **The breathing life of all reveals itself**
> **in the way you live your life.**

Hinduism teaches meditation. Siddheswarananda, a respected Hindu teacher, says that **concentration is, therefore, the first step in all meditation. As soon as our concentration becomes effective, we begin to realize that sense of harmony that exists between the subject and the object.** Meditation brings about transformation. **During the course of meditation, we incidentally aim at the renovation of our entire being, and the more profound our concentration upon our ideal, the more rapid will our transformation be.** When we meditate, we still the thinking process and learn deep listening. Iyengar agrees on the importance of concentrating. **Without concentration one can master nothing. Without concentration on Divinity, which shapes and controls the universe, one cannot unlock the Divinity within oneself or become a universal man.** Meditation is about freedom—freedom from thoughts. A kind of **mindlessness** ensues that is a far cry from **lunacy or idiocy but a conscious state of the mind where it is free from thoughts and desires.**

The very name *Brahman* has a dual etymology in Sanskrit: "Great (*brih*) Breath (*br*)." Thus the connection between breathing and God-work is ancient in Hinduism. Just as "Spirit" in Latin means breath, so too "Prana" in Sanskrit means spirit, breath, élan, chi, vitality, vital force, energy, or strength. One of the manifestations of prana, life force, in the human body is breathing. Pranayama works with the breath in order to increase prana, life force. There is an intimate relationship between thought and breath. When you calm your breathing, there is simultaneous calming of the mind. "Breathing is connected with letting go." From the Artharva Veda (900 B.C.E.) of the Hindu Scriptures we read this teaching about **the vital breath and its circulation throughout the body.**

> **Breath, the healing power that is your**
> **breath is the shining One, the Queen,**
> **breath is the Directress.**
> **She who directs the**
> **breath is the Life of Creatures.**

When you breathe
you quicken the Atman [divine in you]
and this is born again
this is the source of the unwearied ones
O breath, I bind you to myself like a child of the waters
that I may live.

To guide the breath is to guide thought. This is the principle behind the systems of yoga. The Hindu Scriptures says: **The Self is self-luminous, vibrant energy and vigor, vitality, power, tranquillity, wisdom and love. This is who you really are.** This is the inner self which is hidden at the center of our life; it undergirds all our activities; it is also the place where Brahman sits in our heart-center. We are encouraged to seek it out, to go for the inner place and "be still" there. **Be still and know that I am God,** say the Jewish Scriptures. Many and necessary things can be learned by this stillness. **You are the Atman, the immanent eternal Self within you: one with Brahman, the Universal Spirit. The Atman is your Spirit, individualized Brahman. It is Being-Awareness-Bliss, your true nature.** The formula used in Sanskrit is: **Tat twam asi. You are That.**

Swami Ashkananda recommends that **if children were told from their birth: "You are eternal, you have a place in you that is full of wisdom, full of strength, full of blessedness," this truth would become a power in their lives even when they grow up and their other negative influences begin to prevail. . . . A wonderful beauty of appearance and of character comes to you.** Piero Ferrucci writes: **Contact with the Self spreads beyond its own occurrence, and often lives on in the form of a work of art, a creative solution to a problem, a scientific discovery, an invention, a social or religious movement, a humanitarian initiative.** Through meditation practices we return to this place within us that is "full of wisdom" and strength. By meditation we cut through duality and we return to the oneing of self and the Godhead—a oneing that already exists but is too seldom acknowledged. It can be said that the Hindu concept of attachment is similar to the Western idea of addiction.

Meditation teaches us to *let go,* to detach from our fixations. Ramana Maharshi taught that **you have to quiet your mind down so you can listen to this internal intuitive wisdom. That's what meditation is for. . . . You watch your mind creating all sorts of different thoughts. Then it finally quiets down. Only then do you start to just be; be wise, be love, be present. Then the mind becomes the servant, not the master.**

The true "I" in us is the Atman, the spirit connecting us to Brahman. This being, awareness, and bliss accompany us even when we work. Problems do not overcome us. Our work itself carries power to it. Maharshi says: **You are not attached to the fruits of your action. You are not busy wondering how it's going to come out. You just do it as well as you can and it comes out as it comes out. You are in harmony with the way it is, you are not attached to the outcome. To serve others is a work you do on yourself.** Meister Eckhart calls this **working without a why.**

One technique well developed in Hinduism is the *mantra,* which is a repetition of a word or phrase. Connecting this repetition to moving one's fingers on beads in Catholicism or in Islam, Buddhism, or Hinduism is one way to concentrate one's prayer. With this practice we can go deeper into the depths of our minds and escape the superficialities of everyday problem solving. As one person describes it, "a mantra provides a boat with which you can float through your chattering or racing thoughts without clinging, therefore entering deeper and subtler realms." The ninety-nine names for God in Islam that we discussed in chapter five can be such a mantra device. One could recall all 99 or just one at a time, always returning to that name when distracted. In similar fashion, Catholics who recite the rosary while repeating the "Hail Mary," whose rhythm of words keeps their mind concentrating, nevertheless have a mind freed to meditate on mysteries of Jesus' life and death. It is true that St. Dominic, to whom the rosary is said to have been revealed by Mary, actually borrowed the idea from Islam, which exercised such a rich presence in Dominic's thirteenth-century Spain.

Whatever the practice, meditation is about focusing and concentration. It is about letting what Aquinas calls the "discursive intellect" take a break. Psychologist Claudio Naranjo teaches that concentration is the root skill in all meditation practices. One is to keep the mind fixed on a specific task or object and let distractions go by, no matter which technique is used. Why is this important? Because attention results in awareness and waking up.

When we wake up we connect with what has been there all along—the Divine that dwells in our hearts. In meditation, we manifest our true self, we come to grips with our deepest nature, which is a divine presence within us and all things. Call it our "Buddha-nature" or our "Christ-nature," our "Atman" or "Self," or our "Big Mind."

The Tao Te Ching also instructs in meditation.

> **Empty your mind of all thoughts.**
> **Let your heart be at peace.**
> **Watch the turmoil of beings,**
> **but contemplate their return.**
> **Each separate being in the universe**
> **returns to the common source.**
> **Returning to the source is serenity.**

Taoist teacher Loy Ching Yuen writes:

> **To know Tao**
> **meditate**
> **and still the mind.**
> **Knowledge comes with perseverance. . . .**
> **When enlightenment arrives**
> **don't talk too much about it;**
> **just live it in your own way.**

The Tao Te Ching advises letting be and promises a return to our origins when it counsels:

> **Accept the world as it is.**
> **If you accept the world,**
> **the Tao will be luminous inside you**
> **and you will return to your primal self.**

This promise of luminosity is repeated.

> The Master keeps her mind
> always at one with the Tao;
> that is what gives her her radiance.
> The Tao is ungraspable.
> How can her mind be at one with it?
> Because she doesn't cling to ideas.

The Tao, too, is a kind of void, nothingness, and unnameable.

> Since before time and space were,
> the Tao is.
> It is beyond *is* and *is not*.
> How do I know this is true?
> I look inside myself and see.

As ancient and as vast as the Tao is, it also dwells within us. This is not unlike the Brahman/Atman teaching from Hinduism. There is a centering that takes place when one connects to the Tao (or Brahman or Godhead or the Void or Nothingness) and this stabilizes one in the midst of struggle or turmoil.

> She who is centered in the Tao
> can go where she wishes, without danger.
> She perceives the universal harmony,
> even amid great pain,
> because she has found peace in her heart.

Like Jesus who taught the domain of God "is not here and not there," or like Hinduism that teaches "nati, nati, not this, not this," so the Tao is not to be directly perceived.

Words that point to the Tao
seem monotonous and without flavor.
When you look for it, there is nothing to see.
When you listen for it, there is nothing to hear.
When you use it, it is inexhaustible.

Solitude is not an enemy but an opportunity to connect deeply.

Ordinary men hate solitude.
But the Master makes use of it,
embracing his aloneness, realizing
he is one with the whole universe.

The Taoist tradition also recommends a ceasing from judgment, a letting go and letting be.

If you close your mind in judgments
and traffic with desires,
your heart will be troubled.
If you keep your mind from judging
and aren't led by the senses,
your heart will find peace.

How do we go about this? The Source is within us and at hand, beckoning our return.

Use your own light
and return to the source of light.

Like Aquinas and the other teachings we have considered about meditation, we learn that what is at stake is letting go of "discursive" reasoning so that the full mind can develop.

My teachings are easy to understand
and easy to put into practice.
Yet your intellect will never grasp them,
and if you try to practice them, you'll fail. . . .
If you want to know me,
look inside your heart.

The kind of knowing the Tao countenances is a kind of letting go, what Eckhart calls a **transformed knowledge.** He says that **God is not found in the soul by adding anything, but by a process of subtraction.** The Tao says:

In the pursuit of knowledge,
every day something is added.
In the practice of the Tao,
every day something is dropped. . . .
True mastery can be gained
by letting things go their own way.
It can't be gained by interfering.

Letting go is the way.

If you want to be given everything,
give everything up. . . .
If you open yourself to loss,
you are at one with loss
and you can accept it completely.

Judaism also boasts its traditions of meditation and of returning to the source. Rabbi Abraham Joshua Heschel talks about the limits of knowledge and the power of wonder to carry us into self-transcendence. **There are more songs in our souls than the tongue is able to utter.** How do we arrive at these songs in our souls? We let the discursive mind go. **When detached from its original insights, the discursive mind becomes a miser, and when we discover that concepts bring no relief to our outraged conscience and thirst for integrity, we turn to the origin of thought, to the endless shore that lies across the logical.** Wonder for Heschel is that form of thinking that sustains insight. Insight comes from the land of the ineffable, and insights **are the roots of art, philosophy and religion, and must be acknowledged as common and fundamental facts of mental life.** Wonder is **an act that goes beyond knowledge [and an attitude] that does not come to an end when knowledge is acquired.** Wonder takes us to the shores of transcendence. **This, then, is an insight we gain in acts of wonder: not to measure meaning in terms of our own mind, but to sense a meaning infinitely greater than ourselves.**

The mind with which we comprehend ideas is not the only mind we need to utilize. **Transcendence can never be an object of possession or of comprehension.** It is a universal, not a private or a sectarian, experience. **The experience of meaning is an experience of vital involvement, not having an idea in mind, but living within a spirit surpassing the mind; not an experience of a private reference of meaning, but sharing a dimension open to all human beings.** What brings us together is itself ineffable. Words fail us. Silence and letting go is a requisite. **We meet in a stillness of significance . . . The relationship of a human being to ultimate meaning can never be conceived as a possession. . . . Our words do not describe it, our tools do not wield it. But sometimes it seems as if our very being were its description, its secret tool.**

The tradition of *Kabbalah* teaches us to get in touch with emptiness and nothing-ness. **If you think of yourself as something, then God cannot clothe himself in you, for God is infinite. No vessel can contain God, unless you think of yourself as Ayin. . . . Think of yourself as Ayin and forget yourself totally. Then you can transcend time, rising to the world of thought, where all is equal: life and death, ocean and dry land.** For this to happen, we must return to our origins. Thought, which has its limits, must cease. That is why meditation is helpful—to carry us beyond thought. **Thought expands and ascends to her origin. Upon reaching there, she is stopped and can ascend no further. Thought reveals itself only through contemplating a little without content, contemplating sheer spirit. . . . you understand—then you lose what you have understood.**

Meditation is a return to our origins. **How should you train yourself in the quality of Binah, Understanding? By returning to God. If you meditate on re-turning every day, you stimulate Binah to illuminate each day. In consequence all your days join in returning, that is, you integrate yourself within Binah, who is called Returning. Each day of your life is adorned with the mystery of supernal return.** One must quiet the busy mind. **If your mind races, return to the place, return to where you were before the thought. Return to the site of oneness.** This place of unity will be found in the cave or altar of the heart. **Those who practice aloneness and unify the divine name kindle the fire on the altar of their hearts. . . . Here lies the secret of the unification that a person per-forms in the morning and evening prayers, raising all the sefirot and unifying them into a single cluster.**

Solitude is helpful. **To attain you must be alone, so that your contemplation not be disturbed. In your mind, cultivate aloneness to the utmost. . . . If you sense any sound or movement that breaks your meditation, or if any material imagining arises within you, then your soul's contemplation will be severed from the upper worlds. . . . for through the sweetness of melody, aloneness de-scends upon them and they strip their souls. Then the musicians stop the melody, and the prophets remain in that supernal state of union and they**

prophesy. Solitude is not something to fear; it is a path into our deep soul. **If one attains the mystery of equanimity, one will attain the mystery of aloneness. Having attained the mystery of aloneness, this person will attain the holy spirit.**

One must also cultivate an ethical life. **If you wish to attain aloneness, you must first return to God from having strayed and missed the mark. . . . Train yourself to eliminate negative habits such as anger, depression, impatience, and chatter. . . . experience a pure spirit speaking within you words of Torah, wisdom, devotion, purity, and holiness—on its own, without your will.**

Meditation is a journey into the depths of one's soul. **Your deep soul hides itself from consciousness. So you need to increase aloneness, elevation of thinking, penetration of thought, liberation of mind—until finally your soul reveals itself to you.** But what is the soul? Why is it so difficult to access? Like Eckhart, the *Kabbalah* teaches about the mystery of the soul and its relation to nothingness. **No one knows anything at all about the human soul; she stands in the status of nothingness, as it is written: "The superiority of the human over the beast is Ayin." By means of this soul, the human being ascends higher than all other creatures and attains the glory of Ayin.** The richness of what lies in the soul is very great. **Nor can we estimate our own inner abundance. Our inner world is sealed and concealed, linked to a hidden something.**

Your soul will ultimately disclose itself to you. **Your soul hides itself from consciousness. So you need to increase aloneness, elevation of thinking, penetration of thought, liberation of mind—until finally your soul reveals itself to you, spangling a few sparkles of her lights.** One learns to be still and wait for whatever is to come. One is not in control. Wisdom will come when she chooses. **That which abides in thought yet cannot be grasped is called wisdom: Hokhmah. . . . Hakkehmah. Since you can never grasp it, hakkeh, "wait," for mah, "what" will come and what will be. This is the sublime, primordial wisdom emerging out of Ayin. Think of yourself as Ayin and forget yourself totally. . . . all is equal: life and death, ocean and dry land.**

The *Kabbalah* offers a way to meditate. **Be totally alone . . . do it at night . . . empty your mind of all mundane vanities . . . be filled with the awe of Shekhinah . . . wear clean garments, all white . . . focusing your awe and love . . . light many candles, until your eyes shine brightly . . . then you are ready to receive the abundant flow, and the abundant flows upon you, arousing you again and again. Now turn your thoughts to visualizing the Name.**

In Islam, prayer and remembering hold high priority. The special name for this prayer is *Zhikr*. Zhikr is a remembering of God's blessing. It has been called a central method of sanctification, and a way to open oneself to the baraka (blessing and grace) that is all around you and inside you all the time. The Qur'an says that **the recollection of God makes the heart calm,** and Muhammad was once asked: "What is the shortest way to God?" His response was: **Always repeat the name of God in solitary places.** Zhikr (or dhikr) is recollection, remembrance of the divine, repetition of a divine name or holy phrase. From the Qur'an: **Let neither trade nor traffic beguile [divert you] from the remembrance (zhikr) of Allah.** In order to reflect one's true being, the mirror of the divine attributes, it is necessary to awaken one's own heart. The medicine is Zhikr. Spiritual attainment is never absorbed through the head; it can only be received through the heart.

As we have seen in so many other traditions, the key to the Zhikr prayer is breath. As Ana Matt puts it: "The Zhikr is said in rhythm with the breath. Correct breathing is said to help cleanse the mind of lower thoughts and develops magnetism. The breath runs from the surface physical plane into the innermost plane and connects us with our soul. It gives life to the body and mind. The Sufis say that the breath is the soul and the soul is the breath. 'Every breath that goes in remembering God is alive and connected to God.'"

In Islam, too, God both takes form and is fundamentally formless. Form is necessary to manifest the invisible. But forms can become idols—forms of creatures but also forms of religion and worship when they are cut off from their *formless* underpinnings and their true meaning. Rumi teaches that forms of prayer can take us far from God. We must stay with the heart. The woman saint Attar said: **God does not look upon your outward forms.** Kabir reminds us that what actually happens is that the **formless God takes a thousand forms in the eyes of His creatures: He dances in rapture, and waves of form arise from his dance.**

We can and must make connection with Divinity, and Divinity is always one. As Rumi puts it:

I have put duality away
and see the two worlds as one.
One I seek, One I know
One I see, One I call . . .
He is the outward, he is the inward.

Out beyond duality,
we have a home, and it is Glory . . .
This is the time of union,
the time of eternal beauty.

Abandon your stagnant pool
for the running waters of life. . . .
from the world of separation to the world of union.

The Shahadah is the Islamic prayer of unity: **La illaha illa 'llah hu" (Nothing exists save God)**. It is like the Jewish prayer: **Hear, O Israel, the Lord thy God, the Lord is One.** On hearing these words one might think they mean that none is worshipable but God. But the deeper meaning is that there is only one reality. It is about the oneness of all Being. Prayer is our coming to imitate God by becoming one also. "God is One and so man, who is created in 'His Form,' must become integrated and unified." This prayer is not unlike the Buddhist realization of "anata"—that all things are interconnected and not separate entities. Not even God.

Zhikr allows one to let go and become centered and focused. Fixed attention on Zhikr can cause doubt and worry to cease and unite diffuseness and scatteredness. It can unite all one's separate moments into a unity. This unification is a goal of Sufi practice. Shams of Tabriz put it this way:

Let go of your worries and be completely clear-hearted,
Like the face of a mirror, that contains no images.
When it is empty of forms, all forms are contained in it.

One practice of Zhikr is the repetition of the word "Allah," or one of the ninety-nine Names of God that we saw above. Each name is considered to be charged with spiritual power. The names are repeated over and over for a long period of time, either silently or aloud. By this practice you come into a direct experience of the presence of God. It can be an ecstatic state or a very silent, tranquil state, extending through the whole body and mind, setting free immense spiritual powers for transformation and overcoming negative habit patterns.

Another practice is to concentrate on the breath. On inhaling, whisper "Ah"; on exhaling whisper "lah" (or you could substitute another name for God if you wish). Slow the breath down, making it protracted and profound. Inhaling, stand erect, connecting to the sky; exhaling, bow toward the earth.

Zhikr is meant to take one who prays into silence. A wordless place where the silent remembering is a remembering of the heart. Shibli says: **The last mystery of recollection is complete silence. . . . Worshiping has ten parts, of which nine are silence.** Rumi also praises silence:

> **Secretly we spoke,**
> **that wise one and me.**
> **I said, Tell me the secrets of the world.**
> **He said, Sh . . . Let silence**
> **Tell you the secrets of the world.**

Hafiz also celebrates holy silence.

> **Noise**
> **Is a cruel ruler**
> **Who is always imposing curfews,**
> **While stillness and quiet**
> **break open the vintage bottles,**
> **Awake the real Band.**

Hafiz advises us to let go of words:

> When the words stop
> And you can endure the silence
> That reveals your heart's pain
> Of emptiness
> Or that great wrenching-sweet longing.
> That is the time to try and listen
> To what the Beloved's eyes
> most want to say.

Hafiz pictures what emptying and being emptied can feel like.

> Today love has completely gutted me.
> I am lying in the market like a filleted grouper,
> Speechless,
> Every desire and sinew absolutely silent
> But I am still so fresh.

Hafiz gets practical about letting go and embracing solitude—and about the goal in mind, one of finding the jewel inside.

> Not many teachers in this world
> Can give you as much enlightenment in one year
> As sitting all alone, for three days,
> in your closet would do.
> That means not leaving,
> better get a friend to help with
> a few sandwiches
> and the chamber pot.

And no reading in there or writing poems,
that would be cheating;
Aim high—for a 360-degree detox.
This sitting alone, though, is
not recommended
If you are normally sedated
Or have ever been under a doctor's
surveillance because of your brain.
Dear one,
Don't let Hafiz fool you—
A ruby is buried here.

The most direct summary of this way of letting go and of mindfulness might be found in Eckhart's words: **The soul grows by subtraction, not by addition.**

11.

HOLY IMAGINATION: ART AND RITUAL AS PATHS TO MINDFULNESS

The fierce power of imagination is a gift from God.
—The Kabbalah

We have considered emptying forms of meditation—those that empty us and take us to the *formless* center of our existence. Another kind of meditation centers on the experience of creativity and the focusing and gathering in that the discipline of creativity requires of us. This meditation takes us to the God of *form*. The two kinds of meditation are not exclusive. Creativity often takes solitude and silence and emptying. And true emptying often leads to creativity. But the first kind strives to still the mind (by not striving); the second fills the mind by digging deep into the imagination and honoring the images that are there as gifts of the Holy Spirit. It gathers them up and then releases them into our work and into the world.

The *Kabbalah* calls imagination a **fierce power** and **gift from God** that leads us to the Divine. **The fierce power of imagination is a gift from God. Joined with the grandeur of the mind, the potency of inference, ethical depth, and the natural sense of the Divine, imagination becomes an instrument for the holy spirit.** Intellectual work and study are a means to feeding holy imagination. The *Kabbalah* offers advice on how to study: **First, go over the language of the text many times, taking notes to remember fluently. . . . Second, study with great concentration, according to your ability. Even if it seems that you do not understand, do not stop, because God will faithfully help you discover hidden wisdom.**

Rabbi Heschel encourages the spiritual practice of study when he writes: **Torah study is a way of coming upon the presence of God.** In fact, Heschel claims that **in Judaism study is a form of worship, but it may also be said that worship is in a sense a form of study; it includes meditation. It is not enough to rely on one's voice. It takes a constant effort to find a way to the grandeur of the words in the Prayer Book.** Heschel calls for a **genuine reverence for the sanctity of study**—indeed, the school **is a sanctuary, not a factory.**

Learning is not about knowledge but about wisdom and **the unique attitude of the Jew is not the love of knowledge but the love of studying.** Studying means **being involved in wisdom.** The teacher is a kind of midwife to both the student and the tradition. **At the hands of a clumsy practitioner, ideas will be still-born. . . . At the hands of a master, a new life will be born.** A relationship develops between teacher and student that carries spiritual depth to it. **It is not enough for the pupil to appropriate the subject matter; the pupil and the teacher must go through significant moments, sharing insight and appreciation.** In education we ought to **cultivate the soul, not only the mind.** Education is not preparation for life because **learning is life, a supreme experience of living, a climax of existence. . . . Termination of education is the beginning of despair. Every person bears a responsibility for the legacy of the past as well as the burden of the future.**

Growing up in Eastern Europe, Heschel learned that education was not about comfort or class or money. **In almost every Jewish home in Eastern Europe, even in the humblest and the poorest, stood a bookcase full of volumes. . . . Books were neither an asylum for the frustrated nor a means for occasional edification. They were furnaces of living strength, timeproof receptacles for the eternally valid coins of spirit. . . . Poor Jews . . . sat there like intellectual magnates. . . . The stomachs were empty, the homes barren, but the minds were crammed with the riches of Torah.** Just as nature feeds wonder that leads to wisdom, so, too, does learning. That makes study and the discipline for learning a kind of yoga, a certain spiritual practice.

A good example of the *form* kind of meditation can be found in the *Zohar,* where Rabbi Judah proposes a way to know even the mysterious and hidden Godhead.

> **Indeed, he is known in the gates.**
> **He is known and grasped**
> **to the degree that one opens the gates of imagination!**
> **The capacity to connect with the spirit of wisdom,**
> **to imagine in one's heart-mind—**
> **this is how God becomes known.**
> **Therefore "Her husband is known in the gates,**
> **through the gates of imagination.**
> **But that he be known as He really is?**
> **No one has ever been able to attain such knowledge of him."**

This rather optimistic stance on the accessibility of the human to the Divine by way of imagination opens the door to the work of art and thinking, farming and building, crafts and dance as authentic avenues to the Divine. The mind, too, to the extent that it is engaged creatively, becomes a sacred temple wherein the Divine roams. Study becomes a yoga, a spiritual pathway to the Sacred. Indeed, in Judaism the center of thought is in the heart.

Archeologist Marija Gimbutas traces many of our earliest art forms to the advent of the Neolithic Age when the ram became the first domesticated animal and became especially sacred to the Bird Goddess. The symbol of fleece and the association of the Goddess with the arts of spinning and weaving came from this period. Very likely the idea that the Goddess is spinner and weaver of human life and death, happiness and wealth, also traces to this period. The discovery of the art of pottery **opened avenues for the creation of new sculptural forms as well as new ways of expressing symbols through pottery painting. Asoki (bird-shaped vases) and anthropomorphic or bird-woman vases appeared. Streams, chevrons, triangles, net-patterned bands, spirals, winding snakes, and snake coils became dominating motifs in pottery painting.**

Commenting on the late Neolithic passage grave of Gavrinis in Brittany, Gimbutas observes that the Goddess bespeaks immense fertility and generativity. **The piled-up signs seem to say that the creativity of the Goddess is inexhaustible and comes from the cosmic deep, which is implied by a variety of adjacent aquatic configurations.**

The principal and most recurring themes apropos of the Goddess have to do with **the mystery of birth and death and the renewal of life, not only human but all life on earth and indeed in the whole cosmos. Symbols and images cluster around the parthenogenetic (self-generating) Goddess and her basic functions as Giver of Life, Wielder of Death, and, not less importantly, as Regeneratrix, and around the Earth Mother, the Fertility Goddess young and old, rising and dying with plant life.**

One of the most important aspects of Goddess art is the lack of militarism anywhere. It is as if art substituted for war in our ancient past. **The Goddess-centered art with its striking absence of images of warfare and male domination reflects a social order in which women as heads of clans or queen-priestesses played a central part. Old Europe and Anatolia, as well as Minoan Crete, were a gylany. A balanced, nonpatriarchal and nonmatriarchal social system is reflected by religions, mythologies, and folklore. . . .**

Lascaux caves and other ancient ritual and art grottos from as far back as thirty thousand years ago reveal how primal art was to human survival—and how gifted our early ancestral artists were. When I visited the Lascaux caves a few years ago, I was astounded at the beauty and the depth and the overall form of the work. It was truly a Sistine Chapel by and for prehistoric humans. Holy imagination goes back a very long way in our ancestral tree.

Among the rituals of indigenous peoples holy imagination abounds. The costumes, the headdresses, the masks, the chants, the musical instruments, the colors, the fire—all these come from the imagination and speak to it. I remember once visiting the Field museum in Chicago and standing in front of a huge wall of masks that were originally ritual masks from the Native American tribes of the Seattle northwest area. Each of these dozens of masks told a different story about a different mood the human soul undergoes. I realized why that culture did not need psychology: It already had a rich way to tell soul experience and to do it in the midst of community, in the midst of ritual.

The prayer of indigenous people everywhere is rich in imagination. Consider storytelling, for example. Jeanette Henry and Rupert Costo, in their book *A Thousand Years of American Indian Storytelling*, talk about storytelling. **Storytelling, from ancient times and among all peoples of the earth, had a special role in the life of the people. Storytelling educated the young; it provided entertainment for the grown men and women; it made possible the knowledge of a people's history which was passed on by word of mouth from generation to generation; and it served to teach lessons about how to be good people, with care for others and respect for all of life.**

In other words, the art of storytelling was a primary form of education, instruction, immersion into the universe and into the community and into the ancestral history. Thus, it was also what formed *a common ethic*. How to survive. And why survive. Aboriginals in Australia tell me that it is **from our Dreamtime that we learn rules for living in our environment,** Dreamtime, of course, being the inherited creation stories and ongoing Creation stories of the Aboriginal people.

Storytelling among the indigenous peoples was not just words. Many art forms were employed—**in the telling of a story, one experienced the antics of a mime, the music of a song, the sounds of a chant, and the gestures of a skillful actor or actress.** And many stories were spun on and on, embellished as they extended far into the night. **It was fun. It was marvelous, and a splendor of the spirit to experience.**

The oldest human tribe we know is the Australian Aboriginals. Kevin Gilbert tells what really goes on around a campfire of the Aboriginal peoples. **When Europeans see a group of Aboriginals sitting around a camp-fire singing a corroboree song, they say "corroboree" or "Blackfellas yackaaing." But to** *understand* **what they are doing introduces a whole new area for examination. For instance, most people know what transcendental meditation is about, or yoga positions, or they understand something of the process when some people kneel down, clasp their hands together and look up into the sky, saying, "Our Father which art in Heaven." The Aboriginal way is the creative continuum:**

> **At night as I sit by my camp-fire**
> **the Great Serpent Spirit a'star**
> **I sing songs of love to the Presence within**
> **as It plays with the sparks on my fire.**

So, that which is seen as a bit of a sing-a-long, a "yackaaing" by Blacks, is a deeply sacred and spiritual experience. So much so that, if an uninvited man or woman enters the circle unbidden, they can well court a death sentence, for within that circle the Great Creator Essence is present.

A Creation story of the desert areas in the west of South Australia tells how the Creator, Bunjil, made all of Creation but was lonely. **He felt the need for companions with whom to sing and dance, and so he decided to make a man. He searched for the finest clay, fashioned a man to his own likeness, and added some finely shredded tree-bark for the hair. Bunjil was so pleased with his creation that he immediately made another.**

When both figures were finished he breathed on them to give them life. . . . Bunjil stayed with the two men for a long time. He taught them to sing and dance, and under his guidance they gradually became wise in all

things. Eventually they, in their turn, could pass on Bunjil's wisdom to all the Aborigines who followed them.

Notice how in this story it is of the very purpose and essence of humanity that we sing and dance—this pleases God and relieves God's loneliness. Indeed, we were created for celebration and artistic expression through song and dance.

Among the Hopi peoples of the southwestern United States, art is integral to the sacred ceremonies and therefore to the universe itself. **All aspects of life, whether the rituals of daily existence or the sacred religious ceremonies, whether on a physical or a spiritual plane, have the same universal goals—harmony, fertility, and regeneration. Universal harmony, fertility, and regeneration have always been and still are the dominant themes of Hopi painting, for artistic expression is but one aspect of Hopi life and it must be an integral part of the Hopi world. In the Hopi world it is impossible to separate the activities of daily life, religious observance, and artistic creation.** The people who preceded the Hopi, the Anasazi, etched petroglyphs on cave walls; the symbol, design and subject matters depicted parallel those of the Hopi. It was not until the end of the nineteenth century that Hopi painting, under Western influences, stepped outside religious ceremonies themselves. "Painting was always a communal occupation." Painting was for the people, for the community—not for the artist's ego. Hopi art, which is among the oldest art in America, includes pottery, baskets, textiles, altar cloths, masks, ceremonial ritual, kachina dolls, and designs etched into kivas, caves, and rocks. The architecture of Old Oraibi dates to 1150 C.E. and is the oldest continuously inhabited village in North America.

A contemporary movement of Hopi artists is combining the ancient art of their people with some European influences and calls itself Hopid. Poet Mike Kabotie names their experience in a poem called "Hopid."

Among rocky plateaus
shifting sands, whirlwinds
junipers and sagebrushes
their afterbirths dry.
Born, baptized by a rich life
during violent world chaos
but sweet was theirs;

nourished to adolescence,
maise their mother,
Children of Bear, Kachina
and Hopi clans
　　Then
into the cold
grey concrete, asphalt
confusions they were cast;
BIA books, crosses, time-punches
　　unrelated
refined by blinding lights,
slick wheels;
bourbon, wine an escape
　　their addiction.
But young, proud and reckless
they return back to
their womb kiva,
　　sandstone dwellings
now antennaes, 'lectricwebs
but sewerless barren rocks
their security.
Among their people,
tapping infinite creativity
power unknown, they travel
　　among priestly clouds
　　mysterious stars
coordinating abstract thoughts
with skilled hands,
　　Artist hopid their identity.

Notice how, in this ancient tradition also, creativity is **tapping into the infinite,** into a mysterious, cosmic power and priesthood. The artist is an intellectual, passing thoughts through skilled hands into the world.

Among the songs of the Mesoamerican peoples are the following hymns about the Toltecatl-artists.

> **The true artist, capable, practicing, skillful,**
> **maintains dialogue with his heart, meets things with his mind.**
> **The true artist draws out all from his heart.**
>
> **The good painter is wise,**
> **God is in his heart.**
> **He puts divinity into things;**
> **he converses with his own heart.**

One poet describes himself and his creative process in the following manner.

> **Who am I?**
> **I live flying.**
> **I compose hymns,**
> **I sing the flowers:**
> **butterflies of song.**
> **They leap forth from within me,**
> **my heart relishes them.**
> **I have arrived among the people,**
> **I have come down,**
> **I, the bird of spring. . . .**
> **My song arises over the earth,**
> **my song bursts out.**

From the Muslim tradition, Sufi mystic Ibn Al-Arabi endorses the imaginative and form kind of meditation when he writes:

> My heart has become capable of every form:
> it is a pasture for gazelles,
> and a monastery for Christian monks,
> And a temple for idols,
> And the Pilgrims' ka'ba,
> and the tablet of the Torah,
> and the Book of the Koran.
> I follow the religion of Love:
> whatever way love's camel takes,
> That is my religion, my faith.

Sufi mystic Hafiz also honors creativity. He addresses the question: What is Art?

> Art is the conversation between lovers.
>   Art offers an opening for the heart.
> True art makes the divine silence in the soul
>   break into applause.
>
> Art is, at last, the knowledge of
>   Where we are standing—
>   Where we are standing
>   In this Wonderland
> When we rip off all our clothes
> And this blind man's patch, veil,
> That got tied across our brow.

Notice how he honors the relation between silence and breaking the silence and how art rips off the veil that covers "the Wonderland" so that all can receive its revelation. Art is revelation of "grand news" that comes from the divine within us.

> **Someone inside of us is now kissing**
> > **The hand of God**
> **And wants to share with us**
> > **That grand news. . . .**
> **Art is the conversation between lovers.**

Hafiz names the difference between a mature and an immature artist.

> **The difference**
> **between a good artist**
> **and a great one is:**
> **The novice will often lay down his tool or brush**
> **Then pick up an invisible club**
> **on the mind's table**
> **and helplessly smash the easels and Jade.**
> **Whereas the vintage man**
> **no longer hurts himself or anyone**
> **and keeps on sculpting Light.**

The true artist "keeps on sculpting light." How appropriate this image is for a post-modern period like ours when the current physics tells us all matter is light. But how it resonates also with the birthing of the Christ light and Buddha light and God light that we discussed in chapter three above. Art brings more light into the world.

> **Hafiz encourages all art**
> **For at its height it brings Light near to us.**

Hafiz was himself an artist—a great master of words and images and poetry. When he speaks about his own experience, we naturally listen carefully.

> My master once entered a phase
> That whenever I would see him
> He would say,
> "Hafiz, How did you ever become a pregnant woman?"
> And I would reply,
> "Dear Attar, you must be speaking the truth,
> But all of what you say is a mystery to me.". . . .
> And Attar replied, . . .
> "Though if you want to know the Truth
> I can so clearly see that God has made love with you
> And the whole universe is germinating
> Inside your belly
> And wonderful words,
> Such enlightening words
> Will take birth from you
> and be cradled against thousands of hearts."

It is interesting that Meister Eckhart also wrote of his experience with pregnancy. He says: **I, even though a man, was pregnant with nothingness. And out of this nothingness God was born.** Hafiz sees art as our sharing in the divine power, evidence of our being sons and daughters of God.

> All the talents of God are within you.
> How could this be otherwise
>   When your soul
>   derived from His genes!

I love that expression,
"All the talents of God are within you."
Sometimes Hafiz cannot help but applaud
    Certain words that rise from my depths
Like the scent of a lover's Body.

But if our creativity is sharing in the divine work, then it is together that we do the
work, as Hafiz sees it in the following poem, a poem about our being *co-creators*.

    It used to be
That when I would wake in the morning
    I could with confidence say,
    "What am 'I' going to
    Do?"
That was before the seed
    Cracked open.
Now Hafiz is certain:
There are two of us housed
    In this body,
Doing the shopping together in the market and
    Tickling each other
While fixing the evening's food.
    Now when I awake
All the internal instruments play the same music:
"God, what love-mischief can 'We' do
    For the world
    Today?"

Islamic mysticism invites its practitioners into their depths where ecstasy follows—*wajdd*, which literally means "finding," that is, to find God. Ecstasy and in-

toxication are encouraged in the Sufi tradition. A form of Zhikr that readily leads Sufis to ecstasy is dance.

Whirling dervishes dance their way into union with the Divine. It is a different form of meditation from sitting and meditating, but the results are not all that different. Nor are the intentions. Dance requires breath. (In several African languages the word for "dance" and the word for "breath" is the same. And also the word for "spirit.") Dance is communal. Dance can be a true letting go and emptying experience. Dance connects us to all beings, for all atoms are dancing. God too is dancing. Kabir sings:

> Dance, my heart; dance today with joy.
> The strains of love fill the days and nights with music,
> and the world is listening to its melodies:
> Mad with joy, life dances to the rhythm of this music.
> The hills and the sea and the earth dance.
> The world of the human being dances in laughter and tears.
> Why live aloof from the world in lonely pride?
>
> Behold! My heart dances in the delight of a hundred arts;
> and the Creator is well-pleased.

Kabir believes that Creation was launched by Divinity dancing.

> God dances in rapture,
> and waves of form arise from his dance.

Rumi too celebrates the holy dance, the remembrance of our deep connections to all beings, the joining of ourselves to the cosmic dance.

When you dance
       the whole universe dances.
The world dances around the Sun.
The morning light breaks,
       Spinning up with delight.
How could anyone
Touched by your love
       Not dance like a weeping willow?
Today I spin wildly
       throughout the city;
I am the cup-bearer,
My head is the cup.
Perhaps a scholar will see me
       and drop his books.
Perhaps the world will see me
       and forget all its sorrow.

The dance moves the heart to oneness and to transcendence and to the ecstasy of union.

A secret turns within my breast,
And with its turning
       the two worlds turn.
I don't know head or feet,
Up or down—all is lost
       in the awesome turning.

Hafiz also invokes dance. He says: **Dear ones, let's anoint this earth with dance!** For Hafiz, God is the ultimate dancer, whose favorite words are: **Come dance with me.**

Every child has known God,
Not the God of names,
Not the God of don'ts,
Not the God who ever does anything weird,
But the God who only knows four words
And keeps repeating them, saying:
"Come dance with Me."
Come dance.

Imagination plays a central role in Celtic spirituality. Surely that is one reason Celtic people and indigenous people who live close to nature are bound so closely to nature: Nature feeds their imagination. Thomas Berry has said that poetry and art depend on our relation to the rich diversity of species, shapes, colors, sounds and songs that our planet offers us. To destroy such diversity is to starve our imaginations.

W. B. Yeats believed that it was only with Greek and Roman culture that man became all-important. Until then, other questions occupied the human soul. **One was less interested in man . . . than in divine revelations, in changes among the heavens and the gods, which can hardly be expressed at all, and only by myth, by symbol, by enigma. One was always losing oneself in the unknown and rushing to the limits of the world. Imagination was all in all.**

John O'Donohue puts the connection between soul work and imagination this way: The soul, he says, **is the place where the imagination lives.** What does the imagination do? It is at home between worlds, it is at home at the edge. Imagination is **the creative force in the individual. It always negotiates different thresholds and releases possibilities of recognition and creativity that the linear, controlling, external mind will never even glimpse. The imagination works on the threshold that runs between light and dark, visible and invisible, quest and question, possibility and fact. The imagination is the great friend of possibility. Where the imagination is awake and alive, fact never hardens or closes but remains open, inviting you to new thresholds of possibility and creativity.**

M. C. Richards, another Celtic artist and scholar, who is potter, poet, painter, and philosopher, in her classic work *Centering* tells us of the intimate relationship between throwing a pot on the wheel and meditation. Pottery can teach us the **discipline of freedom,** including the freedom to play. **We must be able to have fun, we must feel enjoyment, and sometimes long imprisonment has made us numb and sluggish. . . . We become brighter, more energy flows through us, our limbs rise, our spirit comes alive in our tissues.** In art, we learn to let go. **We** redeem our energies not by wrestling with them and managing them, for we have not the wisdom nor the strength to do that, but by letting the light to shine upon them. We also let things be themselves—including unpleasant things. The discipline comes in when we have to pay attention to what we don't like, aren't interested in, don't understand, mistrust, . . . when we have to read the poetry of our enemies—within or without. In art, we wed body and spirit so thoroughly that redemption comes in a bodily way. It is in our bodies that redemption takes place. It is the physicality of the crafts that pleases me: I learn through my hands and my eyes and my skin what I could never learn through my brain.

For Richards, art as meditation leads to seeing what is—and this has real implications for our work at social healing and compassion. How can we not see what our eyes behold? As our perception become more and more coordinated, we grow in justice. She talks about moral imagination that is developed by the discipline of art. From the child's ability to imagine grows as well the adult's capacity for compassion: the ability to picture the suffering of others, to identify. In one's citizenship, or the art of politics, it is part of one's skill to imagine other ways of living than one's own.

M.C. wrote a poem about what potters do. It ends this way.

Potters like sun and stars
perform their art—
endowed with myth,
they make the meal holy.

Notice the cosmology in this poem; and the rendering of holiness that artists are about. Matter reveals its brilliance in our hands. Speaking of clay, she notes: Through all the molecules streams a light of the numinous, the wondrous, the awesome. Every spoonful of clay emits light. Behold! Surprises happen when one creates. Our task is to learn the revelation that is unfolding. There is also a response to sudden impulses, undefined—this way or that way—oh look, what is the clay saying now?—guided toward an "uninvited" image.

There can be, as well, enthusiasm for not being in conscious control—ah, the energy of the brush, the thrust of the potter's knife, the whip of a bowl off-center, new gestures of fun for the body. . . . In the little color-and-word books, we improvise, dance with the words, let them BE (not to use them, but to celebrate them). The color is put on the paper on both sides first, then the paper is folded and cut and sewn and a little book is made. It is meant to help in the process of "writing." The free use of color may liberate the flow of un-rehearsed magical words. She explains her goal: By example and practice, I try to teach that creativity is built in—like the sun—it shines in everything we are and do—Look!

Take your time. . . . that drip has a soft energy to it. That sweetly and carefully made box holds another kind of spirit. We can't lose. We have to fall in love.

In ancient Egypt, a hymn to the God Ptah in the third millennium B.C.E. tells of the intrinsic creativity of all of space and life.

> **All work and crafts,**
> **the movement of arms and legs,**
> **every stirring tendril**
> **conforms to this process of Ptah:**
> **space unfurls**
> **heart reveals**
> **voice clarifies**
> **life creates.**

Dona Marimba Richards recognizes the profound spirituality of community imagination and makes explicit the link in the African spiritual consciousness between ritual, music, and the making of community. **Few have understood what music is to us. Black music is sacred music. It is the expression of the divine within us.** She emphasizes how music connects the African soul to the cosmic powers and the divine spirit within those powers. Through music and ritual, cosmos, Divinity, and the human get it together. **Ontologically, we gain meaning, force, and being through relationship with the universal life force; by feeling ourselves to be a part of the whole. Our music manifests that relationship, as it puts us in tune with the universe. It explains to us the mysterious workings of the universe and ourselves as cosmic beings. . . . As in ritual, in music the human and the Divine meet.**

With music there comes dance. Dance has the same effect in bringing spirit and soul together in a cosmic context. **Through dance we experience reality as immediate to us; that is, we are identified with the universe. . . . We have experienced cosmic interrelationship. . . . Dance, for us, is a religious expression. When we dance, through Rhythm, we express ourselves as cosmic beings. Music transcends us to ultimate realities. Dance and Song; Rhythm and Music, then, are part of the matrix of the African Universe.**

Dona Marimba Richards names the black experience in the Americas as a "nothingness" experience that was transformed by way of creativity. Nothingness was not achieved through meditation but through politics and degradation. Slavery stripped the African to the bone. **The African universe was disrupted. . . . the benefits of African culture were stripped away—not one by one—but brutally, in one sudden and total act. Family, language, kinship patterns, food, dress and formalized religion were gone. What replaced them was the order of slavery. The objective of the new order was to demonstrate our lack of value.** Slavery was a system designed to dehumanize and annihilate the soul and a people. It brought a people to a state of Nothingness. **Herein lies the miracle of black existence in New Europe: out of "nothingness" we built a world. In an environ-**

ment that denied Black being, we insisted on being. Being triumphed over non-being—the forces of non-being brought forth hidden power and imagination from within the Black soul. Indeed, soul itself took on a power; and so, too, did imagination and creativity. Oppressed by dehumanizing circumstances we still found something in which to recognize enough of ourselves to revitalize our souls—to create new selves. They took from us everything they could, but there was something left inside that slavery couldn't touch. Key to this survival was creativity—creating "new selves" and a vision of the sacred. We created a vision of the sacred in a spiritually barren environment. . . . We reached beyond European Christianity into the depths of this religiosity—this spirituality—and discovered the Divine within us. Expression was key to this spirituality—creative expression. From the very first we gave expression to that Divinity for it was our humanity. . . . The expressions that emerged were our language, our music, our dance, our thought patterns, our laughter, our walk, our spirituality. These were the vehicles through which the African ethos expressed itself in America.

By taking the drums away from the slaves in North America, slave owners were trying to disempower and disconnect the Africans from their spiritual roots. It was live or die, survive or disintegrate, create or be annihilated. The African American chose creativity. They attempted to isolate us, to cut us off from our source of spirit. . . . In order to survive spiritually, we had to create meaning. We had to create order in the midst of chaos . . . we were forced therefore to create something different. Some form within a modality compatible with the African world-view, through which we could make contact with the Source.

Unlike modern European philosophers, the African world view is not ill at ease with the concept of "soul." Indeed, soul is the essence of the human in the African view. It is that aspect of the person that expresses her union with the universal order and through it with all Being (Ikra, Ka, Se, Emi). To "touch" our soul is to touch us most deeply. Leonard Barrett calls soul a "force." He writes: "Soul-force is that power of the Black man that turns sorrow into joy, crying into laughter, defeat into victory. It is patience while suffering, determination while frustrated and hope while in despair." Soul combines feeling and intellect—it goes beyond the rationalistic European definition of mind as reason alone. **It is that ability of the human being to feel which is, in terms of the African world-view, essentially human.** Mollette puts it this way: "The Afro-American aesthetic places a very high value upon emotionally motivated behavior; or another term that might be used to describe it would be spiritually motivated behavior."

It is imagination and the arts that tap into soul and that soul uses as an instrument for expression, a means of telling its wisdom. **Our deepest feelings are expressed through music, dance, and song; our most brilliant conceptions. Our profound and complex philosophy of life is expressed through these vehicles, and that is because we express ourselves, our essence, our souls through music, dance, and song.** This, and the fact that African cosmology does not separate life from religion, the "secular" from the "sacred," is why one can say that **Black music is sacred music. It is the expression of the Divine within us.** It expresses the interbeing, the profound unity between self and the community, the community and the universe. By it one feels a part of the whole. **In music the human and the Divine meet. . . . When we see beauty in the world, we sing. When we want to express how much faith we have in spirit, we sing. When the world is ugly and life is hard, we sing.** The result is an extraordinary contribution of creative imagination to culture at large. *Black suffering* **gave birth to the blues. Just as Black suffering and Black hope gave birth to the spirituals. As Africans, we say everything in music.**

Dance, too, along with the drum and music, is part of the spiritual language that is too complex for the verbal expression alone. Furthermore, ancestors and spirits join into the dance. In dance, the relation of interbeing and cosmology comes alive. As Dona Richards puts it: **Through dance we experience reality as immediate to us; that is, we are identified with the universe. . . . We have experienced cosmic interrelationship. . . . Dance, for us, is a religious expression. When we dance, through Rhythm, we express ourselves as cosmic beings.**

Rhythm is what causes the dance—it is *Ntu,* the Universal Life Force (or Spirit) that revitalizes. Drum locates the Rhythm and communicates it, **until finally we are able to find it within us. . . . The fact that Rhythm exists "outside" of us, "before" us, and yet can only be manifested in and through us, is a statement of the organic interrelationship of the cosmic order. . . . In Rhythm all reality, all being is joined. Ntu animates the entire universe. To be touched by it is to know that all being is spirit.** To find Ntu and Rhythm **is to be in tune with the universe.** It is said that **the Drum is Africa.**

Ritual is a culminating expression of the community's joy and suffering, strength and revitalization. It is also a gathering where the ancestors join in so that life and death merge. It is about remembering. **If we "remember," then the physically deceased members of the family continue to be part of the family, and we are assured of immortality. . . . It is through the ancestors that we keep in touch with our sacred origins.** Rituals of spiritual union with the ancestors are to be performed daily. Ritual is the art of arts. **Universally, in ritual the African combines life with artistic expression. Ritual is, in a sense, the ultimate philosophical expression of the African world-view, for it is the modality within which the unity of the human and Divine is expressed, in which the unity of spirit and matter is perceived and in which the Eternal Moment is achieved.**

Howard Thurman understood the Negro Spirituals as connecting creativity and the *imago dei* (image of God) in humanity. In these songs he saw human creativity and spirit at work—a co-working. **This is the discovery made by the slave that finds its expression in the song—a complete and final refusal to be stopped. The spirit broods over all the stubborn and recalcitrant aspects of experience, until they begin slowly but inevitably to take the shape of one's deep desiring. There is a bottomless resourcefulness in man that ultimately enables him to transform "the spear of frustration into a shaft of light." Under such a circumstance even one's deepest distress becomes so sanctified that a vast illumination points the way to the land one seeks. This is the God in man; because of it, man stands in immediate candidacy for the power to absorb all the pain of life without destroying his joy.** Thurman described the power of the spirituals in this manner: **It is an optimism that uses the pessimism of life as raw material out of which it creates its own strength.** Thus strength itself, the power to survive, is the product of the creative process. Humor, too, is part of this creative survival mechanism. Laughter as well as music comes **leaping out of an elemental faith in life itself, which makes a sense of ultimate defeat not only unrealistic but impossible.**

Hinduism also honors creativity, art, and ritual-making. The Chandogya Upanishad says: **Where there is creating, there is progress. Where there is no creating, there is no progress: Know the nature of creating. Where there is joy, there is creating. Know the nature of joy. Where there is the Infinite, there is joy.** A few years ago I visited the island of Bali, having been urged to go there for years by friends of mine who were keen on ritual's role in celebrating community. I was not disappointed. One day our tour guide consisted of two young men driving an old car. They had set up on the dashboard of their car an altar made of fresh flowers and said they did that every day. The Hindu tradition of ritual-making was everywhere. Even on rainy days mothers with fruit balanced on their heads would be walking their cleanly clothed children to the rituals. How they managed to be so clean was a miracle! But the ritual-making was the motivation behind it all.

The Bhagavad Gita says: **When you offer with love a leaf, a flower, or water to me, I accept that offer of love from the giver who gives herself. Whatever you do, or eat, or offer, whatever you do, do as an offering to me.** A ritual is meant to be a centering device.

> **Make every act an offering to me;**
> **Regard me as your only protector.**
> **Make every thought an offering to me;**
> **Meditate on me always.**

Nikhilananda explains how the rituals work in the prayer life of ordinary Hindu worshipers: **Meditative worship . . . is described as a mental activity; the mind of the worshiper should flow without interruption toward the object of worship. It may also lead to introspection and finally to liberation. . . . The highest tangible result of ritual with meditation is . . . where one enjoys the most exalted form of phenomenal bliss.**

A hymn from the Vedas depicts an attitude of creativity put to the use of service of others.

Lord of light!
fill me with sweet honey,
So that I may speak the glorious word
to the masses of mankind.

A Commentator remarks: **The truths revealed through the words of the Veda are not secrets to be carefully kept from the public. The sage who knows them feels called upon to declare them to his fellowmen, irrespective of their social or cultural status.**

In the Hindu tradition of karma yoga the goal is to realize that whatever one does, one's work is a form of worship. Daily actions are a spiritual discipline. As one author puts it, **the practitioner of Yoga does not renounce the world, for that would mean renouncing the Creator. She does not renounce action. She cuts the bonds that imprison her by dedicating the fruits of her actions to God.** To connect one's work to the Atman in one, to the spirit at one's core, is to transform the work. **Nothing is secular anymore.** Your work becomes **an offering to God. Your whole waking life has become one continual spiritual practice. . . . Everything that you do is a form of worship.** This is true creativity: to transmit one's inner core to others. Piero Ferrucci put it this way: **Contact with the Self spreads beyond its own occurrence, and often lives on in the form of a work of art, a creative solution to a problem, a scientific discovery, an invention, a social or religious movement, a humanitarian initiative. A person's inner state is transmitted to others.**

One of the great images of Indian mythology is Shiva Nataraja, the Dancing Shiva. He is pictured with four arms dancing in a circle of fire, dancing at the heart of creation. **It is a cosmic dance: it represents the power which permeates the whole universe. The idea is that God is dancing in the heart of creation and in every human heart.** Surely there lies in this archetype an invitation to every human heart to dance and to join the cosmic and divine heart-dance that is truly going on. Finding the divine dance in us allows us to find the divine dance all around us.

Christian mystics also celebrate the profound connection between spirit and creativity. Meister Eckhart goes so far as to say that when we give birth we are giving birth to the Christ. **It would mean little to me that the "Word was made flesh" for man in Christ, granting that the latter is distinct from me, unless he also was made flesh in me personally, so that I too would become the Son of God.** In the spark of the soul God is birthed on a regular basis: **There is where the birth takes place; there is where the Son is born . . . not once a year or once a month or once a day but all the time, that is, beyond time in that space where there is neither here and now nor nature and thought.** Eckhart urges us to be creative, for that is how we share the gifts we have received. **Human beings should be communicative and emanative with all the gifts they have received from God. . . . People who do not bestow on others spiritual things and whatever bliss that is in them have never been spiritual. People are not to receive and keep them for themselves alone, but they should share themselves and pour forth everything they possess in their bodies and souls as far as possible, and whatever others desire of them.**

Eckhart understands creativity to be that which **flows out but remains within.** He sees all of Creation as imbued with the divine creativity, for all of it has "flowed out but remained within" Divinity. Creation flows out from our deepest places, from our innermost souls. **Whatever can be truly expressed in its proper meaning must emerge from inside a person and pass through the inner form. It cannot come from outside to inside of a person but must emerge from within. It lives truly in the most spiritual part of the soul. There all things are present, living and seeking within the soul what is spiritual, where they are in their best and highest meaning.** Eckhart compares the work of creativity in us with the work of the Holy Spirit in the womb of Mary, the mother of Jesus.

In the twelfth century the German abbess Hildegard of Bingen not only praised the work of creativity but demonstrated her commitment to it. She was a major musical genius who wrote an opera (including the libretto and the music); painted or directed the painting of thirty-six "illuminations" as she called them; authored ten books; and engaged her nuns in plays and in many forms of healings by growing herbal gardens and more. Hildegard said **wisdom is present in all creative works.** No one could say Hildegard did not practice what she preached.

She quotes God speaking:

> **I have exalted humankind**
> **with the vocation of creation.**
> **I call humankind to the same norm.**

We do not create alone but in consort with all Creation.

> **God gave to humankind the talent**
> **to create with all the world.**

Our creativity demands a special responsibility on our part.

> **Humankind, full of all creative possibilities,**
> **is God's work.**
> **Humankind alone is called to assist God.**
> **Humankind is called to co-create.**

Our work of co-creation means we are an instrument through which Spirit flows. **The marvels of God are not brought forth from one's self. Rather, it is more like a chord, a sound that is played. The tone does not come out of the chord itself, but rather, through the touch of the musician. . . . I am, of course, the lyre and harp of God's kindness.**

For Hildegard, God is music. **O Trinity, you are music, you are life,** she writes. The Holy Spirit actually **kindles the hearts of humankind. Like tympanum and lyre it plays them, gathering volume in the temple of the soul.** She hears all the elements of creation singing out in praise of the Creator. **All of creation is a song of praise to God.** The human soul itself is a **symphony** but so is all of Creation: **All of creation is a symphony of the Holy Spirit which is joy and jubilation.**

Hildegard ends her first book *Scivias*, in which she not only includes an opera but also thirty-five paintings, with Psalm 150.

> **Praise God with the sound of trumpet;**
> **Praise God with lyre and harp.**
> **Praise God with strings and organ.**
> **Praise God with cymbals sounding forth well.**
> **Praise God with cymbals of jubilation.**
> **Let every spirit praise the Lord.**

Thomas Aquinas also honors creativity. He sees our creativity as the image of God at work in us when he says: **Although a created being tends to the divine likeness in many ways, this one whereby it seeks the divine likeness by being the cause of others takes the ultimate place.** Aquinas marvels at our powers of creativity or causality derived from the Creator when he says: **The dignity of causality is imparted even to creatures.** He observes that praise and singing and dancing all come from burning heart-experiences because **it is impossible that anyone hide the words of God, when their heart is inflamed by love. . . . the effect of the excitement is that one who preferred to be silent is moved to speak. "Those whom the Spirit fills, it causes both to burn and speak."** What most excites us and moves us to creativity is, in fact, what it is we meditate on. Aquinas believes that the same Holy Spirit that hovered over the waters at the beginning of creation hovers over the mind of the artist at work. **God's spirit is said to move over the waters as the will of artists moves over the material to be shaped by their art.**

Images are not tangential to our knowledge—they lie at its source. **The image is a principle of our knowledge. It is that from which our intellectual activity begins, not as a passing stimulus, but as an enduring foundation.** Thus artists are involved in laying *enduring foundations* for our minds. When humans give birth they are co-creating with the Divine. **Sometimes the images in the human imagination are divinely formed, so as to express divine things better than do those that we receive from sense objects. Prophetic visions would be an example of this.**

Recent scholarship concerning the origins of Christianity has revealed a profound *creativity* at its core. While some may nostalgically long for the certainty that the Bible once afforded regarding a literal message about the birth of Jesus in Bethlehem and his death and resurrection, what is being discovered is something perhaps more marvelous: It is the profound imagination of the writers of the gospels who created powerful stories and powerful social visions inspired by the historical Jesus and the spirit that he set loose. The making of wisdom speeches, for example, in John's Gospel, is not a deception since such an art form was highly prized in the ancient world. The Q document is that collection of Jesus' sayings that gave birth to the gospels that we know today. It evolved into three versions. What Burton L. Mack in his book *The Lost Gospel: The Book of Q & Christian Origins* calls *mythmaking* by the gospel writers Mark and the writers of the late Q document is a powerful art form. He says: "Upgrading the mythology of Jesus from child of wisdom to Son of God may seem to be a small step, but note the consequences. Jesus was no longer imagined as a sage whose knowledge was divine. He was imagined as an otherworldly being, heir of the father's kingdom in battle with the accuser for the authority to rule over the kingdoms of the earth, whose hour for full disclosure would come in the future, at which time he would turn the father's kingdom over to his followers so they could rule over the twelve tribes of Israel. This is quite a myth."

This same spirit of creativity flows through the gospels of Mark, Thomas, Matthew, and Luke. One can say that *Christianity was built on creativity*. The Jesus story unleashed a powerful imagination, one that birthed a "new social vision," which caught the imagination of an era and ended up creating its own epoch.

In theological terms, one might call this a theology of the Holy Spirit. Indeed, "the holy spirit was a term used by the people of Q to make the connection between their mythology and their situation. As a concept it differed from Jesus, wisdom, and the son of man in that it did not have the status of a primary agent. Instead, it served as a manifestation of the primary agent wisdom. The spirit of wisdom would make it possible for the least in the kingdom of God not to lose their footing, vision, courage or ability to speak when pressured by the real world." While Christians must face anew the question all humanity asks today, namely, "What myths shall we live by?" one must marvel at the myths that the various Christian communities chose and elaborated on nineteen centuries ago. For their choices did indeed seize the imaginations and lives of countless people and cultures over the centuries, creating a vision that still inspires.

We have seen the profound role that holy imagination and creativity play in so many of our spiritual traditions around the world, especially our most ancient ones. There is a consensus that true community and true connection to Spirit, to the imago dei in us, to ancestors who have come and to those who will come, are tapped into when we undergo creativity. African-American philosopher bell hooks believes that the future meeting ground for persons of all classes and races will be the meeting ground of aesthetics. "On the terrain of culture, one can participate in critical dialogue with the uneducated poor, the black underclass who are thinking about aesthetics. One can talk about what we are seeing, thinking, or listening to; a space is there for critical exchange. It's exciting to think, write, talk about, and create art that reflects passionate engagement with popular culture, because this may very well be 'the' central future location of resistance struggle, a meeting place where new and radical happenings can occur."

Ritual was once a communal telling of story in most imaginative ways. In so many places in the West there either is no ritual or what passes for it is rote, mechanical, law-based (remember Francis Bacon who substituted "law" for "form" in the modern era), and dull. It does not arouse or lead to ecstasy. It does not touch the heart but remains so often in the head. No imagination is allowed. Indeed, when a fundamentalist group took over a school board recently in a New Hampshire town, their first decree was: "No teacher in the public school system could use the word 'imagination' in the classroom." This effort to outlaw imagination tells us a lot about the power of imagination. It stands as a threat to powers that put control before everything else.

Working with imagination is a cleansing and purifying experience. It requires letting go because not all images are fit for a particular ritual or occasion. It requires intuition and insight along with discernment. It requires centering and the discipline that goes with that and with learning. All the arts are meant to be spiritual practices. Indeed, we can see ourselves as the art of God. We are the flute through which the divine breath (spirit) flows. God is **the Artist of artists** as Thomas Aquinas put it. Art is the only language we have other than silence to utter what is deepest in our souls, be it grief or ecstasy, pain or pleasure.

12.
JOY

Joy comes from God. . . .
From joy all beings have come and
unto joy they all return.
—The Upanishads

All the spiritual traditions of the world promise joy. Joy is not the opposite of suffering or pain—joy is what sees us through both.

In Hinduism we learn that **joy comes from God. Who could live and who could breathe if the joy of Brahman filled not the universe? . . ."Father, explain to me the mystery of Brahman." Then his father spoke to him of the food of the earth, of the breath of life, of the One who really sees, of the One who really hears, of the Mind that knows, and of the One who truly speaks. . . . Then he saw that Brahman is joy (ananda, bliss); for from joy all beings have come and unto joy they all return.**

In the Upanishad, we read that **He who knows the joy of Brahman fears no more.** Bliss (ananda) and Brahman go together and undergird all reality, all relationships. **Bliss pervades all objects; that is why there is attraction between husband and wife, parents and children, creature and creature, God and man. Furthermore, Brahman is bliss because it is infinite.** Another Hindu teacher, Ma Ananda Moye, says: **Laugh as much as you can. . . . it is important that your laughter come from the deepest place of your heart; it should go from head to foot. . . . Your laughter will diffuse joy everywhere.**

Joy comes from contemplation, so much so that the Maitri Upanishad tells us that **words cannot describe the joy of the soul whose negative habits are cleansed in deep contemplation—who is one with her Atman, her own Spirit. Only those who feel this joy know what it is.**

Joyful contemplation is carried into everyday life including the life of worship. Popular worship in India is generally pervaded by a spirit of joyousness and merriment. Nikhilananda describes it this way: **It is associated with worship of images and with symbols, music, singing, dancing, processions, prayer, joyousness, merriment, feasting, fasting. . . . The atmosphere of the temple is not gloomy or heavy but is filled with song and shouts of joy. This is mainly because a Hindu really feels in the temple the presence of the Deity, who is the embodiment of Bliss.** The overall theme of the Hindu Scriptures is a call to joy. **Life depicted in the Vedas and Puranas, major texts of Hinduism, is a joyous affirmative, optimistic and creative life. Divinity is not only Existence, not only Intelligence, but also Joy.**

> By attaining him, the Essence,
> one is filled with joy.

The Bhagavad Gita speaks to joy when it declares that when one realizes the Supreme Brahman one **becomes fully joyful. He never laments or desires to have anything. He is equally disposed toward every living entity. In that state he attains pure devotional service unto me.** We are instructed that **in every state devotional service is joyful.** And the Lord who is called the "Supersoul" and Overseer is also called the **Transcendental Enjoyer.** The Bhagavad Gita promises joy to those who find goodness in others. **Those who have the powers of their soul in harmony, and the same living mind for all; who find joy in the good of each being—they reach in truth my very Self.** The Katha Upanishad warns that there are two paths that present themselves to human beings: **There is the path of joy and there is the path of pleasure. Both attract the soul . . . The two paths lie in front of every person. Pondering on them, the wise person chooses the path of joy; the fool takes the path of pleasure.** The Upanishads speak of elderhood, or the third stage of human existence, as a time for spiritual practice and reflecting. They say it is also a time of deep enjoyment.

In the Vedas, the mood of worship is anything but gloomy. **Worship, like song and poetry, is an overflow of the joy of the soul:**

> **Agni, the joyous, much beloved. . . .**
> **we worship with joyous hearts.**
> **Like joyous streams bursting from the mountain**
> **The hymns of prayer have proceeded to the Deity.**

> **Sing, sing forth your sons, O Priyamedhas, sing!**
> **Let children also sing!**
> **Song of him like the strong castle;**
> **now loudly let the violin sound,**

Let the lute send its resounding voice,
Let the string send its tunes around;
To God is our hymn upraised.

We worship with joyous hearts the joyous Deity,
dear to all, effulgent, holy, purifying.

A Commentator remarks: There is a sacredness in our highest joy, correspond-
ing to the infinite joy in the Divine. Hence a medium of approach to the Divine is the joy of the soul. Man is not borne down under the burden of sin. His
is not a worship in penitence. It is the opening of the flood-gates of a joyous
soul before the radiant glory of the Source of all joy. Vedic poetry is typical of
this joyous outpouring of a lofty spirit.

In Judaism, the *Zohar* calls us to joy.

> **Souls of the righteous . . . have places from which to gaze,**
> **to enjoy the joy on high, called Delight of YHVH.**
> **There they are filled by precious flows of rivers of pure balsam. . . .**

Of course, the psalms do also.

> **How I love your palace, Yahweh Sabaoth!**
> **How my soul yearns and pines for Yahweh's courts!**
> **My heart and my flesh sing for joy**
> **   to the living God.**

Indeed, worship is meant to be a time of the community expressing its joy.

> **Shout for joy to honor God our strength,**
> **shout to acclaim the God of Jacob!**
> **Start the music, sound the drum,**
> **the melodious lyre and the harp;**
> **sound the New Moon trumpet,**
> **at the full moon, on our feastday!**

And not just the human community is joyful to be alive.

> **Let the sea thunder and all that it holds,**
> **   and the world, with all who live in it;**
> **let all the rivers clap their hands**
> **   and the mountains shout for joy,**
> **at the presence of Yahweh . . .**

The *Kabbalah* urges us to recognize this joy in everyday events like eating. It all comes from the divine source. **When you eat and drink, you experience enjoyment and pleasure from the food and drink. Arouse yourself every moment to ask in wonder, "What is this enjoyment and pleasure? What is it that I am tasting?" Answer yourself, "This is nothing but the holy sparks from the sublime, holy worlds that are within the food and drink."**

Rabbi Heschel says that **joy is a way to God** and **all joy comes from God.** Nor is there a contradiction between joy and struggle. **The experience of bliss in doing the good is the greatest moment that mortals know. The discipline, sacrifice, self-denial or even suffering which are often involved in doing the good do not vitiate the joy; they are its ingredients.**

Rabbi Heschel teaches that the prophets, too, were saturated in joy. The prophets face God and **to sense the living God is to sense infinite goodness, infinite wisdom, infinite beauty. Such a sensation is a sensation of joy.**

Though pleasure is involved in joy, pleasure and joy are not the same. Pleasure has a self-centeredness to it that joy transcends. Pleasure takes in; joy goes out. **To have joy in an object is to value it for its own sake.** This is what Eckhart means when he talks about "living without a why" and "loving without a why" and "working without a why." He is talking about valuing things and our own actions for their own sake. That is the path to joy as distinct from mere pleasure.

The *Zohar* instructs that to find joy one ought to be looking for goodness or blessing. **Your ears should be tuned to hear the good . . . Your mouth should produce nothing but good . . . Speak positively, always with benevolent words.** When we take in joy, it should take us over and radiate from us. **Your face should always be shining. Welcome each person with a friendly countenance. . . . The light of your face should never change; whoever looks at you will find only joy and a friendly expression. Nothing should disturb you.**

The Buddha said: **Waken yourself, watch yourself, and live joyfully.** Thich Nhat Hanh believes that meditation practice can bring joy alive in us.

> **Breathing in, I calm my body.**
> **Breathing out, I smile.**
> **Dwelling in the present moment,**
> **I know this is a wonderful moment!**

He encourages us to become the joy we take in. **Wearing a smile on your face is a sign that you are master of yourself. "Dwelling in the present moment." It is a joy to sit, stable and at ease, and return to our breathing, our smiling, our true nature . . . peace and joy right now, when will we have peace and joy—tomorrow, or after tomorrow?** Joy is our true nature and finding the eternal now is doable. It returns us to our origins of joy. So, too, a walking meditation can be taking us into joy. **We make steps as if we are the happiest person on earth . . . We have to walk in a way that we only print peace and serenity on the earth. . . . Walk as if you are kissing the earth with your feet. We have caused a lot of damage to the earth . . . stop and look at it—a tree, a flower, some children playing . . . only if we do not think of the future or the past, if we know that life can only be found in the present moment.** To be in the present is to be open to joy. **Happiness can always be found in the present moment. Practicing meditation is to go back to the present moment in order to encounter the flower, the blue sky, the child. Happiness is available.** We are called to plant joy in ourselves. **Plant the seeds of joy, peace, and the understanding in yourself in order to facilitate the work of transformation in the depths of your consciousness.** We can be confident of joy because, as Steven Levine says, **it is from the joy of simply being that healing arises in the mind and brings us home to the heart of understanding.** This happens because our natural state is to be in the moment and this leads to joyousness.

The Muslim faith teaches the primacy of gratitude. Prayer is meant to spring from the presence of God in the heart and the gratitude that wells up there. Rumi speaks to the joy that comes from ecstatic prayer when he says:

> The Sufi is dancing
> > like the shimmering rays of the Sun,
> Dancing from dusk till dawn.
> They say, *This is the work of the Devil.*
> Surely then, the Devil we dance with
> > is sweet and joyous,
> > and himself an ecstatic dancer!

Hafiz also celebrates the joy of life.

> Children can easily open the drawer
> That lets the spirit rise up and wear
> Its favorite costume of
> Mirth and laughter.
>
> We are not in pursuit of formalities
> or fake religious laws,
> For through the stairway of existence
> We have come to God's door.
>
> We are people who need to love, because
> Love is the soul's life,
> Love is simply creation's greatest joy.
>
> Through the stairway of existence,
> O through the stairway of existence, Hafiz,

Have you now come,
Have we all now come to
The Beloved's Door.

Thus, for Hafiz, it is the gift of existence itself that so moves us to love and joy. He draws a simple conclusion from this fact.

If you think I am having more fun
than anyone else on this planet
You are absolutely correct.

He calls us to the serious duty to celebrate.

There is only one rule on this wild Playground,
    Every sign Hafiz has ever seen reads the same.
They all say:
"Have fun, my dear, my dear, have fun,
    in the Beloved's divine Game,
O in the Beloved's
    Wonderful Game."

Thomas Aquinas believed that the very reason why things exist is the joy of God that so overflowed that it needed company with which to share it. He says: **Sheer joy is God's and this demands companionship.** Aquinas stresses the generosity of God in making creatures that mirror the divine goodness. **God is so good that it would be out of character for Divinity to keep its knowledge of itself to itself and never to give itself intimately, for goodness of itself is generous.** Joy and ecstasy go together, and for Aquinas there is a great deal of ecstasy in the world because there is a great deal of love. **Divine love produces ecstasy, that is, it puts lovers outside of themselves. . . . For love brings it about that lovers are directed not only toward themselves, but also toward others.** Joy is a result of love—**Delight or enjoyment implies repose of the lover in the beloved object. . . . The only person who truly has joy is one who lives in love.** Joy makes the heart grow and it is also a remedy for sadness. **Joy expands the heart, while sorrow contracts it. . . . Delight drives out sadness.** So important is joy to our being human that **joy is a human being's noblest act.**

What about the joy of God? **God is most joyful and therefore supremely conscious.** In this statement Aquinas is connecting joy and consciousness—not only in God but by implication also in ourselves. Joy represents full consciousness. **God delights. God is always rejoicing and doing so with a single and simple delight. In fact, it is appropriate to say that love and joy are the only human emotions that we can attribute literally to God. . . . Love and joy exist properly in God. The divine joy gathers up within itself and consummates all joys. . . . It is unique to God that the divine joy is identical with the divine being.**

Meister Eckhart also speaks to the joy of God when he says: **God enjoys the God-self. In the same enjoyment in which God enjoys the Godself, God enjoys all creatures. With the same enjoyment with which God enjoys himself, he enjoys all creatures, not as creatures, but he enjoys the creatures as God. In the same enjoyment in which God enjoys himself, he enjoys all things.** Moreover, **God has sheer delight and laughter over a good deed.** God is a joyful God who **finds joy and rapture to the full.** God and the soul are meant to laugh at one another just as the Trinity also laughs in its innermost being. **When the Father laughs to the Son and the Son laughs back to the Father, that laughter gives pleasure, that pleasure gives joy, that joy gives love, and love gives the persons [of the Trinity] of which the Holy Spirit is one.** Eckhart compares the divine joy to that of a horse running about in a meadow that **pours forth its whole strength in leaping about in the meadow.** In the same way **it is a joy to God to pour out the divine nature and the divine being completely into the divine likeness, since God is the likeness itself.** The divine joy is so great, Eckhart feels, that it is ineffable and incomprehensible.

Eckhart relates joy and the creative process: If we have sorrow in our heart it is because we are **not yet mothers.** Our giving birth to the Christ in our creative works delights God and angels—and also ourselves to such an extent that **you will have such great joy as a result of each of those good deeds that take place in this world that your joy will attain the greatest constancy, so that it will never change. Therefore, Jesus says, ". . . and that joy no one shall take from you."** Furthermore, when we enter the divine essence, true joy is ours. **Then I have true joy, and neither sorrow nor torment can take it from me. For then I am removed into the divine essence in which there is no place for sorrow.**

Julian of Norwich, who urges us to think of God as **our Lover**, builds much of her theology on the experience of joy. She writes: **I saw the Soul so large as if it were an endless world and a joyful kingdom.** She sees Christ's face in the following manner.

> **Glad and happy and sweet to our souls**
> **is the joyful, loving face of our Lord.**
> **For he always fixes his eyes upon us**
> **who live in love-longing;**
> **and he wants our soul to smile at him**
> **in return for his favors.**

She says that Jesus **is true lasting joy.** She saw three faces to Jesus: One was a suffering face such as he had during his dying. **Though this face was mournful and troubled yet it was glad and joyful for he is God.** The other two faces were of empathy and compassion. But **the joyful face was shown more than the other two and continued the longest because this face will exist endlessly.** Julian believes that most people ignore the joyful face of Christ just as they ignore the God who is **All-Love.** Yet we are to be recipients of a **new joy which will be flowing copiously out of God into us fulfilling us. Our Lord is with us, taking care of us and leading us into the fullness of joy.** Julian recognizes our capacity for joy as being the awareness of God's presence everywhere. **The fullness of joy is to behold God in everything.**

The Goddess tradition emphasizes joy. Hallie Austen writes that **the essence of the Goddess is joy and love of life, particularly life as we experience it through the earth and her cycles. The sight of sunrise or sunset reflected in water, the smell of gardenias, a loved one's touch, the music of windchimes, the taste of the first ripe fruit—all these are part of our birthright, our natural heritage. So also is pleasure in simply existing, in enjoying the small and large movements of our bodies, in everyday tasks as well as in exuberant dance.** Animals remind us of the joy of living. Marija Gimbutas learned that the celebration of life was what lay at the essence of the goddess culture. This love of life is the very meaning of *eros,* a passion for living. We need to take the erotic back from the pornographers and return it to our daily living where joy and passion go together.

Luisah Teish speaks of the goddess Orisha Oshun in the following manner: **With her we learn to love ourselves. We paint ourselves as brightly as the birds that fly. Through her we learn to love the gifts of the earth, brass and amber, and to become one with them. We place them on our bodies and share substance with them through our sweat. She brings us in contact with the essence of flowers. We make perfume and become one with the plant spirits by rubbing them on our bodies, into our skin. They are absorbed in our pores and we make love to them and with them . . . Our mouths utter sounds, we cry out ancient rhythms, haunting and sweet. We feed the hunger, heal the wounds, and give birth to outrageous beauty.**

Kokomon Clottey is a drummer from Ghana living in Oakland, California, who gathers people together in circles of "mindful drumming." He is struck by the American phrase "pursuit of happiness." How can it be, he asks, that people are bent on pursuit of happiness? **We are happiness. Why need we pursue it outside ourselves?**

Perhaps a similar observation is behind Aboriginal poet Kath Walker's criticism of white culture for lacking joy, for taking joy away from the primal peoples and for missing out on the joy that permeates creation itself. Her poem is called "The Unhappy Race."

> **White fellow, you are the unhappy race.**
> **You alone have left nature and made civilized laws.**
> **You have enslaved yourselves as you enslaved the horse and other**
> **   wild things.**
> **Why, white man?**
> **Your police lock up your tribe in houses with bars,**
> **We see poor women scrubbing floors of richer women.**
> **Why, white man, why?**
> **You laugh at "poor blackfellow," you say we must be like you.**
> **You say we must leave the old freedom and leisure,**
> **We must be civilized and work for you.**
> **Why, white fellow?**
> **Leave us alone, we don't want your collars and ties,**
> **We don't need your routines and compulsions.**
> **We want the old freedom and joy that all things have but you.**
> **Poor white man of the unhappy race.**

13.

SUFFERING

Nobody knows the trouble I've seen,
Nobody knows my sorrow.
Nobody knows the trouble I've seen,
Glory, Hallelujah!
—Negro Spiritual

Suffering is a universal experience and our spiritual traditions have always tried to deal with it in one way or other.

Noel King comments on suffering and the African experience. "Suffering, according to all the great religions, is the stuff of human growth, and Africa has accumulated capital in the world bank of suffering that none, not even the Jews, can surpass. She has undergone invasion and subjugation by colonialism, then by economic neo-colonialism, which has reduced some of the richest peoples in the world to destitution."

Howard Thurman acknowledges the presence and the depth of the suffering in our midst—much of it brought about by human choices. **In the language of faith, the kingdoms of this world often conflict with the Kingdom of God. It cannot be denied that a part of the fact of human society is the will to destroy, to lay waste, and to spend. There is so much that casts down and so little that uplifts and inspires.**

While not attempting to explain suffering, Thurman sees suffering in terms of love: **So much of human misery is poured out upon the innocent and helpless that life seems to be possessed of a vast, hideous deviltry. Of course, there has never been a completely satisfying answer to human suffering, particularly as to the why of it. It is clear that the profoundly significant reflection upon the misery of life must begin not with an idea of omnipotence but with the concept of love.**

Yet Thurman also felt that suffering does not, ultimately, have the last word in life. **The contradictions of life are not in themselves either final or ultimate. This points up the basic difference between pessimism and optimism. The pessimist appraises the facts of experience, and on their face value is constrained to pass a final judgment on them. If there are contradictions between good and evil—between that which makes for peace and that which makes for turbulence—then these contradictions are regarded from this point of view as being in themselves ultimate and final; and because they are ultimate, inescapable, and therefore binding.** For Thurman, life will have the last word and life does not opt for ultimate despair or infinite pain. **Men do reap what they sow; not only because it is so written in the Book, but also because it is a part of the nature of** life. In the last analysis life cannot be fooled . . . it is a dynamic weapon in the hands of the disadvantaged. It makes it possible for them to ride high to life, and particularly to keep their spirits from being eaten away by gloom and hopelessness.

The inequities of life, what he calls the "contradictions of life," are temporary: **If perchance the contradictions of life are not ultimate, then there is always the growing edge of hope in the midst of the most barren and most tragic circumstances. It is a complete renunciation of the thoroughgoing dualism of the point of view just discussed. It is a matter of supreme significance that men are never quite robbed of all hope.**

Hope, Thurman believes, ultimately prevails, for it is what nourishes the human spirit and its dreams. **There is something present in the spirit of man, sometimes even taking the form of great arrogance, sometimes quietly nourishing the springs of resistance to a great tyranny—there is something in the spirit of man that knows that the dualism, however apparently binding, runs out, exhausts itself, and leaves a core of assurance that the ultimate destiny of man is good. This becomes the raw material of all hope, and is one of the taproots of religious faith for the human spirit. . . . we are under judgment not to give each other up . . . man's destiny is a good destiny . . . the dream of peace continues to nourish the hope of the race. This dream persists, even though we do not know what peace on earth would be like because it has never been experienced.**

Dr. Martin Luther King, Jr., spoke candidly of his suffering and relates it to the redemptive suffering of Jesus. **My personal trials have taught me the value of unmerited suffering. . . . I have lived these past few years with the conviction that unearned suffering is redemptive. There are some who still find the cross a stumbling block, others consider it foolishness, but I am more convinced than ever before that it is the power of God unto social and individual salvation. So like the Apostle Paul I can now humbly say, "I bear in my body the marks of the Lord Jesus."** King believed that it would take **voluntary suffering** that goes with nonviolence to put an end to unjust suffering. **There is no easy way to create a world where men and women can live together. . . . It will be done by people who have the courage to put an end to suffering by willingly suffering themselves rather than inflict suffering upon others.**

In the African-American experience, the Spirituals were "sorrow songs" written from the pits of despair during slave times. Consider for example the following song:

> Nobody knows the trouble I've seen,
> Nobody knows my sorrow.
> Nobody knows the trouble I've seen,
> Glory, Hallelujah!

Thurman says that **all the reaches of despair are caught up and held in a trembling wail** in the following song:

> I couldn't hear nobody pray,
> Oh, I couldn't hear nobody pray.
> Oh, way down yonder by myself,
> And I couldn't hear nobody pray.

And again,

> I've got to walk my lonesome valley,
> I've got to walk it for myself.
> Nobody else can walk it for me,
> I've got to walk it for myself!

So prevalent is suffering and its memory in the African-American consciousness that not only the spirituals developed during slavery but the blues developed in this century call to the heart's grief and sorrow. Ma Rainey's song "Blues Oh Blues" states simply:

Oh blues, oh blues, oh blues, oh blues, blues, oh blues.
I'm so blue, so blue, I don't know what to do.
Oh blues, oh blues, oh blues.

Angela Davis points out that this song follows in the tradition of West African *Nommo*—in naming the blues twenty times in this song, the singer is "using the power of the word to magically assert control over circumstances otherwise far beyond her reach. This magical, aesthetic assertion of control over the blues is an implicit expression of the real need to transform the objective conditions that are at the root of these blues: a camouflaged dream of a new social order. This is the powerful utopian function of the blues." In "Poor Man's Blues" singer Bessie Smith addresses the wealthy.

Mr. rich man, rich man, open up your heart and mind
Give the poor man a chance help stop these hard, hard times.
While you're living in your mansion, you don't know what hard times
    mean
Poor working man's wife is starving, your wife is living like a queen.

Bessie Smith influenced Billie Holiday, whose song "Strange Fruit" is, among other things, an exercise in not forgetting or covering up.

Southern trees bear a strange fruit
Blood on the leaves, blood on the root
Black bodies swinging in the Southern breeze
Strange fruit hanging from the poplar trees
Pastoral scene of the gallant South
The bulging eyes and the twisted mouth
Scent of magnolia sweet and fresh

Then the sudden smell of burning flesh
Here is a fruit for the crows to pluck
For the rain to gather, for the wind to suck
For the sun to rot, for the tree to drop
Here is a strange and bitter crop.

Clearly, one of the African-American responses to suffering was by way of creativity, music and lyrics that *tell the truth* of what the heart goes through.

Much of the Buddha's teachings are a response to the reality of suffering. As a young prince he was sheltered from the painful lot of most of humanity not only by his privileged class but also by his youth. It was on wandering away from his palace as a young man that, on encountering poverty, disease, death and old age for the first time, he gave up his comfortable princely role and went to seek understanding. The result of his search is what we call Buddhism today. Yet, as Ana Matt puts it, "The important thing is to find a way to end suffering and attain liberation. Buddhism was never intended to be a religion or a system of metaphysics. It was intended to be a psychology, a way to overcome suffering."

The Four Noble Truths of Buddhist teaching all address the issue of suffering. The first tells us that **life is inherently unsatisfactory.** The Buddha's Second Noble Truth is that **human beings suffer because we live in an almost constant state of desire.** The Buddha's Third Noble Truth is that nature has given us the ability to train our minds to bring us new levels of satisfaction and freedom. The Buddha's Fourth Noble Truth tells us how to end our suffering. Said the Buddha: **I teach one thing and one thing only, suffering and the end of suffering.**

What is the way out of suffering? We have seen it throughout this book: mindfulness. A capacity to live the Now fully and not project and not carry the past or the not-yet into our consciousness. This calls for radical letting go and a willingness to face all thoughts that flow through our minds and let them go. It means a return to our origins, that is, to our "true nature" or "Buddha nature," where we were once free of all thoughts and truly open. Thich Nhat Hanh put it this way: **When we are mindful, touching deeply the present moments, we can see and listen deeply and the fruits are always understanding, acceptance, love, and the desire to relieve suffering and bring joy.** Mindfulness is not learned so much from books as from meditative practice. **The living Dharma (teaching) is not a library of scriptures. . . . It is mindfulness manifested in your daily life. The seed of mindfulness in each of us is the "womb of the Buddha." We are all mothers of the Buddha because we are all pregnant with the potential for awakening.**

The Buddha spoke of the path of liberation: **This is the way for the purifica-**

tion of beings, for the overcoming of sorrow and lamentation, for the destroy-ing of pain and grief, for reaching the right path, for the realization of Nir-vana, namely the four Foundations of Mindfulness. The series of meditation exercises described in the Mahasatipatthana Sutra are called the Four Foundations of Mindfulness. Wes Nisser sees them as deep-ecology practices, ways of exploring our nature as part of greater nature. **These exercises can establish us in our connection with each other, and with all other forms of life on earth.**

The first of these, says the Buddha, is **mindfulness centered on the body.** The breath is key. **Breathing in I calm the entire body . . . breathing out I calm the entire body,** says the Buddha. The second Foundation of Mindfulness is paying attention to our sense impressions or basic feelings of pleasant or unpleasant. "Freud called them drives or instincts. The Buddha called them 'underlying tendencies.'" Our inherited nervous systems works on the principles of stimulus-response. We can let them run our lives or we can pay attention to them. "If we remain unconscious of them, we have no freedom at all." The Buddha's way was to pay them our attention. If we do not examine them, what is pleasant will lead us to craving and what is unpleasant will lead us to aversion. But maybe craving and aversion is not a cycle we want to submit to. **What the Buddha is advising us to do is to become aware of our *automatic reactions* to pleasure and pain.** To do this gives us more freedom to respond to what is. Nisker believes that this method of paying attention to pleasure and pain is, in fact, to confront the reptilian brain we have inherited. **The reptilian brain regulates functions such as breath, body temperature, pain perception, hunger, sensuality, and a basic nervous system program of stimulus-response.** Because this region of our brain is **hard-wired to react to basic feelings of pleasant or unpleasant, with virtually no flexibility,** to confront it with a meditative practice is to introduce flexibility.

We confront excessive desire by facing its underpinnings of craving and aversion. We learn to let go. Buddha is reported to have said: **Develop a mind that clings to nothing.** Learning not to cling is the key to the second Foundation of

Mindfulness. Clinics exist that can help persons with physical pain to let go of some of it through mindfulness training.

The third Foundation of Mindfulness is about focusing on mind-states understood as the feeling-tones of the mind or the "heart-mind." We saw above that 121 classes of consciousness and 89 different mind-states have been identified. We can either let our mind-states dictate to us or we can get a handle on them. "We don't see our mind's condition, because we are *inside* that condition," warns Nisker. The practice is quite simple: To pay attention to the mind-state and be aware of its presence. Thus we learn the difference between our feelings and our self, between our mind's work and our own being. We are more than all of these experiences.

This, briefly, is how Buddha addresses the issue of human suffering. There are ways to find joy and our "Big Mind" and the freedom of our origin in the midst of turmoil and trouble and pain. As Nisker puts it, **Psychological studies of meditators reveal that not only are they more relaxed, but they can also respond more quickly to stimuli. Meditation may also reveal that we are happier than we thought we were. We may discover that ancient conditioning rather than present circumstances is causing our dissatisfaction, and that this moment is quite sufficient or even wonderful, and we simply hadn't noticed.** In the Bhaddakaratta Sutra, the Buddha teaches:

> **Do not pursue the past. Do not lose yourself in the future.**
> **Looking deeply at life as it is in this very moment, the**
> **meditator dwells in stability and freedom.**

How distant is the peace we seek? **This very place is the pure land, this very body, the Buddha.**

Pema Chodron offers her Buddhist perspective on suffering when she asks the question: **Who ever got the idea that we could have pleasure without pain? . . . But pain and pleasure go together; they are inseparable. They can be celebrated. They are ordinary. Birth is painful and delightful. Death is painful and delightful . . . Pain is not punishment; pleasure is not a reward.** She insists on the necessary dialectic that is inherent in pleasure and pain and she calls for our getting used to it. Enter into the misery and learn what it has to teach us. **Inspiration and wretchedness are inseparable. We always want to get rid of misery rather than see how it works together with joy. The point isn't to cultivate one thing as opposed to another, but to relate properly to where we are. Inspiration and wretchedness complement each other. With only inspiration, we become arrogant. With only wretchedness, we lose our vision. Feeling inspired cheers us up, makes us realize how vast and wonderful our world is. Feeling wretched humbles us. The gloriousness of our inspiration connects us with the sacredness of the world. But when the tables are turned and we feel wretched, that softens us up. It ripens our hearts. It becomes the ground for understanding others.**

Chodron teaches that the practice of meditation can make all the difference in dealing with pain and suffering. By returning to our "wisdom mind" we touch what really matters. Meditation practice disciplines the mind to see deeper than the present worry. There lies the ceasing of suffering. **Cultivating a mind that does not grasp at right and wrong, you will find a fresh state of being. The ultimate cessation of suffering comes from that.**

The Dalai Lama, in his book *Ethics for the New Millennium,* offers an ethic that is not grounded in religion but **in the basic human experience of happiness and suffering.** By definition, we are beings who suffer. **A sentient being . . . is one which has the capacity to experience pain and suffering.** Avoidable forms of suffering include war, poverty, violence, crime, illiteracy, and certain diseases. Yet unavoidable sufferings also assail us, including problems of sickness, old age, death, mishaps, accidents, and losses at work and in relationships. The Dalai Lama recognizes that we have choices as to how we will face the sufferings of life. **There is much we can do to influence our experience of suffering.** To fret about our misfortunes is to frustrate ourselves. **As a result, afflictive emotions arise and our peace of mind is destroyed. When we do not restrain our tendency to react negatively to suffering, it becomes a source of negative thoughts and emotions.** The practice of meditation or **inner discipline** can give us a positive view of reality that embraces the suffering and does not run from it or allow it to swallow us up. Therefore, it can be said that **the degree to which suffering affects us is largely up to us.** When he hears disturbing news of his community's travails in Tibet, for example, sadness enters. But **by placing it in context and by reminding myself that the basic human disposition toward affection, freedom, truth, and justice must eventually prevail, I find I can cope reasonably well. Feelings of helpless anger, which do nothing but poison the mind, embitter the heart, and enfeeble the will, seldom arise, even following the worst news.** Wisdom can arise from our experiences of suffering including the wisdom of compassion. **Our experience of suffering reminds us of what all others also endure, it serves as a powerful injunction to practice compassion and refrain from causing others pain. . . . It can serve as the basis of compassion and love.**

Recently I heard a Jewish comedian, who is also a very serious man as most comedians are, say in his public act: "I'm a Jew. I don't need Buddha to teach me that life is about suffering." Rabbi Abraham Heschel came to the United States at the age of thirty-three, having left his homeland of Poland just six weeks before Hitler's invasion. Twenty-five years later, he spoke these words at Union Theological Seminary: **I speak as a person who was able to leave Warsaw, the city in which I was born, just six weeks before the disaster began. . . . I am a brand plucked from the fire of an altar of Satan on which millions of human lives were exterminated to evil's greater glory, and on which so much else was consumed: the divine image of so many human beings, many people's faith in the God of justice and compassion, and much of the secret and power of attachment to the Bible bred and cherished in the hearts of men for nearly two thousand years.** Heschel's personal suffering and that of his community that he felt so deeply gave him courage and strength to carry on the theological journey that was his life—a journey that was as much practical as theoretical.

Key to his theology is an understanding of *the suffering of God*. **God does not stand outside the range of human suffering and sorrow. He is personally involved in, even stirred by, the conduct and fate of man.** In contrast to the "Unmoved Mover," a name that the Greeks gave to God, Heschel insists that **God's participation in human history . . . finds its deepest expression in the fact that God can actually suffer.** God has *pathos,* the ability to be affected by the suffering of others. An apathetic God is a "God of abstraction" who hovers over the world quite indifferent to it, but a God of pathos holds **intimate concern** for history and **is affected by human acts.** This is the God who awakens and moves the prophets to act in human history on behalf of the compassionate God.

Heschel calls for waiting and for patience as well as for action. **We have entered not only the dark night of the soul, but also the dark night of society. We must seek out ways of preserving the strong and deep truth of a living God theology in the midst of the blackout.**

For the darkness is neither final nor complete. Our power is first in waiting for the end of darkness, for the defeat of evil; and our power is also in coming upon single sparks and occasional rays, upon moments full of God's grace and radiance.

We are called to . . . defy absurdity and despair, and to wait for God to say again: Let there be light. And there will be light.

The Hebrew psalms are often a lament at the state of either personal or community suffering. Sometimes they are a shout to God.

> Wake up, Lord! Why are you asleep?
> Awake! Do not abandon us for good,
> Why do you hide your face,
> and forget we are wretched and exploited?
> For we are bowed in the dust,
> our bodies crushed to the ground.
> Rise! Come to our help!
> Redeem us for the sake of your love.

And other times a more personal plea for support.

> My guilt is overwhelming me,
> it is too heavy a burden;
> my wounds stink and are festering,
> the result of my folly;
> bowed down, bent double, overcome,
> I go mourning all the day.
> My loins are burnt up with fever,
> there is no soundness in my flesh:
> numbed and crushed and overcome,
> my heart groans, I moan aloud. . . .
> Yahweh, do not desert me,
> do not stand aside, my God!
> Come quickly to my help,
> Lord, my savior!

Sometimes just the telling of one's misery is all that is prayed.

> Yahweh my God, I call for help all day,
> I weep to you all night;
> for my soul is all troubled,
> my life is on the brink of Sheol;
> I am numbered among those who go down to the Pit,
> a man bereft of strength:
> a man alone, down among the dead,
> among the slaughtered in their graves,
> among those you have forgotten,
> those deprived of your protecting hand.
> You have plunged me to the bottom of the Pit,
> to its darkest, deepest place. . . .
> You have turned my friends against me
> and made me repulsive to them;
> in prison and unable to escape,
> my eyes are worn out with suffering. . . .
> You have turned my friends and neighbors against me,
> now darkness my one companion left.

Clearly the invitation from these and many other psalms and lamentations in the Hebrew Bible are invitations to enter our hearts and face the sorrow that is there, express it, put it out so that it does not fester. Grieve the moment, grieve what the heart-mind holds even when it is painful.

In medieval Christianity in the thirteenth century there lived a remarkable woman who was part of the Beguine movement, which allowed women an alternative lifestyle to that of either being married or being a nun. Mechtild of Magdeburg was a Beguine who moved from town to town and worked with the young and the poor. She also kept a journal her entire adult life and in it she pictures the dark night of suffering in the following language.

> **There comes a time when both body and soul**
> **enter into such a vast darkness**
> **that one loses light and consciousness**
> **and knows nothing more of God's intimacy.**
> **At such a time, when the light in the lantern burns out**
> **the beauty of the lantern can no longer be seen.**
> **With longing and distress we are reminded of our nothingness.**

What does she do? She prays to God who also takes the burden and clasps it close to him/her **so that you may more easily bear it.** But this does not work either. **Still I feel that I can bear no longer the wounds God has given me, unanointed and unbound. My enemies surround me. O Lord, how long must I remain on earth in this mortal body as a target at which people throw stones and shoot and assail my honor with their evil cunning?** Like all Beguines, Mechtild was attacked by male church officials, including the pope, for being wanton women because they were neither married nor cloistered. Mechtild continues to name her pain. **I am hunted, captured, bound, wounded so terribly that I can never be healed. . . . Even if all the hills flowed with healing oils, and all the waters contained healing powers, and all the flowers and all the trees dripped with healing ointments, still I could never recover.** She calls on Christ to demonstrate the divine pathos and lie in the wounds of her soul.

> **Lord, I will tear the heart of my soul in two**
> **and you must lie therein.**

> You must lay yourself
> in the wounds of my soul.

And God replies: **I will always be your physician, bringing healing anointment for all your wounds. If it is I who allow you to be wounded so badly, do you not believe that I will heal you most lovingly in the very same hour?**

Mechtild reflects on what suffering teaches us: **From suffering I have learned this: That whoever is sore wounded by love will never be made whole unless she embrace the very same love which wounded her.** Like the Buddha, Mechtild is recommending that we not put distance between ourselves and our suffering, not make suffering the "other." She recognizes that we are given two wines to drink in life: the white wine of joy and the red wine of sorrow. Until we have drunk deeply of both, we do not know life. Mechtild also finds support from the example of Jesus who had to undergo cruel and unjust suffering. **Life without sorrow would be fool's folly. That is why God Himself took this path, one of sorrow and pain. God shows us that it is still a wonderful, noble, and holy way.** She also teaches letting go.

> **Do you wish to have love?**
> **If you wish to have love, then you must leave love.**

To assist us in letting go, she recommends emptying meditation, which in turn leads to acts of compassion.

> **Love the nothing, flee the self.**
> **Stand alone. Seek help from no one.**
> **Let your being be quiet.**
> **Be free from the bondage of all things.**
> **Free those who are bound,**
> **Give exhortation to the free.**

Care for the sick, but dwell alone.
When you drink the waters of sorrow
you shall kindle the fire of love
with the match of perseverance—this is the way
to dwell in the desert.

When Meister Eckhart teaches about suffering he sounds very Buddhist. **The impediments are in us. . . . It is always you yourself that hinder yourself, because your attitude toward things is wrong. Therefore begin first with yourself and let yourself go. Truly, if you will not flee first from yourself, wherever else you may flee, there you will find impediments and restlessness, wherever it may be.** Eckhart strongly recommends our returning to our origin to rediscover our freedom. **If this will returns to its original source from itself and all Creation even for a moment, this will is again its truly free nature and is free.** Eckhart trusts this return to our core being because **after all, you bear essentially all truth within yourselves.** Letting go is key to suffering but so, too, is letting the suffering be itself.

However, Eckhart also recognizes the pathos of God. **It is God who carries the burden. . . . However great suffering is, if it comes through God, God suffers from it first.** When we can learn to let God have our suffering, an equanimity follows. **Your joy reaches to the greatest evenness; it never alters. Therefore Christ says: "No one can take your joy away from you." And when I am correctly translated into the divine being, God becomes mine as well as everything he has. This is why he says: "I am God, your lord." I have rightful joy only when neither sufferings nor torments ravish it from me. . . . In God there is neither wrath nor grief, but only love and joy.** Letting go of willfulness is the key to entering into the divine equanimity.

Of course both Mechtild and Eckhart, in speaking about suffering, are working from their Christian tradition wherein Jesus suffered deeply at the end of his all-too-brief existence. A lesson to learn from the Jesus story is that suffering is indeed inevitable—it is not only the evil who suffer but even the best among us, that all things suffer in this universe, even Divinity when it passes through in any of its manifestations. The Christian cross has often served to remind people of this reality. Also, the cross in Christianity is a sign of the generosity of God who was stripped of the privileges of Divinity (Phil. 2:5) to become one of us and therefore subject to daily suffering. This reality can assist us to connect more deeply with the Divine and experience its likeness to ourselves more fully. The Divine does not bask in its own privilege but chooses to join human and cosmic history, whatever the price.

Dante began his journey through hell to purgatory and into heaven on Good Friday. There is a deep lesson in this acknowledgment of how the darkness of suffering is a prelude to joy. Psychologist Rollo May believes that many people choose to remain in hell, that is, to see themselves as victims, rather than to move beyond. **To be a victim has real benefits in terms of power over one's family and friends and other secondary gains.** It takes a real choice and commitment to venture out of hell.

But the other extreme is to deny that hell exists, to deny the depth of one's own pain and suffering. Yet, as May points out, **all through history it is true that only by going through hell does one have any chance of reaching heaven.** This was true with Odysseus visiting the underworld and of Aeneas going into the nether-world and of Job undergoing trial upon trial and of Jesus undergoing crucifixion and visiting Hades upon his death. It is true of the artist searching and struggling for her or his music, voice, word, vision. The Inferno or hell of Dante and of the rest of us "consists of suffering and endless torment that produces no change in the soul that endures it and is imposed from without." But in the Purgatorio suffering is temporary and a means of purification. "Both must be traversed before arriving at the celestial 'Paradiso.'"

Julian of Norwich expresses this act of "oneing" that Jesus, nature, and the rest of us undergo in suffering.

I saw a great oneing
between Christ and us
because when he was in pain
we were in pain.
All creatures of God's creation
that can suffer pain
suffered with him.

The sky and the earth failed
at the time of Christ's dying
because he too was part of nature.
Thus those who were his friends
suffered pain
because they loved him.

But at times, sorry to tell, this same cross has been laid on its side to become a sword and a weapon that instead of relieving suffering in the world brought more to bear on others. The perversion of the cross at certain times in Christian history is a scandal that will not go away by wishing it away. It is a reality that must always be defended against, one that believers need to hold before them as the option that it is. Power can corrupt anything—even our memories of our best leaders and guides. We need to guard ourselves against becoming suffering-makers instead of suffering-relievers.

Consider, for example, these lamentations from Aztec poets responding to the destruction of their world by the Spanish Conquistadores.

> **Our cries of grief rise up**
> **and our tears rain down,**
> **for Tlatelolco is lost. . . .**
> **How can we save our homes, my people?**
> **The Aztecs are deserting the city:**
> **the city is in flames, and all**
> **is darkness and destruction. . . .**
> **Weep, my people:**
> **know that with these disasters**
> **we have lost the Mexican nation.**
> **The water has turned bitter,**
> **our food is bitter! . . .**
> **Nothing but flowers and songs of sorrow**
> **are left in Mexico and Tlatelolco,**
> **where once we saw warriors and wise men.**

14.
BEAUTY

> How did the rose
> Ever open its heart
> And give to this world
> all its beauty?
> It felt the encouragement of light
> Against its Being.
> Otherwise, we all remain
> too frightened.
> —Hafiz, *It Felt Love*

Beauty heals; beauty inspires; beauty is often a name we give the Divine. Modern Western culture has often forgotten this truth. When we do, we pay a price such as the willful destruction of beauty and the craving for pseudo-beauties that an addictive culture wishes to seduce us into.

Among the most ancient peoples, beauty is expected in the simplest personal rituals that persons give birth to, whether it is the clothes and costumes with which one fashions one's body for festivals and celebrations or it is the personal offerings made in ritual prayer to Brahman in India. In Bali, the simplest people are busy making beautiful altars and dressing beautifully and gathering food and arranging its beauty all day long. Beauty rules in some cultures.

Beauty is invoked in the most ancient of spiritual writings on earth such as those from ancient Kemet or Egypt. In Egypt, around 1550 B.C.E., hymns were created to the god Aten. Beauty plays a great role in their praise.

> **Beautiful you rise, O eternal living god!**
> **You are radiant, lovely, powerful,**
> **Your love is great, all-encompassing. . . .**
> **You nourish the hearts by your beauty;**
> **One lives when you cast your rays,**
> **Every land is in festivity.**

And again,

> **Beautiful you rise in heaven's horizon,**
> **O eternal, living Creator!**
> **When you have risen in eastern horizon,**
> **You fill every land with your beauty. . . .**
> **You yourself are lifetime, one lives by you.**
> **All eyes are on your beauty until you set,**
> **All labor ceases when you rest in the west.**

Beauty is at the heart of the indigenous peoples' understanding of the universe. The Mesoamerican poet Ayocuan speaks in praise of the poet Tecayebuatzin.

> The beautiful flowers, the beautiful songs
> come from the interior of heaven. . . .
> Your beautiful song
> is a golden rattlesnake-bird,
> you send it aloft most beautifully,
> you sing from the flowering branches.
> Are you by chance a precious bird
> of the Giver of Life?
> Have you by chance spoken with the God?

The Navaho people sing the following song:

> The earth is beautiful
> The earth is beautiful
> The earth is beautiful
> Below the East, the earth, its face toward the East, the top of its head
>   is beautiful
> Its legs, they are beautiful
> Its body, it is beautiful
> Its chest, it is beautiful
> Its breath, it is beautiful
> Its head-feather, it is beautiful
> The earth is beautiful.

Not long ago I was privileged to be part of a Sundance ceremony led by a Lakota community in the northwestern United States. After two days of dancing in the outer circle with the other "lay people," I was invited by the elders to join the Sundance dancers in the middle of the circle. It was a powerful experience: the sun, the sacred pole representing the axis mundi, the center of the universe; the singing; the blowing of the eagle whistle; the drumming, the earth underneath our feet; and above all the community energy as everyone gave their all to support the men and women who were doing a sacrifice for the community. After an hour or two of dancing there was an hour break and the male dancers withdrew into a secluded area for that break time. As we were getting ready to return to the dancing circle, one of the young Lakota men who was adjusting his long orange skirt (what all of us dancing men were wearing) said to me quite nonchalantly: "Well, I have to adjust my skirt so I can be as beautiful as possible since we are going out to mirror the beauty of the universe."

All our acts are meant to be about beauty—we are here to mirror the beauty we have found on arrival, the beauty of the universe. It is taken for granted that that is what ritual is about: mirroring the beauty of the universe. A psychology of microcosm/macrocosm offers us a way to speak about beauty and how humans mirror the beauty of the rest of Creation.

From the Islamic tradition, Hafiz asks:

> How did the rose
> Ever open its heart
> And give to this world
> all its beauty?
> It felt the encouragement of light
> Against its Being.
> Otherwise, we all remain
> too frightened.

Beauty enlarges our heart and builds our courage so we overcome fear. Beauty invariably links to light and to brilliance—what we spoke of in chapter three about light also applies to this chapter about beauty. God is called **The Beautiful One.**

> Indeed, dear ones,
> Hafiz is so very willing
> To share all his secrets
> About how to know the Beautiful One.
>
> I hold the Lion's Paw whenever I dance. . . .
> And the sun and moon
> Will someday argue over
> Who will tuck you in at Night!

Beauty is everywhere, in the simplest activities.

> Is your caravan lost?
> It is,
> If you no longer weep from gratitude or happiness,

> Or weep from being cut deep with the awareness
> Of the extraordinary beauty
> That emanates from the most simple act
> and common object.

The great work of Zikr and remembrance means remembering beauty.

> Remembrance lowers the cup into
> His luminous sky-well.
> The mind often becomes plagued and can deny
> The all-pervading beauty of God
> When the great work of Zhikr [remembrance]
>   is forgotten.

What happens to us when we encounter the divine beauty? It takes its toll on us.

> God's beauty has split me wide open.
> Throw Hafiz on a scale,
> Wrap me in cloth,
> Bring me home.
> Lift a piece of my knowledge to your lips
> So I can melt inside of you
> and sing.

To commit to beauty is often to fight powerful structures and share solidarity with the oppressed—the "beautiful, rowdy prisoners." It demands bigness of heart.

> The small man
> builds cages for everyone

he knows.
While the sage,
who has to duck his head
when the moon is low,
keeps dropping keys all night long
for the beautiful
rowdy
prisoners.

The prophet Muhammad says:

God is beautiful, and He loves beauty.
All that is beautiful comes from the beauty of God.

The great woman saint Rabi'a wrote the following prayer to Allah: **O my Lord, if I worship thee for fear of hell, burn me in hell; and if I worship thee for hope of Paradise, exclude me thence; but if I worship thee for thine own sake, withhold not from me thine eternal Beauty.** We share in the divine beauty, and for this reason we should take care of our bodies. The Qur'an says: **God shaped you and made our shapes beautiful.**

The Sufi Ibn Al-Arabi develops the connection between beauty and compassion and recognizes a theophany or divine revelation in beauty, calling it the "secret of Creation." **This conjunction between Beauty and Compassion is the secret of the Creation—for if divine "sympathy" is creative, it is because the Divine Being wishes to reveal his beauty, and if Beauty is redeeming, it is because it manifests this creative Compassion. Thus the being invested by nature with this theophanic function of Beauty will present the most perfect Image of Divinity.**

The Mevlevi Dervishes offer the following advice on how beauty returns us to our origin and source.

Each beautiful thing, a flower, the song of a bird,
awakens in our soul the memory of our origin.
Learn how to listen to the voice of beautiful things,
to make us understand the voice of our soul.

Beauty is recognized in today's science as playing an essential role in the universe. Nobel Prize winner Werner Heisenberg delivered an address in 1970 on "The Meaning of Beauty in the Exact Sciences." In that talk he called mathematics **the archetype of the beauty of the world** and he invoked the philosopher Plotinus from the third century who said: **Beauty is the translucence, through the material phenomena, of the eternal splendor of the "One."** Swedish astronomer Arne Wyler believes that the future of biology will marry the beautiful and the functional. Single-celled protozoans boast an architecture that is, as one observer puts it, "two billion years ahead of its time. The amoebas had the architectural ideas of R. Buckminster Fuller before there was anyone around capable of having an idea." Wyler comments: **Most of us would agree with Cudmore that the world of those protozoans is one of incomparable beauty. . . . Those single-celled life forms have developed an ability to construct the most exquisitely shaped "houses of glass" for their protection. The blind god of chance surely has no need for such beauty, since only the quality of function matters in the battle for survival of the fittest.** Wyler observes that physicists are ahead of biologists in their search **for understanding the deeper implications of simplicity, elegance, and beauty in the mathematics that seemingly govern the behavior of inanimate matter.**

Who can see the photos of the birth and death of stars, the exploding of supernovas, the edges of the universe that the Hubble telescope and other technical achievements have made available today and not be moved by the beauty of the universe in which we live? Microcosm and Macrocosm, we are surrounded by beauty. Ernesto Cardinale asks the following question:

Why not an infinite beauty and an infinite love?
It's a constant in nature,
beauty.
Whence poetry: song and delight in all that exists.

**The earth could have been just as
functional, practical,
without beauty. Why then?**

He adds that we can argue about the meaning of the universe and we can argue about the reason for the universe, but we cannot argue about the beauty of the universe.

Geologian Thomas Berry has written movingly of the intrinsic grace of our existence in this universe. **If we have a wonderful sense of the Divine, it is because we live amid such awesome magnificence. If we have refinement of emotion and sensitivity, it is because of the delicacy, the fragrance, and indescribable beauty of song and music and rhythmic movement in the world about us.** Beauty feeds our imaginations. **If we have powers of imagination, these are activated by the magic display of color and sound, of form and movement, such as we observe in the clouds of the sky, the trees and bushes and flowers, the waters and the wind, the singing birds, and the movement of the great blue whale through the sea. . . . If we lived on the moon, our mind and emotions, our speech, our imagination, our sense of the Divine would all reflect the desolation of the lunar landscape.**

Among medieval Christian mystics, Thomas Aquinas especially developed the teaching of the beauty of the Divine. He calls God **the Creator of beauty** and says: **The highest beauty is in the Godhead, since beauty consists in comeliness: but God is beauty itself, beautifying all things. The Creator of beauty has set up all the beauty of things. . . . The beauty of a creature is nothing other than a likeness of the divine beauty sharing in things.** Aquinas calls God **supersubstantial beauty [who] bestows beauty on all created beings.** The numinosity and radiance or sheen that God bestows on things is a **sharing of God's likeness and constitute those "beautifying" reflections that make beauty in things.** God does not hoard beauty to the Godself, rather **God is a fountain of total beauty. . . . From this beautiful One beauty comes to be in all beings.**

Aquinas sees beauty as part of our reason for existence and as an imitation of the Divine One. **All things have been made in order that they imitate the divine beauty in whatever way possible.** Aquinas proposes that beauty by its nature yearns to be conspicuous—we need to share our beauty just as Divinity and the rest of nature do. **It is necessary for good things to be conspicuous, because to be conspicuous pertains to the nature of beauty.** We ought not to hide our beauty under a bushel.

According to Aquinas, the experience of beauty is one of the experiences that renders us human: **We can take delight in the very beauty of sense-objects.** Citing the psalmist who talks of the **beauty of the house of God,** Aquinas links beauty to light or glory (*doxa*) that we discussed in chapter three above. **Among all these things, that is, good works, gifts of God, and the saints themselves, are the beauty of the house of God, inasmuch as divine grace shines in them. This grace beautifies like a light.** Aquinas names the following conditions of beauty— **first, integrity or completeness, for broken things are ugly; second, due proportion and harmony; third, brightness and color.** In addition, he names variety as belonging to beauty. **Variety belongs to beauty, as the Apostle says: "In a great** house there are not only vessels of gold and silver, but also of wood and clay." Furthermore, beauty has a cosmic dimension to it. **Beauty establishes the integrity of things in themselves, and also their participation in the whole, each in its own style, not with uniformity.**

Beauty is our origin; beauty is our destiny; beauty is our path along the way. We are here to learn this and to make it happen.

Hildegard of Bingen says:

> **Glance at the sun.**
> **See the moon and the stars.**
> **Gaze at the beauty of earth's greenings.**
> **Now, think.**
> **What delight God gives to humankind with all these things.**
> **Who gives all these shining, wonderful gifts, if not God?**

Meister Eckhart says: **Grace pours all beauty directly into . . . the kingdom of the soul.** He calls beauty salvific when he declares: **This, then, is salvation: When we marvel at the beauty of created things and praise the beautiful providence of their Creator.**

The Vedas celebrate the **Path of Splendor** wherein the sage **perceives the divine presence in all that is splendid and beautiful in the universe. . . . The Path of Splendor is the path of the sage as a poet. Spiritual consciousness on this plane is essentially poetic consciousness. The poet-sage expresses his exquisite astonishment before the visions of glory and wonder. The source of all splendor is light. Hence light is the central object of admiration for the poet-sage. Light is also the symbol for all splendor and glory of the spirit.**

A Vedic hymn follows:

**All shine by his shining,
And by his splendor all the world is splendid.**

In response to this poem, a Commentator says: **The universe reflects divine splendor. . . . The eternal Law manifests itself in nature, making its beauty and glory. In its application to life eternal law makes virtuous conduct—goodness. Hence the beautiful and the good are but two aspects of Law, cosmic and moral. Cosmic lawlessness is chaos, and moral lawlessness evil.** Beauty affects our ethics, in the Hindu tradition: **the three principal values or ultimates [are] Goodness, Beauty, and Truth.** In addition, **God (Indra) is called a dancer. Dancing, the beauty of movement—the rhythm of life, is attributed to the Divine.**

Similarily, Kabir says:

**Do not go into the garden of flowers!
O Friend! go not there;
In your body is the garden of flowers.
Take your seat on the thousand petals of the lotus,
and there gaze on the Infinite Beauty.**

Rabbi Heschel believes that modern society has stunted beauty and withdrawn from the sublime because everything has become utilitarian. *The obsession with power* **has completely transformed the life of man and dangerously stunted his concern for beauty and grandeur. . . . When man looks only at that which is useful, he eventually becomes useless to himself.** To return to the sublime would be to reignite our capacity for the spiritual. **What we encounter in our perception of the sublime, in our radical amazement, is a spiritual suggestiveness of reality, an** *allusiveness* **to transcendent meaning. The world in its grandeur is full of a spiritual radiance.**

This experience of the sublime and of transcendent beauty provides **the root of man's creative activities in art, thought, and noble living.** Therefore, beauty is a necessary part of being human. One reason Heschel believes we have lost an experience of the sublime is that our modern scientific worldview exalts the quantitative over the qualitative, and the sublime is not quantitative but qualitative. We have lost a sense of wonder. **The immense preciousness of being . . . is not an object of analysis but a cause of wonder.** Ethics also requires this sense of the sublime, for **there is no sense of responsibility without reverence for** *the sublime in human existence.* From beauty, then, we undergo radical amazement and wonder and it is in these encounters that the nobility of our species comes to life and fruition. Here transformation and transcendence meet.

Psychologist Rollo May told the story of how he was invited to be on a talk show to discuss his new book but when he told the title of the book—*My Quest for Beauty*—his appearance was canceled. Why is that? Our culture is not at home with the power or the meaning of beauty. **Most people in our culture suppress their reactions to beauty; it is too soul-baring,** he writes. Yet, when people come to their last days, they become very sensitive to beauty. I remember a story my sister told of being with my father when he was about to go into the hospital for cancer. He was in her backyard, staring at the beauty of the Wisconsin hills. He did not want to leave. He did not want to let the beauty go. May comments: **When people are on the verge of death they think, strangely enough, about beauty. Many of these thoughts are about how beautiful is this earth that they are about to leave.** May tells of a friend who was dying of cancer in his forties. He spent his last days in a deck chair on the sun-porch, thinking and saying out loud, "How beautiful each day is!" The psychologist Abraham Maslow, having undergone a severe heart attack, wrote a letter to May from his home on the Charles river in Cambridge. "My river has never seemed so beautiful," he wrote. Death heightens our awareness of beauty. How wonderful it would be if we incorporated this awareness daily into our lives *before we die.* **We are part of a universe of beauty,** says May. We have a right to celebrate that, and a need. What after all is beauty? May says: **Beauty is the experience that gives us a sense of joy and a sense of peace simultaneously. Other happenings give us joy and afterwards a peace, but in beauty these are the same experience. Beauty is serene and at the same time exhilarating; it increases one's sense of being alive. Beauty gives us not only a feeling of wonder; it imparts to us at the same moment a timelessness, a repose—which is why we speak of beauty as being eternal.**

15.

SACRED SEXUALITY

He brings me to the winehall,
Gazing at me with love.
Feed me raisincakes and quinces!
For I am sick with love.

O for his arms around me,
Beneath me and above!
O women of the city,
Swear by the wild field doe
Not to wake or rouse us
Till we fulfill our love.

The sound of my lover
coming from the hills
quickly, like a deer
upon the mountains
Now at my windows,
walking by the walls,

> here at the lattices
> he calls—
> *"Come with me,*
> *my love,*
> *come away. . . ."*
> —Song of Songs, 2:4–10

Is sexuality sacred? Surely it is meant to be.

The late monk Bede Griffiths was interviewed shortly before he died in his beloved ashram in India a few years ago, and he was asked about sexuality. His answer was as follows: **Sexuality is too powerful a force to deny or put aside on the one hand; but it is also too powerful a force to let run our lives on the other. So what shall we do?** *We must consecrate it,* he said. An act of consecration is not an act of *making sacred* but an act of *reminding* us of the sacredness of sexuality. A power like sexuality can be taken for granted and consecrating it makes taking for granted more difficult.

Sexuality is *already* sacred, for it is part of the glory of the universe, a rather recent invention of our universe that profoundly increased the novelty and diversity of creatures. It is sacred because it is so deep a part of creativity and of our human personalities. It is sacred because it is God-given and because sacred beings receive their existence from it: children, the carrying on of our tribes and species and selves, the family; but also the sacred being called human imagination, play, communication, love.

Why need we consecrate sexuality if sexuality is already sacred? The power of sexuality is such that we can fall either into control—using this power as a weapon for our own ends—or into being controlled—letting this power dictate our lives and choices. In other words, addiction.

Etymologically, the word "consecrate" means "to make holy with" or "to be holy with." Thus the consecration of sexuality makes us mindful of the blessing that sexuality is. It is a sacramentalizing of sexuality. When we fail to honor the sacredness of sexuality, when we "secularize" it or remove the sense of awe and sacred from it, then we make our lives less than human, less than everything we need to be. We render sexuality something external and superficial, we withdraw our spiritual energy from it, and it becomes a kind of loose cannon (no Freudian pun intended), a power that runs our lives for us. A quite pitiful situation follows wherein we either run on energy that is sexually deficient or we run on energy that is too sexually volatile and that blocks out other energy sources in our lives. Finding the "middle way," the way of both honoring our sexual energy and also making room for other

energy sources in our lives, can be a lifetime process. One more reason for consecrating our sexuality. The traditional ritual for this consecration has been known in
the West as either 1) marriage or 2) vows of celibacy. Today (and no doubt in olden
days as well) there is also a degree of promising or "living together" or "getting to
know one another" that precedes a marriage commitment.

If sexuality is as basic to personal, social, tribal, and species survival as it seems
to be, then surely spiritual traditions the world over have had something to say
about it that might still be of interest to us today.

Ancient teachings of sexuality among indigenous peoples and among goddess civilizations do not connect sexuality merely to individual psychology. Rather, sexuality is placed in a cosmic context. Sexuality is part of what we share in common not only with animals but with plants, flowers, trees, and the seasons. Archeologist Marija Gimbutas put it this way: **In prehistoric art, pregnant women, double eggs, and excited men are not sex symbols in the twentieth-century sense. Our European forebears were more philosophical; there was no element of obscenity in their art. Prehistoric fertility symbols are symbols of potency, abundance, and multiplication, concerned with the perpetuation of life and the preservation of life forces constantly threatened by death.**

Fertility symbols are seasonal, representing dying and awakening nature. Mother Earth rises as a young goddess in all her splendor in the spring and becomes an old hag in the fall, but her spring/summer pregnancy is the holiest time there is. Male divinities are allegorized as emerging and dying vegetation spirits.

Gimbutas insists that fertility is not the same thing as sexuality—especially in a time of the burgeoning of agriculture. **Fertility was not sexuality; it was multiplication, growing, flourishing. To this class of symbols belong the male deities of rising, flourishing, and dying vegetation: the young, strong, flourishing god and the old, sorrowful, dying god.**

There seem to be powerful lessons here for our reunderstanding of sexuality and the sacred. What made sexuality sacred in the past was its link to the sacred cycles of the earth; what made it sacred was its link to cosmic forces greater than all of us. There lay its sublimity, its awe and wonder. Says Gimbutas: **Fertility is only one among the goddess's many functions. It is inaccurate to call Paleolithic and Neolithic images "fertility goddesses," as is still done in archeological literature. Earth fertility became a prominent concern only in the food-producing era; thence it is not a primary function of the Goddess and has nothing to do with sexuality.** The idea that the goddess needed a husband was introduced in Greece where sexual love was linked to a patriarchal ideology. Greek

Hera became the wife of Zeus, but Zeus seduced or raped hundreds of other god-
desses and nymphs in order to establish himself. **Everywhere in Europe, the Earth
Mother lost her ability to give birth to plant life without intercourse with the
Thunder God or god of the Shining Sky in his spring aspect.**

The earth is sacred. Therefore the actions of earth are sacred. All things are interconnected. Among these is sexuality. **The process of seasonal awakening,
growing, fattening, and dying was seen as connecting humans, animals, and
plants: the pregnancy of a woman, the fattening of a sow, the ripening of fruits
and crops were interrelated, influencing each other. . . . The pregnancy or the
fatness of a woman or an animal was considered to be as holy as the pregnancy
of the earth before her flowering in the spring. Each protuberance in nature,
be it a mound, a hill, on a menhir or on a female body—belly, buttocks,
breasts, knees—was sacred.**

In the *Zohar* the Jewish tradition celebrates the balance and equality of male and female when it declares: **Any image that does not embrace male and female is not a high and true image.** And again,

> **Come and see:**
> **The blessed Holy One does not place his abode**
> **in any place where male and female are not found together.**
> **Blessings are found only in a place where male and female are found,**
> **A human being is only called Adam**
> **when male and female are as one.**

Further, the *Zohar* honors the presence of *Shekinah* in the midst of human lovers when it tells the story of the birth of Moses.

> ***Shekinah* was present on their bed**
> **and their desire joined with her.**
> **Therefore *Shekinah* never left the son they engendered,**
> **confirming what is written:**
> **"make yourselves holy and you will be holy". . . .**
> **Their desire focused on joining *Shekinah*;**
> **so *Shekinah* joined in the very act they were engaged in.**

It is said that *Shekinah* is present **where two or more are gathered together.** Interestingly, Christ-followers have applied this saying to the Christ: Where two are three are gathered in his name he is in their midst. In both cases, *Shekinah* and the Christ, lovers are being told that they are not alone. Holy forces and sacred spirits and presences beyond themselves are also at work and play when sexuality is celebrated.

The *Kabbalah* calls sexual union **very holy** and even uniquely holy. It, too, celebrates the sacredness of human sexuality and the presence of *Shekinah* in its midst when it declares:

> **When sexual union is for the sake of heaven,**
> **there is nothing as holy or pure.**
> **The union of man and woman, when it is right,**
> **is the secret of civilization.**
> **Thereby, one becomes a partner with God in the act of Creation.**
> **This is the secret meaning of the saying of the sages:**
> **"When a man unites with his wife in holiness, the divine presence is**
> > **between them."**

The writer of the *Kabbalah* gets very impassioned in defending the sacredness of sexuality against Aristotle, who said the sense of touch is shameful, and Moses Maimonides, a Jewish medieval philosopher who followed Aristotle on this topic. **If that Greek scoundrel believed that the world was created with divine intention, he would not have said what he said. But we, who possess the holy Torah, believe that God created everything as divine wisdom decreed. God created nothing shameful or ugly. If sexual union is shameful, then the genitals are too. Yet God created them! How could God create something blemished, disgraceful or deficient? After all, the Torah states: "God saw everything that he had made, and behold: very good!"**

The *Kabbalah* interjects ethics into sexuality when it uses the phrase "when it is right" and again when it says: **Sexual union is holy and pure, when performed in the right way, at the right time, and with the right intention. Let no one think that there is anything shameful or ugly in such union. God forbid!**

Much of Judaism's celebration of sexuality comes from the great love poem of the Bible, the Song of Songs (or Song of Solomon). That great poem, or rather collection of poems, while often allegorized to be about God's love for the soul, is, in fact, about how the divine love is present when humans are in love and expressing their love. There are three voices in the poem: a singular female, a singular male and a chorus or group of speakers. The woman has the most to say, and many scholars believe that a woman or women were crafters of most of the poetry in it. The poem captures the wildness, the gentleness, the surprise, the anguish, the sensuousness, the fear of losing, the wonder, the cosmology of human sexual love. It still works, after all these centuries. I know this because just recently I did a weekend retreat at which we enacted this poem in one evening, creating the chorus and speakers from among the retreatants. The leader of the choral rendition of the Song of Songs was Mr. David Granville, who is director of the arts council for the city of Buffalo and a graduate of our program in Creation Spirituality. Sitting in the audience, hearing the Song recited in 1999, and feeling my and other retreatant responses to it, I tasted still again what a powerful poem it is. And what a need this is for our society: to hear sexuality honored in a sacred context again.

Interestingly, the poem "does not seem to be about marital love" but about love. The poem is soaked in Creation imagery—clearly whoever wrote it understood human love in the context of the other love going on in the cosmos. There are references to over twenty-five varieties of trees, shrubs, flowers, herbs, fruits, nuts, spices, and nectars, and among the animals celebrated are the mare, dove, gazelle, deer, nightingale, turtledove, fox, lion, leopard, and raven. Metaphors of human arts and architecture mingle with these other symbols of nature. Eroticism is spoken of in images of eating and drinking, entering the garden and playing in a bed of leaves. Indoors, outdoors, in the city and in the country, these lovers pursue and are pursued by their passion for each other. "The Song eloquently expresses some of the paradoxes of erotic love: conflict that intensifies passion, painful separation that heightens the pleasure of union, intimate bonding with the other that gives the individual courage to stand alone."

There is an amazing level of gender balance in the poem: The woman is not passive or withdrawing but very active in the whole poem. Sometimes coy, she is also indignant, defiant toward her brothers who try to coax her out of love. "Self-assertion" is how one scholar names the attitude both lovers hold against a sometimes hostile world, one that does not want to hear about love. Their romance is a secret affair that can be consummated only out of the way of public scrutiny. This makes for some of the drama the poem contains. The Song offers "a thoroughly nonsexist view of heterosexual love. Women in the Song speak as assertively as men, initiating action at least as often; so too, men are free to be as gentle, as vulnerable, even as coy as women. Men and women are mutually praised for their sensual appeal and beauty."

Furthermore, there is no anthropocentrism. A relationship of equality seems to exist between the human and the rest of nature. "Consonant with this mutuality between the sexes, in the world of the Song no domination exists between human beings and the rest of nature; rather, interrelationship prevails." There is no hierarchical domination in the Song. It "expresses mutuality and balance between the sexes, along with an absence of stereotyped notions of masculine and feminine behavior and characteristics."

In the Song, women are central and not on the sidelines as in so much of biblical literature. "Unlike most of the Bible, the Song of Songs views us women speaking out of their own experiences and their own imaginations, in words that do not seem filtered through the lens of patriarchal male consciousness." What is obvious is that the Song "is primarily concerned not with marriage or religious ritual but with the various emotions of erotic love." It contains no mention of the name of God in it. Following are two of the lyric poems that make up the Song.

He brings me to the winehall,
Gazing at me with love.
Feed me raisincakes and quinces!
For I am sick with love.

O for his arms around me,
Beneath me and above!

O women of the city,
Swear by the wild field doe
Not to wake or rouse us
Till we fulfill our love.

The sound of my lover
coming from the hills
quickly, like a deer
upon the mountains
Now at my windows,
walking by the walls,
here at the lattices
he calls—
"Come with me,
my love,
come away
For the long wet months are past,
the rains have fed the earth
and left it bright with blossoms
Birds wing in the low sky,
dove and songbird singing
in the open air above
Earth nourishing tree and vine,
green fig and tender grape,
green and tender fragrance
Come with me,
my love, come away."

In what may be a gross understatement, Marcia Falk proposes that the Song, ancient as it is, may have "something new to teach about the redemption of sexuality and love in our fallen world." The Song's treatment of nature together with human sexuality, of equality of the sexes, of the shamelessness of eroticism, of dangers and fears associated with sexual relationship, of the Divine without being named—all this is still a challenge for our spiritual traditions: to include the sexual with the sacred. Still another domain that remains unexplored, one that the Song address indirectly, is that of homosexual love. It is hard to imagine that religion that cannot deal with the sacred aspect of heterosexual love is in any position to pronounce about homosexual love either.

This past year, as themes for our Techno Cosmic Masses, we celebrated on Father's Day "The Return of the Sacred Masculine," and on another Sunday "The Return of the Divine Feminine" and on another "The Return of the Green Man." Each ritual was deeply felt and entered into by a great variety of worshipers ranging from Christian to pagan, from Jewish to Buddhist, from Baptist to Catholic. For the Divine Feminine Mass we gathered hundreds of pictures of the Goddess in her many, many guises from all around the world, pictures including Tara and Mary, the Black Madonna and the Neolithic cave paintings. I was profoundly moved, praying and dancing as we were, in the context of this ancient and sacred and *neglected* holy parthenon. How important it was that both women *and* men welcomed the Goddess back, the sense of the Divine Feminine that has been so neglected especially in the modern era.

Equally so for the return of the Sacred Masculine. It is evident to anyone who looks at our culture at all seriously that the young men are in trouble. They lack mentors, they lack direction, they often lack fire. I believe that our relegating the Sacred Masculine to the "Father in heaven" and then telling our young men that, by the way, the heavens are dead, inert, and a junkyard for the machine parts of the universe—this lie more than any other has rendered men spirit-less and without a sense of their own Sacred Masculinity. With the illusion of a machine universe and a dead and deadening universe now displaced by today's Creation story from science, we can open the heavens up again to the profound beauty, wonder, life and death adventures that are transpiring there. This in turn will open up our souls so that they can expand again and grow deeply. There lies one important avenue for the return of the Sacred Masculine.

For the Green Man Mass, several male liberation groups participated and offered leadership in drumming, chanting, and exchange of poetry, this with the pictures of the many Green Men from the medieval Cathedrals being displayed on the screens and with deep dancing in the sacred presence of this almost forgotten image that connects the male and nature, the human and the vegetative world.

Sexuality is so deep and so great a gift that it is about far more than sex. It is about the sacred, it is about the Divine, it is about Creation. That is the message from the *Song of Songs* in the Hebrew Bible, but it is also the message from spiritual traditions the world over. Our sexuality deserves to be resacralized. It is time to bring the sacred to it and allow it to lead us to the sacred once again.

Perhaps, if Christians were more at home with the *sacredness* of our sexuality, our culture would be less invested in the pornography industry than it is. Perhaps, too, we would have more energy for service in the world, for a repressed sexuality or a second chakra ignored will result in less energy in one's remaining chakras. We would have less passivity and less couchpotatoitis.

The sins that the Catholic church has committed against the sacredness of sexuality seem to me to be greater than what we commit in the name of love. In a poem called "Mission Boys and Mission Girls," a Lakota poet named Tim Giago lays bare some of the sickness he experienced as a boy raised in a Catholic school.

> **Even at the movies on Sunday night,**
> **We were segregated by the priests,**
> **And could only watch across the gym floor,**
> **Our girl friends on the other side.**
> **We felt the pains of youthful love,**
> **The emptiness of separation,**
> **But we were never told why.**
> **Why was it wrong for us to love?**

To want to be together,
Made to feel our love was evil,
Instead of a natural feeling
An Indian boy felt for an Indian girl,
With all of the emotions,
A Lakota heart could suffer.
The scars that came were deep,
Many of us never recovered,
From the trauma of growing up,
With a rope around our necks,
Ignorant of the emotions caused by love,
Yet trying to fulfill a deep commitment,
We never really understood.

These attitudes toward youth and sexuality demonstrate a sickness that unfortunately is still with many ecclesiastics to this day. As I write this, this very morning the headlines in the local paper are that a Roman Catholic bishop of the diocese in which I am writing this book has admitted to having sexually abused one of his priests several times. This priest is suing the bishop, and the bishop has stepped down from being bishop. I am struck by the hypocrisy and silliness of a church that demands celibacy of all its clergy but does not teach them how to be celibates. The scandal is exacerbated by the hypocrisy of a church that is becoming daily more and more homophobic when so many of its clergy, bishops, and cardinals are homosexual, some practicing and some not. This is the same church that just the previous week disbanded a thirty-year ministry carried on by a priest and a sister to educate Catholic parishioners about homosexuality called New Ways ministry. This same church, a year ago, disbanded an entire parish in Rochester, New York, that was vital and alive and inclusive. Why? Because the parish accepted homosexual persons into its liturgies. With this latest episcopal scandal I am reminded of the heterosexual scandal in Ireland a few years back wherein a bishop admitted to having fathered a son with an American divorcée and was expelled from the episcopacy. The result of this hypocrisy in Ireland has been the virtual abandonment of the institutional church by the young generation who are wisely seeking their Celtic spiritual roots and other forms of community and spirituality.

When will all this sexual nonsense cease? Only when sexuality is allowed into the realms of the sacred again. In all these blatant failures and hypocritical stances by the Roman Catholic church, including its immoral defense of forbidding birth control, I am reminded of the Celtic poet early in this century who predicted that the church, having weathered high seas and storms for nineteen centuries, would crash on a rock in the twentieth century. The name of the rock would be: Sexuality.

Among the indigenous traditions that teach a different view of the sacred and the sexual than mainstream Christianity is the Celtic tradition. According to John O'Donohue, the old Irish tradition boasted **a wonderfully vibrant acknowledgment of the power of Eros and erotic love.** He cites from "The Midnight Court," an eighteenth-century poem that offers a **ribald celebration of the erotic** lacking any **intrusion of the frequently negative language of morality, which tries to separate sexuality into pure and impure.**

> **Amn't I plump and sound as a bell,**
> **Lips for kissing, and teeth for smiling,**
> **Blossomy skin and forehead shining,**
> **My eyes are blue and my hair is thick**
> **and coils and streams about my neck;**
> **A man who's looking for a wife**
> **Here's a fact that will keep for life;**
> **Hand and arm and neck and breast**
> **Each is better than the rest;**
> **Look at that waist! My legs are long**
> **Limber as willows and light and strong.**

In an understatement, O'Donohue admits that **modern Ireland has had a complex and painful journey toward the recognition and acceptance of Eros.** After all, it was the Irish church that picked up where the Jansenists of France left off: telling us the body was our problem and sex was the enemy. O'Donohue believes that the true mystical tradition calls for a **transfiguration of the senses** in preference to any denial of them. Another Celtic scholar also notices a great distinction between the dominant Roman view on the body as represented by St. Augustine and the attitudes of the Celtic mind. Thomas Cahill comments that the Celtic **sensuous reveling in the splendors of the created world** would most likely have unnerved Augustine, who would have sniffed heresy in the "Breastplate" poem. There is absolutely no negative treatment of the temptations of the flesh in St. Patrick's own story. **Patrick is silent about sex as are the Gospels**—though he does react with outrage when his female converts are made into sex slaves by the soldiers of Coroticus. Cahill observes: **It may simply be that Patrick, in his zeal to baptize—to wash clean—Irish imagination, was not as sex-obsessed as his continental brethren and felt little need to stress these matters. Before his mission, Irish sexual arrangements were relatively improvisational. Trial "marriages" of one year, multiple partners, and homosexual relations among warriors on campaign were all more or less the order of the day. Despite Patrick's great success in changing the warrior mores of the Irish tribes, their sexual mores altered little. Even the monasteries he established were not especially notable for their rigid devotion to the rule of chastity.** Remember, too, that Celtic monasteries, such as that in which Hildegard of Bingen was raised, were mixed communities of men and women. One more evidence that the sex-obsession of the Roman Christians did not fit the mindset of the Celtic Christians.

Ninth-century Celtic philosopher John Scotus Erigena also sounds unlike Augustine. Says one scholar: "Augustine's preoccupation with the body and with heresy hardly finds an echo in Erigena. Unlike Augustine, Erigena never discusses sexual desire." Unlike Augustine and Jerome, and, as we saw, *like* Jesus and *like* St. Patrick.

In the Middle Ages, Thomas Aquinas broke with the Fathers of the church, including the Augustinian mainstream teaching about sexuality. He supported the mainstream Jewish teaching when he linked the goodness of our sexuality to the goodness of Creation itself. He criticized Origen's teaching that souls were *imprisoned in their bodies out of punishment.* Aquinas strongly objects: **If, then, the union of soul and body is something penal in character, it is not a good of nature. But that is impossible, for that union is intended by nature, since natural generation terminates in it. Again, on Origen's theory, it would follow that a person's being would not be a good according to nature, yet it is said, after human beings were created: "God saw all the things that God had made, and they were very good."** Aquinas also takes on Gregory of Nyssa around the subject of the goodness of our sexuality. Gregory taught that the generation of our species in the Garden of Eden did not happen by lovemaking but somehow in the manner that angels generate. Aquinas says absolutely not. **What is natural to human beings was neither acquired nor forfeited by sin. . . . God made man and woman before sin. But nothing is void in God's works. Therefore, even if human beings had not sinned, there would have been sexual intercourse to which the distinction of sex is ordained.**

Aquinas calls our sexuality **a very great blessing** and points out that in the Creation story in Genesis the generation by plants is not singled out as a blessing but human generation is. Far from seeing intercourse as a spiritual problem, Aquinas says that **natural love is nothing else than the inclination implanted in nature by its Author. To say that a natural inclination is not well regulated is to derogate from the Author of nature.** In other words, to insult the holiness of our sexuality is to insult God.

Augustine taught that every act of sexual intercourse contained sin in it, since we "lose control." But Aquinas vehemently disagrees. **The blessing of God [regarding reproduction] in Genesis is repeated in the case of the human race . . . to prevent anyone from saying that there was any sin whatever in the act of begetting children.** Thus, the very argument Aquinas uses for our sacred sexuality is that our sexuality comes from the Author of all creation. **Certainly all the power to procreate present in us is from God. Sexual intercourse is natural to human beings by reason of their animal life, which they possessed even before sin, just as it is natural to other perfect animals. The bodily parts we possess make this clear.**

Rather than going along with the dominant teaching of *regret for our bodies* that Origen, Gregory of Nyssa, Augustine, and many other Fathers of the church taught, a teaching based on their devotion to Plato and Neoplatonism, Aquinas spent his entire life trying to fight this anti-matter bias that had developed in Christian thinking—a bias in no way present in the teachings or person of the historical Jesus. Dominic Crossan, one of the Jesus Seminar scholars, points out that *sarcophobia*, the fear of the flesh, grew and grew among Christian theologians beginning with St. Paul himself even though the historical Jesus had none of it. Aquinas tells us that this is why he consciously and deliberately chose to follow the scientist Aristotle over the dualistic Plato: because Aristotle does not denigrate matter like Plato and the Neoplatonists do. But this choice on Aquinas's part—a choice to opt for the blessing that matter is—met with powerful opposition. Aquinas paid a great price for this effort to return to Jesus' more Jewish attitude of seeing our whole nature as a blessing. The three condemnations of his work that came about swiftly on his death were all centered on his teaching of the "consubstantiality" of soul and body, spirit and matter.

Aquinas taught that marriage is meant to be a relationship of **friendship— there is a virtue proper to both husband and wife that renders their friendship delightful to each other.** He calls for a special love between couples. **Superabundant love is not designed by nature for many but for one only. This is evident in sexual love, according to which one man cannot at the same time love many women in an excessive manner. Therefore, the perfect friendship of the virtuous cannot extend to many persons.** He is calling marriage an invitation to "perfect friendship" and "superabundant love."

Hildegard of Bingen also took a stand in favor of sacred sexuality when she fought the fight waging in her day on behalf of making matrimony a sacrament. The power structure of the celibate religious orders was split over this great debate. If marriage was declared a sacrament, would that not denigrate from the ideal of celibacy and monastic life? Would that not suggest that it was more spiritually lofty to be married than to take vows of poverty, stability, obedience and celibacy? These arguments did not persuade Hildegard. She sided with married couples, and with help from persons like herself that argument carried the day. Marriage was declared a sacrament—not nostalgia for sexual innocence however that nostalgia be wrapped. It is evident that not all church authorities since Hildegard's day have agreed with her or with the church's teaching on the holy sacrament that marriage and sexual love are.

Hildegard celebrates the equality of male/female relationship. **Now it came to pass that man lacked a help-mate that was his equal. God created this help-mate in the form of a woman—a mirror image of all that was latent in the male sex. In this way, man and woman are so intimately related that one is the work of the other. Man cannot be called man without woman. Neither can woman be named woman without man. The woman is the labor of the man. The man is an aspect of comfort for the woman. One does not have the capacity of living without the other.**

Julian of Norwich also celebrates our sensual nature. **Our sensuality is grounded in nature, in compassion and in grace. This enables us to receive gifts that lead to everlasting life. For I saw that in our sensuality God is.** Julian, following the tradition of Aquinas and repudiating that of Neoplatonism, declares that there exists a **beautiful oneing that was made by God between the body and the soul.** Indeed, so aware is God of this union and so intimate is he to it, that **God is the means whereby our substance and our sensuality are kept together so as to never be apart.** Julian sees our sensuality as the throne of the Christ in our soul. **Our sensuality is the beautiful city in which our Lord Jesus sits and in which He is enclosed.**

Like Aquinas and the Jewish tradition, Julian attributes her gentle regard for our bodies to the regard Divinity holds for Creation itself.

Nature and Grace
are in harmony with each other.
For grace is God
as nature is God.

Nature is all good and beautiful in itself,
and grace was sent out
to liberate nature and destroy sin
and bring beautiful nature
once again to the blessed point
from whence it came:
that is, God.

Nature has been evaluated
in the fire of trying experiences
and no flaw or fault
has been found in it.

Muhammad sanctified marriage. The Qur'an celebrates marriage in the following manner: **Of Allah's signs it is that he has created mates for you of your own kind that you may find peace of mind through them, and he has put love and tenderness between you.** Husband and wife make one soul. **He it is who has created you from a single soul and made therefrom its mate, that he might incline toward her and find comfort in her.** One scholar comments that "the tone of marriage in Islam is thus one of mutual respect, kindness, love, companionship, and harmonious interaction. In her husband, the wife has a friend and partner to share her life and concerns, to cherish and protect her, and to help her bear responsibilities . . . while a man has in his wife a companion and helper who can give him peace, comfort, and repose in his struggle with the rough-and-tumble of the world's life."

Among the Sayings of the Prophet is the following: **When a man looks upon his wife and she upon him, God looks mercifully on them. When they join hands together, their sins disappear in the interstices of their fingers. When he makes love to her, the angels encircle the earth. Voluptuousness and desire are as beautiful as the mountains.**

In India, many Hindu temples honor sacred sexuality in their carvings and statues. Most temples in India dedicated to Siva have a lingam in their inner shrine. Father Bede Griffiths relates a telling story of how Europeans react to sacred temples in India that bring the sacred and the sexual together: **This has caused much feeling of horror and disgust among Europeans, especially Christians, but properly understood there is nothing "obscene" about it. It represents on the one hand the "source of life" and on the other hand the absolute "formless" Divinity, the stone barely shaped in contrast with the wealth of imagery elsewhere.** Often in the very center of the shrine—the *garbha griha*—that represents the "cave of the heart" there may be nothing but a lingam representing the absolute Godhead. Griffiths comments: **The sexual origin of the lingam is, of course, obvious, but this only brings out the extraordinary depth of understanding in ancient India. Sex was always regarded as something "holy"—I think that it still is, except where the Indian spirit has been corrupted by the West. The lingam was therefore a natural symbol of the sacred "source of life."**

Father Bede tells the story of sitting by a river at a shrine which contained only a roughly carved lingam and yoni, the male and female organs. **The natural reaction of a European is to think that this is something "obscene"; but to me it seemed a touching expression of the sense of the "sacred," the awareness of the essential holiness of nature and of faith in her generative powers.** He draws a larger conclusion from this observation. **Perhaps this is the deepest impression left by life in India, the sense of the sacred as something pervading the whole order of nature. Every hill and tree and river is holy, and the simplest human acts of eating and drinking, still more of birth and marriage, have all retained their sacred character.** What follows from this is a pervasive sense of *the beauty of life*. Sexuality is part of beauty. But as we saw in the previous chapter, if a culture loses beauty as a significant philosophical and theological category, then how can it understand sexuality?

Griffith connects beauty and the sacred in India. **It is this that gives such an indescribable beauty to Indian life, in spite of the poverty and squalor. Wealth** and sanitation are of little value if this sense of the sacred is to be lost in the process. Perhaps there is nothing which the Western world needs more urgently to recover than this sense of the sacred. . . . It is there that the West needs to learn from the East the sense of the "holy," of a transcendent mystery which is immanent in everything and which gives an ultimate meaning to life.

An African proverb honors the cosmology of sexuality when it says:

**Think of how a baby is formed in the womb;
there is power greater than husband and wife.**

The African view of sexuality is summarized by Pere Tsasa, who believes that "life is essentially a participation and a sharing." Sexuality and fecundity are intrinsic to participation and sharing. Indeed, they are our response to the gifts of God, cosmos, ancestors, parents, and community. One who receives is called to share one's gifts. "It is thus that participation in the life received from God, the ancestors, the parents, the community, and the cosmos demands that the duty of motherhood-fatherhood, or fecundity, be assumed." This same power of fecundity is about sharing. "Having gratuitously received the gift of life the individual feels the desire to have others also participate in the joy of living, the desire to give freely the life that she/he has freely received."

In Taoism, sex was considered a vehicle for enlightenment. Sex was to be properly harnessed because sexuality and spirituality went together. Because the sexual act was an act of meditation, spiritual preparation before intercourse and attention and focus during the act were expected for the supreme results of physical and spiritual health. The key is that the partners hold back their sexual fluids. One learned to do this by controlling the breath and by applying pressure to a certain pressure point. Spiritual discipline was required. "To the ancient Taoist, sex was a means to salvation, and he advocated that it be practiced in calm surroundings. The practitioner was cautioned never to forget that coitus was only a means to an end and that the end was health, well-being, and long life."

Delores Lachapelle, in her book, *Sacred Land, Sacred Sex,* states that because Taoism understood everything in terms of cosmology, and understood the creation of the universe itself to be sexual, that is, to have contained both Yin (female) and Yang (masculine) energies working together, Taoism developed "the most sophisticated methods of any culture for dealing with sexual energy within the human community itself and between humans and nature." Lovemaking could itself be taught as a ritual and Chinese sexual rituals rendered sex itself "numinous." Taoism talks of our "lower mind" and "other brain" located four fingers below the navel and insists that our "sacred middle" is the very place where the flow of energy happens between us and the cosmos. In other words, the second chakra is honored as a holy and sacred place to tune in to the grace of creation. Ejaculation is exclusively for having children; other sex should be accomplished without ejaculation. The benefits for birth control are obvious. By pressing the *tu-mo* acupressure point (located halfway between the anal opening and the scrotum) not only is ejaculation thwarted but orgasm is increased. The sexual organs themselves are given poetic names in the ancient sexual manuals of Taoism. The male organ is called "the jade peak" and the women's organs are called "jade cavern," "jade gate," "anemone of love." The womb is called "cinnabar cave" and the opening to the womb, "flower heart."

Wouldn't it be a wonderful thing to include these teachings of spiritual discipline and birth control and joy for our bodies as part of the sexual instruction of our young people?

16.
DYING, RESURRECTION,
REINCARNATION

Your existence my dear, O love my dear,
Has been sealed and marked
"Too sacred," "too sacred," by the Beloved—
To ever end!
Indeed, God has written a thousand promises
All over your heart
That say,
Life, life, life
Is far too sacred to
ever end.
—Hafiz, *God's Bucket*

Death and its aftermath are included as important teachings in all the world's spiritual traditions as far back as we can trace them. The oldest ones, of course, are not recorded in written texts but in pottery, ceramic and cave wall paintings, and in burial mounds.

Marija Gimbutas summarizes her life's work in the archaeological field amidst these ancient pots and testimonies this way: **Throughout prehistory images of death do not overshadow those of life: they are combined with symbols of regeneration. The Death Messenger and the Death-wielder are also concerned with regeneration.** Many versions of symbols of regeneration were created during the Neolithic period. **Graves and temples assumed the shape of the egg, vagina, and uterus of the Goddess or of her complete body. The megalithic passage graves of Western Europe quite probably symbolized the vagina (passage) and pregnant belly (*tholos,* round chamber) of the Goddess.**

The Goddess herself played an important role in the passage from life to death. **The Life and Birth Giver can turn into a frightening image of death**—these include images of the Goddess as a bird of prey or a poisonous snake. In mid-fifth century B.C.E. masks of the Goddess of death were fearsome. Above all, the subjects of life, birth, death, and regeneration were felt and presented in terms of the cosmic cycles in nature. That was the key statement about death: that we were following the life cycles of Creation itself. **Whirls, crosses, and a variety of four-corner designs are symbols of the dynamism in nature which secures the birth of life and turns the wheel of cyclic time from death to life, so that life is perpetuated.** A bias in favor of transformation lies with the Goddess, for **in these series of transformations, the most dramatic is the change from one life form into countless others: from a bucranium to bees, butterflies, and plants, epiphanies of the Goddess of Regeneration.**

Not all death and regeneration ceremonies we have evidence of would be something we would want to imitate today. According to Gimbutas, there is evidence of human sacrifice in several sacred cave sights, sacrifices that were part of the Regeneration Mysteries. For example, in Scaloria in Manfredonia, southeastern Italy, remains from about 5600 B.C.E. include 137 skeletons arranged in a mass burial with peculiar cuts at the base of their skulls. **Perhaps Death and Regeneration Mysteries were celebrated here. The cycle of regeneration is mirrored in the cave's** uterine shape, the life water below, and the stalagmites in a constant process of formation.

Another cave containing human sacrifice near Bamberg, Germany, dates to around 5000 B.C.E. There, 36 girls and women between one and 45 years of age, and two men were found and recognized to be sacrificial victims. **The vases deposited in the cave were decorated with hourglass and triangle motifs suggesting that the sacrificial ritual was connected to regeneration.**

Crypts abound from these early days that indicate a belief in resurrection of some kind. At Knossos in Crete, for example, subterranean rooms are decorated with the double ax symbolizing a horizontal hourglass or butterfly of resurrection. In these rooms, initiation ceremonies most likely took place—ceremonies which depicted for persons going through passages in life their own ongoing death and resurrection. **It seems probable that pillar crypts symbolized the womb of the Goddess Creatrix, where transformation from death to life took place and where initiation rites were performed. The participants returned to the womb—that is "died"—and after the ceremonies were reborn again.** Gimbutas believes that the phallic pillars in Neolithic Sardinia, Corsica, and Malta that were connected with tomb and temple architecture were not so much symbols of sexual procreation as of vitality **for sustaining life and assuring regeneration.**

Mesoamerican poets raise questions around death that are universal.

> Where do we go, oh! where do we go?
> Are we dead beyond, or do we yet live?
> Will there be existence again?
> Will the joy of the Giver of Life be there again?
> Do flowers go to the region of the dead?
> In the Beyond, are we dead or do we still live?
> Where is the source of light, since that which gives life hides itself?

The poet Nezahualcoyotl goes from sadness to hope in his poems about death.

> Thus we are,
> we are mortal,
> men through and through,
> we all will have to go away,
> we all will have to die on earth.

> Within myself I discover this:
> indeed, I shall never die,
> indeed, I shall never disappear.
> There where there is no death,
> there where death is overcome,
> let me go there.

The poet finds a sense of resurrection in acts of art and beauty.

> My flowers will not come to an end,
> my songs will not come to an end,
> I, the singer, raise them up;
> they are scattered, they are bestowed.

Among the Hopi people the experiences of emergence and rebirth pervade every progressive cycle of life. The spiritual rebirth of the community nurtures the rebirth of every individual. Ceremonies held in the kiva, which represents the Earth Mother, assist this spiritual rebirth. The Hopis draw their teachings from their observation of nature around them. **All of Hopi life is part of a rhythmic cycle of generation, growth, and regeneration.** Just as seeds and seasons regenerate, so do humans. This is why the ceremonies follow the seasons so carefully. The Hopis bury their dead in a seated position facing east, the direction of sunrise, so that the Spirit may rise easily and begin its journey to the Spirit world. A ladder is included as a ladder plays an important role in the kiva ceremonies as well, the climb to and fro, into and from Mother Earth.

Continuous renewal of life lies at the heart of Hopi belief. Responsibilities await the dead. **Hopi life must follow a path which coincides with the cycle of the natural world, a cycle of fertilization, birth, youth, maturity, death, and rebirth. On earth the Hopis must follow a divinely ordered Path of Life and at death they must follow the sacred path to the Spirit World where the protection and sustenance of the Hopi peoples on earth is their principal responsibility.**

In 1855, the great Chief Seattle, speaking of the **mournful memory** of his people absent from their land, had this to teach about the experience of death and regeneration. **When the last Red Man shall have perished from this earth and the memory of my tribe shall have become a myth among the White Men, these shores will swarm with the invisible dead of my tribe ... And when your children's children think themselves alone in the field, the store, the shop, upon the highway or in the silence of the pathless woods, they will not be alone. ... At night when the streets of your cities and villages are silent and you think them deserted, they will throng with the returning hosts that once filled and still love this beautiful land. ... The White Man will never be alone. ... Let him be just and deal kindly with my people, for the dead are not powerless. ... Dead, did I say? There is no death, only a change of worlds!**

When death is separated from cosmology, confusion ensues. Psychologist Stanislav Grof, in his work *Books of the Dead: Manuals for Living and Dying,* rightly points out that the modern era, with its scientific and industrial revolutions, brought about for humanity "a progressive alienation from [our] biological nature and loss of connection with the spiritual source." Three basic areas in particular that link humans to the rest of nature—"birth, sex, and death—were subjected to deep psychological repression and denial. At the same time, the spiritual awareness that had provided a sense of meaningful belonging to the cosmos was replaced by atheism, or superficial religious activities of decreasing vitality and relevance." Of course much has emerged in our culture as a response to this denial, including the work of Dr. Kübler-Ross on death and dying, Ernest Becker's work *The Denial of Death* and Raymond Moody's work *Life After Life,* which collected stories from 150 individuals who underwent "near-death" experiences.

As Grof points out, Moody's work and that of many others who have entered that burgeoning field of afterlife experience are not so much doing something new as connecting to ancient traditions. "The literature of ancient cultures, who had a remarkably sharp awareness of the spiritual and philosophical importance of death, abounds in eschatological passages." Ancient texts we can now study include the African collection of prayers, hymns, litanies, funerary texts, and incantations known as *The Egyptian Book of the Dead* or *Pert em hru* or *Manifestation in the Light* or *Coming Forth by Day.* From the East we study *The Tibetan Book of the Dead* or *Bardo Thodol* or *Liberation by Hearing on the Afterdeath Plane.* Reconstructed from pictures and texts on funeral vases in Mesoamerica is what we call the *Maya Book of the Dead.*

What is common to all these texts is that they provide what Grof calls "maps of the inner territories of the psyche" and these maps have taken on a new meaning with today's research that is focusing on non-ordinary states of consciousness. "Systematic study of the experiences in psychedelic sessions, powerful non-drug forms of psychotherapy, and spontaneously occurring psychospiritual crises showed that in all these situations, people can encounter an entire spectrum of unusual experiences, including sequences of agony and dying, passing through hell, facing divine judgment, being reborn, reaching the celestial realms, and confronting memories from previous incarnations." Grof urges us to pay attention to these experiences before we die. He echoes what many spiritual traditions teach: Meditate on death and befriend it in order to live deeply this life. Grof says: "The experiential practice of dying, or "dying before dying," has two important consequences. It liberates the individual from the fear of death and changes his or her attitude toward dying, and so prepares him or her for the experiences at the time of biological demise, and by eliminating the fear of death, it transforms the individual's way of being in the world." The use of these texts prepares one both for dying *and for living* or for enlightenment.

In Africa or Kemet (Egypt), the funerary texts were originally written exclusively for kings. We find them inscribed on the walls of certain pyramids. "These so-called 'Pyramid Texts' were produced between 2350 and 2175 B.C.E., and are among the oldest written records, not only in Egypt, but in the whole of human history." They point to a keen interest in afterlife that led to the practice of mummification, which dates to about 3100 B.C.E.

About 1700 B.C.E., the practice of burial with funerary texts was extended to other members of the nobility besides the pharaohs. "Coffin texts" were scrolls painted on the sides of wooden coffins. The oldest and youngest of the funerary texts we possess from Egypt span a period of five thousand years. "From the first to the last, the texts of *Pert em hru* reveal the unalterable belief of the Egyptians in the immortality of the soul, resurrection, and life after death." Two traditions emerge in this storytelling. One honors the sun god Ra, who traveled in a dazzling solar boat across the large arc of the Egyptian sky by day. At the end of the day the barge sank beyond the mountains of the West and entered an underworld known as *Tuat*. Tuat was a dangerous and fearful place full of treachery, demons, darkness, firepits of the damned—all enemies of Ra. Those who worshipped Ra believed that they would accompany him after death in the solar boat.

The second tradition, which is older, concerns the god Osiris who was killed and dismembered by his evil sibling Seth, who scattered his bodily members around the Nile delta. He was reassembled and resurrected by his divine sisters, Isis and Nephthys, and became the god and ruler of the Egyptian underworld. His followers expected to join him after death in a paradise modeled after the Nile Valley, which included eternal life, feasting, cruising on the celestial river, worshiping the deities. In the myth it was Osiris's son Horus who grew up to avenge his father's murder by slaying and castrating his uncle Seth. "The death and resurrection of Osiris was for the Egyptians an important archetypal pattern for survival after death. The battle between Horus and Seth became a metaphor for the cosmic battle between the forces of light and darkness, or good and evil."

In Egypt, the theme of death and rebirth was not about life after death exclusively. Initiation ceremonies in the temple mysteries of Isis and Osiris "gave neophytes the opportunity to confront death long before old age or disease made it mandatory, and to conquer it and discover their own immortality." Through these rituals the participants overcame their fear of death but also learned to alter deeply their way of living in this lifetime.

The African view of life and death is an inclusive view. As Dr. Asante puts it, **African civilizations have posited a world of the unborn, the living, and the dead as a common society. Those unborn and those who have died become ancestors and are weighty presences in African societies.** Notice that the not-yet-born as well as the deceased are part of the ancestral African tree. This certainly makes for a large sense of community, an "extended family," indeed! There is a real practice of interconnectivity and interrelationship when one grasps the unborn, the born, and the deceased in one lineage. This grasping or connecting is done primarily, of course, in ritual.

Every African ritual includes a *libation,* which is a calling on the ancestors to be present. Biased European observers of African religion talk about "ancestor worship," but no African scholar I know agrees with that language. To remember and call in is not the same as to worship. Kenyan scholar Jomo Kenyatta talks about "communion with ancestors." Literally translated from his language, a libation is "to pour out or to sprinkle beer for spirits." African philosopher John Mbiti describes the libation this way: "The departed, whether parents, brothers, sisters or children form part of the family, and must therefore be kept in touch with their surviving relatives. Libation and the giving of food to the departed are tokens of fellowship, hospitality, and respect; the drink and food so given are symbols of family continuity and contact."

What is going on is the power of remembering. "African peoples do not feel ashamed to remember their departed members of the family. Remembering them . . . is not worshipping them." Ghana psychologist William E. Abraham also elaborates on the libation tradition. It is a *respect* that is invoked by libations, respect for the ancestors. "The basis of the respect is twofold: first that the ancestors are our predecessors, our elders, and for this reason alone command our respect; and second that in their spiritual state they note more than we can, being in unhindered touch with the essence of things." It is also a kind of "family reunion" insofar as it is a remembering ceremony. The rites speciously called "ancestor-worship" are not "rites of worship but methods of communication." In the West, this honoring of ancestors is called "the communion of saints."

The book we know as the *Tibetan Book of the Dead* or *Bardo Thodol,* while based on ancient oral traditions, was put to writing by the great guru Padmasambhava in the eighth century C.E. This teacher is honored for having introduced Buddhism to Tibet and for having laid the foundations for a mix of the ancient indigenous tradition, called Bon, and Buddhism. It appears that the old religion of Bon was very concerned with life after death and had developed elaborate rituals, including sacrificing of animals and the inclusion of food, drink, and precious objects to accompany the deceased on the next journey.

The *Bardo Thodol* associates states of consciousness with the process of death and rebirth. A "bardo" is such a state of existence. We undergo it in the womb, in the dream state, in ecstatic equilibrium during deep meditation, at the moment of death, and while seeking rebirth. While the text can be interpreted as a guide for the dying, it applies to living as well. According to Buddhist understanding, death and rebirth happen constantly in our lives. (This same teaching is found in Christian mystics.) Meditation also induces such states. Thus it can be said that this book is "simultaneously a guide for the dying, for the living, and for serious spiritual seekers." These teachings are considered guides to liberation and illumination. Three bardos are described in the book: experience at the time of death; those following death; and those in the process of seeking rebirth.

The moment of death is described as a time of unreality and confusion, a losing touch with the familiar world and polarities of good and evil. There is "earth sinking into water," which occurs as one loses touch with the physical world. Next comes "water sinking into fire," when vivid emotions dissolve and objects of our love and hatred flow away. Then comes "fire sinking into air," wherein an openness occurs toward what is to come: an experience of cosmic luminosity, "an overwhelming vision of Dharmakaya, or the Primary Clear Light of Pure reality." At the time of death, a special breakthrough is often experienced. Sogyal Rinpoche describes it this way: **The Mother Luminosity is the name we give to the Ground Luminosity. This is the fundamental, inherent nature of everything, which underlies our whole experience, and which manifests in its full glory at the mo-**

ment of death. It is an experience of profound unity. "All dualities are transcended. Agony and ecstasy, good and evil, beauty and ugliness, burning heat and freezing cold, all coexist in one undifferentiated whole."

In the next two bardos one encounters divine and demonic presences as one journeys from the moment of death to the time of another rebirth. The bardo seeking rebirth has a body with unusual qualities, including unimpeded motion and the ability to penetrate solid objects. Those whose previous life was a good one will experience delightful pleasures, while those whose karma was negative will find themselves amidst many raging beasts and enemies. A Judgment Day awaits in which the Judge of the Dead examines the past actions of the individual and assigns that person, according to his or her merits or demerits, to realms into which one will be reborn. Hopefully, the next incarnation will happen in a state where more spiritual depth might be undergone while on earth.

In his most basic teachings called "The Four Noble Truths," the Buddha put great emphasis on teaching about death and suffering. **Monks, what is the noble truth about suffering? Birth is suffering, old age is suffering, death is suffering, grief, lamentation, discomfort, unhappiness and despair are suffering; to wish for something and not obtain it is suffering; briefly, the five factors of attachment are suffering.** In teaching the cessation of craving, learning to let go and let be, the Buddha was instructing us to move beyond the fear of death. **Monks, what is the noble truth about the cessation of suffering? Just the complete indifference to and cessation of that very craving, the abandoning of it, the rejection of it, the freedom from it, the aversion toward it.**

Buddha emphasized contemplating death in order to wake up. As Wes Nisker puts it, **Meditating on death brings us face-to-face with those characteristics of existence that we mostly try to avoid—the impermanence of all things, the inevitable suffering of conditioned beings, and the impersonality of the natural processes that govern all life.** Zen masters say: **Die before you die.** If we do this, when death comes we will not be such strangers. Breathing in and breathing out can itself be a practice of death. After all, isn't death our final exhalation?

Trungpa Rinpoche once gave a public lecture titled "Death in Everyday Life." Death *is* an everyday experience if we pay attention to it. Pema Chodron says: **We are raised in a culture that fears death and hides it from us. Nevertheless, we experience it all the time. We experience it in the form of disappointment, in the form of things not working out. We experience it in the form of things always being in a process of change. When the day ends, when the second ends, when we breathe out, that's death in everyday life.** Meditation helps us deal with death because **relaxing with the present moment, relaxing with hopelessness, relaxing with death, not resisting the fact that things end, that things pass, that things have no lasting substance, that everything is changing all the time— that is the basic message.** Chodron believes that **to live is to be willing to die over and over again.**

By meditating on death we learn more about the truth of life, including its impermanence and preciousness. We learn letting go and how impossible it is to cling even if we want to. But we also learn how uncommon each breath—and therefore each minute—we participate in life truly is. We learn that **the kingdom/queen-dom of God is already among us.** We learn what Eckhart taught: **Live for the sake of living.**

The pre-Columbian mythology of Mesoamerica celebrated the cycles of spiritual death and rebirth especially through the figure of Quetzalcoatl. This god, whose name means "Plumed Serpent," was understood to have created the Fifth Sun. He was also known as God of the Wind, Lord of Dawn, and Lord of the Land of the Dead. There is an understanding of Quetzalcoatl both as an historical figure (like the historic Jesus or Buddha) and as a Cosmic figure (like the Cosmic Christ or the Living Buddha). The living Quetzalcoatl was said to have been a wise, good, and pure ruler of the City of the Gods established after the fifth sun was created. However, his demonic rival got him inebriated and while in this state of intoxication, he committed incest with his sister Xochiquetzal, who was goddess of love and beauty. When he regained his sobriety and realized what he had done, he went on a very strict regimen of penance, which concluded with his throwing himself into a funeral pyre in an act of self-immolation. Eight days later, his heart rose like a flaming star and his soul journeyed through the land of the Dead. He redeemed two humans from death with his own blood and these became the first human inhabitants of earth.

Quetzalcoatl then ascended to heaven and was transformed into the planet Venus, the morning star. Thus he appears regularly in the western sky as the evening star. He then goes underground, and reappears in the eastern sky as the morning star, uniting with the rising sun. **The Quetzalcoatl myth is thus an expression of the universal theme of death and resurrection, sin and redemption, and the transfiguration of a human into god.**

What distinguishes this story from that of Isis and Osiris in Egypt is the inclusion of Venus—which is to be expected since at the latitude of Mesoamerica Venus shines in the dawn sky with great brilliance. Thus we see that this myth, like so many others involving death and rebirth, is *cosmic* in character—death and rebirth are cosmic events. To understand death and rebirth requires a cosmology. The astronomy of the Mayan people was very well developed—the eight days of Quetzalcoatl's journey underground corresponds to the disappearance of Venus that occurs after 250 days of visibility. Like the Tibetan Book of the Dead, his journey includes enounters with demonic forces that want to destroy him. But, like the Tibetan story, he also meets friendly forces on that journey. With his transformation into Venus, he consummates his journey in a state of spiritual fullness.

The Hindu tradition has long taught reincarnation. In the Baghavad Gita we hear the following instruction: **One who has taken his birth is sure to die, and after death one is sure to take birth again. Therefore, in the unavoidable discharge of your duty, you should not lament.** Arjuna is instructed on why we should not fear death: birth follows death. **As the embodied soul continuously passes, in this body, from boyhood to youth to old age, the soul similarly passes into another body at death. A sober person is not bewildered by such a change.** Life does not die, it only changes. **As a person puts on new garments, giving up old ones, the soul similarly accepts new material bodies, giving up the old and useless ones.** We have long existed and shall long exist. **Never was there a time when I did not exist, nor you, nor all these kings; nor in the future shall any of us cease to be.**

The difference between humans and gods is that the latter remember their various incarnations. **The Personality of Godhead said: Many, many births both you and I have passed. I can remember all of them, but you cannot, O subduer of the enemy!**

Yet life goes on, as the following Veda announces:

> **The Inspired self is not born nor does he die;**
> **he springs from nothing and becomes nothing.**
> **Unborn, permanent, unchanging, primordial,**
> **he is not destroyed when the body is destroyed.**

To realize the infinite is to be **freed from the jaws of death.** Another Vedic hymn honors that experience in the following manner.

> **I have known this Mighty Being**
> **refulgent as the sun beyond darkness;**
> **By knowing him alone one transcends death,**
> **there is no other way to go.**

We can trust death because the indwelling of Brahman in our spirit cannot die. An instruction from the Upanishad puts it this way: **The Spirit who is in the body does not grow old and does not die, and no one can ever kill the Spirit who is everlasting. This is the real castle of Brahman wherein dwells all the love of the universe. It is Atman, pure Spirit, beyond sorrow, old age, and death.**

In his spiritual autobiography called *Play of Consciousness,* Swami Muktananda talks about the land of the ancestors in language very similar to how African people talk about the ancestors. He says: **The world of the ancestors is as real as the mortal world; I have seen it with my own eyes.** We can and ought to relate to this ancestral world. **There can be no doubt that the various ritual offerings of water and foodstuffs that we make to our ancestors do actually reach them in a subtle form.** Our prayers truly affect our ancestors as well. **The subtle form of the offering reaches the world of the ancestors through the mantras we repeat.** Muktananda describes why it is we need to reverence our ancestors: It is they who sacrificed so much for us. **They do not think of eating, but of giving food to their children; they do not think of sleeping, but of letting their children sleep. Anything special that comes their way they give to their children to eat, and then they eat what's left. What don't parents do for their children? This is why we are always indebted to our ancestors. It is essential for a virtuous son to make offerings to his ancestors at this time.** When ancestors are invoked at ceremony and ritual, *they do come.* Is this teaching different from the commandment from Moses: **Honor thy father and thy mother?** Is not the connection to ancestors also our reverencing and gratitude to them? Is this not the meaning of the communion of saints as well?

Swami Muktananda tells a story of a meditation that took him face to face with death. In his meditation he was overwhelmed with the power of light, a **light so fierce that I could not stand it.** He lost all control and felt he was dying. **I lost all control over my body. Just as a dying man opens his mouth, spreads his arms, and makes a strange sound, so I fell down making this sort of noise.** Losing consciousness for an hour and a half, he then rose like a man from sleep. **I got up**

and laughed to myself, saying, "I just died, but now I'm alive again." I got up feeling very much at peace, very happy, and full of love. I realized that I had experienced death when I saw the unmanifest divine radiance as bright as millions of suns. I had been very frightened, but from this experience I now understood death. I realized that death is nothing but this condition. Once I had seen that sphere of unmanifest Light, I lost all fear. This experience corresponds to many stories I have listened to from people who have undergone near-death experiences.

Science today is also introducing us to new and ancient thoughts about life, death, and rebirth. There are at least three areas where this is so. First is the new cosmology wherein we are learning—much to our surprise—that not only so-called "living beings" but *all* beings undergo this pattern of living, dying, and resurrecting. I am speaking of stars, of suns, of supernovas, of fireballs. Each has their lifetime in which they strut their stuff. But it seems to come to an end for all of them. But their endtime is not final. Rather, they resurrect *in a new form.* (Once again we see that the modern idea of Francis Bacon—that form is absolute and eternal—is grossly misleading. It has no doubt filled humans with more than the usual dread of dying, and therefore with more than the usual lust for greed and power and pseudo-immortalities to put death aside.) But now we are learning that even the heavens are not eternal. But neither are they just random events. They don't just disappear. They give off progeny. Supernova explosions unleash atoms and galaxies and stars, which in turn give birth to such as *us:* earth with its amazing plethora of life forms and shapes and shades and colors. And four-legged ones and finned ones, winged ones and two-legged ones. If this is not resurrection, rebirth, or reincarnation, what is?

A second arena in which science addresses itself to the subjects of death and rebirth is in its understanding of evolution. Is reincarnation not a story of evolution? And is evolution not a story of reincarnation? Indeed, might we say that every incarnation is a kind of reincarnation because all being is some kind of recycling of being? Wes Nisker sees it that way. He writes: **Life itself seems to reincarnate in form after form, with new methods of locomotion, perception, or types of consciousness. The human condition can be seen as our shared incarnation, part of our common "evolutionary karma". . . . Within nine months we develop from a single cell to a complex mammal. . . . We share more than ninety-eight percent of our genes with chimpanzees, sweat fluids reminiscent of seawater, and crave sugar that provided our ancestors with energy three billion years before the first space station had evolved. We carry our past with us.** Thich Nhat Hanh writes in *The Heart of Understanding,* **As I look more deeply, I can see that** in a former life I was a cloud. And I was a rock. This is not poetry; it is science. This is not a question of belief in reincarnation. This is the history of life on earth.

Consider this poem from Rumi.

> Think of your soul as the source and created things as springs.
> While the source exists, the springs continually flow. . . .
> From mineral substance you were transformed to plant,
> and later to animal. How could this be hidden?
> Afterwards, as a human being,
> you developed knowledge, consciousness, faith.
> See how this body has risen from the dust like a rose?
> When you have walked on from human you will be an angel . . .
> Pass, then from the angelic and enter the Sea.
> Your drop will merge with a hundred Seas of Oman . . .
> Although your body has aged, your soul has become young.

He also says:

> We began
> as a mineral. We emerged into plant life
> and into the animal state, and then into being human,
> and always we have forgotten our former states,
> except in early spring when we slightly recall
> being green again. . . .

These poems from a thirteenth-century Sufi mystic sound uncannily like the recitation of the story of evolution that we hear today.

A third instance of science awakening to the theme of death and rebirth has to do with the systematic study of non-ordinary states of consciousness. As Stanislav

Grof puts it, **In deep meditation, psychedelic sessions, experiential psychother-apy, trance states, spontaneous psychospiritual crises ("spiritual emergen-cies"), and other similar situations, the experiences typically transcend biography and the psyche reveals its deeper dynamics. This results in a rich spectrum of phenomena that bear a close similarity to those described in spir-itual literature of all ages.**

The activation of the memory of the birth trauma or "perinatal" level of the psyche results in **profound experiences of dying and being born or reborn.** These experiences bear **a strange amalgam that combines concrete memories of biological birth with elements that are clearly archetypal and transpersonal in nature, and have a very strong spiritual overtone.** They come in four ways. The first is an experience of **the amniotic universe. Its biological basis is the situation of the original symbiotic unity with the maternal organism during foetal exis-tence. . . . It can also be associated with oceanic or cosmic experiences and states of mystical unity.** The second matrix corresponds to experiences of **cosmic engulfment and "no exit" or hell.** It relates to the beginning of uterine contrac-tions for the fetus. The beginning of labor is felt to be **a dangerous whirlpool, or as entering an ominous underworld labyrinth.** It develops into a **claustrophobic nightmare, a situation of extreme physical and emotional suffering from which there is no way out. Any contact with the Divine seems forever lost, and all of existence appears to be meaningless, absurd, and monstrous. In spiritual terminology, this is hell or the dark night of the soul.**

The third matrix concerns the propulsion through the birth canal after the cervix opens. **It is subjectively experienced as a determined death-rebirth strug-gle.** Its characteristics include crushing pressures, tension, suffocation, murderous aggression, strong sexual arousal. The visions that accompany it include fierce bat-tles, sexual and sadomasochistic scenes, **and encounter with purifying fire. Here subjects frequently identify with archetypal figures representing death and re-birth, such as Jesus, Osiris, Dionysus, Attis, Adonis, or Quetzalcoatl.** Grof sees this passage as parallel to the religious category of purgatory.

The fourth perinatal matrix concerns the actual moment of birth and emergence into existence. **The propulsion through the birth canal is completed and is followed by explosive relief and relaxation. Subjectively, this sequence is experienced as psychospiritual death and rebirth.** Visions of blinding light occur, rainbow halos, peacock designs, or glorious celestial beings. **There is a sense of spiritual liberation, divine epiphany, redemption, and salvation. The universe seems indescribably beautiful and radiant, and evil appears ephemeral and unimportant.**

Another field contributing to a fuller appreciation of life-death-rebirth knowledge is that called *thanatology* or the study of death and dying. What is being found from today's studies seems to complement and affirm the ancient traditions we have been considering. **Modern consciousness research has validated many of the claims of the great mystical traditions. It has shown that the spiritual scriptures, rather than being products of primitive minds dominated by wishful and magical thinking, describe with great accuracy experiences in nonordinary states of consciousness.** What we now understand as the cartography of near-death experiences—condensed life reviews, traveling through a dark tunnel, meeting with dead relatives or ancestors, encountering brilliant light and beauty, scenes of divine judgment—these experiences Groff believes **represent the most convincing proof that what happens in near-death experiences is more than the hallucinatory phantasmagoria of physiologically impaired brains. The similarity between these observations and the descriptions of the bardo body in the Tibetan Book of the Dead is truly astonishing.**

In Judaism, the emphasis is on *this life*. Still, in the Kabbalah, we hear mention of reincarnation from a Jewish mystical perspective. **The purpose of the soul entering this body is to display her powers and actions in this world, for she needs an instrument. By descending to this world, she increases the flow of her power to guide the human being through the world. . . . At first before descending to this world, the soul is imperfect; she is lacking something.By descending to this world, she is perfected in every dimension.** Notice in this passage how entering Creation is not an *im*perfection but a *perfection*. This is very different from the Hellenistic Neoplatonic traditions.

In the Zohar we hear talk of a life beyond this one.

It has been taught:
Happy are the righteous
for their days are pure and extend to the world that is coming.
When they leave this world, all their days are sewn together,
made into radiant garments for them to wear.
Arrayed in that garment,
they are admitted to the world that is coming
to enjoy its pleasures.

We also hear of reincarnation or resurrection.

Clothed in that garment,
they are destined to come back to life.
All who have a garment will be resurrected,
as it is written:
"They will rise as in a garment."

> Woe to the wicked of the world
> whose days are faulty and full of holes!
> There is not enough to cover them when they leave the world.

What would "coming back to life" mean? It means joining the ancestors in a very beautiful place.

> All the righteous
> who are privileged to wear a radiant garment of their days
> are crowned in that world with crowns worn by the Patriarchs
> from the stream that flows and gushes into the Garden of Eden,
> as it is written:
> "YHVH will guide you always
> and satisfy your soul with sparkling flashes."
> Happy is the destiny of Jacob!
> He had such faith that he could say:
> "I will lie down with my fathers."
> He attained that level, nothing less!
> He surpassed them, dressed in his days and in theirs!

Islam also deals with issues of death and rebirth. The Holy Qur'an says Allah will restore all things to life: **How can you disbelieve in Allah? You were without life and he gave you life, then he will cause you to die, then he will restore you to life and then to him will you be made to return.** And again, **Allah plans to preserve alive those considered dead and shows you his Signs that you may understand.** The Qur'an speaks of the resurrection day as the Day of Judgment or the "Hour" of the individual and stresses how there is no doubt that such a day will arrive. Because Allah is the "Self-Subsisting and "All-Sustaining" One, **it is he Who brings the dead to life and that he has power of all things; and that the time appointed for everything is bound to come there is no doubt in it, and that Allah will raise up those who are in their graves.**

On that Judgment Day, **those whose scales are heavy with good works will prosper; and those whose scales are light will have ruined their souls; in hell will they abide.** God will ask of us: **You tarried only a short while, if you did but understand. Did you imagine that we had created you without purpose, and that you would not be brought back to us?**

Death and resurrection also take place in this lifetime according to the Qur'an. **Only those respond to Allah's call who listen; and Allah will raise those who are dead and to him shall they be brought back.** Allah awakens people. **O ye who believe, respond to Allah and his Messenger when he calls you that he may bring you to life, and know that Allah surely supervenes between a man and his mind and that he it is unto whom you shall be gathered.**

Rumi sings about death and resurrection as a dawning.

> When you see my procession, don't cry, "Gone, gone."
> For me it is a time of meeting and reunion.
> As you lower me into the grave, don't say, "So long."
> The grave is a veil before the gathering of paradise.
> When you see that lowering down, consider a rising.
> What harm is there in the setting of a sun or moon?
> What seems a setting to you is a dawning.

Hafiz sings out about death and resurrection also.

> If your life was not contained in God's cup
>   How would you be so brave and laugh,
>   Dance in the face of death? . . .
> Your existence my dear, O love my dear,
>   Has been sealed and marked
> "Too sacred," "too sacred," by the Beloved—
>   To ever end!
> Indeed, God has written a thousand promises
>   All over your heart
>   That say,
>   Life, life, life
> Is far too sacred to
>   ever end.

In the African-American experience, the experience of slavery rendered death an everyday event. Slavery brought death so near that sorrow songs and freedom songs about death and resurrection abounded. The composers of the Spirituals knew death intimately. Howard Thurman points out that **their contact with the dead was immediate, inescapable, dramatic. The family or friends washed the body of the dead, the grave clothes were carefully and personally selected or especially made. The coffin itself was built by a familiar hand. . . . During all these processes, the body remained in the home—first wrapped in cooling sheets and then "laid out" for the time interval before burial.** Songs like the following spoke to the reality of the "death rattle" and the physical panic that was often observed of those dying.

> **I want to die easy when I die**
> **I want to die easy when I die.**
> **Shout salvation as I fly,**
> **I want to die easy when I die.**

Notice how swiftly the poet goes from *dying* to *flying*. A soaring, a release, is anticipated. So, too, is a struggle.

> **Chilly water, chilly water,**
> **Hallelujah to that lamb.**
> **I know that water is chilly and cold,**
> **Hallelujah to that lamb.**
> **But I have Jesus in my soul,**
> **Hallelujah to that lamb.**
> **Satan's just like a snake in the grass**
> **Hallelujah to that lamb.**
> **He's watching for to bite you as you pass**
> **Hallelujah to that lamb.**

One song addresses the grief of those left behind.

> You needn't mind my dying,
> You needn't mind my dying,
> You needn't mind my dying,
> Jesus goin' to make up my dying bed.

> In my dying room I know,
> Somebody is going to cry.
> All I ask you to do for me,
> Just close my dying eyes.

> In my dying room I know,
> Somebody is going to mourn.
> All I ask you to do for me,
> Just give that bell a tone.

Thurman indicates that the load of slavery was often so heavy that hope itself was lost. And yet, there was **a maniacal kind of incurable optimism that arose out of great overwhelming vitality as deep as the very well-springs of life.** Consider the following song.

> I'm so glad trouble don't last alway.
> My Lord, O my Lord, what shall I do?
> Christ told the blin' man,
>   to go to the pool and bathe,
> O my Lord, what shall I do?

Or again:

> I'm troubled in mind,
> If Jesus don't help me, I surely will die;
> O Jesus, my Savior, on thee I'll depend.
> When troubles are near me, you'll be my true friend.

Thurman points out that death often seemed like the only hope to slaves as year passed into year. Death and resurrection come to mind as one thing.

> Children, we shall be free
> When the Lord shall appear.
> Give ease to the sick, give sight to the blind,
> Enable the cripple to walk;
> He'll raise the dead from under the earth,
> And give them permission to talk.

Some songs are about release, the release that death gives. But, as Thurman points out, at least one song **belongs to that moment of heartfelt realization when it finally dawned on the soul of the slave that he _was_ free. Even here God is given the credit.**

> Slav'ry chain done broke at las'—
> Goin' to praise God 'til I die.
>
> "I did know my Jesus heard me
> 'Cause de spirit spoke to me
> An' said, 'Rise, my chile, your chillun,
> An' you too, shall be free!'"

What Thurman finds common in this very nuanced and deeply developed thanatology among the slaves was the fact that **the note of transcendence of death is never lacking—whether it is viewed merely as release or as the door to a heaven of endless joys. . . . The great idea about death itself is that it is not *the master of life*. It may be inevitable, yes; gruesome, perhaps; releasing, yes; but triumphant, NEVER. With such an affirmation ringing in their ears, it became possible for them, slaves though they were, to stand anything that life could bring against them.**

John O'Donohue describes the Celtic understanding of death and rebirth as a great **hospitality to death. When someone in the village dies, everyone goes to the funeral. First everyone comes to the house to sympathize. All the neighbors gather around to support the family and to help them. It is a lovely gift.** The tradition of the *caoineadh* is that people—usually women—would come in and keen the deceased with a high-pitched wailing cry that spoke to the heart of deep loneliness. It was a grieving ritual that let peoples' deepest feelings out. The Irish wake is meant to assure that the deceased is not left alone the night of their death. Neighbors and friends gather with the family to tell stories and to remember but also to be present for the gradual exit of the soul at death, assuring that the soul does not travel without support of the community. There is also an understanding that the dead stay on and live near the place and fields of their living places. Also, ancestors often arrive at the time of death. **When a person is close to death, the veil between this world and the eternal world is very thin. . . . Your friends who now live in the eternal world come to meet you, to bring you home.**

Death for the Celtic people was linked up with the rhythm and habits of nature. **For the Celts, the eternal world was so close to the natural world that death was not seen as a terribly destructive or threatening event.** Thus, the following poem which sees death as a return.

> **I am going home with thee, to thy home, to thy home,**
> **I am going home with thee, to thy home of winter.**
> **I am going home with thee, to thy home, to thy home,**
> **I am going home with thee, to thy home of autumn of spring and of**
> **summer.**
> **I am going home with thee, thy child of my love to thy eternal bed to**
> **thy perpetual sleep.**

Scotus Erigena sees all of Creation involved in a return to its source and origins. The sun returns daily; the seasons return, seeds become plants, which in turn flower, produce seeds, and die. Humans undergo a special return by grace called *deificatio* or deification wherein we enter the Godhead itself. This return begins in this lifetime. Erigena writes: **All of us men, without exception, shall rise again in spiritual bodies and with the wholeness of natural goods, and shall return to the ancient condition in which we were first created; but not all will be transformed into the glory of deification, which surpasses all nature and paradise. Therefore just as general resurrection is one thing and special transformation another, so return to paradise is one thing and eating of the tree of life is another.**

Perhaps it is in this context of the concern over life, death, and regeneration as well as rituals of initiation and of burial that the Christian teaching of resurrection takes on its force. Here the observation by psychologist Otto Rank that Christianity is a Goddess religion takes on special meaning. While Jesus Seminar scholars refuse to ascribe the resurrection stories of the gospels to the historical Jesus, the prominent role that these stories play would seem to indicate not only a keen interest in the subject of life, death, and what lies beyond but also some kind of response to the Goddess religions of the day that depicted assurances about life after death. Christianity democratized immortality or resurrection, promising it for all persons and all classes of persons.

There is also in the Christian teaching a rejection of any need for future human sacrifice to carry on the community's longing for regeneration. The story that Jesus was the last lamb slain in the Age of the Ram is a powerful one: There need be no more blood-lettings in the hope of regeneration.

Each of these dimensions of death finds an expression in the earliest writings of the Christian Bible, the letters of Paul. He experienced on the road to Damascus a regenerated Jesus or a risen Christ, and he made this resurrection experience a basis of his theology. **Christ is risen from the dead, and the first fruits of them that sleep; for by a human came death, and by a human came the resurrection of the dead.** Paul sees Christ's resurrection as a way that we are woken up in this life to live well. **Christ is risen from the dead by the glory of the Father, so we also must walk in the newness of life; and as he, rising from the dead, dies now no more, so let us reckon that we are dead to sin, that we may live together with him.** Paul (or the author of Ephesians) links this current resurrection to enlightenment. **Rise, you who sleep, and rise from the dead; and Christ shall enlighten you.** Paul teaches death as an initiation rite. We are to enter into the tomb with Jesus at Baptism. This means that we die before we die. Paul also taught about Jesus as the last slain victim, the last sacrifice in an era that offered animal sacrifices.

Others in the Christian tradition, of course, took Paul up on these issues around death and regeneration. These writers like to stress death as a Now experience, death as an initiation experience. The Gospel of Thomas speaks to the first resurrection when it relays this exchange between Jesus and his disciples. **His disciples said to him: On which day will the repose of the dead come about? And on which day will the new world come? He said to them: What you expect has come but you, you recognize it not.** This same gospel refers to death as a return to our origins in the following exchange. **The disciples said to Jesus: Tell us in what way our end will be. Jesus said: Have you therefore discerned the beginning in order that you seek after the end? For in the place where the beginning is, there will be the end. Happy is he who will stand boldly at the beginning, he shall know the end, and shall not taste death.**

Thomas Aquinas talks about the **first resurrection** and the **second resurrection.** He says, commenting on the text from Ephesians cited above, **This is the first resurrection: "Blessed and holy is one who has part in the first resurrection."** Aquinas teaches: **Christ's resurrection is instrumentally effective not only with respect to the resurrection of bodies, but also with respect to the resurrection of souls.** And he says, **there is a double resurrection, one of the body, when soul rejoins body, the other spiritual, when soul reunites to God. Christ's bodily resurrection produces both in us—though he himself never rose again spiritually, for he had never been separated from God.** And Saint Francis of Assisi talks about our **first death** and our **second death.**

Meister Eckhart also sees death as a return—a return to the Godhead whence we all came. Our origin was a place where there was total unity and harmony. Speaking of our origin, he says: **When I was still in the core, the soil, the stream, and the source of the Godhead, no one asked me where I wanted to go or what I was doing. There was no one there who might have put such a question to me.** Then he relates what happens when we return there. **When I come into the core, the soil, the stream, and the source of the Godhead, no one asks me where I'm coming from or where I've been. No one has missed me in the place where "God" ceases to become.**

For Eckhart, we return to our origin not just at death but also in this lifetime.

He calls this return *breakthrough*. In meditation we return to our **unborn selves**. Here we taste eternal life. **I am cause of myself according to my being, which is eternal, but not according to my becoming, which is temporal. Therefore also I am unborn, and following the way of my unborn being I can never die. Following the way of my unborn being I have always been, I am now, and shall remain eternally. What I am by my [temporal] birth is destined to die and be annihilated, for it is mortal; therefore it must with time pass away. In my [eternal] birth all things were born, and I was cause of myself and of all things.** Eckhart teaches that at death **life dies but being goes on.** His language about his "unborn self" in which "all things were born" echoes intimations of reincarnation.

Eckhart, like so many other teachers about death and rebirth that we have considered, believes that we die in this lifetime many times. His word for this death is **letting go;** and for the rebirth it is **breakthrough.** Letting go is another word for death, another avenue to rebirth. It occurs daily and not just at our physical demise. Letting go leads to breakthrough. Breakthrough is resurrection.

Breakthrough happens when we come awake, when we see things as they are, when we are *broken through* by the spirit. It happens in meditation and it happens in our processes of creativity and birthing. **A great master says that his breakthrough is nobler than his flowing out [meaning his creation], and this is true. When I flowed out from God, all things spoke: God is. But this cannot make me happy, for it makes me understand that I am a creature. In the breakthrough, on the other hand, where I stand free of my own will and of the will of God and of all his works and of God himself, there I am above all creatures and am neither God nor creature. Rather, I am what I was and what I shall remain now and forever.** What happens in these acts of breakthrough? **In this breakthrough I discover that I and God are one. There I am what I was, and I grow neither smaller nor bigger, for there I am an immovable cause that moves all things. . . . Here God is one with the spirit, and that is the strictest poverty one can find.** How often do we undergo breakthrough? Many times every day, according to Eckhart, for the person who is aware.

Eckhart sees breakthrough as a second birth, a rebirth into God. **This birth does not take place once a year or once a month or once a day but all the time. . . .** It is the divine being in us, the Cosmic Christ (or Buddha Nature) that is being born. **As often as this birth takes place, the only begotten Son is born.** We become that divine child. **Out of the purity he eternally begat me as his only begotten Son in the same image of his eternal Fatherhood, that I might become a father and beget him by whom I was begotten.** In this rebirth we become a **new Creation,** just as Jesus showed us and himself became a new Creation on his resurrection.

The *fact* of resurrection is integral to Christian faith but the *what* of it is very diversely understood. Just what form or forms resurrection takes—even the forms it took with the risen Christ in Jesus—has always been diversely held. Today, for example, people ask about the relation of resurrection to reincarnation. How different and how alike are these teachings? The Christian church has only condemned reincarnation on one occasion, that being a version put forward by Origen, a theologian in the third century. Ideas of reincarnation do appear, sometimes in the most unlikely places. Julian of Norwich, for example, writes that **we were all created at the same time; and in our creation we were knit and oned to God.**

In addition, at least three classical theological positions in Christianity speak to traditions of reincarnation. One is purgatory. If purgatory be separated from a vengeful fall and redemption ideology, a place of extreme punishment for our sins, then it becomes a teaching close to reincarnation. For what the purgatory tradition is saying is this: We are here to learn love. And if we don't learn it this time around we will learn it later—in purgatory—some time around. It may be, then, that this life as we know it is for many *their purgatory.* Quite a few people I have met would tend to agree with this assessment. It is interesting that Julian of Norwich sought for a vision of both hell and purgatory, but she could not see them. She reports: **I understood this to mean that God and all the holy ones no more talk about them than they do about the devil.**

A second bridge between reincarnation and Christian theology is around the theme of the communion of saints. That teaching is about our ancestors. It addresses the question: Where are they? What are they doing? Do they care about us? What about their beauty, their grace, their goodness—does it continue on after their death? If so, how? The Christian teaching about the communion of saints is that those who went before us are indeed still active, though in a different form. They care, they participate, their radiance shines and continues. They are in our midst, they are present at prayer and at gatherings, they can be called upon for help with spirits, angels, and the Divine. They are accessible. No beauty is lost. Or as Hildegard put it, **no warmth is lost in the universe.** Their beauty and warmth are with us still, though it behooves us to call on them, to be mindful and remembering of them.

Theologian John Dominic Crossan, operating from the perspective of the Jesus Seminar, has this to say about the resurrection of Jesus. "Resurrection does not mean, simply, that the spirit or soul of Jesus lives on in the world. And neither does it mean, simply, that the companions or followers of Jesus live on in the world. *It must be the embodied life that remains powerfully efficacious in this world.*" Crossan insists on the inspiration that the risen Christ gives to the communities gathered in his name. "Bodily resurrection means that the *embodied* life and death of the historical Jesus continues to be experienced, by believers, as powerfully efficacious and salvifically present in the world. That life continued, as it always had, to form communities of like lives."

Four

RELATING TO

THE FUTURE:

WHAT THE DIVINE

IS ASKING

OF US

Wisdom is not just about consciousness and spirituality is not exclusively about relating to Creation, Divinity, and self. Both wisdom and spirituality are about affecting society, transforming the contexts in which people live and strive to live, breathe, and try to earn a living. Wisdom, after all, is said to walk the streets and be available to all. All spiritual traditions agree that humans are here for a greater purpose than mere coping, and face deeper challenges than merely securing one's comfort living in the world. We are here, it is agreed, for service and compassion, for justice and celebration. And for us to take on these tasks takes perseverance and self-knowledge, courage and heart work. In short, it takes a development of the spiritual warrior in us. We treat these subjects below in two chapters:

17. Service and Compassion (including Justice and Celebration)
18. Spiritual Warriorhood

17.

SERVICE AND COMPASSION
(INCLUDING JUSTICE
AND CELEBRATION)

We can reject everything else:
religion, ideology, all received wisdom.
But we cannot escape the necessity of love and compassion.
This, then, is my true religion, my simple faith. . . .
Our own heart, our own mind, is the temple.
The doctrine is compassion.
—Dalai Lama,
Ethics for the New Millennium

Compassion is about both relieving suffering *and* about celebration (which also re-lieves suffering by putting it in a context of gratitude). The subject of celebration has arisen in previous chapters dedicated to holy imagination, art, and ritual; to joy, to beauty, and to sacred sexuality as well as the chapters on Creation and on community. It permeates our living in the world. In compassion, we share in the divine celebration of existence. In this sense, celebration finds a kind of crescendo in the milieu of compassion.

The spiritual traditions of the world agree that compassionate service constitutes a true expression of the divine intention for human beings. We serve in order that people may more fully celebrate their existence. There is a general agreement that compassion is, on the one hand, natural to our state of being and, on the other hand, something we must struggle to reconnect to.

The Buddha said: **Fill your mind with compassion!** Buddhist teacher Kalu Rimpoche says **the essence of Mind is spacious and pure, like the open, blue sky. Its nature is luminous clarity [and] its energy or manifestation is compassion.** Philosopher Jack Kornfield cites the Buddhist Scriptures, which say that compassion is the **quivering of the pure heart** that occurs "when we allow ourselves to be touched by the pain of life." With compassion comes a greatness of heart. "We all share a longing to go beyond the confines of our own fear or anger or addiction, to connect with something greater than 'I,' 'me,' and 'mine,' greater than our small story and our small self. It is possible to stop the war and come into the timeless present to touch a great ground of being that contains all things."

Sunyata means the complete interrelatedness of all beings, and *karuna* or compassion flows from this intuition of interrelatedness. Together, they comprise the heart of Buddha's teaching. Compassion gives concrete expression to *sunyata* in the phenomenal world. Compassion, then, is our response to interconnectivity. It arises when we allow our heart to be touched by the pain and need of another. Buddhist scholar T. R. V. Nurti observes that "what makes Buddha a loving God is his great compassion and his active and abiding interest in the welfare not only of suffering humanity but of all beings. . . . This great compassion is not of a sentimental kind, grand but blind. It is born of the realization of the universality and unity of all being."

Thich Nhat Hanh applies the practice of compassion concretely when he says: **Compassion is a mind that removes the suffering that is present to the other. . . . Anyone who has made us suffer is undoubtedly suffering too. We only need to follow our breathing and look deeply, and naturally we will see his suffering.** It is not enough to mouth words like "I love him very much" without engaging in action to relieve another's suffering. **We all have the seeds of love and compassion in our minds, and we can develop these fine and wonderful sources of energy.** Thich Nhat Hanh and some fellow monks started a movement in Vietnam called "Engaged Buddhism." It was a question of moving from meditating in a meditation hall to going to where the worst suffering was in progress. The decision was a both/and. Because of the intense suffering during the war, these Buddhists decided **to do both [things]—to go out and help people and to do so in mindfulness. We called it engaged Buddhism. Mindfulness must be engaged. Once there is seeing, there must be acting. Otherwise, what is the use of seeing?** One result of Engaged Buddhism was overcoming meaninglessness in one's own life. **Being in touch with the kind of suffering we encountered during the war can heal us of some of the suffering we experience when our lives are not meaningful or useful. . . . You see that you can be a source of compassion and a great help to many suffering people. In that intense suffering, you feel a kind of relief and joy within yourself, because you know that you are an instrument of compassion. . . . You become a joyful person, even if your life is very hard.**

Earlier in chapter nine we learned of the power of Vipassana meditation to alter a prison in India in a most compassionate way. A *Los Angeles Times* reporter told me recently that the largest youth prison in America, located near Los Angeles, was a violent hellhole for years. Inmates sixteen to nineteen years of age would become ever more violent and gangs ruled the place for years. Then recently, in desperation, the warden invited three Buddhist monks in to teach meditation. This was new to most of the inmates. They learned meditation and the entire energy of the prison changed from violence to being a basically human place to be. Consider how inexpensively this prison was reformed; consider how learning to meditate will serve these young people their whole lives and the communities to which they return when their incarceration is finished.

Pema Chodron teaches that **in order to feel compassion for other people, we** have to feel compassion for ourselves. In particular, to care about people who are fearful, angry, jealous, overpowered by addictions of all kinds, arrogant, proud, miserly, selfish, mean, you name it—to have compassion and to care for these people means not to run from the pain of finding these things in ourselves. In fact, our whole attitude toward pain can change. Instead of fending it off and hiding from it, we could open our hearts to allow ourselves to feel that pain, feel it as something that will soften and purify us and make us far more loving and kind.

Because meditation teaches us to let go, it becomes a training ground for compassion. **Meditation is probably the only activity that doesn't add anything to the picture . . . Meditation is a totally nonviolent, nonaggressive occupation. Not filling the space, allowing for the possibility of connecting with unconditional openness—this provides the basis for real change. . . . This is our birthright—the wisdom with which we were born, the vast unfolding display of primordial richness, primordial openness, primordial wisdom itself.** Mindfulness is about the expansion of our minds, about stretching our hearts so that they do reach their capacity for compassion. Indeed, Chodron identifies mindfulness and compassion. **The ground of not causing harm is mindfulness, a sense of clear seeing with respect and compassion for what it is we see. . . . Mindfulness is the ground; refraining is the path.**

Stephen Levine offers meditations that heal mind and heart, past and present and teaches a "Guided Loving Kindness Meditation" which includes breathing in and out and speaking silently in the heart the following phrase: "May I be free from suffering. May I be at peace." He comments: "Each breath deepening the nurturing warmth of relating to oneself with loving kindness and compassion. Each exhalation deepening in peace, expanding into the spaciousness of being, developing the deep patience that does not wait for things to be otherwise but relates with loving kindness to things as they are." One can substitute another's name for oneself in this same exercise. The results of learning compassion to ourselves flow out to compassion toward others. "The power of loving-kindness is so great that when we concentratedly project it out to others, they often can feel it. It is a subtle but tangible energy which can be consciously directed, like awareness in the heart, or the sun through a magnifying glass, to a shimmering point of light."

Jack Kornfield writes about the human heart: **The human heart has the extraordinary capacity to hold and transform the sorrows of life into a great stream of compassion. . . . Let yourself feel how the beauty of every being brings you joy and how the suffering of any being makes you weep.** It is important that we remember that compassion is about sharing our common joy and beauty as well as sharing our common pain and suffering.

As we saw at the beginning of this chapter, the Dalai Lama names compassion as the center of his ethics. He says we do not need more guilt; rather, **a reorientation of our heart and mind away from self and toward others.** We must work on ourselves so that we develop contentment, for without it restlessness and greed and **aggressive competitiveness** take over. The word for compassion in the Dalai Lama's language carries no connotation of *pity* toward another. Rather, it means **a combination of empathy and reason. It denotes a feeling of connection with others, reflecting its origins in empathy.** It leads not to emoting but to taking action, to service, to getting involved in relieving the burdens of one another's suffering, a giving of our time and talents to assisting others. This in turn brings happiness to ourselves.

The holy Qur'an begins with the holiest names of God and this verse is the most repeated passsage throughout the Qur'an. It is repeated five times a day in the Muslim's daily prayer. What is this name for God? **In the name of Allah, the Compassionate and Merciful.** Compassion, then, is a favorite among all the names for Allah. It follows that those who follow Allah are meant to follow a way of compassion.

Sufi Ibn Al-Arabi believes the divine compassion, including both love and sadness, launched Creation itself. God is both passionate and compassionate. **The origin of the universe derives from the divine sadness.** The primordial solitude made God **yearn to be revealed in beings who manifest him to himself insofar as he manifests himself to them. "I was a hidden treasure, I yearned to be known. That is why I produced creatures, in order to be known in them."** This sadness produced a sigh. **From the inscrutable depths of the Godhead this sadness calls for a sigh of compassion. . . . In its hidden being every existent is a Breath of the existentiating divine compassion.**

With our awareness of the divine compassion comes responsibility. **Some pray that God "have compassion with them. But the intuitive mystics ask that divine compassion be fulfilled through them." This means: "Let us be compassionate ones. . . ." For the mystic has come to know that the very substance of his being is a breath of that infinite compassion; he is himself the epiphanic form of a divine name.** In our compassion, we give back to God. **The compassion does not move only in the direction from the Creator to the creature whom he feeds with his existentiating Breath; it also moves from the creature toward the Creator . . . so that the created universe is the theophany of his names and attributes, which would not exist if the creature did not exist.**

There is a story told about Muhammad that a man was spending all his time in the mosque praying. Muhammad asked: **Then who feeds him? "His brother"** was **the reply. Then his brother is better than he,** said the prophet. As Sheikh Muzaffer puts it: "To be a dervish (or Sufi) is to serve and to help others, not just to sit and pray. To be a real dervish is to lift up those who have fallen, to wipe the tears of the suffering, to caress the friendless and the orphaned." The following statements from Muhammad demonstrate his teaching that to be a believer is to be a person who puts compassion into action.

> A man does not believe until he loves for his brother what he loves
>   for himself.
> God will not show mercy to him who does not show mercy to others.
> The believer is not one who eats his fill when his neighbor beside
>   him is hungry.
> You see the believers in their mutual pity, love, and affection like one
>   body. When one member has a complaint, the rest of the body is
>   united with it in wakefulness and fever.
> The believers are like a single person: if his eye is affected all of him
>   is affected, and if his head is affected all of him is affected.

Since God is the author of all one has received, it is expected that caring for the needy take precedence. Alms of 2.5 percent of all one has including income and possessions is expected. One of the purposes of fasting is to sensitize one to others' hunger. There are no old peoples' homes in Muslim countries since the aged are to be taken care of by the extended family. In the Qur'an we read: **They are righteous who believe in God . . . and who donate goods and money for love of God to relatives and orphans, and to the poor and the wayfarer, and to the needy, and for freeing slaves; and who are constant in prayer and give alms for welfare, and those who fulfill their promises when they make them, and who are patient in suffering, adversity, and hard times. They are the truthful ones and they are the conscientious.**

Generosity and hospitality are expected toward relatives but also toward strangers. The Qur'an says: **Be benevolent toward parents, and kindred, and orphans, and the needy, and the neighbor who is a kinsman, and the neighbor who is not related to you, and your associate and the wayfarer, and those who** are under your control. Surely, Allah loves not the proud and boastful, who are niggardly and enjoin people to be niggardly, and conceal that which Allah has given them of his bounty. There are warnings against hypocrisy: **Woe unto those also who pray but are unmindful of their prayer and pray only to be seen of people and they hold back the least beneficence.** We are urged to imitate the compassion of Allah who **is the most forgiving, ever merciful.** Belief is not a theory in the head, it is action toward our neighbor. **How shouldst thou know what the scaling of the height is? It is the freeing of a slave, or feeding, on a day of scarcity, an orphan near of kin, or a poor person reduced to penury; and to be of those who believe and exhort one another to steadfastness and exhort one another to mercy.**

In Judaism, too, compassion constitutes an imitation of God. Rabbi Heschel says: **Humanity is a reminder of God. As God is compassionate, let humanity be compassionate.** God is known as "the Compassionate One," Yahweh is **a God of tenderness and compassion, slow to anger, rich in kindness and faithfulness.** God feels the suffering of every creature, the pathos of our human condition and that of all sentient beings. Heschel comments: **There is a very famous text saying that even when a criminal is hanged on the gallows, God cries. God identifies himself with the misery of man.** An ancient rabbinic teaching gets to the heart of the interdependence that lies behind compassion when it says:

> **When you are filled with compassion,**
> **there is no self to oppose another**
> **and no other to stand against oneself.**

Psalm 145 sings: **God's compassion is over all that he has made.** Thus compassion rules the universe and is the source of creation itself. **Just as God is called compassionate and gracious, so you must be compassionate and gracious, giving gifts freely,** advises one commentator on the Torah.

Psalm 82 pictures God holding a court amidst other gods. These other gods are judged responsible for lack of justice in the land.

> **Give justice to the weak and the orphan;**
> **maintain the right of the lowly and the destitute.**
> **Rescue the weak and the needy;**
> **deliver them from the hand of the wicked.**

Here justice and compassion come together. Compassion is not about pity but about justice and action. Compassion means action. The *Kabbalah* says: **Imitate your Creator. Then you will enter the mystery of the supernal form, the Divine** image in which you were created. If you resemble the divine in body but not in action, you distort the form. . . . For the essence of the divine image is action. Imitation of God concerns *actions*. What are these actions? **Imitate the acts of Keter, the thirteen qualities of compassion alluded to by the prophet Micah: "Who is a God like you, delighting in love? You will again have compassion upon us."** The *Kabbalah* offers a definition of compassion when it declares: **Let your neighbor's honor be as precious to you as your own, for you and your fellow are one and the same. That is why we are commanded: "Love your neighbor as yourself." You should desire what is right for your fellow; never denigrate him or wish for his disgrace. . . . You should feel as bad for such suffering as if it were your own. Similarly, rejoice over another's good fortune as if you were basking in it.**

We have to be aware and on the lookout for the suffering of others. **Your eyes should . . . always be open to notice those who suffer, to be compassionate toward them as much as possible. When you see a poor person suffering, do not close your eyes in the slightest. On the contrary, keep him in mind as much as you can; arouse compassion for him—from God and from people.** This compassionate awareness should extend to all beings. **Be good to all creatures, disdaining none. Even the most insignificant creatures should assume importance in your eyes; attend to it. Do good to whomever needs your goodness. . . . God nourishes everything, from the horned buffalo to nits, disdaining no creature—for if he disdained creatures due to their insignificance, they could not endure for even a moment.** All creatures are looked over by Wisdom. **Wisdom spreads over all created things: mineral, vegetable, animal, and human. Each was created in Wisdom. . . . Do not kill any living creature, unless it is necessary.**

We are called to **mend the cosmos** by our actions—even our ordinary actions like the way we eat can be an act of mending of the cosmos. In the *Zohar*, compassionate love is called "an offering to God." We are called to its practice.

**"Does not everyone know that I based the world solely on love?
I have said, 'The world is built by love.'"
It is love that sustains the world!
The angels on high then declare:
'Master of the world!
Look at so-and-so who is eating and drinking his fill.
He could share something with the poor
but he gives them nothing at all!'**

Rabbi Heschel recognizes compassion as the essence of God. **Being compassionate [is his very] nature.** God is **all concern** and **absolutely personal.** Pathos or caring is at the very heart of who God is. **Justice is God's nature.** And so, too, is the capacity to suffer. **God does not stand outside the range of human suffering and sorrow. He is personally involved in, even stirred by, the conduct and fate of man.... God's participation in human history ... finds its deepest expression in the fact that God can actually suffer.** Heschel is putting distance between the God of Abraham's concern and involvement for people and certain Greek gods who distanced themselves from the pathos of humanity. We are to imitate the divine care and concern, the divine pathos and compassion by our deeds. This is what the prophets call us to—divine pathos and compassion.

Hinduism teaches the path of *seva* or service. Service is compassion in action. It is also prayer. Ramakrishna teaches: **The presence of God is felt not only when you shut your eyes; God can also be seen when one looks around. Service to the hungry, poor, sick, and ignorant, in the proper spirit, is as effective as any other spiritual discipline.**

Nikhilananda emphasizes that Hinduism should not be held responsible for the poverty of India any more than Jesus can be held responsible for the arrogance in Christian history. **Hinduism does not repudiate the world, negate social values, or forbid the enjoyment of legitimate pleasures.** Most of India's poverty, he believes, is due to centuries of foreign domination. India's fabulous wealth invited foreign conquerors, from the Greeks to the modern Europeans. Western colonialism raped India, stripping her of rich natural resources and reducing her people to continual frustration and servanthood.

When one looks at the life and commitment of Hindu saints like Gandhi, Vivekananda, Sri Aurobindo, the organization Bramo Samaj and many others, one realizes that Hinduism indeed teaches a compassionate path.

In Karma yoga one's daily actions are meant to be a spiritual discipline. Karma yoga is work done without the desire for personal gain. The Bhagavad Gita says: **To the work alone you have the right, never to its fruit.**

The Bhagavad Gita recommends service to all beings when it teaches that those

> **whose minds are engaged within,**
> **who are always busy working for the welfare of all living beings . . .**
> **achieve liberation in the Supreme.**
> **My dear Arjuna, he who engages in my pure devotional service . . .**
> **he who works for me, who makes me the supreme goal of his life,**
> **and who is friendly to every living being—he certainly comes to me.**
> **By controlling the various senses and being equally disposed to**
> ** everyone,**
> **such persons, engaged in the welfare of all, at last achieve me.**

According to the Vedas, the **Path of Action is as important as the Path of Knowledge.** This path is called **Karma yoga. This leads to the building up of the body and the sharpening of the mind and to living a full life with health and vigor and in the joy of being.** It also means **accepting the battle of life and fighting it with a will to victory and survival.** This struggle applies **to moral and spiritual life. Hence, the battle of life is the battle between good and evil, calling up all that is most energetic and valiant in man to its service.**

The spiritual Hindu is to **dedicate all his actions to the Lord and take refuge in him,** and this in turn frees one from the bondage of karma (action). Thus one **becomes a Liberated Soul.** It is a matter of intention, not of renunciation—**the yogi does not renounce action. He cuts the bonds that tie himself to his actions by dedicating their fruits either to the Lord or to humanity. He believes that it is his privilege to do his duty and that he has no right to the fruits of his actions.**

Mahatma Gandhi is a prime example of one who put this spirituality of work and service into practice. He said: **Man's ultimate aim is the realization of God, and all his activities—social, political, religious—have to be guided by the ultimate aim of the vision of God. The immediate service of all human beings becomes a necessary part of the endeavor, simply because the only way to find God is to see him in his creation and be one with it. This can only be done by service of all.**

Gandhi's commitment to nonviolent action can be seen as a living out of the compassion he learned from his spiritual heritage, as Ivengar puts it: **The yogi uses all his resources—physical, economic, mental, or moral—to alleviate the pain and suffering of others. He shares his strength with the weak until they become strong. He shares his courage with those that are timid until they become brave by his example. He denies the maxim of the survival of the fittest, but makes the weak strong enough to survive. He becomes a shelter to one and all.** Gandhi saw in the Gita **a grammar of action.** He equated service with action and humility. **A life of service must be one of humility. . . . True humility means** strenuous and constant endeavor entirely directed toward the service of humanity. God is continuously in action without resting for a single moment. If we would serve him or become one with him, our activity must be as unwearied as his. . . . This restlessness constitutes true rest. This never-ceasing agitation holds the key to peace ineffable.

Ma Yoga Shakti is a contemporary writer and practitioner of the Hindu way of life. She comments about American culture in a recent interview. "America has grown like Vindhyachal (a mountain range in India). The gods are overburdened with happiness, like children in America. Who has time to enjoy all the [television] channels, all the food, all the Coca Cola? America also needs a lesson in humility to make it sweet. It needs, like the Vindhyas [mountains], *to learn to bow low in service* . . . In India nobody cares for TV, they're happy with chanting and meditating, singing and chanting. You can't purchase this joy in shops. By singing the glories of God you make your heart free."

Work from the heart emanates from God. **I am seated in everyone's heart . . . The Supreme Lord is situated as Paramatma in everyone's heart, and it is from him that all activities are initiated. . . . Thus, the Lord is not only all-pervading; he is also localized in every individual heart.**

A key concept in African religion is *Maat,* which Dr. Asante defines as **the influence of right and righteousness, justice and harmony, balance, respect, and human dignity.** *Maat* is about living out the harmony or balance we find in creation itself. It is also clearly about living out our shared reality of interdependence. **In all cases the ideas of religion [in Africa] kept the societies close to the fundamental principles of harmony between humans, humans and the environment, and humans and the spirit world.** A tomb inscription from the sixth dynasty of Egypt (2300 B.C.E.) says:

> I rescued the weak from one stronger than he
> As much as was in my power.
> I gave bread to the hungry, clothes to the naked,
> I brought the boatless to land.
> I buried him who had no son,
> I made a boat for him who lacked one.
> I respected my father, I pleased my mother,
> I raised their children.
> So says he whose nickname is Sheshi.

The "Zulu Personal Declaration" of 1825 in South Africa understands compassion well when it says:

> My neighbor and I have the same origins;
> We have the same life-experience and a common destiny;
> We are the obverse and reverse sides of one entity;
> We are unchanging equals;
> We are the faces which see themselves in each other. . . .

My neighbor's sorrow is my sorrow;
His joy is my joy.
He and I are mutually fulfilled when we stand by each other in
    moments of need.
His survival is a precondition of my survival.

African-American mystic Howard Thurman discourses on the glory of Mahatma Gandhi's achievements in throwing off British colonialism. **Occasionally there comes into view on the horizon of the age a solitary figure who, in his life, anticipates the harmony of which he speaks. No one dreamed that Mahatma Gandhi would be able to introduce into the very center of a great modern empire such as Britain a principle contrary to empire, and abide. For Gandhi to have come out of the womb of a religion outside the Christian faith and address himself to an empire whose roots were nurtured by that faith is the most eloquent testimony of the timeless, universal character of what was working in him.**

Thurman also reflects on the compassion that Jesus represents to the downtrodden of the world. Who was Jesus? What did he know and teach about compassion? He was poor and a member of the lower class. (This makes him quite different from Buddha, who began his life and his search as a prince.) **Jesus was a poor Jew. . . . mother of Jesus was one whose means were not sufficient for a lamb and who was compelled there to use doves or young pigeons . . . The masses of the people are poor . . . in his poverty he was more truly Son of Man than he would have been if the incident of family or birth had made him a rich son of Israel . . . Jesus was a member of a minority group.** Thurman believed that Jesus' "strategy" to appeal to the oppressed was an appeal to spirit and heart. It is there that the true struggle is engaged. **No external force, however great and overwhelming, can at long last destroy a people if it does not first win the victory of the spirit against them. . . . Jesus came back to the inner life of the individual . . . the "inward center" as the crucial arena where the issues would determine the destiny of his people.**

Thurman identifies Jesus' strategy to be applicable to all cultures and all oppressed people. That strategy is simply put: **Jesus expressed his alternative in a brief formula—the Kingdom of Heaven is in us. . . . He recognized with authentic realism that anyone who permits another to determine the quality of his inner life gives into the hands of the other the keys to his destiny. If a man** knows precisely what he can do to you or what epithet he can hurl against you in order to make you lose your temper, your equilibrium, then he can always keep you under subjection. . . . The solution which Jesus found for himself and for Israel, as they faced the hostility of the Greco-Roman world, becomes the word and the work of redemption for all the cast-down people in every generation and in every age.

Speaking with the passion of slavery fresh in his memory (he was raised with his grandmother who was an ex-slave), Thurman applies Jesus' strategy to the needs of his own people. **The basic fact is that Christianity as it was born in the mind of this Jewish teacher and thinker appears as a technique of survival for the oppressed. . . . "In him was life; and the life was the light of men." Wherever his spirit appears, the oppressed gather fresh courage; for he announced the good news that fear, hypocrisy, and hatred, the three hounds of hell that track the trail of the disinherited, need have no dominion over them.**

Thurman names the contradictory role that organized Christianity has so often played in movements of oppression. He sees the church as having betrayed Jesus. **Persecution and suffering has become the cornerstone of a civilization and of nations whose very position in modern life has too often been secured by a ruthless use of power applied to weak and defenseless people. One of your famous Christian hymn writers, Sir John Newton, made his money from the sale of slaves to the New World. He is the man who wrote "How Sweet the Name of Jesus Sounds" and "Amazing Grace." The name of one of the famous British slave vessels was "Jesus."**

Thurman traces our capacity for compassion to the understanding that **the source of life is God. The mystic applies this to human life when he says that there is in man an uncreated element; or in the Book of Job where it is written that his mark is in their foreheads. In the last analysis the mood of reverence that should characterize all men's dealings with each other finds its basis here. The demand to treat all human beings as ends in themselves, or the moral imperative that issues in respect for personality, finds its profound inspiration** here. To deal with men on any other basis, to treat them as if there were not vibrant and vital in each one the very life of the very God, is the great blasphemy.

Thurman writes about compassion as a **whole-making** tendency we need to find within ourselves. Tempted as we are to lash out at others and to blame others, the search for compassion is a lifelong search. **I have looked long and hard at the early alienations of my youth; I have lived, as many others, through the frustration of alienation and rejection. I have had to discover, after the pattern of the grain in my wood, the difference between solitariness and loneliness. I have had to wrestle with many spiritual crises growing out of what seemed to be the contradictory demands of love and hate, of vengeance and mercy, and of retaliation and reconciliation. In all of these experiences there is a part of me that seeks ever for harmony, for community, for unity and creative synthesis in conflicting relations; and an equally articulate urgency within me for withdrawal, for separateness, for isolation, and for aggression . . . Thus I am driven to seek, if happily I may find, a basis for this "whole-making" tendency in myself.**

Thurman tells an amazing story about parenting his children around issues of racism in the South. One day in Daytona Beach, Florida, his two daughters saw a playground attached to a public school and wanted to play in it. His father said they couldn't, and when they protested, he said he would explain why at home over lemonade. When the moment came, he instructed his children in the following manner: **At present, only white children can play there. But it takes the state legislature, the courts, the sheriffs and policemen, the white churches, the mayors, the banks and businesses, and the majority of white people in the state of Florida—it takes all these to keep two little black girls from swinging in those swings. That is how important you are! Never forget, the estimate of your own importance and self-worth can be judged by how many weapons and how much power people are willing to use to control you and keep you in the place they have assigned to you. You are two very important little girls. Your presence can threaten the entire state of Florida.**

Thurman offers a creative twist to the lesson of the crucifixion of Jesus and compassion. Instead of just seeing Jesus as saving us, he makes the point that humans who truly suffer—in his example the slaves who composed the song "Were you there when they crucified my Lord?"—identify with Jesus. Thus compassion is theirs toward the Christ and not just the other way around. **The suffering of Jesus on the cross was something more. He suffered, he died, but not alone—they were with him. They knew what he suffered; it was a cry of the heart that found a response and an echo in their own woes. They entered into the fellowship of his suffering. There was something universal in his suffering . . ." 'Were you there when they crucified my Lord?' . . . The inference is that the singer was there: "I know what he went through because I have met him in the high places of pain, and I claim him as my brother."** When Thurman and his wife visited Mahatma Gandhi in 1935, Gandhi requested that they sing this song to him. Thurman commented on that special moment. **The insight here revealed is profound and touching. At last there is worked out the kind of identification in suffering that makes the cross universal in its deepest meaning.**

Jesus was ethically radical. He disturbed his culture's presuppositions concerning home, family, economics, and power. Crossan says this about Jesus. "The earthly Jesus was not just a thinker with ideas but a rebel with a cause. He was a Jewish peasant with an attitude, and he claimed that his attitude was that of the Jewish God. . . . There is only one Jesus, the *historical* Jesus, who incarnated the Jewish God of justice for a believing community committed to continuing such incarnation ever afterward." As we have seen, that Jewish God is a God of compassion. Crossan sees Jesus as one who resisted exploitation of others and through whom the God of compassion worked "in the healing and in the eating as nonviolent resistance to systemic evil." Referring to Psalm 82, which we saw above, Crossan believes that "justice is spelled out as protecting the poor from the rich, protecting the systemically weak from the systemically powerful. Such injustice creates darkness over the earth and shakes the very foundations of the world."

Scholars believe that early Christian communities like that which wrote the Gospel of Thomas were ethically radical. "The dominant ethos among Thomas Christians was a kind of social radicalism . . . including (though not primarily) homelessness, willful poverty, begging, the rejection of family and local piety, and a critique of the political powers that be." Jesus' many references to the **reign of God** are a deliberate reproach to the empire and reign of Roman rule under which he and his people struggled to live.

Another early Christian community, called the Q community, offered what one scholar calls "a new social vision." It was this vision that drew so many people to follow Jesus and to create powerful stories around his story. Behavior was more important than beliefs in this early community. It was a behavior that called for "pursuit of sane and simple living." It was not an attempt to fight Roman power or to reform Jewish religion that attracted these people. At the heart of their belief was the understanding that "all of nature is God's domain and all kinds of people are under his care." In addition, compassion is to be lived.

In Luke's Gospel, Jesus is reported to have said: **Be you compassionate as your Creator in heaven is compassionate.** As we have seen above, this is at the heart of

Jewish understanding of God and of humanity's need to imitate God. Jesus also speaks about **loving your enemies.** Paul summarizes Jesus' teaching this way: **The whole of the law is summarized in a single command: "Love your neighbor as yourself."** The Gospel of Matthew summarizes Jesus' teaching as well as the prophet Isaiah's teaching about the works of compassion. God and human are one when we serve one another. **I was hungry and you gave me food; I was thirsty and you gave me drink; I was a stranger and you made me welcome; naked and you clothed me, sick and you visited me, in prison and you came to see me. . . . I tell you solemnly, in so far as you did this to one of the least of these brothers or sisters of mine, you did it to me.**

In this same spirit, Thomas Aquinas articulates a Jewish and a Christian understanding of compassion when he writes:

> **Through compassion human beings imitate God.**
> **In every work of God, viewed at its primary source, there appears**
>   **compassion.**
> **God is said to be rich in compassion because God possesses an**
>   **infinite and unfailing compassion, which human beings do not.**

What role does Aquinas see compassion playing in the life and teachings of Jesus? **Compassion is the fire the Lord came to send on the earth.** Furthermore, **compassion is Christ himself** and **the will of Christ is twofold, namely, of compassion and justice. But it is first indeed concerned with compassion both of itself and in itself, since "God's compassion is over all God's works."**

How does Aquinas see human compassion? **To be compassionate is to have a heart that suffers from the misfortune of others because we think of it as our own.** But compassion means action. **We are truly compassionate when we work to remove the misfortune of others.** Compassion springs from love. **The love of neighbor requires that not only should we be our neighbor's well-wishers, but also their well-doers, according to 1 John 3:18: "Let us not love in word, nor in speech, but in deed, and in truth." And in order to be a person's well-wisher and well-doer, we ought to succor their needs.** Aquinas invokes the temporal and spiritual works of mercy to lay out a plan for compassion. The former include feeding the hungry, giving drink to the thirsty, clothing the naked, sheltering the homeless, visiting the sick, ransoming the captive, and burying the dead. Under the latter he includes praying for help from God and offering assistance by way of teaching, counseling, comforting, reproving, pardoning, and bearing with others.

He believes that two principal obstacles lie in the way of compassion: First is **a contempt for the wretched.** Some people believe that others are not worthy of their attention and concern. The second obstacle is **assurance of one's own power.** When people want to lord over others, there is no room in them for compassion. Power trips drive compassion aside. So, too, does fear.

Meister Eckhart also finds the fulfillment of the spiritual journey to be in compassion and justice. **Compassion means justice [and] the person who understands what I say about justice understands everything I have to say.** In Jesus' Sermon on the Mount in Luke's Gospel, Jesus says: **Be you compassionate as your Creator in heaven is compassionate.** Eckhart comments: **In every work which God works in a creature, compassion goes with it and ahead of it, especially in the inwardness of the creature itself. . . . Every work in a creature supposes the work of compassion and is grounded in it as in its root, the power of which preserves all things and works powerfully in them.**

Eckhart calls for compassion to oneself. **How then can anyone be compassionate toward me or toward you who is not compassionate toward himself?** Christ, he says, wants us **to be compassionate even to our own body and soul.** Late in his life, Eckhart tried to resolve a theological debate between Franciscans and Dominicans: Is knowledge better than love? His way out of the dilemma was to invoke compassion. **I say that beyond these two, beyond knowledge and love, there is compassion. In the highest and purest acts that God works, God works compassion.** He also wrestles with the meaning of *soul.* First he says that **all human science can never fathom what the soul is in its ground.** The soul is ineffable and fathomless like God is. It is wrapped in mystery. **What the soul is in its ground, no one knows.** However, he surprises even himself when he declares at the culmination of his sermon: **The soul is where God works compassion.** What he is saying is that soul is not a thing-in-itself, not a substance no matter what: Soul is a space where compassion happens, a space where divine compassion operates through us. That would mean that to the extent that we are not compassionate we lack soul. This would seem to be an understanding of soul that Buddhists can live with.

We return to compassion when we meditate because compassion is a return to our origins. We were born of compassion.

But **compassion means justice.** Justice cuts to our very being. **For the just person as such to act justly is to live; indeed, justice is his life, her being alive,** her being, insofar as she is just. One does justice work because it is the thing to do, not for any particular reward. **The just person lives and works without reason or gain.** Eckhart sounds like Hindu philosophers expounding on working without a why. **God's ground is my ground and my ground is God's ground. Here I live on my own as God lives on his own. . . . You should work all your works out of this innermost ground without why.** Our actions need to be living, not dead, actions. **Those deeds which do not flow from within your inner self are all dead before God.**

And Julian of Norwich says that **the ground of compassion is love and the working of compassion keeps us in love. . . . Compassion protects, increases our sensitivity, gives life and heals.**

18.

SPIRITUAL
WARRIORHOOD

Now since a person's real work in this world
is the work of the Blessed Holy One,
he must be as strong as a lion on every side
so that the Other Side will not overpower him
or be able to seduce him.
—The Zohar

There is an invitation in many spiritual traditions to develop our *spiritual warriorhood.* The truth of the spiritual warrior has been misplaced whenever religions have taught their young to kill and coerce, to build empires in the name of the gods instead of wrestling with the demons in self and social structures. The changes needed in self and social structures to live out the spiritual agenda laid out in this book are not possible without a strengthening of our hearts and a reburst of courage. The spiritual warrior needs to be nurtured anew. This is possible.

It is, I am convinced, what many young people are seeking whether they have the words or not: something to live for, something to give their lives for. The illusory goals of shopping and making money will not cut it with most young people. Deep down they resent this trivializing of their existences. Deep down they know what Thomas Aquinas taught, that we are "capax universi," capable of the universe, and they want to know their place in it, their dignity derived from it, and their responsibility to it. All this is part of the spiritual warrior's vocation.

It is not just the young who must seek authentic warriorhood today. As a species, we need to be strong to resist the onslaught of myths of progress, consumerism, and consequent degradation.

Thomas Berry writes about the role of the warrior and hero in the Native American consciousness. **The Indians have never accepted human life as ordinary, as something that can be managed in a controlled or painless manner. They realized that life tests the deepest qualities within the human personality, qualities that emerge in heroic combat not merely with others, but also with oneself and with the powers of the universe. The sacred function of enemies was to assist one another to the heroic life by challenge, even by the challenge of death.** The existence of challenges instead of mere comforts and acquisition of comforts is what brings alive the warrior in us. Today, with so many "enemies" confronting us internally and externally—greed and envy, violence and self-pity, fear and sloth, is it any wonder that the return of the spiritual warrior is called for? Fasting, service, sundancing, and other generous acts of giving to the community are all ways to develop warriorhood. The warrior takes on enemies, both internal and external.

A warrior defends what is beautiful; a warrior defends Creation and its light; a warrior defends what the community cherishes; a warrior assists the community to survive. A warrior's heart must be strong but also creative; it must be connected to the whole; it must know quiet and solitude as well as busyness and engagement. It must be familiar with nothingness and it must have tasted joy. It must know service as well as sacrifice. In short, it must know spirit.

The violence of our culture and its cultural institutions instructs us to take for granted from an early age that all warriorhood is about killing for the empire or the nation or the corporation or even for our religions. The very term "warrior" to most people smacks of the military.

But that has not always been the case. I am reminded of a Native American student in our university who had been a soldier in the Vietnam War. On returning home to his tribe, his elders said to him: "You have been a soldier. Now we will make you a warrior." His training to be a warrior took four years. I asked him what was at the heart of this training, and he related this story. The elders taught him to play the flute, which he learned to do very proficiently. When they felt he was ready to play before the whole tribe, everyone gathered. As the evening came to an end, and all were touched by his playing, each elder came up to him with a knife in his hand and cut a chunk of wood out of his flute. At the end of the evening, he had no flute. When I quoted Eckhart to him, **the soul grows by subtraction,** he exclaimed: "That is it! All my training as a warrior was like that."

Spiritual traditions the world over embrace the archetype of warriorhood, for it takes a stout heart, a determined mind, a focused intention, a *very awake person,* to be a successful warrior. A warrior defends what he or she cherishes when it is threatened. A warrior is a lover defending the beloved. A prophet is a warrior—the energy of the prophets of Israel was very much a warrior energy. A warrior responds to moral outrage, feels injustice in the gut like a kick to one's solar plexus, and responds with ingenuity and creativity. It may be that not only our nation-state and corporate state worldviews have limited our understanding of warriorhood but also our sexism. A patriarchal culture needs to deny women their warriorhood, deny women their masculine and assertive role.

"Femininity," being "ladylike" and going shopping and doing homemaking without any options—all this is part of putting down the inherent warriorhood of women. It serves the purposes of entrenched power to teach people to stifle their spiritual warriorhood and channel its energy exclusively to soldierhood or warmaking on behalf of the powerful.

St. Teresa of Avila was a spiritual warrior—she took on the established church of her day, outmaneuvering the powerful Inquisition itself, and the privileged classes who were quite literally dumping their unmarried daughters into convents, convents which she committed her considerable energies to cleaning up. By so doing, she took on powerful forces in sixteenth-century Spain. She did not flinch. She was a warrior. It is interesting that in her writings she offers at least fifty images of soul and about 90 percent of these are masculine. She calls her soul a castle, a garrison, an army, a king—all images that rose in her psyche that bespeak her warriorhood.

Hildegard of Bingen was also a spiritual warrior, taking on as she did many powers of her day, including bishops, archbishops, abbots, merchants, clergy, and even the pope. No shrinking violet there. No introspective conscience rotting on the inside, no passive/aggressive Christian who is sentimental on the outside but violent on the inside, Hildegard called her sisters and others to their noble roles to fight injustice and embrace compassion.

St. Thomas Aquinas embraces spiritual warriorhood when he celebrates the virtues of courage, magnanimity, and zeal. Zeal, he says, comes from an intense experience of the beauty of things. Thus our real energy for being spiritual warriors derives from our being in love: our awareness of how precious beauty is and how real our defense of it must be. Surely there are profound lessons here for an era that must commit to an ecological revolution, one that is nonviolent but committed. Aquinas says that the virtue of magnanimity (a "big soul" in Latin), relates especially to *trust*. A warrior is magnanimous and trusts a power greater than himself or herself. Courage is necessary for magnanimity as well. Magnanimity urges us to do great things and to **brave great dangers for great things, for instance the common welfare, justice, divine worship, and so forth.**

Aquinas was fond of citing the prophet Jeremiah who said, **The Lord is with me like a brave warrior.** The prophet needs protecting against enemies both internal and external. Aquinas outlines the elements of spiritual warriorhood when he names three elements that saints need for making peace: **First, the strength of di-**

vine power. Psalm 125 says: "Those who believe in the Lord are like Mount Sion which will never be shaken. . . ." Second, the purity of one's own conscience, as in Proverbs 3: "You will walk confidently along your way, and your foot will not stumble." Third, the removal of hostile evil, as in John 16: "Be confident, I have overcome the world."

In the Hebrew Bible, Yahweh is praised as a warrior for having destroyed Pharaoh's army and liberated the Jewish people.

> Yahweh is my strength, my song,
> he is my salvation.
> This is my God, I praise him;
> The God of my father, I extol him.
> Yahweh is a warrior;
> Yahweh is his name.
> The chariots and the army of Pharaoh he has hurled into the sea. . . .
> Your right hand, Yahweh, shows the majestic in power,
> your right hand, Yahweh, shatters the enemy.

This same theme is commemorated in Psalm 24.

> Let the king of glory in!
> Who is this king of glory?
> Yahweh the strong, the valiant,
> Yahweh valiant in battle!

The prophet Isaiah tells how Yahweh Sabaoth is **marshalling the troops for battle to punish the world for its evil-doing, and the wicked for their crimes, to put an end to the pride of arrogant men and humble the pride of despots.** God calls forth warriors to accomplish the divine anger at injustice.

> I, for my part, issue orders
> to my sacred warriors,
> I summon my knights to serve my anger,
> my proud champions.

In Judaism the spiritual warrior is identified with the Messiah as in the following text from Wisdom literature.

> **When peaceful silence lay over all,**
> **and night had run the half of her swift course,**
> **down from the heavens, from the royal throne, leapt your all-powerful**
> **Word;**
> **into the heart of a doomed land the stern warrior leapt.**
> **Carrying your unambiguous command like a sharp sword,**
> **he stood, and filled the universe with death;**
> **he touched the sky, yet trod the earth.**

It is interesting that Christians employ this text on Christmas eve as applicable to the birth of the Christ. Thus Jesus is seen as a spiritual warrior.

In the *Zohar* the warrior energy is invoked.

> **Now since a person's real work in this world**
> **is the work of the Blessed Holy One,**
> **he must be as strong as a lion on every side**
> **so that the Other Side will not overpower him**
> **or be able to seduce him.**

The prophetic tradition of Israel might be seen in the light of spiritual warriorhood. As Rabbi Heschel puts it, what is uppermost in the prophets' mind is injustice— **the presence of oppression and corruption. The urgency of justice was an urgency of aiding and saving the victims of oppression.** This was the work of the prophets. They sought out leaders, kings, princes, false prophets, and priests as the ones responsible for the sins of the community. Taking on the leaders was a warrior-like task. Isaiah says:

The Lord enters into judgment
With the elders and princes of his people:
It is you who have devoured the vineyard,
The spoil of the poor is in your houses.
What do you mean by crushing the people,
By grinding the face of the poor?
Says the Lord of hosts.

Yet Heschel reminds us that all people are to be prophets. **To do justice is what God demands of every man: it is the supreme commandment, and one that cannot be fulfilled vicariously.**

Buddhism has much to teach about spiritual warriorhood. The warrior trains his or her heart by learning to let go and be emptied in order to see what is. Pema Chodron puts it this way: **For practitioners or spiritual warriors—people who have a certain hunger to know what is true—feelings like disappointment, embarrassment, irritation, resentment, anger, jealousy, and fear, instead of being bad news, are actually very clear moments that teach us where it is that we're holding back. They teach us to perk up and lean in when we feel we'd rather collapse and back away.** Notice, it is *hunger* that marks a warrior, hunger for the truth. The emptying that goes on prepares us to get more involved, not less.

The reptilian brain that we carry within us yearns to be tamed and bridled. We need to give it our attention, in the process getting to know our deeper and often more violent selves, and move beyond the aggressive instincts that may have served us when we were hunters and gatherers in a hostile environment but that play havoc with our contemporary efforts at making community. Pema Chodron writes how important courage is in a time like ours. **When the rivers and air are polluted, when families and nations are at war, when homeless wanderers fill the highways, these are traditional signs of a dark age. Another is that people become poisoned by self-doubt and become cowards.**

How do we resist becoming cowards? How many ways do we have of hiding our cowardice behind addictions of all kind, behind not standing up and being heard, behind busyness or "I'm too busy with my family" excuses, behind pseudo-religiosity, behind making money? Behind small-mindedness and chatter and living lives of shopping, television addiction, and trivia pursuits?

Buddhism teaches us to be warriors insofar as it teaches mindfulness. Mindfulness leads to compassionate action. Chodron puts it this way. **The ground of not causing harm is mindfulness, a sense of clear seeing with respect and compassion for what it is we see.** Thich Nhat Hanh also believes that mindfulness can make one strong and solid. **Mindfulness, if practiced continuously will be strong enough to embrace your fear or anger and transform it. We need not** chase away evil. We can embrace and transform it in a nonviolent, nondualistic way. Nonviolence takes a warrior's heart and mind.

Chogyam Trungpa talked about the **spiritual warrior's tender heart.** That is a beautiful phrase, the *tender heart* of the warrior. So often soldiers are taught to stifle their hearts and to develop steel around their heart. But a spiritual warrior is to have a heart that is both tender and strong. As Jack Kornfield puts it, **true compassion arises from a sense that the heart has the fearless capacity to embrace all things, to touch all things, to relate to all things.** Reaching out to the great cosmos, to its vast beauty and its vast pain, takes strength. A strong heart, a **fearless capacity.**

Joanna Macy teaches an ancient prophecy from Tibet concerning the Shambhala warriors. **Great courage—moral and physical—is required of the Shambhala warriors, for they must go into the very heart of the barbarian power, into the pits and pockets and citadels where the weapons are kept to dismantle them.** What weapons do they train to use? **The weapons are compassion and insight.** Compassion opens you to pain and gives you the energy to move. **But that weapon by itself is not enough. It can burn you out, so you need the other— you need insight into the radical interdependence of all phenomena.** Joanna believes that now is the hour of the Shambhala warriors.

The tradition of "jihad" in Islam has often been distorted to mean "holy war" against others. In fact, Muhammad himself was explicit about its true meaning. He said, on returning from a battle: **We are returning from the lesser *jihad*, to the greater *jihad*, the struggle with our own selves.** *Jihad* means spiritual warfare, that is, to go to battle with one's own demons and princely adversaries inside oneself. It means effort on the spiritual path, that which is necessary to struggle against evil. As one commentator puts it. **The first and most essential *jihad* which the Muslim must carry on is within himself in a never-ceasing effort at self-improvement and self-purification. This is known as *jihad bil nafs* (striving with the self).** It means the struggle against injustice but there is to be no religious strife. The Qur'an states explicitly: **Let there be no compulsion in religion.**

Sufi mystic Hafiz speaks on behalf of the spiritual warrior on several occasions. He warns us that life includes struggle and that soldierhood alone, battle without love, can render a person mad.

> **It is a naive man who thinks we are not**
>> **Engaged in a fierce battle,**
> **For I see and hear brave foot soldiers**
>> **All around me going mad,**
> **Falling on the ground in excruciating pain.**
> **You could become a victorious horseman**
> **And carry your heart through this world**
>> **Like a life-giving sun**
> **Though only if you and God become sweet Lovers!**

Becoming a lover is the key to warriorhood. But to do this also requires that we know ourselves and cleanse ourselves of our past wounds. Compassion toward self is thus presumed in the warrior. A taming of the beasts. In doing this, the jewel within the heart is released anew.

> The warriors tame
> The beasts in their past
> So that the night's hoofs
> Can no longer break the jeweled vision
> In the heart.

To ignore this taming of past hurts is to invite "barfing everywhere." It opens the door to a new future. We learn to live beyond the past.

> The intelligent and the brave
> Open every closet in the future and evict
> All the mind's ghosts who have the bad habit
> Of barfing everywhere.

Hafiz recognizes the cosmos itself yearning to express itself in our chakras, through our spine.

> For a long time the universe
> Has been germinating in your spine.

But to have the courage to face both past and future requires saintliness.

> But only a Pir [saint] has the talent,
> The courage to slay
> The past-giant, the future-anxieties.

Where does the warrior learn wisdom? First, he or she learns self-knowledge and humility and unmasking in a circle with others; next, she or he learns generosity.

>   The warrior
> Wisely sits in a circle
> With other men
> Gathering the strength to unmask himself,
>   Then Sits, giving,
> Like a great illumined planet on
>   the Earth.

The generosity we learn as warriors mirrors the generosity of the sun itself.

>   Even after all this time
>   The sun never says to the earth,
>   "You owe me."
>   Look what happens
>   with a love like that,
>   It lights up the whole sky.

The danger exists that we will run away from this invitation to courage and saintliness and prefer the comfort religion promises.

>   Love wants to reach out and manhandle us,
>   Break all our teacup talk of God. . . .
>   The Beloved sometimes wants
>   To do us a great favor:
>   Hold us upside down
>   And shake all the nonsense out.
>   But when we hear
>   He is in such a "playful drunken mood"
>   Most everyone I know
>   Quickly packs their bags and hightails it
>   Out of town.

In Hinduism, the Bhagavad Gita centers around the story of a young soldier named Arjuna. He is overwhelmed by grief and compassion while engaging in a battle and seeing people he admired slaughtered. He wants to give up living. One could say that the entire story is one of instructing Arjuna on how to grow from being a soldier to being a warrior. The key is inner work, yoga, discipline, and learning. He is told: **Therefore the doubts which have arisen in your heart out of ignorance should be slashed by the weapons of knowledge. Armed with yoga, of Bharata, *stand and fight.*** The young soldier must move from fighting an external enemy to dealing with internal ones. He must take on new weapons, more internal than external, weapons of knowledge and self-discipline. He must grow up, be strong, stand and fight. The final chapter of the Gita summarizes the work of the warrior in this way:

> **Heroism, majesty, firmness, skill,**
> **And not fleeing in battle also,**
> **Generosity, and leadership,**
> **Are the natural-born actions of warriors.**

In India, Kali is a side of the Divine Mother that has been called the warrior aspect of the feminine. She refuses to separate death from life, and she demands that the false self be sacrificed. She calls one to become aware of the shadow and not suppress it but confront it. Shakti power is a purifying power that is aggressive. Spiritual vigor is called forth. In the *Chandi* book of the Hindu Scriptures, the Divine Mother says: **Wherever there is oppression in the world, I shall descend and destroy it.**

The Vedas offer many prayers for **valor, manliness, spiritual power, conquering power, wrath, fearlessness, vigor, and other qualities of heroism.** One such prayer follows.

> **O Hero! give manly vigor to our men.**
> **urge us to heroic power**
> **I pray for soul-force which none can bend.**
> **Fight, warrior, strong in truth.**

In our century, surely Mahatma Gandhi and Martin Luther King were spiritual warriors who drew on the traditions of both India and the Jewish prophets including Jesus. Each got killed for their warriorship and nonviolent leadership. Dorothy Day and many members of the women's movement have displayed credentials of warriorhood as well.

Julia Butterfly Hill is a twenty-five-year-old woman who spent the past two years living in an ancient redwood tree in northern California to protect it from the Pacific Lumber Company's threat to cut it down and sell it. Life in the tree was forever cold and damp and very cramped. She left the tree only after Pacific Lumber agreed not to cut it down. Charles Hurwitz, the chairman of the corporation that owns Pacific Lumber, tried to cajole Hill, threatening to remove her from the forest and take her to court. She held her own, however, and did prevail. She sent Hurwitz letters and Christmas cards, but got no response. Yet she says: "Hurwitz is a master chess player. He's brilliant—if he ever got in touch with his heart, he could do amazing work." She says of her testimony, "I asked God to use me as a vessel, so I guess you have to be careful what you ask for. My hope is people can learn to feel their connection to the magnificence of creation. . . . Pacific Lumber talks about economics, but how can anyone place a price (on a tree like Luna)?" Luna is her name for the tree she inhabited. Clearly, Hill is a modern-day warrior. She even understands the role of her adversary. Her stout heart and determination carried her far. She is living proof that warriorhood is alive and well and we can all participate in its responsibilities and challenges.

In her autobiography *The Legacy of Luna,* Julia Butterfly tells a story that explains the difference between a soldier and a warrior. When she first climbed the tree, she was joined by a young man—but he only lasted three weeks in the tree. Why? Because he was so radically angry at the loggers, his "enemies," that he **just seemed to sink deeper and deeper into despair and anger. . . . Day by day, he seemed to grow more drawn. His already deep-set eyes and his striking cheekbones and thick eyebrows were a part of him when I met him, but as the onslaught wore on, his cheeks and eyes sunk in more and more. He started** looking like a skeleton, his skin stretched tight over the bones underneath. His life seemed to be draining away in front of my eyes. After twenty-five days, this young man left the tree-sit.

Why was Julia able to endure? She had a spiritual practice that took her beyond her anger. **I began to pray. I knew that if I didn't find a way to deal with my anger and hate, they would overwhelm me, and I would be swallowed up in the fear, sadness, and frustration. I knew that to hate and strike out was to be a part of the same violence I was trying to stop. And so I prayed. "Please, Universal Spirit, please help me find a way to deal with this, because if I don't, it's going to consume me."**

Julia was the warrior; her companion was merely a soldier. Julia comments: **You see that a lot in activists. The intense negative forces that are oppressing and destroying the earth wind up overcoming many of them. They get so absorbed by the hate and the anger that they become hollow. I knew I didn't want to go there. Instead, my hate had to turn to love—unconditional agape, love. One day, through my prayers, an overwhelming amount of love started flowing into me, filling up the dark hole that threatened to consume me. I suddenly realized that what I was feeling was the love of the earth, the love of Creation.**

It takes a warrior to do many kinds of work in our culture. A parent is a warrior. A parent must do strong things at times, pay mindful attention, be alert, loving and defensive of one's children, protecting them from onslaughts from advertisers and media, communications that would distort a child's view of creation. And yet, a parent must also let her or his child go to experience life on their own. There is a special art, therefore, to being a parent, an art that is not different from any other act of compassion: an art that combines heart and head, love and intelligence, communication and silence.

An educator is a warrior, one hungry for truth, on the lookout for ideas that stimulate and excite and put minds into motion. An educator has to be alert to oneself to see that one is always learning and not complacent, that one basks in the moments of truth that come one's way and encourages students to do the same. A true teacher finds rest in truth and joy and does not confuse learning with elitist education.

An administrator is called to be a warrior—especially at this time in history when so many bureaucracies interfere with Spirit happening.

Indeed, all work demands warriorhood, for the need to bring Spirit, values, compassion, and the new cosmology to our professions is a demanding work. Ordinary people are called to warriorhood especially where we work. This is one of the lessons learned in the Native American sundance: that ordinary people can and will be generous and heroes *for the sake of the community.* We can deal with our past hurts and the wounds we inflict on others and will if invited to do so.

Five

CONCLUSION: WHERE

DO WE GO FROM HERE?

HOW DEEP ECUMENISM

EXPLODES OUR

IMAGINATIONS WITH

EIGHTEEN NEW

MYTHS AND VISIONS

I began this book telling a story of a young man attending one of our Techno Cosmic Masses. His operative line was, "Finally, Religion 1999." The key to his exclamation of joy was the deep ecumenism of the ritual in which he participated.

The year 2099 is only one hundred years away. What will humanity look like a century from today? How deep will our ecumenism have traveled? What will the earth look like? What will our spiritualities and religions look like? Will our species survive until then? Will we have lassoed solar energy so that our energy needs are indeed renewable and sustainable? Will we have tamed the violence, envy, greed and resentment in the human heart that is so often the cause of war, slavery, and injustice? Will we have limited the human population so that other populations might survive and thrive and bless us with their presence? Will we have preserved our forests, cleaned our waterways, returned fishes to the oceans, healed the ozone hole, formed laws to regulate our transnational corporations, drawn wisdom from our various spiritual traditions, and accomplished what the Dalai Lama called for early in this book—put forth a reasonable spirituality that all humans could draw on?

This book has been an effort to do just that. In it I have mixed sacred texts and mystical teachings from Judaism and Islam, Hinduism and African, Christian and African American, Goddess and Native American, Celtic and Buddhist and scientific sources. I have done so within a framework of categories that I believe are key to our species' survival.

This book is in no way complete. It is, as I proposed in the introduction, not meant to be exhaustive but rather suggestive. This book may be an example of what future Scriptures will and must contain: wisdom from all our Wisdom traditions, a bias in favor of what we have in common; a religious humility that lets traditions other than our own speak for themselves; a use of primary sources; God as experience, not doctrine; an inclusion of science as part of our wisdom inheritance and our future; and the grouping of the wisdom of our ancestors around issues or themes that concern us all.

Perhaps what we need instead of rivalry and propaganda between religions is a kind of gentle competition among religions to see who can teach these themes the best and the quickest to our young people: Service/compassion/letting go/justice/community/reverence for creation/awe, etc.! And, why not teach them together? Public schools are forbidden to teach religion in America. But there is no reason under heaven that forbids them to teach Creation, service, compassion, joy, meditation, creativity/imagination, sacred sexuality, wisdom, multiple names for Divinity, beauty, suffering, death and rebirth, ethics—and how humanity has traditionally and in diverse ways responded to these realities.

Indeed, if we choose not to teach these things—which is a choice currently in vogue—then we are asking for despair, meaninglessness, drugs, alcohol, suicide, violence, and the thousand other ways of self-hatred and screaming for attention that the young, hurting soul, will indulge in. Just as beauty yearns to be conspicuous, so, too, does our soul's suffering.

For some time now, I have been urging Deep Ecumenism. I named it this in my book *The Coming of the Cosmic Christ* in 1989. I have employed Deep Ecumenism in many books since, including my study on *The Reinvention of Work* (where I was amazed at the depth of contribution that our spiritual traditions make to an understanding of work); in my study on evil, *Sins of the Spirit, Blessings of the Flesh,* where I related the seven chakras of the East to the traditional seven Capital Sins of the West; in my dialogues with scientist Rupert Sheldrake on *Natural Grace* and on *The Physics of Angels.* I have practiced Deep Ecumenism by participating in prayers and rituals, including sweat lodges, sundances, vision quests, and in dialogues with persons of many faiths and in our University of Creation Spirituality and at Naropa Institute of Oakland and Boulder.

But doing this book has taken me into a whole new level of appreciation for Deep Ecumenism. A whole new reality has emerged to speak to me face-to-face. I believe one reason for this deepening of the encounter has been the themes I have chosen. They are not just speaking to us from many faith traditions—they are shouting to be heard, shouting to be investigated. They will not tolerate lack of curiosity, complacency, or just sheer inertia. Our survival as a species depends on their coming alive in our hearts, bodies, minds, and rituals. They are the stuff of authentic community.

The Problem of Religion:
Did Christianity Betray Jesus?

Rabbi Abraham Heschel refuses to let religion off the hook as easily as most people—he does not blame all the troubles of the modern era on science. Rather, he sees religion itself as the problem. **It is customary to blame secular science and anti-religious philosophy for the eclipse of religion in modern society. It would be more honest to blame religion for its own defeats. Religion declined not because it was refuted, but because it became irrelevant, dull, oppressive, insipid. When faith is completely replaced by creed, worship by discipline, love by habit; when the crisis of today is ignored because of the splendor of the past; when faith becomes an heirloom rather than a living fountain; when religion speaks only in the name of authority rather than with the voice of compassion—its message becomes meaningless.**

I hear Heschel calling for our substituting a living spirituality for our tired, institutional forms of religion. I also hear this from the Dalai Lama, and from all the mystics I have cited in this book from whatever tradition they draw on. Religion based on *experience* instead of religion based on authority or institutional ego. Is this not the battle Jesus was fighting in his day? And Gandhi in his? And King in his? And Muhammad in his? And Isaiah in his?

When I hear Heschel's words with my heart as well as my head I am sure I know where they come from. They derive from the horrors of a so-called Christian Europe that indulged in the Holocaust and other atrocities of this century. He needs to say what he says and say it loudly again and again. I hear similar language from the African-American experience of slavery. Howard Thurman says, **Christianity betrayed Jesus.** I hear it from Gandhi, who had to wrestle his nation back from the "Christian" English empire. Indeed, in his encounter with Howard Thurman in the mid-thirties, Gandhi challenged Thurman as to how he could be a Christian when Christian empires enslaved his people. I also hear this language from Native Americans. In a book of poetry called *The Aboriginal Sin* by Tim Giago, Jr., an Oglala Sioux, stories are told of his upbringing on the Pine Ridge reservation by Catholic nuns and priests. The stories are chilling. Here are a few stemming from the *sin of being an aboriginal.*

Holy Rosary Indian Mission, established in 1888 on the Pine Ridge Reservation, in the name of the Christian God, did the following to young Indians. "We were forbidden to speak our native tongue under penalty of a severe whipping. Our identities as individuals were erased by a militaristic type of discipline and behavior. We slept in dormitories, marched to and from all activities in company groups, ate by companies in a dining hall. But the single most dreadful change that tore at the very core of all Indian children was the separation and isolation from our parents, grandparents, and family. All the traditional beliefs, the cultural distinctions, were thus secreted from us." The author states that many children experienced this school as "nothing but a religious concentration camp for Indian kids." Sending their children there was not a choice but a survival mechanism for many of the parents of the children, for it offered their kids room and board during the tough depression times—times that were even more severe on Indian reservations than in the rest of the country.

We have a contemporary telling of the ugliness of Christian missionary work by Malidoma Somé who was literally kidnapped from his West African village by Jesuit missionaries at the age of seven and kept in a seminary along with other kidnapped youth until he escaped at the age of sixteen. Having missed his tribal education all those years, he suffered profoundly from anger and hostility until, at the age of nineteen, he underwent the rite of passage that he had missed when interned by the Catholic church.

The anger that indigenous and enslaved people hold against Christian imperialism ought not to melt away easily. There are profound changes that Christianity must undergo if it is to rediscover its spirit and the true spirit of its source—Jesus himself. While apologies are better than cover-up, forgetfulness and silence, they are not at all adequate to the damage that has been inflicted on individuals and entire cultures. The only appropriate request for forgiveness can and must be *a reinventing of one's religious system,* that is to say, the replacement of religion with spirituality. This deconstruction of Christianity is happening today with the work of the Jesus Seminar scholars and others. The reconstruction can also happen with the remythologizing that we have laid out in this book. Allow me to explain.

DECONSTRUCTING OUR SOURCES: THE HISTORICAL JESUS AND THE COSMIC CHRIST

I am struck when I learn that the first Buddhist texts were written down five hundred years after the Buddha lived and that much of the Qur'an was written after the prophet lived. I am surprised to hear how many of the world Scriptures that we know began as storytelling and not textual gathering, and this in cultures where oral memory was strong and practiced with intensity. The fact that we have this pattern in all our Scripture-based religions is good news. While each religion is tempted to go the way of fundamentalism for simple answers, that would, in fact, betray the very spirit of Moses, Jesus, Buddha, Muhammad, *all of whom* reached out to the less than orthodox of their day and all of whom interfered with religion and society as it was in their day just as prophets do.

I think the findings of today's historical scholars about biblical sources are very important, for they remind us how important the community is as a source itself of group memory. They remind us that literalism and textualisms are addictions that are very recent. Stories get embellished, retold, improved upon, imaginatively and excitedly added to. That is human nature. That is not an effort to deceive. It is part of what enthusiasm does to a person's or a community's soul.

For Christians today, a return to our sources is an especially exciting return because so much new has emerged this century with discoveries of lost sacred texts and gospels and with the culmination of historical scholarship around the sources of our faith. With these discoveries we are far more equipped to hold back our projections onto the historical Jesus and to let him be who he was—not what we want to make him over to be for us. Who is this historical Jesus as we now know him? Dominic Crossan writes: "The historical Jesus was a peasant Jewish Cynic. His strategy, implicitly for himself and explicitly for his followers, was the combination of *free healing and common eating*, a religious and economic egalitarianism that negated alike and at once the hierarchical and patronal normalcies of Jewish religion and Roman power. He announced the unmediated or brokerless Kingdom of God." Another Jesus scholar, Marcus Borg, sees Jesus as a teacher of wisdom whose goal through his aphorisms and parables is "to subvert conventional ways of seeing and living, and to invite his hearers to an alternative way of life"—especially as regards attitudes of "conventional wisdom" toward economics, power, sexuality, and relationship.

We are learning that about 85 percent of what we were told are the words of Jesus actually came from the excited community rather than from him. Finding which words ascribed to Jesus were really his and which were not has the effect of freeing up our ability to relearn the ancient tradition of the Cosmic Christ (like cosmic wisdom and the Living Buddha) and to respond to our calling to become Cosmic Christs ourselves. Indeed, was this not the purpose of Jesus' teachings and life, to draw us into our divine dignity and responsibility for compassion? The Cosmic Christ tradition is not unimportant simply because all its words do not come directly from Jesus' mouth. Indeed, much of the *spirit* of this tradition comes from those hearts and minds who met Jesus and were awakened by him or those who knew him. With our newly found ability to distinguish between the historical Jesus and the Cosmic Christ, and to honor each while not surrendering our own responsibility to develop their meanings, our spiritual imagination will be reinvigorated to launch new models of worship, meditation, art, politics, economics, education. In short, a renaissance becomes possible for our species. Hopefully, movements similar to the Jesus Seminar in Christian and biblical circles will gain ground among students of other religious traditions as well. There is a healthy freedom vis-à-vis our sources when we can know where the sources derived from. Ideologies receive some checks and balances.

The sad stories that are told by cultures conquered by Christian empires are testimony to the power of ideology to wage war and to conquer. A critical attitude toward our sources is one way to diffuse this tendency to project onto Divinity our reptilian brain's desire to vanquish and devour.

By giving proper attention to our mystical sources as well as our Scriptural ones, we are inviting the mystic in us to develop, we are honoring our ancestors, and we are awakening our own souls. After all, those sections of our Scriptures that embellish the words of Jesus (or of Buddha or of Muhammad, etc.), were composed by artists and mystics moved by spirit to create and speak wisdom. In this book I have cited often some of my favorite ancestors who are Christian mystics: Hildegard of Bingen, Julian of Norwich, Meister Eckhart, Thomas Aquinas, John of the Cross, Martin Luther King, Jr., Howard Thurman, and others. These people were losers in Christian history. Rarely has their understanding of the Cosmic Christ been grasped or taught. Their wisdom, however, shouts to us today. By knowing them, we know ourselves and our own capacity for depth—and our own responsibility to go deep no matter what institutional authorities declare.

Who says that the same spirit that moved the makers of Scripture and the mystics of our tradition is somehow retired or on vacation in our day as if all wisdom has been expressed or all need for connections to the Divine has been fulfilled? Quite the opposite is the case, I feel. The Spirit is more at work today than ever precisely because our species is at such a moral and survival crossroads. Artists of all kinds are needed today to let art-for-art-sake ideologies go and learn to serve the community anew with truth-telling. This truth-telling must be about the beauty of our existences *and* about the ugliness and evil that confronts us and in which we participate.

Jesus too was a mystic, "a Middle Eastern mystic," as Aramaic scholar Neil Douglas Klotz puts it. This is a very important insight, for many biblical scholars, more influenced by certain biases of European academia than by Jesus' character (who, after all, never got a degree), ignore mysticism altogether in their analysis of his person.

Another area in which Christians are being called to a new look at their sources derives from language studies around the tribal language that the historical Jesus spoke. An example of this work can be found in the Aramaic version of the prayer we know today as the Our Father or The Lord's Prayer. So often believers can become overly familiar with a text that is recited frequently and the result is a dulling of the mind and heart instead of an awakening of one's soul. Consider the following translation. It is just as accurate—given the flexibility of the language that Jesus spoke and prayed in—as the translations we have memorized from our childhood. Yet it is much more inclusive of a cosmic mysticism.

> **O Birther! Father-Mother of the Cosmos**
> **you create all that moves in light.**
> **Hear the one Sound that created all others,**
> **in this way the Name is hallowed**
> **in silence.**
> **Your rule springs into existence**
> **as our arms reach out to embrace all creation.**
> **Let all wills move together**
> **in your vortex, as stars and planets**
> **swirl through the sky.**
> **Grant what we need each day in bread and insight:**
> **subsistence for the call of**
> **growing life.**
> **Lighten our load of secret debts as**
> **we relieve others of their**
> **need to repay.**

Keep us from hoarding false wealth,
and from the inner shame of
help not given in time.

Many times I have utilized this Our Father prayer in our Techno Cosmic Masses and people always want a copy. They are awakened by it. Jesus' prayer comes alive again and so do they. We need to remember that Jesus, a Middle Eastern mystic, was *listened to* and not read in his day. His words penetrated heart and mind and body—as words tend to do in oral societies more than text-based societies. These words inspired and provoked the responses that resulted in 85 percent of our Christian scriptures.

In his book *The Hidden Gospel: Decoding the Spiritual Message of the Aramaic Jesus,* Neil Douglas Klotz offers new perspectives from the Aramaic of other of Jesus' sayings. For example, while the word we translate as "spirit" is used over one hundred times in the four gospels, and in his language the word can mean spirit, wind, air, or breath, in our translations of the Scriptures we have only used the word "spirit." Following are two sections of the Scriptures that come to new life with alternative translations.

From John 4:24, usually translated **God is a spirit.**

God is breath.
All that breathes resides in the Only Being.
From my breath
to the air we share
to the wind that blows around the planet:
Sacred Unity inspires all.

From Matthew 5:3, usually translated **Blessed are the poor in spirit, for theirs is the kingdom of heaven.**

**Ripe are those who reside in breath,
to them belongs the reign of unity.
Blessed are those who realize that breath is
their first and last possession,
theirs is the "I Can" of the cosmos.**

These translations lend themselves to spiritual practices of meditation and breath work and dance, as Dr. Klotz demonstrates in his books. A return to one's sources newly translated and richly so from Jesus' own language clearly creates an all-new impact on our spirits.

An opportunity facing Christians today derives from the amazing discovery near the town of Nag Hammadi in upper Egypt in 1945 of a library that has turned out to be "every bit as revolutionary for the study of the New Testament as the Dead Sea Scrolls are for the study of the Hebrew Bible." There was found the "Gospel according to Thomas," a gospel lost for one thousand years, and which probably goes back to as early as 50–60 C.E. in its earliest form, to the year 100 in its present form. In that gospel are new sayings and parables attributed to Jesus as well as proof that early Christians circulated texts of Jesus' sayings (not just narratives like the better known four gospels).

It is important to note as well, however, that the authors of this fifth gospel had their agenda and ideologies and put many words into Jesus' mouth that were not his. Clearly, one slant in the gospels that often emerges is what scholar Robert Funk calls "incipient Gnosticism," including an attitude of seeking aloneness versus community. Nevertheless, the Gospel of Thomas is "rooted in the Jewish wisdom tradition, such as we find in Psalms and Proverbs. It is a wisdom gospel made up of the teachings of a sage. But it is moving off in the direction of gnostic speculation such as we find in later gnostic documents." Thus, it carries its own theological agenda with it as do the other gospels and Paul as well. The library found at Nag Hammadi opens the Christian mind and heart to reexamine origins, and scholars are busy at work doing just that. As Elizabeth Castelli and Hal Taussig put it, "No find could be as significant as the library at Nag Hammadi, which offers an unparalleled palette of colors with which to nuance and transform the reigning portrait of early Christianity. Moreover, the texts that form this remarkable library insist that the other ancient sources to which we have already had access . . . can never be read in quite the same fashion again." All this points to "the diversity and irreducibility of early Christian writing." Permission is now at hand to honor diversity in even the earliest of Christian communities. Why not in later manifestations as well?

PRACTICING DEEP ECUMENISM

In practicing Deep Ecumenism according to the spirit of this book and joining in those many movements today which are dedicated to the same spirit we can reconstruct our religious faiths. We can and ought to return to our spiritual sources—not to run empires with and not to propagandize with—but to find joint truth together, common ground on which to face the very survival issues of morality and celebration, grief and forgiveness and letting go. Without this truth-discovery we will not survive. Going down the well of one's own tradition or a chosen one, we do indeed arrive at common waters of wisdom.

But arriving is not enough. We must drink deeply there. We must be refreshed and energized there. We must move beyond to common action, common non-action, common prayer and common celebration, common warriorhood. Then we will be *practicing* Deep Ecumenism.

As a species, we are in a whole new position to know spirit today. The shrinking of our globe by way of instant communications as well as rapid travel, the mixing of ideas and music, dance, and parties by the young culture and its facility with electronic media, all of this holds vast implications for spiritual connecting. The kind of wisdom I have gathered from many sources in this book was not available much before our time. Westerners were so steeped in modernist propaganda that they were oblivious of their own spiritual traditions, much less that of other cultures and times. Witness the Jewish theologian who in the 1970s told his seminar students that "there is no mystical tradition in Judaism." Witness the inquisitors in the Vatican's so-called Congregation of Faith who do not know their mystical tradition when it is being recovered for them. Witness the presence of fundamentalism in all the world religions today, a reactionary movement that belies Creation and the Author of Creation.

Privilege and the ideologies that buttress them die hard. But it is my experience that the new generation, imbued with post-modern worldviews and suspicious of religious denominationalism, is truly seeking a spiritual depth and will respond to elders and others who can deliver and work together to birth an intergenerational wisdom.

REMYTHOLOGIZING FOR THE TWENTY-FIRST CENTURY

As we saw in our chapter on creativity and our chapter on compassion, early Christianity was astoundingly creative and radical. What Jesus and Paul unleashed in creativity was astounding. Eighty-five percent of the gospels, all of Paul's and others' epistles, the Eucharistic liturgy, the Resurrection and Crucifixion and Birth stories, and nineteen hundred years of theological development are traceable to the release of the Christ energy and the Holy Spirit that accompanied it.

Burton Mack, a scholar of the Q community of Christians, says that what was going on among the earliest communities after Jesus' death was "an explosion of creative imagination that we would call myth-making." One wonders if we do not need such an *explosion of imagination* today. But it was not just the myth-making that launched the Christian movement. "It was the attraction of participating in a group experimenting with a new social vision." A new social vision launched the imaginations of the earliest followers of Jesus. A similar laudable vision of reality is lacking in many academic theologians who are more committed to deconstructing than to reconstructing. But myths are at our fingertips for such a vision.

How important is myth? Rollo May insists that "myth is the foundation of values and ethics." Myths support us and inspire us to great things. New social visions—like old ones—are aroused in us by myth. "Every individual seeks—indeed *must* seek if he or she is to remain sane—to bring some order and coherence into the stream of sensations, emotions, and ideas entering his or her consciousness from within or without. Each one of us is forced to do deliberately for oneself what in previous ages was done by family, custom, church and state, namely, form the myths in terms of which we can make some sense of experience."

What myths might carry us into the twenty-first century? Are there social visions that can arouse excitement and spirit comparable to the first century visions? As I indicate in the introduction, no one was more surprised than I was on finishing this book to realize that the eighteen themes that form the chapters of this book can be understood as viable myths for our time. Remember that myths are not stories that are not true; myths are stories that are *too true* and *too large* for facts alone, for the left hemisphere of the brain alone. A myth is not primarily about analysis but about seizing imagination.

EIGHTEEN MYTHS FOR
REMYTHOLOGIZING OUR SPECIES

Following are the myths I propose as fertile ground for artists and ritualists, for economists, theologians, scientists and all workers, for parents and grandparents, for children and all peoples. And certainly, for descendants of all the world's spiritual traditions.

1. The myth that all our spiritual traditions can learn from each other *and* offer something fresh from their experiences and teachings. That is, the myth of Deep Ecumenism.
2. The myth that all Creation is sacred and we humans are part of it, integral to it, though late on the scene. Ecological care and concern is part of being here.

3. The myth that all Creation is on fire with sacredness; that the Buddha nature and the Cosmic Christ and the image of God reside in the very light (photons) present in every atom in the universe.

4. The myth that community already is because all things are interdependent, nothing stands alone. Isolation and rugged individualism are lies that betray the very manner in which the universe operates. The truth is that interdependence exists at the microcosmic and macrocosmic and psychic levels of existence. We need to remove the obstacles that interfere with our realizing this truth about community.

5. The myth that whatever name we give the Source of sources, the Artist of artists, the Creator of Creation, all are accurate and none are sufficient.

6. The myth that the Divine has a feminine as well as a masculine side. And so do we, made in her image.

7. The myth that divine Wisdom roams the world, "fills the whole earth," interacts with us and all Creation and calls us to supper.

8. The myth that the Divine, while present in all forms, is also present as emptiness, nothingness, and formlessness and that we experience emptiness, nothingness, and formlessness and can trust these experiences.

9. The myth that the Divine "I Am" can be spoken by every one of us and by every creature and that this is our way of asserting our divine nobility and exuding a radiance greater than ourselves.

10. The myth that we experience mindfulness, a state of being more and more fully present to the "I Am" and to our deepest self through meditations of various kinds.

11. The myth that our imaginations are holy, that the Holy Spirit works through us when we create and participate in the ongoing Creation of self, society, universe, and mind.

12. The myth that joy is possible even daily—and that we have a right to it as well as a responsibility to search it out, prepare for it, and pass it on.

13. The myth that suffering, while it is everywhere, is real yet endurable. That suffering comes as a teacher of wisdom and compassion and rather than fleeing it, we ought to sit at its feet and learn what it wants to teach us.

14. The myth that Beauty is another name for the Divine, that it is available everywhere, and that our task is to become ever more aware of its presence and be sharers of its energy.

15. The myth that our sexuality is sacred, that the body is no obstacle to Divine presence, that love-making is as holy a meditation as fasting or serving, and that love-making is for the propagation of community and love as much as for propagation of the species (which clearly needs less propagation at this time).

16. The myth that our dying is as adventurous as our living and that what occurs at death and after death, whether we call it reincarnation or resurrection or regeneration, is mysterious but not final. No beauty dies; no grace is lost; no warmth is forgotten.

17. The myth that compassion is the imitation of the Divine and compassion includes celebration and relief of pain and suffering and the active struggle against injustice. That service is something we can commit ourselves to that is worthy of full commitment.

18. The myth that we are all spiritual warriors (or prophets) as well as lovers (or mystics). And this means that we struggle with self and not just with outside enemies when we struggle for social transformation; it also means that we work from the heart and not just from reaction.

These myths, I believe, hold the key to "Religion 2099"—if there need be such a thing. As the Dalai Lama observes, the majority of people don't feel a need for religion. This majority may increase in the coming century. But people clearly do feel a need for spirituality, for connecting with deep living, deep breathing, deep sharing, deep awareness and mindfulness. These myths, as laid out in this book, suggest that *all human experiences* of what we call religion or spirituality and today's cosmology have something to offer regarding these myths. The task now is to live them, to put them into our imaginations through art and story, through ritual and celebration, through grief and caring. And service.

Without the positive or life-supporting myths laid out in this book that are biophilic, our species will continue its downward spiral into necrophilic myths. The myth of ever-more consumption and consumerism—even though it instructs us to eat our childrens' futures—will reign. Rollo May believes that much of the quest for drugs and cults and what he calls "the lonely search for internal identity" happens today because of lack of healthy myths. The animus against myth that derives from rationalistic attitudes of academics also contributes to this bleak, meaningless culture.

What we can learn from this book is that myths still abound in all of our wisdom traditions, myths that we can weave and reweave today under our unique circumstances of living together in these postmodern times on this wounded planet. Myths can save and heal. Myths can assist us to move, as Howard Thurman put it, from our **little walls, little altars, little God, little lives of defending our little barriers to living in a universe that sustains great adventure.** The key to this shift from littleness to greatness will be creativity itself—that which **inspires the mind to multiply experiences in unity—which experiences of unity become over and over and over again more compelling than the concepts, the ways of life, the sects, and the creeds that separate men.** What will result from this movement, this growing up and coming of age of our species? **What we see dimly now in the churning confusion and chaos of our tempestuous times will someday be the common experience of all the children of men everywhere.** There will be a unity amidst our diversity and a diversity within our unity.

NOTES

Note to Reader

The quotes in the notes below are linked to the Bibliography on page 461. The number in boldface refers to the bibliographical work and is followed by the page number.

INTRODUCTION

page 3. "Humanity will find . . . call wisdom." **26.** 126, 241; "I believe that we must find. . . ." Jean-Claude Carriere, "Global View: A Conversation with the Dalai Lama," *Tricycle,* Fall, 1995, 39; "Everything starts with us. . . ." Jean-Claude Carriere, *Violence and Compassion, Dialogues on Life Today* (New York: Doubleday, 1996), 92.

page 6. "A powerful, expressive modality. . . ." **1.** 197f.

page 7. "the dispersal . . . Arabic as language." **1.** 198; "the reality is. . . ." **52.** 33.

page 8. "now more than ever . . . other faiths." **52.** 184, 222.

page 9. "We have, of course, to guard. . . ." **36.** 99.

page 10. "all paths lead. . . ." **29.** 64.

Chapter 1. DEEP ECUMENISM AND THE UNIVERSALITY OF EXPERIENCE

page 15. "It is my belief. . . ." **84.** 152.

page 16. "the truly wise person. . . ." **92.** 39.

page 17. "Neither a Hindu nor. . . ." **50.** 31; "The god of Hindus resides. . . ." **50.** 31; "Do not look here. . . ." Luke 17:20f.; "Once you experience. . . ." **50.** 170.

page 18. "Many are the paths. . . ." *Bhagavad Gita* iv.11; "the great religions. . . ." **67.** xxii; "I am the thread . . . one of the pearls." **67.** 192; "The worship of. . . ." **56.** 17; "I see people who talk. . . ." **43.** 53.

page 19. "Islam considers. . . ." Seyyed Hossein, *Sufi Essays* (London: George Allen and Unwin Ltd. 1972), 169; "Surely, of the Believers. . . ." **49.** 13; "Indeed We gave. . . ." **49.** 16; "We gave

Jesus. . . ." **49.** 40; "We believe in Allah. . . ." **49.** 22; "We make no distinction. . . ." **49.** 46; He has sent down. . . ." **49.** 48.

page 20. "All religions. . . ." Coleman Barks, *Rumi: One-Handed Basket Weaving* (Athens, GA: Maypop, 1991), 30; "For those in love," **80.** 51; "I have learned. . . ." **51.** 32.

page 21. "What do sad people. . . ." **51.** 119; "The great religions are. . . ." **51.** 177.

page 22. "Through the practice . . . touch your own." **41.** 7; "All men of wisdom. . . ." **50.** 155.

page 23. "A strange necessity. . . ." **88.** x; "It is my belief. . . ." **84.** 152; "We were thus released. . . ." **84.** 22.

page 24. "Every truth without exception. . . ." **31.** 31. "This is very important. . . ." **37.** 29.

page 25. "The only genuine proof. . . ." **58.** 107.

Chapter 2. CREATION—ALL OUR RELATIONS

page 28. "cosmic religion" **37.** 30; "had not learned. . . ." **37.** 32.

page 29. "A mistake. . . ." **31.** 75; "They shall be drunk. . . ." **31.** 124; "Each and every creature. . . ." **31.** 124; "God's work. . . ." **31.** 125f.; "The ultimate end. . . ." **31.** 125; "The principal good. . . ." **31.** 122; "The whole universe. . . ." **31.** 123.

page 30. "Every creature participates. . . ." **31.** 120f

page 31. "words of God. . . ." **30.** 58f.; "all creatures. . . ." **30.** 59; "God is. . . ." **30.** 66; "This word was with. . . ." **1.** 3–4; "In him all things. . . ." Colossians 1:16–17; "isness is God. **16.** 89; "become flesh and. . . ." John 1:14.

page 32. "God is creating. . . ." **29.** 24f.

page 33. "Creation is allowed. . . ." **90.** 57; "As the Creator. . . ." **90.** 51; "God's Word. . . ." **90.** 49.

page 34. "Yahweh, what variety. . . ." Psalm 104.24–26; "Good and very good." Genesis 1:4, 1:31; "Simply I learned about. . . ." Wisdom 7:17–22.

page 35. "The heavens. . . ." Psalm 19. 1–4.

page 36. "By the word of Yahweh. . . ." Psalm 33:8f; "Creation is . . . ." *Pirke Avot* 6: 2. Cited in **43.** 100; "All things the Lord. . . ." Daniel 3: 57–80.

page 38. "O mankind. . . ." **49.** 8; "In the creation. . . ." **49.** 26; "In every abode. . . ." R. W. J. Austin, trans., *Ibn Al'Arabi: The Bezels of Wisdom* (New York: Paulist, 1980), 101.

page 39. "Although you are one. . . ." **73.** 569; "The Spirit of the Lord. . . ." Wisdom 1:7; "If hundreds of thousands of suns. . . ." **73.** 563; "O Lord of the universe. . . ." **73.** 566; "You are the original. . . ." **73.** 583; "Understand. . . ." **73.** 460; "O son of Kunti. . . ." **73.** 463; "There is no end. . . ." **73.** 550; "Know that all opulent. . . ." **73.** 551; "Everywhere are His hands. . . ." **73.** 656; "I enter into each planet. . . ." **73.** 728.

page 40. "All creation is. . . ." **47.** 54; "creation is not. . . ." **7.** 146.

page 41. "miracles of wildness. . . ." **9.** 125; "We need to tire. . . ." **9.** 126; "We all possess. . . ." **9.** 126; "God lies on a. . . ." **29.** 88; "Even when there are. . . ." **81.** 92f.

page 42. "Awaken to the fact. . . ." **81.** 29.

page 43. "When we look into. . . ." **41.** 11; "In East Asia. . . ." **40.** 45; "One thing is made up. . . ." **40.** 5; "If you are not able. . . ." **40.** 8f; "all beings. . . ." **41.** 43.

page 44. "A Buddha is. . . ." **41.** 22; "Our true home. . . ." **41.** 22; "The technique. . . ." **41.** 17; "The reign of God. . . ." Luke 17:21.

page 45. "The difference between. . . ." **12.** 131; "The first ringing assertion. . . ." **12.** 116; "This sense of the world. . . ." **12.** 133; "all the world. . . ." **12.** 135; "I arise today. . . ." **12.** 117.

page 46. "God is both above. . . ." **64.** 179.

page 47. "The African universe. . . ." **74.** 5; "both spiritual and material beings. . . ." **74.** 5; "The spiritual is the foundation. . . ." **74.** 6; "This we see all around. . . ." **74.** 83f.

page 48. "We regard all. . . ." **45.** 124; "Peace comes within. . . ." **10.** 38f.

page 49. "One of the Natural. . . ." **10.** 40; "Another of the Natural. . . ." **91.** 66f; "We have the wind. . . ." **91.** 31; "revelation comes. . . ." **31.** 59.

Chapter 3: LIGHT

page 50. "Beautiful you rise. . . ." **2.** 75.

page 51. "Fifteen billion years . . . sparkling worlds." **82.** 7, 47; "numinous energy. . . ." **82.** 17.

page 52. "outshines even. . . ." **82.** 49; "Ecosystems differ. . . ." **14.** 299; "Solar energy. . . ." **14.** 299.

page 53. "The so-called free market. . . ." **14.** 300; "Radio waves. . . ." **79.** 284f.; "Because of music's. . . ." **79.** 286.

page 54. "Beautiful you rise. . . ." **2.** 75.

page 55. "Primeval without equal. . . ." **2.** 66.

page 56. "The Shining One." **70.** 100; "The Celtic mind. . . ." **70.** 4f.; "strength of heaven. . . ." **70.** 3f. (translation by Kuno Meyer); "Light is the mother. . . ." **70.** 56; "The eye of the great God. . . ." **70.** 56 (translation by A. Carmichael).

page 57. "We need a light. . . ." **70.** 4; "In the Celtic tradition. . . ." **70.** 5.

page 58. "The Creator gave us. . . ." **91.** 113f.

page 59. "When the world was. . . ." **78.** 14; "So the hunters held. . . ." **78.** 136; "had found something. . . ." **78.** 84.

page 61. "The splendor of the sun. . . ." **73.** 726; "Krishna is the source. . . ." **73.** 661; "Your glory is. . . ." **73.** 568; "Radiant in his light. . . ." **54.** 78; "The cosmic waters . . . all this world." **71.** 335.

page 62. "The light that illuminates. . . ." **67.** 17; "The light that shines. . . ." **54.** 113; "light in the heart." **54.** 134; "Your form is difficult. . . ." **73.** 567.

page 63. "God said:. . . ." Genesis: 1:3–5; "Yahweh my God. . . ." Psalm 104.1–2; "king of glory. . . ." Psalm 24:8; "the heavens declare. . . ." Psalm 19:2; "radiance of Shekinah. . . ." **59.** 100; "the human body. . . ." **59.** 173; "blinding spark. . . ." **59.** 49.

page 64. "Sparks burst. . . ." **59.** 119; "In our case. . . ." **58.** 97; "Sparks of holiness. . . ." **58.** 149; "When you desire to eat. . . ." **58.** 150.

page 65. "We constantly aspire. . . ." **58.** 152; "Love and sparks. . . ." **58.** 144; "The angel of YHVH. . . ." **59.** 102; "This is the light. . . ." **59.** 51.

page 66. "Rabbi Isaac said. . . ." **59.** 52f.

page 67. "A reflection of light. . . ." Wisdom 7:26; "All that came to be. . . ." John 1:3–5; "I am the light. . . ." John 8:12; "As long as I am. . . ." John 9:5; "The word was. . . ." John 1:9; "Jesus said: If they say. . . ." **33.** 502.

page 68. "I am the light. . . ." **33.** 515; "The word was made. . . ." John 1:14; "We all. . . ." 2 Corinthians 3:18; "the Lord of glory. . . ." 1 Corinthians 1:8. Cf. James 2:1; "Lie down in the fire. . . ." **92.** 113.

page 69. "God is light. . . ." **31.** 324; "nothing other than the light. . . ." **31.** 141; "God puts into creatures. . . ." **31.** 104; "The being of things. . . ." **31.** 88.

page 70. "There is no. . . ." **90.** 24; "All creation. . . ." **90.** 32; "mirror of. . . ." **28.** 104; "God says. . . ." **90.** 22; "I, God, remain. . . ." **27.** 10; "I, the fiery life. . . ." **90.** 30; "God says. . . ." **90.** 25; "Who is the Holy Spirit?. . . ." **90.** 37.

page 71. "burning light of. . . ." **28.** 9.

page 72. "God glows. . . ." **30.** 289; "never extinguished. . . ." **30.** 326; "a simple power. . . ." **30.** 365; "is hidden something. . . ." **30.** 373f.; "In the soul. . . ." **30.** 108.

page 73. "There in the lucky dark. . . ." **68.** 19; "Produces within. . . ." **48.** 578; "This flame of love. . . ." **48.** 580.

page 74. "All the acts of the soul. . . ." **48.** 580f.; "Since love is never. . . ." **48.** 582; "in its deepest center. . . ." **48.** 582f.

page 75. Liu I-Ming, "Awakening to the Tao," in Andrew Harvey and Anne Baring, *Daily Encounters with the Divine* (San Francisco: HarperSanFrancisco, 1995), 179.

page 76. "Be you lamps. . . ." Cited in Houston Smith, *The Religions of Man* (New York: Harper & Brothers, 1958), 93. "Always shining. . . ." **41.** 145; "made of. . . ." **41.** 147; "The trees, the birds. . . ." **41.** 147; "The road to Buddhahood. . . ." **55.** 31.

page 77. "God is the light. . . ." Sura 24:35. Translation by A. J. Arberry in **21.** 48.

page 78. "Ah, once more. . . ." **80.** 112; "The sun's eyes. . . ." **51.** 189; "The moon came. . . ." **51.** 159.

page 79. "The sun once glimpsed. . . ." **51.** 205; "The first effect. . . ." **31.** 112f.

Chapter 4: COMMUNITY AND INTERDEPENDENCE

page 80. "In tribal religions. . . ." **45.** 171f.

page 81. "Soil is. . . ." Wes Jackson, *New Roots for Agriculture* (Lincoln, NE: University of Nebraska Press, 1985), 10.

page 82. "Reality is. . . ." **82.** 26; "in a bonded relationship . . . for instant by instant. . . ." **82.** 35; Sahara study: "Change in Earth Orbit Blamed for Arid Sahara," *San Francisco Chronicle,* July 13, 1999, A8; "moonlight is created. . . ." **81.** 103; "The universe is not. . . ." **81.** 103; "Through this story. . . ." **82.** 5.

page 83. "Each particle. . . ." **82.** 29; "the great news. . . ." **81.** 99; "Sustainable communities. . . ." **14.** 297; "all members. . . ." **14.** 298; "multiple feedback loops," **14.** 299.

page 84. "so that the ecosystem. . . ." **14.** 299; "one of the hallmarks. . . ." **14.** 301; "the web of life. . . ." **14.** 302.

page 85. "The loneliness. . . ." **89.** 15; "an integrated basis. . . ." **89.** 85; "would never accept. . . ." **89.** 24; "the community cannot. . . ." **89.** 105.

page 86. "unique form of torture . . . fiber of the American character. . . ." **89.** 88f; "greatly enlarge. . . ." **89.** 57.

page 87. "For both thinkers. . . ." **25.** 158f; "like Thurman . . . is rooted. . . ." **25.** 159; "an individual. . . ." **25.** 163; "The redemptive love of God. . . ." **25.** 166; "Jesus eloquently. . . ." **25.** 142; "an expression. . . ." **25.** 166.

page 88. "Only a refusal. . . ." **25.** 144.

page 89. "prior to. . . ." **2.** 112; "and the ultimate. . . ." **2.** 111; "Among the Yoruba. . . ." **1.** 199; "because an undisciplined. . . ." **1.** 200; "I am most healthy. . . ." **1.** 201; "While we recognize. . . ." **1.** 204.

page 90. "This is one. . . ." **1.** 203, 60.

page 91. "The relationship. . . . **74.** 7; "The universe was created. . . ." **74.** 6f.

page 92. "the possibility of. . . ." **45.** 171; "In tribal religions. . . ." **45.** 171f; "In the Hopi world. . . ." **8.** 175.

page 93. "Everything teems. . . ." **58.** 153; "There is one. . . ." **58.** 154; "Only he who. . . ." **62.** 110; "We should be. . . ." **62.** 110; "To have faith. . . ." **62.** 110f; "requires bold initiative. . . ." **62.** 111f; "The endeavor. . . ." **62.** 107.

page 94. "is a movement. . . ." **62.** 106; "A Jew never. . . ." **62.** 187; "every act of worship. . . ." **62.** 187; "our kinship. . . ." **62.** 187; "The cosmos is. . . ." **62.** 187.

page 95. "the community. . . ." **41.** 118; "The Sangha. . . ." **40.** 48. "In the Buddhist. . . ." **40.** 47; "Your greater Sangha. . . ." **40.** 121.

page 96. "We have, in my view. . . ." **52.** 8; "the same degree of harmony. . . ." **52.** 13; "we come to see. . . ." **52.** 42; "there is no self-interest. . . ." **52.** 47.

page 97. "God has arranged. . . ." **90.** 65, 41; "relation is. . . ." **30.** 198; "Equality of being." **30.** 91–101.

page 98. "All believers are brothers. . . ." **49.** 518; "The believers are like . . . his children kindly." **30.** 194f.; "He from whose. . . ." **39.** 195.

PART II. OUR RELATION TO DIVINITY

page 100. "All the names. . . ." **30.** 175.

Chapter 5: NAMES FOR GOD

page 101. "God has. . . ." Bhagavad Gita 13.13 (or 13.14). Translation by Christopher Isherwood; "The one Being. . . ." **7.** 30; "there is only one. . . ." **43.** 53.

page 106. "Sweet Uncle. . . ." **51.** 4; "Dear ones. . . ." **51.** 141.

page 107. "I pray God. . . ." **30.** 221.

page 109. "And the Divine One. . . ." **31.** 182f; "God becomes. . . ." **30.** 76.

page 110. "My beloved is. . . ." **48.** 412; "Inasmuch as the soul. . . ." **48.** 464.

pages 110–113: "My beloved is . . . all things give." **48.** 465–473.

page 114. "The One Existence. . . . **7.** 30; "To that God who is in the plants. . . ." **37.** 24; "It can be called . . . woven in the Creator" **37.** 43, 51; "A true yogi. . . ." **73.** 337; "For one who sees. . . ." **73.** 339; "Such a yogi. . . ." **73.** 340; "And of all yogis. . . ." **73.** 359.

page 115. "the supreme giver. . . ." **7.** 210–212.

page 116. "One should meditate. . . ." **73.** 423.

Chapter 6. The Feminine Face of Divinity

page 117. "The Goddess in all her. . . ." **35.** 321.

page 119. "The Goddess. . . ." **35.** 321. Carol Christ, *Rebirth of the Goddess* (New York: Addison-Wesley, 1997), 66.

page 120. "The land of Ireland. . . ." **70.** 86; "Irish mythology. . . ." **23.** 26; "children of . . . Mother Goddess." **23.** 29; "Thoughout Irish. . . ." Mary Condren in **23.** 29; "For the pagan Celt. . . ." **23.** 37f.

page 120. For women as priests and possibly bishops, see **23.** 142. 147.

page 121. "Creation, including birth. . . ." **3.** xix; "The Goddess is she. . . ." **3.** xix; "In most primal. . . ." **3.** 30; "As genetrix of the sun. . . ." **3.** 34; "While numerous legends. . . ." **3.** 32.

page 122. "Myths around the world. . . ." **3.** 32.

page 123. "protects women. . . ." **3.** 44; "In the lands. . . ." From the Lotus Sutra, **3.** 44.

pages 124–125. "Buddha! Emanator!. . . .**3.** 46; "Homage to Tara. . . ." **3.** 122; "They emphasize. . . ." **3.** 124.

pages 126–127. "The Great Mother. . . ." **63.** 25; "always present. . . ." **63.** 6; "flows through. . . ." **63.** 25; "The Tao is great. . . ." **63.** 25; "Every being . . . the very nature of things." **63.** 51.

page 128. "She presides. . . ." Quote from Asungi in **3.** 140. "I am Nature. . . ." **3.** 48.

page 130. "O Child of God. . . ." M. D. Chenu, *Nature, Man and Society in the Twelfth Century* (Chicago, IL: University of Chicago Press, 1968), 19. "As mother and earth. . . ." Eloise McKinney-Johnson, "Egypt's Isis: The Original Black Madonna," *Journal of African Civilizations*, vol. 6, n. 1, April, 1984, 68.

page 131. "Isis, out of the Nile . . . an issue of sex." China Galland, *Longing for Darkness: Tara and the Black Madonna* (New York: Viking, 1990), 156f.

page 132. "Mary, ground of. . . ." **90.** 115; "Mary, the heavens gift. . . ." **90.** 116; "Mary, O luminous mother. . . ." **90.** 117; "Mary, Your womb exalts . . . forth into light." **90.** 118f.

page 133. "whatever was irregular. . . ." cited in **5.** 204; "The Virgin of the twelfth. . . ." **5.** 206; "the whole rebellion . . . by guile of Devil." **5.** 203.

page 134. "To Kwannon the Compassionate One. . . ." **5.** 203; "as a demagogic tool. . . ." **15.** 178; "In the Chicano movement. . . ." **15.** 180.

page 135. My *Virgen de Guadalupe* . . ." **15.** 50; "She is not neuter. . . ." **15.** 51.

page 136. "God is not only . . . maternal breast" **92.** 109; "surrounded with . . . compassion." Matthew Fox, *Wrestling with the Prophets* (San Francisco: HarperSanFrancisco, 1995), 93; "Divinity is like. . . ." **90.** 21; "From all eternity. . . ." **29.** 88; "we are all meant. . . ." **30.** 336f.; "Just as God is truly. . . ." **22.** 94f.

page 137. "The mother of our songs. . . ." **43.** 5.

page 138. "Whatever we see. . . ." **43.** 55; "Pray to the Divine. . . ." **43.** 56; "Transcendent, the original. . . ." **43.** 58f.; "Become completely. . . ." **43.** 61; "Mighty Mother . . . Obeisance to Her!" **7.** 141.

page 139. "O God (Brahman). . . ." **7.** 142; "Daughter of Heaven. . . ." **71.** 163; "See now, the shining. . . ." **71.** 168; "Dawn comes shining. . . ." **71.** 169.

page 140. "By you this universe. . . ." **3.** 78; "Wherever there is. . . ." Linda Johnsen, *The Daughters of* *the Goddess: The Women Saints of India* (St. Paul:Yes International Publishing, 1994), 117. Vivekenanda cited in **56.** 58.

page 142. "Lady of all the essences. . . ." **3.** 74; "When you have a Goddess. . . ." **13.** 165, 166.

Chapter 7: WISDOM: ANOTHER FEMININE FACE OF THE DIVINE

page 144. "Sophia I loved. . . ." Wisdom 8:2; "Once you have grasped. . . ." Sirach 6:27f.

page 145. "She is fairer. . . ." Wisdom 7:29; "My dwelling place. . . ." Sirach 24:5, 6, 9, 26; "awe is the beginning. . . ." Psalm 111:10; "Whoever loves her. . . ." Sirach. 4:12; "friend of the prophets. . . ." Wisdom 7: 27, 8.1; "She is an inexhaustible. . . ." Wisdom 7: 14.

page 146. "Glory to God. . . ." Luke 2:14; "the mother of all. . . ." Wisdom 7:11f.; "age after age . . . all things new" Wisdom 7:27; "To love her. . . ." Sirach 4:12; "Sophia I loved. . . ." Wisdom 8:2; "Once you have grasped her. . . ." Sirach 6:27f.; "Sophia goes about. . . ." **6.** 16; "Yahweh created. . . ." Proverbs 8:22–31.

page 147. "There is more material . . . is ignored." **11.** 15; "organic part. . . ." **11.** 52.

page 148. "The figure of Sophia. . . ."; **11.** 53; "No creature. . . ." **59.** 37.

page 149. "We are preaching. . . ." 1 Corinthians 23:30, 2:6–8. Translation in **11.** 33; "new creation" 1 Corinthians 5:17; "The Creator of all things. . . ." Sirach 24:8.

page 150. "The Word was made. . . ." John 1:14; "Jesus in John. . . ." **11.** 41; "dwell in the house. . . ." **28.** 100f.

page 151. "One obtains. . . ." **18.** 159; The spirituality of our Islamic. . . ." **18.** 159; "Woman is a. . . ." **18.** 160; "All people are equal. . . . God's trust." **59.** 70.

page 153. "The believers, men. . . ." **49.** 182; "is seen more perfectly. . . ." Annemarie Schimmel, *Mystical Dimensions of Islam* (Chapel Hill: The University of North Carolina Press, 1975), 431; "Patriarchy was able. . . ." **57.** 70.

page 154. "The perfection of wisdom. . . ." Edward Conze, ed. *Buddhist Texts Through the Ages.* (New Delhi: Munshiram Manoharlal, 1992), 146; "Spotless, unobstructed, silent. . . ." ibid., 147.

page 155. "The Lord dwells. . . ." **43.** 44; "There is a Light. . . ." **54.** 113; "In the center. . . ." **54.** 120f.; "The heart is. . . ." **43.** 8; "The first peace. . . ." **43.** 14; "You thought yourself. . . ." **43.** 146f.

Chapter 8: FORM, FORMLESSNESS, NOTHINGNESS

page 157. "Love God as God is. . . ." **30.** 180; "and all the other . . . surpasses all things." **31.** 183.

page 158. "It may be that. . . ." Owen Barfield, *Saving the Appearances: A Study in Idolatry* (New York: Harvest/HBJ, n.d.), 94; Laws vs. habits of the universe: Rupert Sheldrake, *The Rebirth of Nature* (New York: Bantam, 1991), 125–129; "the ground of. . . ." **81.** 93.

page 159. "There was something . . . origin of all things." **63.** 25; "When you have names. . . ." **63.** 32.

page 160. "Look, and it can't. . . ." **63.** 14.

page 161. "There is nothing. . . ." **37.** 54; "It is without. . . ." **37.** 49; "From the lowliest. . . ." **47.** 44; "Such is thy. . . ." **7.** 182.

page 162. "There are two forms. . . ." **71.** 731; "The problem of. . . ." **67.** 24.

page 163. "is nameless . . . nameless nothingness." **30.** 178, 179; "God is nothing. . . ." **30.** 194. "The mystery. . . ." **29.** 43; "The naked God. . . ." **29.** 42; "Be silent. . . ." **29.** 44; "How should you love God?. . . ." **30.** 180.

page 164. "The Divine One. . . ." **29.** 40; "the Godhead is. . . ." in Andrew Harvey and Anne Baring, op. cit., 13.

page 165. "Through creatures. . . ." **31.** 203; "Every name. . . ." **31.** 207; "Concerning God all things. . . ." **31.** 201; "The cause at which. . . ." **31.** 195; "We are united. . . ." **31.** 195; "The mind's greatest achievement. . . ." **31.** 196; "Divinity is. . . ." **31.** 196; "God is said to be. . . ." **31.** 207.

page 166. "We have to rid ourselves. . . ." **40.** 101; "It is impossible. . . ." **40.** 8; "In the phenomenal. . . ." **40.** 10; "The difference between. . . ." **17.** 39; "Nontheism is finally. . . ." **17.** 40.

page 167. "Sunyata is. . . ." **55.** 37. "There is no independently. . . ." **69.** 189.

page 168. "We begin to realize. . . ." **69.** 190.

page 169. "is the designation. . . ." **59.** 176; "Ayin, Nothingness. . . ." **58.** 66f; "All is one. . . ." **58.** 68; "God is the annihilation. . . ." **58.** 69; "Human consciousness. . . ." **59.** 37; "The essence of serving. . . ." **59.** 72.

page 170. "The blessed Holy One. . . ." **59.** 66; "The Blessed Holy One. . . ." **59.** 65.

Chapter 9: THE DIVINE "I AM": HUMANITY'S SHARE IN DIVINITY

page 171. "The human is. . . ." **1.** 204.

page 172. "I am she. . . ." **35.** 318f.

page 173. "I; I am; I am alive. . . ." **2.** 371.

page 174. "O son of Kunti . . . are within me." **73.** 375–379.

page 175. "I am the goal. . . ." **73.** 478; "I give heat. . . ." **73.** 480; "I am the Supersoul . . . exist without me." **73.** 532–549.

page 176. "I am the wind. . . ." **70.** 96f.; "I am because. . . ." **70.** 97; "Christ with me. . . ." Anthony Duncan, *Celtic Christianity* (Shaftesbury, England: Element, 1992), 49.

page 177. "I see his blood. . . ." **12.** 132f.

page 178. "in a culture. . . ." **21.** 64f.; "The Incarnation accomplished. . . ." **31.** 155; "Wherever two or three. . . ." **21.** 69.

page 180. "God says: I am. . . ." **90.** 22; "I am the one. . . ." **90.** 31.

page 181. "Our Lord Jesus. . . ." **22.** 47; "God said: 'This I am. . . .'" **22.** 104.

page 182. "I am a child. . . ." Kevin Gilbert, ed., *Inside Black Australia* (Ringwood, Victoria, Australia, 1988), 60; "I am the tree. . . ." ibid., 188.

page 184. "living Buddha. . . ." **41.** 34f.; "From a Buddhist perspective. . . ." **41.** 37; "When we look. . . ." **17.** 75f.

page 185. "God is life. . . ." **31.** 69.

III. RELATING TO OURSELVES:
PATHS TO ENCOUNTER AND ENLIGHTENMENT

Chapter 10. MEDITATION AND MINDFULNESS

page 189. "Meditation is. . . ." **41. 3.**

page 190. "In that respect. . . ." **30.** 178; "stopping, calming . . . and bring joy." **41.** 3, 14; "The technique. . . ." **41.** 17.

page 191. "Every angel. . . ." **30.** 165.

page 192. "It is not a matter. . . ." **41.** 24; "The living Dharma. . . ." **41.** 40; "A Buddha is. . . ." **41.** 22, 23; "live in a way. . . ." **41.** 48; "Meditation means. . . ." **40.** 45; "mindfulness is. . . ." **40.** 5; "Emptiness means. . . ." **40.** 26f.; " 'luminous,' 'immaculate'. . . ." **69.** 198.

page 193. "I believe that. . . ." **69.** 114; "We mistake each emotion. . . ." **69.** 121; "They are first. . . ." **69. 123.**

page 194. "A meditator knows. . . ." **69.** 123; "Thus any feeling. . . ." **69.** 124; "You should know. . . ." Thich Nhat Hanh, *The Miracle of Mindfulness* (Boston: Beacon Press, 1975), 15; "One should not lose. . . ." ibid., 21; "It alone. . . ." ibid., 23.

page 195. "As meditators we might. . . ." **17.** 182; "Through practice, we realize. . . ." **17.** 120; "In its true state. . . ." **55.** 33. See W. Y. Evans-Wentz, ed., *The Tibetan Book of the Great Liberation* (London: Oxford University Press, 1968), 211, 215, 218.

page 196. "What you find repulsive. . . ." **17.** 122; "Breathe it in . . . the human condition." **17.** 122f.

page 197. "The first requirement . . . 'And play there.'" **31.** 210; "Playing has no. . . ." **31.** 211; "Abandon discursive reasoning. . . ." **31.** 212f; "The heart is said. . . ." **31.** 211; "chaste silence. . . ." **31.** 213.

page 198. "He is a poor person. . . ." **30.** 213; "For a human being . . . unborn being. . . ." **30.** 214, 217; "How then should one. . . ." **30.** 180; "When all the images. . . ." **30.** 185; "If people . . . return to it." **30.** 241f.

page 200. "When you want. . . ." **21.** 61f.

page 201. "Concentration is . . . transformation be." Swami Siddheswarananda, *Meditation According to Yoga-Vedanta* (Trichur, India: Prabuddhakeralam Press, 1976), 71, 78; "Without concentration. . . ." **47.** 51; "mindlessness. . . ." **47.** 46.

page 202. "Contact with the Self. . . ." Piero Ferrucci, *Inevitable Grace* (Los Angeles: Jeremy Tarcher, 1990), 336; "The Hindu concept of attachment. . . ." See Swami Rama and Rudolph Ballentine, M.D., *Yoga and Psychotherapy* (Glenview, IL, Himalayan Institute: 1976), 152–154.

page 203. "You have to quiet. . . ." **56.** 150; "You are not attached. . . ." **56.** 149.

page 204. See Claudio Naranjo and Robert E. Ornstein, *On the Psychology of Meditation* (New York: Viking, 1971).

page 205. "Empty your mind. . . ." **63.** 16; "To know Tao. . . ." **43.** 32; "Accept the world. . . . **63.** 28.

page 206. "The Master keeps. . . ." **63.** 21; "Since before time and space. . . ." **63.** 21; "She who is centered. . . ." **63.** 35; "Words that point. . . ." **63.** 35; "Ordinary men. . . ." **63.** 42.

page 207. "If you close your mind . . . the source of light." **63.** 52.

page 208. "My teachings are easy. . . ." **63.** 70. "God is not found. . . ." **30.** 183; "In the pursuit of knowledge. . . ." **63.** 48. "If you want. . . ." **63.** 22f.

page 209. "There are more . . . greater than ourselves." **62.** 162; "Transcendence can never be . . . its secret tool." **62.** 163.

page 210. "If you think. . . ." **58.** 71; "Thought expands. . . ." **58.** 130; "Thought reveals. . . ." **58.** 114; "How should you train. . . ." **58.** 87; "If your mind races. . . ." **58.** 108; "Those who practice. . . ." **58.** 119; "To attain you must. . . ." **58.** 122.

page 211. "If one attains. . . ." **58.** 118; "If you wish to attain. . . ." **58.** 122; "Your deep soul. . . ." **58.** 124; "No one knows anything. . . ." **58.** 69; "Nor can we estimate. . . ." **58.** 153; "Your soul hides. . . ." **58.** 124; "That which abides. . . ." **58.** 70.

page 212. "Be totally alone. . . ." **58.** 103.

page 213. **49.** 234; "Let neither trade nor traffic. . . ." **49.** 343; "The Zhikr is said. . . ." **57.** 29; "God does not look. . . ." Margaret Smith, *Rabi'a the Mystic and Her Fellow Saints in Islam* (Amsterdam: Philo Press, 1974), p. 2; "formless God takes a thousand forms. . . ." **83.** 75.

page 214. "I have put duality. . . ." **44.** 22; "Out beyond duality. . . ." **44.** 36f.; "Abandon your stagnant pool. . . ." **44.** 42; "God is one and so man. . . ." Seyyed Hossain Nasr, op. cit., 167; "Let go of your worries. . . ." **44.** 31.

page 215. "The last mystery of recollection. . . ." **57.** 80; "Secretly we spoke. . . ." **80.** 35; "Noise is a cruel. . . ." **51.** 51.

page 216. "When the words stop. . . ." **51.** 143; "Today love has. . . ." **51.** 195; "Not many teachers. . . ." **51.** 295.

Chapter 11: HOLY IMAGINATION: ART AND RITUAL AS PATHS TO MINDFULNESS

page 218. "The fierce power. . . ." **58.** 116.

page 219. "fierce power . . . the holy spirit." **58.** 116; "First, go over the. . . ." **58.** 161; "Torah study is a way. . . ." **62.** 207; "in Judaism study is. . . ." **62.** 199; "genuine reverence . . . sharing insight and appreciation. . . ." **62.** 202f.; "cultivate the soul. . . . **62.** 205; "learning is life. . . ." **62.** 206.

page 220. "In almost every Jewish home. . . ." **62.** 206; "Indeed, he is known in the gates. . . ." **59.** 65f.

page 221. "opened avenues for the creation. . . ." **35.** xxiii; "the piled-up signs seem. . . ." **35.** 225; "the mystery of birth and death. . . ." **35.** xix; "The Goddess-centered art. . . ." **35.** xx.

page 223. "Storytelling, from ancient times. . . ." Jeannette Henry, Rupert Costo, *A Thousand Years of American Indian Storytelling* (San Francisco: The Indian Historian Press, Inc., 1981), vii; "In the telling . . . it was fun . . ." ibid., ix.

page 224. "When Europeans see a group. . . ." Gilbert, op. cit., xvi; "He felt the need . . . followed them." **78.** 42.

page 226. "All aspects of life. . . ." **8.** 7; "Among rocky plateaus. . . ." **8.** 84.

page 228. "The true artist. . . ." **72.** 208; "The good painter. . . ." **72.** 211; "Who am I?. . . ." **72.** 274.

page 229. "My heart has become. . . ." **43.** 145; "Art is the conversation. . . ." **51.** 52f.

page 230. "Someone inside of us. . . ." **51.** 55; "The difference between. . . ." **51.** 77; "Hafiz encourages. . . ." **51.** 170.

page 231. "My master once. . . ." **51.** 92; "I, even though. . . ." **29.** 71; "All the talents of God. . . ." **51.** 207.

page 232. "It used to be. . . ." **51.** 35.

page 233. "Dance, my heart. . . ." **83.** 80; "Behold! My heart. . . ." **83.** 80f.; "God dances in rapture. . . ." **83.** 75.

page 234. "When you dance. . . ." **80.** 7; "The world dances. . . ." **80.** 44; "A secret turns. . . ." **80.** 45; "Dear ones. . . ." **51.** 6.

page 235. "Come dance with me. . . ." **51.** 223.

page 236. "One was less interested. . . ." W. B. Yeats, in Lady Gregory's *Cuchullain of Muiuthemme* (Gerard's Cross: Colin Smyth, Ltd.), 265–6; "is the place. . . ." **70.** 145; "the creative force. . . ." **70.** 145; "discipline of freedom . . . in our tissues." **75.** 22; "We redeem our energies. . . ." **75.** 35.

page 237. "The discipline comes. . . ." **75.** 64; "It is in our bodies. . . ." **75.** 15; "How can we not. . . ." **75.** 78; "From the child's ability. . . ." **75.** 115; "Potters like sun. . . ." **76.** 12; "Through all the molecules . . . fall in love." **76.** 14f.

page 239. "All work and crafts. . . ." **21.** 60.

page 240. "Few have understood. . . ." **74.** 37; "Ontologically, we gain meaning. . . ." **74.** 37; "Through dance we experience. . . ." **74.** 38f; "The African universe. . . ." **74.** 13; "Herein lies the miracle. . . ." **74.** 14.

page 241. "Oppressed by . . . in America." **74.** 14; "They attempted. . . ." **74.** 23; "soul is the essence. . . ." **74.** 36; "Soul-force is that power. . . ." **74.** 34.

page 242. "It is that ability. . . ." **74.** 35; "The Afro-American aesthetic. . . ." **74.** 35; "Our deepest feelings. . . ." **74.** 36; "Black music is . . . everything in music." **74.** 37; "Through dance we experience. . . ." **74.** 38f.

page 243. "until finally we are able. . . ." **74.** 39; "is to be in tune. . . ." **74.** 9; "The Drum is. . . ." **74.** 9; "If we 'remember,' . . . Moment is achieved. . . ." **74.** 8.

page 244. "This is the discovery. . . ." **85.** 39f.; "It is an optimism. . . ." **85.** 56; "leaping out of. . . ." **85.** 57.

page 245. "Where there is creating. . . ." **54.** 119; "When you offer. . . ." **73.** 487, 489; "Make every act. . . ." **43.** 43; "Meditative worship. . . ." **66.** 170, 171.

page 246. "Lord of light . . . cultural status." **7.** 160f.; "The practitioner of Yoga . . ." **47.** 32; "Nothing is secular. . . ." Swami Ashokananda, *Spiritualizing Everyday Life* (San Francisco, CA: Vedanta Society of Northern California, 1976), 32f.; "Contact with the self. . . ." Piero Ferrucci, *Inevitable Grace* (Los Angeles: Jeremy Tarcher, 1990), 336; "It is a cosmic dance. . . ." **37.** 41.

page 247. "It would mean. . . ." **30.** 311; "there is where the birth. . . ." **30.** 312; "Human beings should. . . ." **30.** 367; "flows out but. . . ." **30.** 65; "Whatever can be truly. . . ." **30.** 399.

page 248. "I have exalted. . . ." **90.** 110; "God gave to humankind. . . ." **90.** 125; "Humankind, full of all. . . ." **90.** 106; "The marvels of God. . . ." **90.** 93.

page 249: "O Trinity, you are music. . . ." **28.** 116; "All of creation is a song. . . ." **28.** 116; "All of creation is a symphony. . . ." **28.** 116.

page 250. "Although a created being. . . ." **31.** 245; "The dignity of causality. . . ." **31.** 255; "it is impossible. . . ." **31.** 267; "God's spirit is said. . . ." **31.** 248; "The image is a principle. . . ." **31.** 301; "Sometimes the images. . . ." **31.** 293.

page 251. "Upgrading the mythology. . . ." **53.** 173f.; "new social vision. . . ." **53.** 225; "The holy spirit was a term. . . ." **53.** 170.

page 253. "On the terrain of culture. . . ." bell hooks, *Race, Gender, and Cultural Politics* (Boston: South End Press, 1990), 31.

Chapter 12: JOY

page 254. "Joy comes . . . all return." **54.** 110, 111.

page 255. "Joy comes . . . all return." **54.** 110f; "Brahman is joy. . . ." **54.** 111, 110; "Bliss pervades all. . . ." **66.** 18; "Laugh as much as. . . ." *L'Enseignement de Ma Ananda Moyi* (Paris: Albin Michel, 1974), 268; Words cannot describe. . . ." **54.** 103; "with symbols, music, singing . . . embodiment of bliss." **66.** 164, 166f; "Life depicted in. . . ." **66.** 10; "Divinity is not only. . . ." **7.** 149.

page 256. "becomes fully joyful." **73.** 837; "in every state. . . ." **73.** 454; "Transcendental Enjoyer." **73.** 668; "These who have the powers. . . ." **73.** 26; "There is the path of joy. . . ." **54.** 57f.; "Worship, like song . . . to the Deity." **7.** 66; "Sing, sing forth. . . ." **7.** 82.

page 257. "We worship . . . lofty spirit." **7.** 86.

page 258. "Souls of the righteous. . . ." **59.** 128.

page 259. "When you eat and drink. . . ." **58.** 150; "Joy is a way . . . are its ingredients." **62.** 213; "To sense the living God. . . ." Abraham Heschel, *The Prophets* (New York: Harper & Row, 1962), 143; "To have joy. . . ." **62.** 214; "Your ears should be tuned. . . ." **59.** 85.

page 260. "Waken yourself. . . ." **69.** 122; "Breathing in . . . tomorrow, after tomorrow?" **42.** 10; "We make steps. . . ." **42.** 28f.; "Happiness can always. . . ." **42.** 32; "Plant the seeds of joy. . . ." **42.** 128; "It is from that joy. . . ." Steven Levine, *Guided Meditations, Explorations and Healings*, 10.

page 261. "The Sufi is dancing. . . ." **80.** 43; "Children can easily open. . . ." **51.** 66.

page 262. "If you think I am having. . . ." **51.** 57; "There is only one rule. . . ." **51.** 331.

page 263. "Sheer joy is God's. . . ." **31.** 100; "God is so good. . . ." **31.** 99; "Divine love produces. . . ." **31.** 109; "Delight or enjoyment. . . ." **31.** 116; "Joy expands the heart. . . ." **31.** 116, 115; "Joy is a human's. . . ." **31.** 120; "God is most joyful. . . ." **31.** 119; "God delights. . . ." **31.** 118f.

page 264. "God enjoys the Godself. . . ." **30.** 76; "God has sheer. . . ." **30.** 151; "finds joy and rapture. . . ." **30.** 155; "When the Father laughs. . . ." **30.** 155; "pours forth its whole strength. . . ." **30.** 155f.; "not yet mothers. . . ." **30.** 329; "you will have such great joy. . . ." **30.** 329.

page 265. "I saw the Soul so large. . . ." **22.** 114; "Glad and happy. . . ." **22.** 116; "is true lasting joy." **22.** 116; "Though this face . . . exist endlessly." **22.** 117; "All-Love." **22.** 118f; "new joy which will be. . . ." **22.** 124; "Our Lord is with us. . . ." **22.** 126; "The fullness of joy. . . ." **22.** 60.

page 266. "the essence of the Goddess. . . ." **3.** 109; "With her we learn. . . ." **3.** 109.

page 267. "White fellow, you are. . . ." Gilbert, op. cit., 98.

Chapter 13: Suffering

page 269. "Suffering, according to all. . . ." Noel Q. King, *African Cosmos: An Introduction to Religion in Africa* (Wadsworth Publishers, 1986), 89; "In the language of faith. . . ." **86.** 279; "So much of human misery. . . ." **86.** 118; "The contradictions of life are. . . ." **86.** 226f; "Men do reap. . . ." **85.** 58.

page 270. "If perchance. . . ." **85.** 60; "There is something present. . . ." **85.** 60f.

page 271. "My personal trials. . . ." **25.** 142; "There is no easy way. . . ." **25.** 148.

page 272. "All the reaches . . . nobody pray." **85.** [26]; "I've got to walk. . . ." **85.** [27].

page 273. "Oh blues, oh blues. . . ." **2.** 772; "Using the power of the word. . . ." **2.** 772; "Mr. rich man. . . ." **2.** 776; "Southern trees bear. . . ." **2.** 776.

page 275. "The important thing is. . . ." **55.** 30; "Life is inherently. . . ." **69.** 21; "human beings suffer. . . ." **69.** 22; "I teach one thing. . . ." **69.** 23; "When we are mindful. . . ." **41.** 14; "The living Dharma. . . ." **41.** 40; "This is the way. . . ." **69.** 30.

page 276. "These exercises. . . ." **69.** 30. "Mindfulness centered. . . ." **69.** 33; "Breathing in I calm. . . ." **69.** 39; "Freud called them. . . ." **69.** 91; "If we remain. . . ." **69.** 92; "What the Buddha is advising. . . ." **69.** 93; "The reptilian brain. . . ." **69.** 95; "Develop a mind. . . ." **69.** 103.

page 277. "heart-mind . . . ." **69.** 120f; "We don't see. . . ." **69.** 123; "psychological studies . . . stability and freedom." **69.** 126; "This very place is. . . ." **55.** 31.

page 278. "Who ever got the idea. . . ." **17.** 61; "Inspiration and wretchedness. . . ." **17.** 61f.; "Cultivating a mind. . . ." **17.** 113.

page 279. "in the basic human experience. . . ." **52.** 33; "A sentient being. . . ." **52.** 133; "There is much we can. . . ." **52.** 137; "As a result . . . the worst news." **52.** 139; "our experience of suffering. . . ." **52.** 143.

page 280. "I speak as a person. . . ." **62.** 11; "God does not stand. . . ." **62.** 130; "God's participation. . . ." **62.** 130; "intimate concern . . . human acts." **62.** 134f; "We have entered not only. . . ." **62.** 217.

page 284. "There comes a time. . . ." **52.** 60f.; "Still I feel. . . ." **52.** 62f.; "I am hunted. . . ." **52.** 64f; "Lord, I will tear the heart. . . ." **92.** 66.

page 285. "I will always be. . . ." **92.** 68; "From suffering I have learned. . . ." **92.** 69; "Life without sorrow. . . ." **92.** 70; "Do you wish to have love?" **92.** 58; "Love the nothing. . . ." **92.** 71.

page 287. "The impediments are in us. . . ." **30.** 173; "If this will returns. . . ." **30.** 203; "after all, you bear. . . ." **30.** 209; "It is God who carries. . . ." **30.** 235; "Your joy reaches to. . . ." **30.** 235f.

page 288. "To be a victim. . . ." **60.** 165; "all through history . . . the celestial 'Paradiso.'" **60.** 162.

page 289. "I saw a great. . . ." **22.** 44.

page 290. "Our cries of grief rise. . . ." **72.** 226f.

Chapter 14: Beauty

page 291. "How did the rose. . . ." **51.** 121.

page 293. "Beautiful you rise. . . ." **2.** 75; "Beautiful you rise in heaven's horizon. . . ." **2.** 76, 78.

page 294. "The beautiful flowers. . . ." **72.** 265f.; "The earth is beautiful. . . ." **43.** 7.

page 296. "How did the rose. . . ." **51.** 121; "Indeed, dear ones. . . ." **51.** 57; "Is your caravan lost?. . . ." **51.** 62.

page 297. "Remembrance lowers the cup. . . ." **51.** 244; "God's beauty has split. . . ." **51.** 195; "The small man. . . ." **51.** 206.

page 298. "God is beautiful. . . ." William Stoddart, *Sufism: The Mystical Doctrines and Methods of Islam* (New York: Paragon House, 1986), 82; "O my Lord, if I worship. . . ." Swami Ghanananda, ed., *Women Saints of East and West* (London: The Ramakrishna Vedanta Centre, 1972), 269; "This conjunction between. . . ." **18.** 145.

page 299. "Each beautiful thing. . . ." **56.** 34.

page 300. "The archetype . . . splendor of the 'One.'" **93.** 73f; "Most of us would agree. . . . inanimate matter." **93.** 71; "Why not an. . . ." Ernesto Cardinale, *Cosmic Canticle* (Willimantic, CT: Curbstone Press, 1993), 40.

page 301. "If we have a wonderful sense. . . ." **4.** 11.

page 302. "the Creator of beauty . . . sharing in things." **31.** 102f.; "supersubstantial beauty. . . ." **31.** 104; "sharing of God's likeness . . . whatever way possible." **31.** 106; "It is necessary. . . ." **31.** 107; "We can take delight . . . not with uniformity." **31.** 298f.

page 304. "Glance at the sun. . . ." **90.** 45; "Grace pours all beauty. . . ." **30.** 195; "This, then, is. . . ." **30.** 412.

page 305. "perceives the Divine presence . . . glory of the spirit." **7.** 165; "All shine. . . ." **7.** 185; "The universe reflects . . . lawlessness evil." **7.** 188; "the three. . . ." **7.** 171; "God (Indra) is. . . ." **7.** 186; "Do not go into the garden. . . ." Andrew Harvey and Anne Baring, op. cit., 110.

page 306. *"The obsession with power. . . ."* **62.** 56f. Italics his. "What we encounter. . . ." **62.** 56; "the root of man's. . . ." **62.** 56. "the immense preciousness. . . ." **62.** 58; "there is no sense. . . ." **62.** 65.

page 307. "Most people. . . ." **61.** 20; "When people are on. . . ." **61.** 69; "We are part of. . . ." **61.** 215; "Beauty is the experience. . . ." **61.** 20.

Chapter 15: SACRED SEXUALITY

page 308. "He brings me to. . . ." **24.** Songs 8 and 9.

page 312. "In prehistoric art . . . vegetation spirits." **35.** 139; "Fertility was not sexuality. . . ." **35.** 317; "Fertility is only one. . . ." **35.** 316.

page 313. "Everywhere in Europe. . . ." **35.** 318; "The process of seasonal. . . ." **35.** 317.

page 314. "Any image that does not. . . ." **59.** 55; "Come and see. . . ." **59.** 56; "*Shekinah* was present. . . ." **59.** 99f.

page 315. "When sexual union is. . . ." **58.** 155; "If that Greek scoundrel. . . ." **58.** 155; "Sexual union is. . . ." **58.** 155.

page 316. "does not seem. . . ." **24.** 182; "The Song eloquently. . . ." **24.** 150; "self-assertion. . . ." **24.** 149.

page 317. "a thoroughly nonsexist view. . . ." **24.** 134; "Consonant with this mutuality. . . ." **24.** 134f; "expresses mutuality. . . ." **24.** 118; "Unlike most of the Bible. . . ." **24.** 117; "is primarily concerned. . . ." **24.** 103; "He brings me to the winehall . . . *my love, come away.*" **24.** Songs 8 and 9.

page 318. "Something new to teach. . . ." **24.** 135.

page 320. "Even at the movies on Sunday. . . ." Tim Giago, Jr., *The Aboriginal Sin* (San Francisco: Indian Historical Press, 1978), 22.

page 323. "wonderfully vibrant . . . pure and impure." **70.** 31f.; "Amn't I plump and sound. . . ." **70.** 31f.; "modern Ireland has had. . . ." **70.** 31; "Sensuous reveling in . . ." **6.** 134.

page 324. "Patrick is silent . . . rule of chastity." **12.** 134f.; "Augustine's preoccupation with. . . ." **64.** 115.

page 325. "If, then, the union of soul and body. . . ." **31.** 152; "What is natural to. . . ." **31.** 152; "natural love is. . . ." **31.** 153; "The blessing of God. . . ." **31.** 283.

page 326. "Certainly all the power. . . ." **31.** 283; "Sexual intercourse is. . . ." **31.** 152; "friendship—there is . . . to many persons." **31.** 39.

page 327. "Now it came to pass. . . ." **90.** 101; "The woman is the labor. . . ." **90.** 102.

page 328. "Our sensuality is. . . ." **22.** 92; "beautiful oneing that was made. . . ." **22.** 93; "God is the means. . . ." **22.** 95; "Our sensuality is the beautiful. . . ." **22.** 97; "Nature and grace are in. . . ." **22.** 108; "Nature is all good and. . . ." **22.** 109.

page 329. "Of Allah's signs. . . ." **49.** 397; "He it is who. . . ." **49.** 162; "the tone of marriage. . . ." **39** 157; "When a man. . . ." Helminski, "Islam: Blind Spot of the West," *Whole Earth Review,* Winter 1985, 15.

page 330. "This has caused much feeling. . . ." **36.** 99f.; "The sexual origin. . . ." **36.** 20; "The natural reaction . . . their sacred character." **36.** 21; "It is this that gives. . . ." **36.** 21.

page 332. "Life is essentially . . . freely received." Pere Tsasa, "African and Religious Values," Conference for Religious Formation Personnel, Zaire, 1978.

page 333. "To the ancient Taoist. . . ." Howard S. Levy and Akira Ishihara, *The Tao of Sex* (Lower Lake, CA: Integral Publishing, 1989), 11. "The most sophisticated methods . . . flower heart." Delores Lachapelle, *Sacred Land, Sacred Sex: Rapture of the Deep* (Silverton, CO: Finn Hill Arts, 1988), 261–263.

Chapter 16: DYING, RESURRECTION, REINCARNATION

page 335. "Your existence, my dear. . . ." **51.** 81.

page 336. "Throughout prehistory images of death. . . ." **35.** xxii; "Graves and temples assumed. . . ." **35.** xxiii; "The Life and Birth . . . Goddess of Regeneration." **35.** xxiii; "Perhaps Death and Regeneration . . . connected to regeneration." **35.** 223.

page 337. "It seems probably that . . . assuring regeneration." **35.** 223

page 338. "Where do we go, Oh!. . . ." **72.** 183; "Thus we are, we are mortal. . . ." **72.** 242; "My flowers will not. . . ." **72.** 243.

page 339. "All of Hopi life. . . ." **8.** 149; "Hopi life must follow a path. . . ." **8.** 175; "When the last Red Man. . . ." **91.** 125.

page 340. "A progressive alienation . . . vitality and relevance." **38.** 5; "The literature of ancient cultures. . . ." **38.** 6; "Systemic study of the experiences. . . ." **38.** 6.

page 341. "The experiential practice of dying. . . ." **38.** 7.

page 342. "These so-called 'Pyramid Texts'. . . ." **38.** 8; "From the first to the last. . . ." **38.** 9; "The death and resurrection of Osiris. . . ." **38.** 11.

page 343. "gave neophytes the opportunity. . . ." **38.** 11.

page 344. "African civilizations have posited. . . ." **2.** 59; "communion with . . . beer for spirits." **2.** 88; "The departed, whether parents, brothers. . . ." **2.** 289; "African peoples do not feel. . . ." **2.** 289; "The basis of the respect is. . . ." **2.** 454.

page 345. "simultaneously a guide for the dying. . . ." **38.** 12; "The Mother Luminosity. . . ." **77.** 263.

page 346. "All dualities are. . . ." **38.** 13.

page 347. "Monks, what is the noble . . . the aversion toward it." **43.** 69; "Meditating on death brings us. . . ." **38.** 78; "We are raised in a culture. . . ." **17.** 43; "relaxing with the present moment. . . ." **17.** 44; "to live is to be. . . ." **17.** 72.

page 349. "The Quetzalcoatl myth is thus. . . ." **38.** 21.

page 351. "One who has taken his birth. . . ." **73.** 110; "As the embodied soul continuously. . . ." **41.** 91; "As a person puts on new garments. . . ." **73.** 104; "Never was there a time. . . ." **73.** 88; "The Personality of Godhead. . . ." **73.** 222; "The inspired self . . . jaws of death." **71.** 566; "I have known. . . ." **7.** 129.

page 352. "The Spirit who is. . . ." **54.** 120f.; "The world of the ancestors. . . ." **65.** 176; "There can be no doubt. . . ." **65.** 175; "The subtle form of. . . ." **65.** 175; "They do not think of. . . ." **65.** 180; "light so fierce . . . I lost all fear." **65.** 197f.

page 354. "Life itself seems to reincarnate . . . complex mammal." **69.** 60f; "We share more than ninety-eight percent. . . ." Dorion Sagan and Lynn Margulis cited in **69.** 61; "As I look more deeply. . . ." **69.** 60f.

page 355. "Think of your. . . ." **44.** 33; "We began as a. . . ." **44.** 34.

page 356. "In deep meditation. . . ." **69.** 27; "profound experiences of dying . . . night of the soul." **69.** 28; "It is subjectively . . . ephemeral and unimportant." **69.** 29.

page 357. "Modern consciousness research. . . ." **69.** 30; "represent the most convincing. . . ." **69.** 31.

page 358. "The purpose of the soul entering. . . ." **58.** 148; "It has been taught . . . leave the world." **59.** 94.

page 359. "All the righteous who are. . . ." **59.** 94f.

page 360. "How can you disbelieve. . . ." **49.** 9; "Allah plans to. . . ." **49.** 14; "It is he who brings the dead. . . ." **49.** 320; "those whose scales are heavy. . . ." **49.** 336; "You tarried only a short while. . . ." **49.** 337; "Only those respond to Allah's call. . . ." **49.** 121; "O ye who believe. . . ." **49.** 166.

page 361. "When you see my procession. . . ." **44.** 48; "If your life was not contained. . . ." **51.** 81.

page 362. "their contact with the dead. . . ." **85.** [19]; "I want to die easy. . . ." **85.** [20]; "Chilly water, chilly water. . . ." **85.** [21].

page 363. "You needn't mind my. . . ." **85.** [22]; "a maniacal kind of. . . ." **85.** 28; "I'm so glad trouble don't last. . . ." **85.** 28f.

page 364. "I'm troubled in mind. . . ." **85.** 29; "Children, we shall be. . . ." **85.** 29; "belongs to that moment . . . An' you too, shall be free!" **85.** 30.

page 365. "The note of transcendence. . . ." **85.** [24].

page 366. "hospitality to death. . . ." **70.** 208; "When a person is close. . . ." **70.** 211; "For the Celts, the eternal . . . perpetual sleep." **70.** 206.

page 367. "All of us men, without exception. . . ." **64.** 180.

page 369. "His disciples said to him. . . ." Hugh McGregor Ross, *The Gospel of Thomas* (Longmead, Shaftsbury, England: Element Books, 1987), 39; "The disciples said to Jesus. . . ." ibid., 20; "This is the first resurrection. . . ." **31.** 361; "There is a double resurrection. . . ." **31.** 361; "When I was still in the core . . . ceases to become." **30.** 77.

page 370. "I am cause of myself. . . ." **30.** 217f.; "A great master says. . . ." **30.** 218; "In this break-through I discover. . . ." **30.** 218.

page 371. "This birth does not take place. . . ." **30.** 330; "As often as this birth. . . ." **30.** 330; "Out of the purity he. . . ." **30.** 331.

page 372. "We were all created. . . ." **22.** 100; "I understood this to mean. . . ." **22.** 59.

page 373. "Resurrection does not mean, simply. . . ." **19.** xxx. Italics his; "Bodily resurrection means. . . ." **19.** xxxi.

Chapter 17: SERVICE AND COMPASSION.

page 377. "We can reject everything. . . ." **52.** 234.

page 379. "Fill your mind. . . ." **43.** 69; "The essence of Mind. . . ." **57.** 29; "when we allow ourselves . . . contains all things." Jack Kornfield, *A Path with Heart* (New York: Bantam, 1993), 29; "What makes Buddha. . . ." Murti, op. cit., 283; "Compassion is a mind . . . his suffering" **42.** 81, 83.

page 380. "We all have the seeds of love. . . ." **42.** 81; "to do both [things]. . . ." **42.** 91; "Being in touch with the kind. . . ." **42.** 125; "In order to feel compassion. . . ." **17.** 93.

page 381. "Meditation is probably the only. . . ." **17.** 105–107; "The ground of not causing. . . ." **17.** 32f.; "May I be free from . . . as they are." Levine, op. cit., 29f.; "the power of loving kindness. . . ."; ibid., 26.

page 382. "The human heart. . . ." Kornfield, op. cit., 226f.; "a reorientation of our heart. . . ." **52.** 162; "aggressive competitiveness." **52.** 165; "a combination of empathy and. . . ." **52.** 73f.

page 383. "In the name of. . . ." **49.** 5; "The origin of . . . known in them." **18.** 184; "From the inscrutable. . . ." **18.** 115; "Some pray that God. . . ." **18.** 117; "does not move. . . ." **18.** 129. "To be a dervish (or Sufi). . . ." **57.** 106; "A man does not . . . wakefulness and fever." **39.** 94–96; "The believers are like. . . ." **39.** 194.

page 384. "Be benevolent. . . ." **49.** 79.

page 385. "Woe unto those. . . ." **49.** 631; "most forgiving. . . ." **49.** 378; "How shouldst thou know. . . ." **49.** 619f.

page 386. "Humanity is a reminder. . . ." **32.** 1; "There is a very famous. . . ." **32.** 19; "When you are filled. . . ." *Pirke Avot* 2:4. **43.** 101; "Just as God is called compassionate. . . ." **32.** 27; "Imitate your Creator . . . upon us." **58.** 83.

page 387. "Let your neighbor's honor. . . ." **58.** 83; "Your eyes should. . . ." **58.** 85; "Be good to all. . . ." **58.** 84; "Wisdom spreads over all. . . ." **58.** 87; "Mend the cosmos." **58.** 149.

page 388. "Does not everyone know. . . ." **59.** 69f.; "Being compassionate is. . . ." **62.** 100; "Justice is God's nature . . . God can actually suffer." **62.** 130.

page 389. "The presence of God is felt. . . ." **56.** 73; "Hinduism does not repudiate. . . ." **36.** xx;

"whose minds are engaged . . . in the Supreme." **73.** 300; "My dear Arjuna. . . ." **73.** 606; "By controlling the various. . . ." **73.** 615.

page 390. "Path of Action . . . to its service." **7.** 219; "becomes a liberated. . . ." **47.** 53; "the yogi does not. . . ." **47.** 33; "man's ultimate aim. . . ." Dhirendra Datta, *The Philosophy of Mahatma Gandhi* (Madison, WI: University of Wisconsin Press, 1953), 73; "The yogi uses all. . . ." **47.** 28; "grammar of action" Erik Erikson, *Gandhi's Truth* (New York: Norton, 1969), 162; "a life of service. . . ." Datta, op. cit., 391; Linda Johnsen, op. cit., 87–89.

page 391. "I am seated in everyone's. . . ." **73.** 730.

page 392. "the influence of right and. . . ." **2.** 59; "In all cases the ideas. . . ." **2.** 59; "I rescued the weak from one. . . ." **2.** 33; "My neighbor and I have. . . ." **2.** 372f.

page 394. "Occasionally there comes into view. . . ." **86.** 279; "Jesus was a poor Jew. . . ." **86.** 125; "No external force. . . ." **86.** 128; "Jesus expressed his alternative. . . ." **86.** 132.

page 395. "The basic fact is that. . . ." **86.** 133; "Persecution and suffering has become. . . ." **86.** 122; "One of your famous Christian hymn writers. . . ." **86.** 123; "the source of life is. . . ." **86.** 238.

page 396. "I have looked long and hard. . . ." **89.** 77; "At present, only white children can. . . ." Howard Thurman, *With Head and Heart: The Autobiography of Howard Thurman* (New York: Harcourt Brace Jovanovich, 1979), 97.

page 397. "The suffering of Jesus on the cross. . . ." **85.** 23; "The insight here revealed is. . . ." **85.** 22.

page 398. "The earthly Jesus was not just a thinker. . . ." **19.** xxx; "in the healing and in the eating. . . ." **19.** 304; "justice is spelled out as protecting. . . ." **19.** 575; "The dominant ethos among Thomas. . . ." **19.** 269; "a new social vision." **53.** 225; "pursuit of sane. . . ." **53.** 120f.; "all of nature is God's. . . ." **53.** 128; "Be compassionate. . . ." **53.** 84, Q Saying n.10.

page 400. "Through compassion human. . . ." **31.** 385; "In every work of God. . . ." **31.** 385; "God is said to be. . . ." **31.** 387; "Compassion is the fire. . . ." **31.** 401; "Compassion is Christ. . . ." **31.** 400; "To be compassionate is to have. . . ." **31.** 392; "We are truly compassionate. . . ." **31.** 392; "The love of neighbor. . . ." **31.** 396f.

page 401. "a contempt . . . one's own power." **31.** 398–400.

page 402. "Compassion means justice. . . ." **30.** 429; "In every work which God works. . . ." **30.** 429f.; "How then can anyone be. . . ." **30.** 436; "I say that beyond these two. . . ." **30.** 442; "all human science . . . works compassion." **30.** 442; "For the just person. . . ." **30.** 472.

page 403. "The just person lives . . . without why." **30.** 472; "Those deeds which do not. . . ." **30.** 473; "the ground of compassion. . . ." **22.** 80f.

Chapter 18: SPIRITUAL WARRIORHOOD

page 404. "Now since a person's real work. . . ." **59.** 89.

page 406. "The Indians have never accepted. . . ." **4.** 190.

page 408. "brave great dangers for great. . . ." **31.** 351; "The Lord is with me. . . ." **31.** 455; "First, the strength of divine. . . ." **31.** 454f.

page 411. "Now since a person's real work. . . ." **59.** 89; "the presence of oppression. . . ." Heschel, *The Prophets,* op. cit., 204.

page 412. "To do justice is what God. . . ." ibid.

page 413. "For practitioners or spiritual warriors. . . ." **17.** 12; "When the rivers and air are. . . ." **17.** 30f.; "The ground of not causing harm. . . ." **17.** 32; "Mindfulness if practiced continuously. . . ." **41.** 124.

page 414. "spiritual warrior's. . . . relate to all things." Kornfield, op. cit., 222; "great courage . . . all phenomena." Joanna Macy, *World as Lover, World as Self* (Berkeley: Parallax Press, 1991), 179f.

page 415. "We are returning from the lesser. . . ." Edmund Helminski, "Islam: Blind Spot of the West," loc. cit., 10; "The first and most essential *jihad*. . . ." **39.** 122; "Let there be no compulsion. . . ." **49.** 41; "It is a naive man. . . ." **51.** 73.

page 416. "The warriors tame. . . ." **51.** 135; "The intelligent and the brave. . . ." **51.** 135; "For a long time . . . planet on the earth." **51.** 135.

page 417. "Even after all this time. . . ." **51.** 34; "Love wants to reach out and. . . ." **51.** 187f.

page 418. "Therefore the doubts. . . ." **73.** 270; "Heroism, majesty. . . ." Bhagavad Gita xviii. 43; "Wherever there is oppression. . . ." Linda Johnsen, op. cit., 117; "valor, manliness. . . ." **7.** 53f.

page 419. "Hurwitz is a master chess player. . . ." Glen Martin, "Tree-Sitter Recounts Life in the Clouds," *San Francisco Chronicle,* December 30, 1999, A21, 24; "just seemed to . . . of my eyes." **46.** 72.

page 420. "I began to pray. . . ." **46.** 66; "You see that a lot. . . ." **46.** 67.

CONCLUSION

page 426. "It is customary to blame. . . ." **62.** 29.

page 427. "We were forbidden to speak. . . ." Giago, op. cit., viif.; "nothing but a religious. . . ." ibid., 1.

page 429. "The historical Jesus was a peasant Jewish. . . ." **20.** 198; "to subvert conventional ways. . . ." Marcus J. Borg, *Meeting Jesus Again for the First Time* (San Francisco: HarperSanFrancisco, 1994), 75.

page 431. "O Birther! Father-Mother of the Cosmos. . . ." Neil Douglas-Klotz, trans., *Prayers of the Cosmos* (San Francisco: Harper & Row, 1990), 12ff.

page 432. "God is breath. . . ." **21.** 41; "Ripe are those who. . . ." **21.** 41.

page 433. "every bit as revolutionary. . . ." **33.** 474; "incipient Gnosticism." **33.** 501, 490; "rooted in the Jewish wisdom. . . ." **33.** 501.

page 434. "no find could be . . . early Christian writing." Elizabeth A. Castelli and Hal Taussig, ed., *Reimagining Christian Origins* (Valley Forge, PA: Trinity Press International, 1996), 11.

page 435. "an explosion of creative imagination. . . ." **53.** 125; "It was the attraction of. . . ." **53.** 225.

page 436. "Every individual seeks. . . ." **60.** 29.

page 439. "the lonely search for internal. . . ." **60.** 16; "little walls, little altars . . . men everywhere." **84.** 151–153.

BIBLIOGRAPHY

1. Molefi Kete Asante, *The Afrocentric Idea* (Philadelphia: Temple University Press, 1998).
2. Molefi Kete Asante and Abu S. Abarry, eds., *African Intellectual Heritage: A Book of Sources* (Philadelphia: Temple University Press, 1996).
3. Hallie Iglehart Austen, *The Heart of the Goddess* (Berkeley: Wingbow Press, 1990).
4. Thomas Berry, *The Dream of the Earth* (San Francisco: Sierra Club, 1988).
5. R. P. Blackmur, *Henry Adams* (New York: Harcourt, Brace, Jovanovich, 1980).
6. Jalaja Bonheim, *Goddess: A Celebration in Art and Literature* (New York: Stewart, Tabori & Chang, 1997).
7. A. C. Bose, *The Call of the Vedas* (Bombay: Bharatiya Vidya Bhavan: 1988).
8. Patricia Janis Broder, *Hopi Painting: The World of the Hopis* (New York: E. P. Dutton, 1978).
9. David Brower, *Let the Mountains Talk, Let the Rivers Run* (San Francisco: HarperSanFrancisco, 1995).
10. Joseph Epes Brown, *The Spiritual Legacy of the American Indian* (New York: Crossroad, 1986).
11. Susan Cady, Marian Ronan, and Hal Taussig, *Wisdom's Feast* (San Francisco: Harper & Row, 1986).
12. Thomas Cahill, *How the Irish Saved Civilization* (New York: Doubleday Anchor, 1995).
13. Joseph Campbell, *Power of Myth* (New York: Doubleday, 1988).
14. Fritjof Capra, *The Web of Life* (New York: Doubleday Anchor, 1996).
15. Ana Castillo, ed., *Goddess of the Americas: Writings on the Virgin of Guadalupe* (New York: Riverhead Books, 1996).
16. Pema Chodron, *Start Where You Are* (Boston: Shambhala, 1994).
17. Pema Chodron, *When Things Fall Apart* (Boston: Shambhala, 1997).
18. Henri Corbin, *Creative Imagination in the Sufism of Ibn Arabi* (Princeton: Princeton University Press, 1969).
19. John Dominic Crossan, *The Birth of Christianity* (San Francisco: HarperSanFrancisco, 1998).
20. John Dominic Crossan, *Jesus: A Revolutionary Biography* (San Francisco: HarperSanFrancisco, 1994).
21. Neil Douglas-Klotz, *The Hidden Gospel: Decoding the Spiritual Message of the Aramaic Jesus* (Wheaton, IL: Quest Books, 1999)

22. Brendan Doyle, *Meditations with Julian of Norwich* (Santa Fe: Bear & Co., 1983).
23. Peter Berresford Ellis, *Celtic Women* (Grand Rapids, Michigan: Eerdmans Publishing, 1996).
24. Marcia Falk, *The Song of Songs* (San Francisco: HarperSanFrancisco, 1990).
25. Walter E. Fluker, *They Looked for a City: A Comparative Analysis of the Ideal of Community Thought of Howard Thurman and Martin Luther King, Jr.* (New York: University Press of America, 1989).
26. Matthew Fox, *The Coming of the Cosmic Christ* (San Francisco: HarperSanFrancisco, 1988).
27. Matthew Fox, *Hildegard of Bingen's Book of Divine Works with Letters and Songs* (Santa Fe: Bear & Co., 1987).
28. Matthew Fox, *Illuminations of Hildegard of Bingen* (Santa Fe: Bear & Co., 1985).
29. Matthew Fox, *Meditations with Meister Eckhart* (Santa Fe: Bear & Co., 1983).
30. Matthew Fox, *Passion For Creation: The Earth-Honoring Spirituality of Meister Eckhart* (formerly, *Breakthrough*) (Rochester, Vermont: Inner Traditions, 2000).
31. Matthew Fox, *Sheer Joy: Conversations with Thomas Aquinas on Creation Spirituality* (San Francisco: HarperSanFrancisco, 1992).
32. Matthew Fox, *A Spirituality Named Compassion* (Rochester, Vermont: Inner Traditions, 2000).
33. Robert W. Funk, et al., *The Five Gospels: What Did Jesus Really Say?* (San Francisco: HarperSanFrancisco, 1993).
34. Marija Gimbutas, *The Civilization of the Goddess: The World of Old Europe* (San Francisco: HarperSanFrancisco, 1991).
35. Marija Gimbutas, *The Language of the Goddess* (San Francisco: HarperSanFrancisco, 1989).
36. Bede Griffiths, *Christ in India: Essays Towards a Hindu-Christian Dialogue* (Springfield, IL: Templegate Publishers, 1984).
37. Bede Griffiths, *The Cosmic Revelation: The Hindu Way to God* (Springfield, IL: Templegate Publishers, 1983).
38. Stanislav Grof, *Books of the Dead: Manuals for Living and Dying* (New York: Thames and Hudson, 1994).
39. Suzanne Haneef, *What Everyone Should Know about Islam and Muslims* (Chicago, IL: Kazi Publications, 1979).
40. Thich Nhat Hanh, *Going Home: Jesus and Buddha as Brothers* (New York: Riverhead, 1999).
41. Thich Nhat Hanh, *Living Buddha, Living Christ* (New York: Riverhead, 1995).
42. Thich Nhat Hanh, *Peace Is Every Step* (New York: Bantam, 1992).
43. Andrew Harvey, ed., *The Essential Mystics: The Soul's Journey into Truth* (San Francisco: HarperSanFrancisco, 1996).
44. Edmund Helminski, transl., *The Ruins of the Heart: Selected Lyric Poetry of Jelaluddin Rumi* (Putney, Vermont: Threshold Books, 1981).
45. Jamake Highwater, *The Primal Mind* (New York: New American Library, 1981).
46. Julia Butterfly Hill, *The Legacy of Luna* (San Francisco: HarperSanFrancisco, 2000).
47. B. K. S. Iyengar, *Light on Yoga* (New York: Schocken Books, 1966).
48. Kieran Kavanaugh and Otilio Rodriguez, trans., *The Collected Works of St. John of the Cross* (Washington, D.C.: ICS Publications, 1973).
49. Muhammad Zafrulla Khan, trans., *The Qur'an* (New York: Olive Branch Press, 1997).
50. Sehdev Kumar, *The Vision of Kabir* (Concord, Ontario, Canada: Alpha & Omega, 1984).

51. Daniel Ladinsky, trans., *The Gift: Poems by Hafiz the Great Sufi Master* (New York: Arkana, 1999).
52. Dalai Lama, *Ethics for the New Millennium* (New York: Riverhead Books, 1999).
53. Burton L. Mack, *The Lost Gospel: The Book of Q & Christian Origins* (San Francisco: HarperSanFrancisco, 1994).
54. Juan Mascaro, trans., *The Upanishads* (New York: Penguin, 1965).
55. Ana Matt, *Buddhism: A Reader* (Berkeley: unpublished manuscript)
56. Ana Matt, *Hinduism: A Reader* (Berkeley: unpublished manuscript).
57. Ana Matt, *Islam: A Reader* (Berkeley: unpublished manuscript).
58. Daniel C. Matt, *The Essential Kabbalah* (San Francisco: HarperSanFrancisco, 1996).
59. Daniel Chanan Matt, trans., *Zohar, the Book of Enlightenment* (New York: Paulist, 1983).
60. Rollo May, *The Cry for Myth* (New York: Delta, 1991).
61. Rollo May, *My Quest for Beauty* (New York: Saybrook, 1985).
62. John C. Merkle, *The Genesis of Faith: The Depth Theology of Abraham Joshua Heschel* (New York: Macmillan, 1985).
63. Stephen Mitchell, *Tao Te Ching* (New York: HarperPerennial, 1991).
64. Dermot Moran, *The Philosophy of John Scottus Eriugena* (New York: Cambridge University Press, 1989).
65. Swami Muktananda, *Play of Consciousness* (South Fallsburg, New York: Syda Foundation, 1994).
66. Swami Nikhilananda, *Hinduism: Its Meaning for the Liberation of the Spirit* (New York: Harper & Brothers, 1958).
67. Swami Nikhilananda, *The Upanishads*, vol. iv (New York: Harper & Brothers, 1959).
68. John Frederick Nims, trans., *The Poems of St. John of the Cross* (Chicago: University of Chicago Press, 1979).
69. Wes Nisker, *Buddha's Nature: Evolution as a Practical Guide to Enlightenment* (New York: Bantam, 1998).
70. John O'Donohue, *Anam Cara: A Book of Celtic Wisdom* (New York: HarperCollins, 1997).
71. Raimundo Panikkar, *The Vedic Experience* (Berkeley: University of California Press, 1977).
72. Miguel Leon-Portilla, ed., *Native Mesoamerican Spirituality* (New York: Paulist, 1980).
73. A. C. Bhaktivedanta Swami Prabhupada, *Bhagavad-Gita As It Is* (Los Angeles: The Bhaktivedanta Book Trust, 1986).
74. Dona Marimba Richards, *Let the Circle Be Unbroken: The Implications of African Spirituality in the Diaspora* (Lawrenceville, NJ: Red Sea Press, 1992).
75. M. C. Richards, *Centering: In Pottery, Poetry and the Person* (Middletown, CT: Wesleyan University Press, 1962).
76. M. C. Richards, *Image Inventing Yellow: The Life and Work of M. C. Richards* (Worcester, MA: Worcester Center for Crafts, 1999).
77. Sogyal Rinpoche, *The Tibetan Book of Living and Dying* (San Francisco: HarperSanFrancisco, 1993).
78. Melva Jean Roberts and Ainslie Roberts, *Dreamtime: The Aboriginal Heritage* (Sydney: Rigby Publishers, 1981).
79. Leonard Shlain, *Art & Physics: Parallel Visions in Space, Time & Light* (New York: William Morrow, 1991).

80. Jonathan Star, trans., *A Garden Beyond Paradise: The Mystical Poetry of Rumi* (New York: Bantam, 1992).
81. Brian Swimme, *The Hidden Heart of the Cosmos* (Maryknoll, NY: Orbis Books, 1996).
82. Brian Swimme and Thomas Berry, *The Universe Story* (San Francisco: HarperSanFrancisco, 1992).
83. Rabindranath Tagore, trans., *Songs of Kabir* (York Beach, ME: Samuel Weiser, Inc., 1988).
84. Howard Thurman, *The Creative Encounter* (Richmond, IN: Friends United Press, 1972).
85. Howard Thurman, *Deep River and The Negro Spiritual Speaks of Life and Death* (Richmond, Indiana: Friends United Press, 1975).
86. Howard Thurman, *For the Inward Journey* (Richmond, IN: Friends United Press, 1984).
87. Howard Thurman, *Jesus and the Disinherited* (Richmond, IN: Friends United Press, 1976).
88. Howard Thurman, *The Luminous Darkness* (Richmond, IN: Friends United Press, 1989).
89. Howard Thurman, *The Search for Common Ground* (Richmond, IN: Friends United Press, 1986).
90. Gabriele Uhlein, *Meditations with Hildegard of Bingen* (Santa Fe: Bear & Co., 1982).
91. Steve Wall and Harvey Arden, *Wisdomkeepers: Meetings with Native American Spiritual Elders* (Hillsboro, OR: Beyond Words Publishing, Inc., 1990).
92. Sue Woodruff, *Meditations with Mechtild of Magdeburg* (Santa Fe: Bear & Co., 1982).
93. Arne A. Wyller, *The Planetary Mind* (Aspen, CO: MacMurray & Beck, 1996).

PERMISSIONS

Passage from Coleman Barks, *Rumi: One-Handed Basket Weaving,* used by permission of the author.

Passage from Stephan Beyer, *Cult of Tara: Magic and Ritual in Tibet,* permission granted by the Regents of the University of California and the University of California Press.

Passage from Brendan Doyle, *Meditations with Julian of Norwich* (Santa Fe: Bear & Co., 1983), used by permission of the publisher.

Passage from Edmund Helminski, *The Ruins of the Heart: Selected Poetry of Jelaluddin Rumi,* originally published by Threshold Books (Aptos Hills, CA 1981), used by permission of the publisher.

Passage from *The Collected Works of St. John of the Cross,* translated by Kieran Kavanaugh and Otilio Rodriguez © 1979, 1991 by Washington Province of Discalced Carmelites, ICS Publications, 2131 Lincoln Road, N.E. Washington, DC 20002-1199, U.S.A. Used by permission of publisher.

"Hopid" poem by Michael Kabote, from Patricia Broder's *Hopi Paintings: The World of the Hopi,* used by permission of Michael Kabote.

Passage from Neil Douglas-Klotz, *The Hidden Gospel: Decoding the Spiritual Message of the Armamaic Jesus* (Wheaton, IL: Quest Books, 1999), used by permission of the publisher.

Passage from Daniel Ladinsky, *The Gift: Poems by Hafiz,* Penguin USA 1999. Translation and copyright Daniel Ladinsky, used by permission of the author.

Passage from Daniel Matt, *Zohar: The Book of Enlightenment* (New York: Paulist Press 1983), used by permission of the publisher.

Passage from Miguel Leon-Portilla, *Native Mesoamerican Spirituality* (New York: Paulist Press, 1980), used by permission of the publisher.

Passage from Raimundo Panikkar, *The Vedic Experience* © Raimundo Panikkar, used by permission of the author.

Passage from Jonathan Star, *A Garden Beyond Paradise*, used by permission of the author.

Passage from Rabindranath Tagore, *Songs of Kabir* (York Beach, ME: Samuel Weiser, 1971), used by permission of the publisher.

Passage from Gabriele Uhlein, *Meditations with Hildegard of Bingen* (Santa Fe: Bear & Co., 1982), used by permission of the publisher.

Passage from Thich Nhat Hanh, *Peace Is Every Step*. Copyright © 1991 by Thich Nhat Hanh. Used by permission of Bantam Books, a division of Random House, Inc.

Passage from Sehdev Kumar, *The Vision of Kabir* (Concord Ont., Canada: Alpha & Omega, 1984), used by permission of the publisher.

Passage from John Frederick Nims, trans., *Poems of St. John of the Cross* (Chicago: University of Chicago Press, 1979), used by permission of the publisher.

Poem by Tim Giago appears by permission of the author (Tim Giago, publisher, *The Lakota Nation Journal*, P.O. Box 3080, Rapid City, SD 57709-3080).

Passages from Kevin Gilbert, ed., *Inside Black Australia* (Ringwood, Victoria, Australia, 1998), used by permission of the publisher.

Strange Fruit, word and music by Allan Lewis, copyright © 1939 (renewed) by Music Sales Corporation (ASCAP). International copyright secured. All rights reserved. Reprinted by permission.

Passages from Daniel C. Matt, *The Essential Kabbalah*, copyright © 1995 by Daniel C. Matt, reprinted by permission of HarperCollins Publishers, Inc.

Passages from Stephen Mitchell, *Tao Te Ching by Lao Tzu, a New English Version, with Foreword and Notes by Stephen Mitchell*, translation copyright © 1988 by Stephen Mitchell, reprinted by permission of HarperCollins Publishers, Inc.

Passage from A. C. Bhaktivedanta Swami Prabhupada, *Bhagavad Gita: As It Is* (Bharatiya Vidya Bhavan, Kulpati K. M. Munshi Marg, Chowpatty, Mumbai 400 007), used by permission of the publisher.

Passage from Marija Gimbutas, *The Language of the Goddess*, copyright © 1989 by Marija Gimbutas, reprinted by permission of HarperCollins Publishers, Inc.

Passage from *Awakening to the Tao* by Liu I-Ming, translated by Thomas Cleary, copyright 1988 by Thomas Cleary. Reprinted by arragement with Shambhala Publications, Inc., Boston, www.shambhala.com

INDEX

ABOUT THE AUTHOR

A visionary activist, and one of the most important religious thinkers and teachers of our time, Matthew Fox has devoted his career to unleashing the suppressed mystical and life-affirming traditions within Christianity and other faiths. His theology of "Creation Spirituality"—the belief that we are born in "original blessing"—has reinvigorated the faith of countless seekers and earned him the headline-making censure of the Vatican, which officially "silenced" Fox in 1989 and precipitated his dismissal by the Dominican Order in 1993. Now an Episcopal priest, Fox is the author of more than twenty books, including *Original Blessing; The Reinvention of Work;* and *The Coming of the Cosmic Christ.* He is founding president of the University of Creation Spirituality in Oakland, California. In 1995, Fox was awarded The Peace Abbey Courage of Conscience Award. Recently, Fox has been nationally praised for his groundbreaking "techno cosmic masses," which combine the world's faiths in a reconstruction of liturgical celebration embracing dance, techno music, and multimedia. He lives in California.

For more information about the work of Matthew Fox and the master's degree in creation spirituality offered at Naropa Oakland and the Doctor of Ministry degree at the University of Creation Spirituality in Oakland, California, call 510-835-4827 or consult the following web site: www.creationspirituality.com